THE GREATER WAR

General Editor ROBERT GERWARTH

The paroxysm of 1914–1918 was the epicentre of a cycle of armed conflict that in some parts of Europe began in 1912 and continued until 1923. Taken together, the volumes in this series recognize not only that the Great War has a greater chronological dimension, but also that it has a greater territorial reach than the well-published struggle on the Western Front.

War in Peace

*Paramilitary Violence in Europe after
the Great War*

Edited by
ROBERT GERWARTH AND JOHN HORNE

OXFORD
UNIVERSITY PRESS

OXFORD
UNIVERSITY PRESS

Great Clarendon Street, Oxford, OX2 6DP,
United Kingdom

Oxford University Press is a department of the University of Oxford.
It furthers the University's objective of excellence in research, scholarship,
and education by publishing worldwide. Oxford is a registered trade mark of
Oxford University Press in the UK and in certain other countries

© Oxford University Press 2012

The moral rights of the author have been asserted

First Edition published in 2012
First published in paperback 2013

Published in the United States of America by Oxford University Press
198 Madison Avenue, New York, NY 10016, United States of America

ISBN 978–0–19–965491–8 (Hbk)
ISBN 978–0–19–968605–6 (Pbk)

Acknowledgements

This book is the result of collaborative efforts over a long period. Most of the authors assembled in this volume met at two themed workshops, held in Dublin in 2008 and 2010. The editors would like to thank the participants and commentators at these workshops who provided extensive critical input. Over the last three years, the collaborative project between the Centres for War Studies in Trinity College Dublin and University College Dublin that led to this volume has received generous funding, first from the Irish Research Council for the Humanities and Social Sciences (IRCHSS), then from the European Research Council (ERC). The editors of this book would like to take this opportunity to record their gratitude to these funding bodies. On a more personal level, we have benefitted greatly from working with the postdoctoral fellows affiliated with this project—Julia Eichenberg, John Paul Newman, and, more recently, Uğur Ümit Üngör, James Kitchen, and Tomas Balkelis—as well as from the skilled administrative help we received from Christina Griessler and Suzanne d'Arcy. We would also like to thank Elaine Cullen for drawing the maps.

Robert Gerwarth and John Horne
Dublin, October 2011

Table of Contents

List of Illustrations

List of Maps

List of Contributors

Tomas Balkelis is a European Research Council funded Postdoctoral Fellow at the UCD Centre for War Studies. After gaining his PhD from the University of Toronto he worked as a lecturer at the University of Nottingham and as an AHRC Postdoctoral Fellow at Manchester University. He is the author of *The Making of Modern Lithuania* (London, 2009) which was recently translated into Lithuanian. He has published articles in *Past and Present* and *Contemporary European History*. He has a particular interest in the history of nationalism and violence in Eastern Europe (Baltics, Russia, and Poland).

Anne Dolan lectures in modern Irish history at Trinity College Dublin. She is author of *Commemorating the Irish Civil War: History and Memory, 1922–2000* (Cambridge, 2003), and, with Cormac O'Malley, is co-editor of *'No Surrender Here!': The Civil War Papers of Ernie O'Malley* (Dublin, 2008). She is currently working on a book on violence in postwar Ireland.

Julia Eichenberg is a DAAD Postdoctoral Fellow at the Humboldt University Berlin. She has published articles on Irish and Polish paramilitaries and has recently published her first book on Polish veterans of World War I, *Kämpfen für Frieden und Fürsorge: Polnische Veteranen des Ersten Weltkriegs und ihre internationalen Kontakte, 1918–1939* (Munich, 2011).

Emilio Gentile is Professor of History at Sapienza University of Rome. He is an internationally recognized historian of fascism whose books, such as the *The Sacralization of Politics in Fascist Italy* (Cambridge, MA, 1996) or *Politics as Religion* (Princeton, NJ, 2006) have appeared in various languages.

Robert Gerwarth is Professor of Modern History at University College Dublin and Director of UCD's Centre for War Studies. He is the author and editor of several books on the history of political violence in twentieth-century Europe, including, most recently, the biography *Hitler's Hangman: The Life of Reinhard Heydrich* (New Haven and London, 2011) and (with Donald Bloxham), *Political Violence in Twentieth-Century Europe* (Cambridge, 2011).

Pertti Haapala is Professor of Finnish History at the University of Tampere, and Director of the Finnish Centre of Excellence in Historical Research. He is the author and editor of several important publications on the Finnish Civil War, most recently of the book *Tampere 1918: A Town in a Civil War* (Tampere, 2010).

John Horne is Professor of Modern European History at Trinity College Dublin and board member of the Research Centre of the Historial de la Grande Guerre, Péronne. He has published widely on the history of the Great War, most recently (ed.) *A Companion to World War One* (Oxford, 2010), and (ed.), *Vers la guerre totale: le tournant de 1914–1915* (Paris, 2010).

John Paul Newman is Lecturer in Modern European History at the National University of Ireland, Maynooth. He works on the social and cultural history of war in the modern Balkans and is currently preparing a monograph on South Slav veterans of the First World War and their impact on state and society in interwar Yugoslavia.

William G. Rosenberg is Professor Emeritus at the University of Michigan. He has published widely on the Russian Revolution, including the book, *Liberals in the Russian Revolution* and (with

Marilyn B. Young; Princeton, 1974) *Transforming Russia and China: Revolutionary Struggle in the Twentieth Century* (Oxford, 1982). He is also the editor of *Bolshevik Visions: The Cultural Revolution in Soviet Russia* (Ann Arbor, 1990).

Marko Tikka is a Lecturer in History at the University of Tampere. He is the author of the book, *Kenttäoikeudet: Välittömät rankaisutoimet Suomen sisällissodassa 1918* (*Court-Martial without Law: Punitive Measures in the Finnish Civil War of 1918*) (Helsinki, 2004).

Uğur Ümit Üngör received his Ph.D. from the University of Amsterdam and is currently Lecturer in History at Utrecht University and the Center for Holocaust and Genocide Studies in Amsterdam. His main area of interest is the historical sociology of mass violence and ethnic conflict. His most recent publications include *Confiscation and Destruction: The Young Turk Seizure of Armenian Property* (London, 2011), and the award-winning *The Making of Modern Turkey: Nation and State in Eastern Anatolia, 1913–1950* (Oxford, 2011).

Serhy Yekelchyk is an Associate Professor of History at University of Victoria. He is the author and editor of several acclaimed books on Eastern Europe such as *Ukraine: Birth of a Modern Nation* (New York, 2007), *Stalin's Empire of Memory: Russian-Ukrainian Relations in the Soviet Historical Imagination* (Toronto, 2004), and, as co-editor: *Europe's Last Frontier? Belarus, Moldova, and Ukraine between Russia and the European Union* (New York, 2008).

1

Paramilitarism in Europe after the Great War

An Introduction

Robert Gerwarth and John Horne

'The war of the giants is over; the wars of the pygmies have begun.'
Winston Churchill, 1919

The end of the Great War did not immediately bring peace to Europe. On the contrary, revolutions, counter-revolutions, ethnic strife, pogroms, wars of independence, civil conflict, and inter-state violence continued from 1917 to 1923 as the seismic forces unleashed by the cataclysm of the Great War transformed the political landscape of much of the old continent. One or more of these kinds of violence affected Russia, the Ukraine, Finland, the Baltic states, Poland, Austria, Hungary, Germany, Italy, Anatolia, and the Caucasus. Ireland experienced a war of independence and civil war in the same period.[1]

Paramilitarism was a prominent feature in all of these conflicts and this book seeks to explore the origins, manifestations, and legacies of this form of political violence as it emerged between 1917 and 1923. By paramilitary violence we mean military or quasi-military organizations and practices that either expanded or replaced the activities of conventional military formations. Sometimes this occurred in the vacuum left by collapsing states; on other occasions it served as an adjunct to state power; in yet others it was deployed against the state. It included

---

[1] Recent literature on some of these conflicts includes: Serhy Yekelchyk, *Ukraine: Birth of a Modern Nation* (Oxford, 2007); Peter Hart, *The IRA at War, 1916–1923* (Oxford, 2003); Michael Reynolds, 'Native Sons: Post-Imperial Politics, Islam, and Identity in the North Caucasus, 1917–1918', *Jahrbücher für Geschichte Osteuropas* 56 (2008), 221–47; idem, *Shattering Empires: The Clash and Collapse of the Ottoman and Russian Empires, 1908–1918* (Cambridge, 2011); Norman Davies, *White Eagle, Red Star: The Polish-Soviet War, 1919–20*, (2nd edn., London, 2003). See also Peter Gatrell, 'War after the War: Conflicts, 1919–23', in: John Horne (ed.), *A Companion to World War One* (Oxford, 2010), 558–75; Alexander V. Prusin, *The Lands Between: Conflict in the East European Borderlands, 1870–1992* (Oxford, 2010), 72ff; Christoph Mick, 'Vielerlei Kriege. Osteuropa 1918–1921', in: Dietrich Beyrau, Michael Hochgeschwender, Dieter Langewiesche (eds.), *Formen des Krieges: Von der Antike bis zur Gegenwart* (Paderborn: 2007), 311, 326; Piotr Wrobl, 'The Revival of Poland and Paramilitary Violence, 1918–1920', in: Rüdiger Bergien and Ralf Pröve (eds.), *Spießer, Patrioten, Revolutionäre. Militärische Mobilisierung und gesellschaftliche Ordnung in der Neuzeit* (Göttingen, 2010), 281–303.

revolutionary and counter-revolutionary violence committed in the name of secular ideologies as well as ethnic violence linked to the founding of new nation-states or to minority groups which resisted this process. It shared the stage with other violence, such as social protest, insurrection, terrorism, police repression, criminality and conventional armed combat.[2]

The term 'paramilitary' was not formulated until the 1930s, when it designated the emergence of armed political formations organized on military lines in fascist states; it was subsequently developed in the 1950s to describe such formations in the wars of decolonization and in postcolonial conflicts.[3] But paramilitary formations have a much older history, whether as local militias, guerrilla movements or armed adjuncts to the forces of order. They have proved significant in periods of defeat, notably in Spain, Austria, and Prussia during the Napoleonic Wars, when standing armies were unable to halt the French advance. In their respective 'wars of liberation', Spanish guerrillas, Andreas Hofer's *Landsturm* in the Tyrolese Alps and the German *Freikorps* of 1812–13 achieved legendary status and their influence was still perceptible following the First World War, if only as a historical reference point for emerging paramilitary movements that sought to legitimate them and emulate the success of anti-Napoleonic resistance.[4] What was distinct about these new movements was that they appeared *after* a century in which national armies had become the norm and modern police formations, penal codes and prisons had helped to firmly establish a largely unchallenged monopoly of force in the hands of the state. This monopoly was eroded as the Great War dissolved into widespread, smaller conflicts.[5] Moreover, the fact that this occurred as part of a major transition in state forms, social structures and political ideologies meant that paramilitary violence was imbued with a double significance, as a force that affected the outcome of military conflicts but also as a new source of political authority and state organization. Its impact was political and symbolic as well as military and operational.

In this sense, our volume aims to think afresh about one of the most important trajectories that led from the violence of war to the relative quietude of the second half of the 1920s. Historians have proposed a number of concepts in order to assess this process. One is the presumed 'brutalization' of postwar societies. But the war experience itself (which was not dissimilar for German, Hungarian, British or French soldiers) does not sufficiently explain why politics were 'brutalized' in *some* of the former combatant states post-1918, but not in others.[6] If the 'brutalization

---

[2] Sven Reichardt, 'Paramilitarism', in: Cyprian P. Blamires (ed.), *World Fascism: A Historical Encyclopedia,* 2 vols. (Santa Barbara, Ca, 2006), here vol. 1, 506–7. See, too: Alex Alvarez, *Governments, Citizens, and Genocide: A Comparative and Interdisciplinary Approach* (Bloomington, Indiana, 2001), 91ff.

[3] 'Paramilitary Forces', in: Trevor N. Dupuy (ed.), *International Military and Defence Encyclopedia,* vol. 5 (Washington and New York, 1993), 2104–7.

[4] Daniel Moran and Arthur Moran (eds.), *People in Arms. Military Myth and National Mobilization since the French Revolution* (Cambridge, 2002).

[5] His-Huey Liang, *The Rise of the Modern Police and the European State System from Metternich to the Second World War* (Cambridge, 1992).

[6] On the brutalization thesis see, among others: George L Mosse, *Fallen Soldiers: Reshaping the Memory of the World Wars* (Oxford, 1990). A similar argument in favour of the 'brutalization thesis'

thesis', once widely endorsed, has come under sustained criticism in recent years, it has not, as yet, been replaced by empirically sound alternative explanations for the widespread escalation of violence after the end of the war.[7] In a cautious attempt to explain the apparent lack of 'brutalization' in the victorious powers of the Great War, Dirk Schumann has recently argued that the relative domestic stability of interwar France and Britain (relative, that is, when measured against the situation in Germany) was partly due to the fact that their violent potential was relieved in the colonies, an option no longer available to Germany after 1918.[8] It remains unclear, however, whether the level of colonial violence in the French and British Empires was greater after the war than before, and the argument presupposes that the war generated a level of personal violence that *had* to be discharged somewhere.

Perhaps a more convincing explanation for the uneven distribution of paramilitary violence in Europe lies in the mobilizing power of defeat. Defeat should be seen not just in terms of the balance of power but also as a state of mind (including the refusal to acknowledge the reversal) which Wolfgang Schivelbusch has termed a 'culture of defeat'.[9] The nation had played a central role during the Great War in organizing and endorsing the mass deployment of violence by millions of European men. By the same token the nation was a potent means of legitimizing, reabsorbing and neutralizing that same violence once the conflict was over. Where the nation had been defeated, however, either in reality or in perception (as with nationalist circles in Italy), it was more difficult for it to play this role; indeed, it may have done precisely the opposite, exacerbating violence and generalizing it to a host of groups and individuals who chose to take it on themselves to redress defeat and national humiliation.[10] The nature of the 'homecoming' in a context of victory or defeat was thus an important variable but one that must be studied empirically on a regional, and not just a national basis. Defeat was infinitely more

---

was put forward by Adrian Lyttleton, 'Fascism and Violence in Post-War Italy: Political Strategy and Social Conflict', in: Wolfgang J. Mommsen and Gerhard Hirschfeld (eds.), *Social Protest, Violence and Terror* (London, 1982), here 262–3. For a critical view that argues against the usefulness of the concept for France, see Antoine Prost, 'Les Limites de la brutalisation. Tuer sur le front occidental 1914–1918', *Vingtième siècle*, 81 (2000), 5–20. On Britain, see John Laurence, 'Forging a Peaceable Kingdom: War, Violence and Fear of Brutalization in Post-First World War Britain', *Journal of Modern History*, 75 (2003), 557–89.

[7] For Germany in particular, see Benjamin Ziemann, *War Experiences in Rural Germany, 1914–1923* (Oxford, 2007); Dirk Schumann, 'Europa, der Erste Weltkrieg und die Nachkriegszeit: Eine Kontinuität der Gewalt?', *Journal of Modern European History* (2003), 24–43. See, too Antoine Prost and Jay Winter (eds.), *The Great War in History: Debates and Controversies, 1914 to the Present* (Cambridge, 2005); Scott Stephenson, *The Final Battle: Soldiers of the Western Front and the German Revolution of 1918* (Cambridge, 2009).

[8] Dirk Schumann, 'Europa, der erste Weltkrieg und die Nachkriegszeit. Eine Kontinuität der Gewalt?', *Journal of Modern European History*, 1 (2003), 23–43.

[9] Wolfgang Schivelbusch, *The Culture of Defeat: On National Trauma, Mourning, and Recovery* (New York, 2003); John Horne, 'Defeat and Memory since the French Revolution: Some Reflections', in: Jenny Macleod (ed.), *Defeat and Memory. Cultural Histories of Military Defeat since 1815* (London, 2008), 11–29.

[10] For the general argument, see Josh Sanborn, *Drafting the Russian Nation. Military Conscription, Total War and Mass Politics, 1905–1925* (DeKalb, Illinois, 2003), 165–200.

real for those who lived in the ethnically diverse border regions of the Central Powers than it was for those in Berlin, Budapest or Vienna and it is no coincidence that young men from these disputed border regions were highly overrepresented in the paramilitary organizations of the postwar years.[11] A recent investigation of the geographical origin of Nazi perpetrators has confirmed that they, too, were disproportionately drawn from the lost territories or contested border regions such as Austria, Alsace, the Baltic countries, the occupied Rhineland or Silesia.[12]

Another prominent concept in historiographical debates relevant to our topic is that of demobilization seen as a political and cultural process rather than a purely military and economic one.[13] 'Cultural demobilization' of course implies a possible refusal or failure to demobilize. The incidence of paramilitarism, and the contexts in which it proved most violent, provide a good means of tracing those states, regions, movements and individuals, especially where the conflict had been lost, which found it hardest to leave the violence of war behind, whether they had experienced it directly as combatants or as adolescents on the home front.[14] The peace of the mid- to late 1920s was relative and short-lived. The legacy of postwar paramilitarism in turn supplies one of the connections between the cycle of European and global violence of 1912–23 and its successor which, on a political and cultural level, began 10 years later.

This book builds on these concepts and debates whilst simultaneously proposing a somewhat different approach to this period than those usually adopted. First, the geographical scale of the violence necessitates a comparative and transnational analysis.[15] As the Great War destroyed the dynastic Empires of Russia, Austria-Hungary and Ottoman Turkey, and created a 'bleeding frontier' in Germany's East, it left 'shatter zones', or large tracts of territory where the disappearance of frontiers created spaces without order or clear state authority.[16] Waves of violence occurred in many of these zones, but not all, and where they did they had identifiable causes

---

[11] For the complex German case, see Richard Bessel, *Germany after the First World War* (Oxford, 1993); Benjamin Ziemann, *War Experiences in Rural Germany, 1914–1923* (Oxford, 2007), and Adam R. Seipp, *The Ordeal of Peace: Demobilization and the Urban Experience in Britain and Germany, 1917–1921* (Farnham, 2009).

[12] Michael Mann, *The Dark Side of Democracy: Explaining Ethnic Cleansing* (Cambridge, 2005), 239.

[13] For the concept of cultural demobilization, see John Horne (ed.), 'Démobilisations culturelles après la Grande Guerre,' theme issue of *14–18 Aujourd'hui-Heute-Today*, 5 (2002).

[14] For Germany in particular, see Ziemann, *War Experiences*; Dirk Schumann, 'Europa, der Erste Weltkrieg und die Nachkriegszeit: Eine Kontinuität der Gewalt?', *Journal of Modern European History* (2003), 24–43. Also important in this respect is Mark Cornwall's recently completed AHRC-funded project 'Victors and Victims: the Male Wartime Generation in East-Central Europe, 1918–1930', which investigated the ways in which the male generation of the Habsburg Empire that passed through the First World War coped with the wartime sacrifice and the transition to peacetime conditions in a way that complements the recent work of cultural historians on war commemoration and demobilization in individual states in Western Europe in the 1920s.

[15] Despite recent attempts to write transnational histories of the Great War, the global history of its immediate aftermath is yet to be tackled. The most recent attempts at transnational histories of the Great War include Alan Kramer, *Dynamics of Destruction: Culture and Mass Killing in the First World War* (Oxford, 2008). On the global ramifications of the Paris Peace Treaties, see Erez Manela, *The Wilsonian Moment: Self-Determination and the International Origins of Anticolonial Nationalism* (Oxford, 2007).

[16] The term 'shatter zone' was first used by Donald Bloxham, *The Final Solution: A Genocide*, (Oxford, 2009), 81.

Map 1. Freikorps activity in the 'shatter zones' of East Central Europe, 1918–21.

that need to be analysed and compared.[17] The fashionable idea that there are certain inherently violent states in Europe (such as Russia, Yugoslavia or Ireland) and others (such as the 'peaceable kingdom' of Great Britain) which are not, obscures more than it reveals. As all twentieth-century historians would recognize, the 'body count' in some parts of the continent has been vastly higher than in others. But such comparisons make no sense unless one examines the material, ideological, political, and cultural factors which explain that difference. The geography of violence, and in this case of paramilitary violence, is one way to do so.

Secondly the interplay between the short and long-term causes of postwar paramilitary violence requires a temporal approach that breaks the conventional time span of the Great War. The focus on the years 1914–18 makes more sense for the victorious 'Western front powers' (Britain, France, the USA), than it does for much of Central-Eastern and South-Eastern Europe or Ireland. The paroxysm of 1914–18 was the epicentre of a cycle of armed conflict that in some parts of Europe began in 1912, with the formation of paramilitary forces in Ulster determined to preserve the Union with Britain, and the first two Balkan wars that reduced Ottoman power to a toe-hold in Europe before setting Bulgaria against its former allies over Macedonia and Thrace.[18] The violence continued until 1923, when the Treaty of Lausanne defined the territory of the new Turkish Republic and ended Greek territorial ambitions in Asia Minor with the largest forced exchange of populations before the Second World War.[19] The end of the Irish Civil War in the same year, the restoration of a measure of equilibrium in Germany after the occupation of the Ruhr and the confirmation of the New Economic Policy on Lenin's death in 1924 were further indications that the cycle of violence had run its course.

Thirdly, the period from 1917 was marked by the articulation of competing ideologies that by 1923 had taken shape in new states and in the system of European international relations. Here, too, the origins lay much further back, as far as the 1870s, a decade of rapid cultural, socio-economic and political change. The transitions to new forms of mass politics that occurred in much of Europe with the franchise reforms of the 1870s and the emergence of mass movements around democratization, socialism and nationalism marked a durable change in the terms of European politics and intellectual debate. Revolutionary socialism and syndicalism challenged a parliamentary democracy that was far from established as the predominant state form. New variants of nationalism (sometimes democratic in flavour, sometimes overtly hostile to liberal democracy) triggered internal crises in the Ottoman, Romanov and Habsburg Empires, whose governments in turn

---

[17] For an overview of the ethnic violence attendant on the collapse of the multi-ethnic empires, see Aviel Roshwald, *Ethnic Nationalism and the Fall of Empires: Central Europe, Russia and the Middle East, 1914–1923* (London, 2001). For the chaos and violence in the Russian countryside, see Sanborn, *Drafting the Russian Nation*, 170–83.

[18] Richard Hall, *The Balkan Wars, 1912–1913: Prelude to the First World War* (London, 2000); Wolfgang Höpken, 'Performing Violence: Soldiers, Paramilitaries and Civilians in the Twentieth-Century Balkan Wars', in: Alf Lüdtke, Bernd Weisbrod, and Richard Bessel (eds.), *No Man's Land of Violence: Extreme Wars in the 20th Century* (Göttingen, 2006), 211, 249.

[19] Ryan Gingeras, *Sorrowful Shores: Violence, Ethnicity and the End of the Ottoman Empire, 1912–1923* (Oxford, 2009).

sought to assert their authority through violent demonstrations of strength, at home and abroad.

At the risk of inevitable simplification, it is therefore possible to trace a continuum of political violence in Southern and Eastern Europe during the half century that followed the Eastern Crisis of the 1870s, and which prefigured many of the forms of violence that emerged subsequently in Central Europe. The dismantling of large swathes of the Ottoman Balkan domains from the 1870s onwards gave rise to aggressively insecure, ethnically exclusive new states that were prey to each other but also to the agendas of greater powers, to secessionist terrorism, and to acts of ethnic murder. Following revolts against Ottoman rule in Herzegovina, Bosnia, Bulgaria, Serbia and Montenegro in 1875–76, the Ottomans repressed the uprisings with a ferocity that aroused indignation throughout Europe. In the embattled Balkan lands, paramilitarism in the form of anti-Ottoman guerillas, the Serbian, Greek, and Bulgarian *comitadji* foreshadowed forms of political violence that would become dominant throughout Eastern and Central Europe after 1917. At least in this respect, paramilitary violence between 1917 and 1923 formed part of a larger cycle of violence that predated and outlasted the Great War itself.[20]

Yet it was the radicalization of politics during and after the Great War that converted these competing movements and doctrines into a pan-European ideological conflict. 1917 saw the redefinition of democracy and nationalism by Woodrow Wilson as an inter-Allied crusade. At the same moment, the Bolsheviks seized power in the name of the legitimacy (and violence) of a class revolution.[21] Whether the successor nation-states of Central and Eastern Europe would assume the democratic form advocated by the Allied leaders at the Paris Peace Conference, and notably by Woodrow Wilson, was a pivotal issue. Already anti-democratic, anti-Bolshevik nationalism provided the language for the remobilization of the radical right during the last year of the war in Germany.[22] With the dissolution of political legitimacy as well as of the dynastic empires, new varieties of counter-revolutionary movements emerged in much of Central and Eastern Europe from the end of 1918, mobilizing paramilitary forces. In the case of Italian fascism, they had taken power by 1923 and begun to remodel the state.

The history of paramilitary violence after the Great War, then, has to be explored in terms of these larger developments—revolution, imperial collapse, and ethnic conflict—and they in turn inform the structure of the following chapters. We believe that it is impossible to understand the violent conflicts of the postwar period without due consideration of the Russian Revolution, the subsequent civil war and its effects on Europe. Related to the Russian Revolution was the

---

[20] Robert Gerwarth and Donald Bloxham (eds.), *Political Violence in Twentieth Century Europe* (Cambridge, 2011).

[21] See the classic studies of Arno Mayer, *Political Origins of the New Diplomacy, 1917–1918* (London and New Haven, 1959), and *Politics and Diplomacy of Peacemaking: Containment and Counterrevolution at Versailles, 1918–1919* (New York, 1967). See also Daniele Rossini, *Woodrow Wilson and the American Myth in Italy. Culture, Diplomacy and War Propaganda* (Cambridge, Mass., 2008).

[22] Heinz Hagenlüke, *Deutsche Vaterlandspartei: Die nationale Rechte am Ende des Kaiserreiches* (Düsseldorf, 1996).

counterrevolutionary movement that emerged in response to defeat in the Great War and left-wing radicalization in much of Central Europe as well as Italy. It is to this that we then turn. Between the two, both geographically and in its genesis and inspiration, lay the predominantly (but never exclusively) ethnic paramilitary violence that was generated by the struggles to establish (and resist) the formation of new nation-states and frontiers in Central-Eastern Europe. They form the subject of the next chapters. However, the comparative chapter by Julia Eichenberg on Poland and Ireland and that by Anne Dolan on British paramilitary violence in Ireland show that comparable circumstances also existed in the far west of the continent. Finally, the coherence of the 1918–23 timeframe is both confirmed and relativized by a consideration of the role of paramilitary violence in fascist Italy where it not only brought the movement to power in 1923 but also left an enduring legacy in the nature of the fascist state. The case of France provides a counter-example in which the emergence of a limited case of paramilitary violence *after* 1923 highlights some of the reasons why the phenomenon of paramilitarism affected many, but by no means all, parts of postwar Europe. We now turn to the arguments underpinning each section of this book in more detail.

THE RUSSIAN REVOLUTION AND PARAMILITARISM

The revolutions—political, social and national—which occurred across the diverse territories of the Russian Empire between the early months of 1917 and the summer of 1918 may not have been inherently violent. The path that led from the February Revolution of 1917 to the Russian Civil War of the summer of 1918 might have taken many directions. But the successful consolidation of power by a determined revolutionary minority of Bolsheviks during the winter of 1917–18 in the midst of a massive military conflict that had already set in train its own dynamics of ethnic struggle, injected a powerful new energy into revolutionary violence, which found its response in the emergence of equally determined counter-revolutionary armies, for whom the violent repression of revolution, and more especially of revolutionaries, constituted their overriding goal. Consequently, new energies of revolutionary and counter-revolutionary violence spread across the territories of European Russia (and beyond into the Caucasus and Central Asia), dwarfing the specific but intense upsurges of revolutionary violence which had occurred in Europe prior to 1914. In some areas, the collapse of state power and the economic upheaval consequent on the revolutions resulted in a breakdown in social order by 1918–19 that prompted primitive forms of military organization in local self-defence. As William Rosenberg shows in chapter two, this provided the most basic impulse to paramilitary organizations in the chaos of the Russian Revolution. The answer of the Bolsheviks, however, was not a formalization of paramilitary politics but rather a new and durable phenomenon in twentieth-century politics: the modern Communist revolutionary, trained in political action and experienced in the necessity of violent action, who built a new state based on the party.[23]

From the Red Guards who played a role in the overthrow of the Provisional Government to the armed groups that conducted 'War Communism' in the countryside and contributed to the Civil War, the Russian revolutionaries developed various formations that operated alongside the Red Army. But paramilitary violence did not legitimate the new regime. Rather, in line with Bolshevik understanding of Marxist theory and with Leninist practice, the party was the source of authority and organization in the new state, and it was the party (not the army) that provided the most important forms of extra-judicial violence, such as the Cheka and the Terror. Indeed, the Bolsheviks' deep-seated hostility to 'militarism', alongside their fear of 'Bonapartism', meant that even a class-based *levée en masse* had its dangers, especially with the violence that pervaded Russia down to 1920. A regular conscript army led by professional officers but framed by political commissars was the preferred solution. It was on this that the new regime relied to solve both the Civil War and its border wars (notably with Poland). The Bolsheviks absorbed paramilitary violence in the growing dominance of the party and had no need of it as a legitimating principle.[24]

Conversely, the White Russian armies had little more than the military to rely on once Tsardom had fallen, especially given the diversity of political perspectives involved. In some parts of Russia, the White cause was largely fought by private armies and irregular forces, such as those of Atman Semenov and Baron von Ungern-Sternberg in Central Asia. Greens and Blacks also drew on the undercurrent of armed groups free from all state control as they played their separate roles in the Civil War. An important question for further research, therefore, is the degree to which paramilitarism was used by the anti-Bolshevik forces and whether it served to legitimize the counter-revolutionary cause following defeat. The exile of the army of Baron Wrangel in Gallipoli in 1920–23 and the spirit of the Gallipoli Society which converted the experience of defeat into the ideal of the 'White Dream' supplied an identity and cause to many of those who would form paramilitary groups in exile (such as the Russian All-Military Union, founded in Yugoslavia in 1924) and mount operations on Soviet territory in the interwar years and during the Second World War.[25]

The Bolshevik Revolution interacted with paramilitary counter-revolutionary violence further afield. Not entirely dissimilar to the situation in the late-eighteen

---

[23] Daniel H. Kaiser (ed.), *The Workers' Revolution in Russia, 1917: the View from Below* (Cambridge, 1987); Steve Smith, *Revolution and the People in Russia and China. A Comparative History* (Cambridge, 2008); Martin Conway and Robert Gerwarth, 'Revolution and Counter-Revolution', in: Gerwarth and Bloxham, *Political Violence*, 140–175.

[24] Mark von Hagen, *Soldiers in the Proletarian Dictatorship: the Red Army and the Soviet Socialist State, 1917–1930* (Ithaca, 1990), 20–40, 327–34; Sanborn, *Drafting the Russian Nation;* idem, 'The Genesis of Russian Warlordism: Violence and Governance during the First World War and the Civil War', *Contemporary European History* 19 (2010), 195–213.

[25] Anatol Shmelev, 'Gallipoli to Golgotha: Remembering the Internment of the Russian White Army at Gallipoli, 1920–3', in: Macleod (ed.), *Defeat and Memory*, 195–213 (esp. 207–8).

century when Europe's horrified ruling elites feared a Jacobin 'apocalyptic' war, many Europeans after 1917 feared that Bolshevism would spread to 'infect' the rest of Europe in 1919–20, prompting paramilitary mobilization against the perceived menace. This occurred not only where the threat was plausible—in the Baltic states and Ukraine, in Hungary and parts of Germany—but also in more peaceable victor states such as France and Britain. Everywhere, the fact of the Bolshevik Revolution and the new regime in Russia injected a counterrevolutionary ethos into the defence of the existing social order, justifying paramilitary violence as a means of self-defence. Reconstructing the imaginary categories of 'communism' and 'revolution' outside Russia is thus vital in order to understand how, and where, paramilitary force was seen as a legitimate defence against revolution—or even as a vector of counter-revolution a question addressed by Robert Gerwarth and John Horne in chapter three.[26]

COUNTER-REVOLUTION AND THE RISE OF MODERN PARAMILITARISM

In parts of Central and Eastern Europe, the politics of class in the context of military defeat and the disintegration of established political authority resulted in a counter-revolutionary mobilization in which paramilitary organizations such as the *Freikorps,* the White Guards or the *Heimwehren* assumed a prominent role. This is the theme taken up by Robert Gerwarth in chapter four. Central to this development was a new political personnel that tried to implement ideas that were not in themselves new (anti-democratic nationalism, authoritarianism) but which now became the object of military conflict. From 1917–18, revolutionary politics of left and right were no longer dominated by the lawyers, intellectuals, and trade-union officials of the pre-1914 era. Instead, power, and more especially the levers of violent action, had passed to new figures, many (if by no means all) of whom had had direct experience of military violence in the First World War, and who depended for their authority on their radicalism of rhetoric and action.

This transition was most emphatic on the extreme right, where the immediate postwar years witnessed the emergence of a new political culture of the armed group. In these paramilitary formations, ex-officers brutalized by the war and (in some areas) infuriated by defeat and revolution joined forces with members of a younger generation, who compensated for their lack of combat experience by often surpassing the war veterans in terms of radicalism, activism, and brutality. Although grimly nationalist in outlook, such paramilitary activists during this period proved to be highly mobile, both nationally and internationally. If, as Ute Frevert has suggested, the Great War generally constituted a powerful transnational experience, a period of multinational contacts and transfers, the same applies to the conflict-ridden

---

[26] The theme of the international revolution has not aroused scholarly interest since the weakening of labour and social history in the 1980s. See, however, A. S. Lindemann, *The 'Red Years': European Socialism versus Bolshevism, 1919–1921* (Stanford, Ca., 1974).

postwar years.[27] German ex-officers were highly sought-after 'military instructors' during the myriad civil wars that raged in China or South America and large numbers of non-Russian anti-Bolshevik volunteers fought alongside the White armies during the Civil War.

In times of rapid socio-economic change and a perceived existential threat at the hands of 'international Bolshevism', paramilitary organizations offered a network that protected its members from social isolation, and a diversion through its permanent activism and the possibility for its members to act out their frustrations in a violent manner. Members of paramilitary organizations were characterized by their downward social mobility, although they had no coherent class background. Whereas the German *Freikorps*, the Italian *arditi*, and Russian White militias contained a disproportionate number of ex-officers and aristocrats, the militias of Lithuania, the Baltics or Ireland tended to be based on peasants and middle class intellectuals.[28]

In contrast to the army, members of paramilitary organizations often had political ambitions and defined themselves as political soldiers. Although they did not promote a clearly defined political programme, they fought against socialists, communists, the newly emerging political systems, and the alleged petty bourgeois mentality of security and respectability. Their worldview was defined mainly by its destructive actions against 'Reds' and ethnic minorities.

The organizational structures of counter-revolutionary paramilitarism were characterized by flat hierarchies and a strong group identity. Discipline and obedience toward the leader was achieved through a form of comradeship that was generated through the voluntary recruitment of members. Paramilitary leaders claimed that violence could cleanse, purify, or regenerate the people and the national mentality. Despite only vaguely defined political aims, they viewed themselves as the idealistic avant-garde who fought for the moral rejuvenation of the nation. It was mainly the violence itself that functioned as a performative act and created meaning for the activists. The experience of violence mobilized passions and resoluteness and was aestheticized by some intellectuals—Marinetti, D'Annunzio, Jünger, von Salomon—as the beauty of surgical cleansing or the efficacy of will and strength. It was the emotional energy produced by acting violently that held paramilitary groups together.

The political logic of such groups was twofold: to resist Bolshevism (and more broadly the 'Reds') as the real and imagined opponent but also to establish a new legitimacy for the counter-revolutionary cause, and eventually for states that might be founded on that basis. In many cases, this ideological violence super-charged ethnic and national conflicts (the Baltic states, Silesia), giving paramilitary violence a central role compared to other forms of violence.[29] However, in the case of Italy,

---

[27] Ute Frevert, 'Europeanizing German History', *Bulletin of the German Historical Institute* 36 (2005), 9–31, particularly 13–15.

[28] On the Baltic states, see Tomas Balkelis, 'Turning Citizens into Soldiers: Lithuanian Paramilitaries in 1918–1920' (forthcoming). On the *arditi*, see: Sven Reichardt, *Kampfbünde*.

[29] Robert Gerwarth, 'The Central European Counter-Revolution: Paramilitary Violence in Germany, Austria and Hungary after the Great War', *Past and Present*, 200 (2008), 175–209.

where paramilitary counter-revolutionary mobilization went furthest, ethnic conflicts were to be found only on the margins. True, in the case of D'Annunzio's occupation of Fiume for 15 months in 1919–20, the margin provided a potent foretaste of the central fascist project, and the 'mutilated victory' that left some irredentist claims unsatisfied remained an important rallying cry.[30] But, as Emilio Gentile shows in chapter six, in the heartlands of Northern and Central Italy, the dissolution of prior state legitimacy, a clash over land-ownership and redistribution in the countryside, and the violence of class conflict in the cities supplied the main cause for fascist paramilitaries.[31]

PARAMILITARISM, ETHNICITIES AND IMPERIAL COLLAPSE

If the Bolshevik Revolution and the subsequent civil war had spread fears of a European class war, the idea of creating ethnically homogeneous nation-states proved to be just as revolutionary a principle and an important source of paramilitary violence in much of Europe at the end of the Great War, especially where it was opposed by empire and dynasty or disputed as a minority by other nationalities. While revolutionary violence post-1917 followed the nineteenth-century clarity of the barricades, of two sides confronting each other in the name of opposing ideologies, ethnic violence was more complicated and much more messy. Much of what appeared to be ideologically driven, or was indeed claimed to be political by actors at the time, was motivated by pre-existing social tensions or a by-product of the more immediate stimuli of envy, greed, or lust.[32]

In post-1917 Europe, national projects were often intertwined with social movements, and in parts of Eastern Europe claiming the nation went hand in hand with demanding the land, so that peasant nationalism emerged as a powerful radical force in the postwar years, notably in Bulgaria, Western Ukraine, and the Baltic states (but not Ireland, where the British had conceded the land to tenant farmers). Nor were labour and socialist movements only internationalist; on the contrary, they often assumed a 'national' form. Fighting to establish or defend the nation entailed multiple kinds of violence. Ethnic and national claims were predominant in the imperial shatter zones of the Ottoman and Romanov Empires (as well as in Ireland), though Bolshevism or anti-Bolshevik counter-revolution played a variable role as well.[33] In chapter seven, Serhy Yekelchyk examines how struggles over the land and local police control were fought by paramilitary forces which in turn helped crystallize Ukranian and Polish national identities in contested regions where the two peoples overlapped.

[30] John Woodhouse, *Gabriele D'Annunzio: Defiant Archangel* (Oxford, 1998).
[31] Emilio Gentile, *The Origins of Fascist Ideology, 1918–1925* (New York, 2005); idem, 'Il Fascismo: una definitzione orientativa', in: Gentile, *Fascismo* (Bari, 2002), 54–73.
[32] Stathus Kalyvas, *The Logic of Violence in Civil War* (Cambridge, 2006), 365–87.
[33] Bloxham, *Final Solution,* 81ff.

Often enough, the politics of ethnic cleansing were inspired by older Darwinian metaphors of social struggle, the perils of racial or national degeneration and the ideal of a purified and healthy community. But the logic of imposing new frontiers to define national communities could generate the same effects even where such an ideological heritage was little in evidence, as in countries such as Ireland or Poland where the nationalism was associated with democratic traditions and religion. The need to purge communities of their 'alien' elements and to root out those who were harmful to the balance of the community were also practical ones that required the use of violence, as the decades after 1917 powerfully illustrate. The ways in which purges were carried through owed much to the context within which they operated, and more especially to the crises of state authority and the exacerbation of inter-community relations by military conflicts and economic change. But they also reflected how certain revolutionary movements developed an internal culture that predisposed them to paramilitarism. The origins of such a culture were complex. In cases such as the counter-revolutionary bands that acted with such savagery across Central and Eastern Europe in the aftermath of the First World War, they owed much to the adoption of a simplified and highly gendered military culture, in which the willingness to give and enact violent orders subordinated the 'normal' value structures of civilian society to unquestioning service for the cause.

Inter-communal violence between opposed ethnic and religious groups (Poles and Germans in Silesia, Unionists and Nationalists in Northern Ireland, Muslims and Christians in the new Turkish Republic) was no less important a source of paramilitary hostility, since each side sought a combination of militia and terrorist force in order to take or protect 'national' terrain. In some cases, notably during the Greek-Turkish War of 1919–22, paramilitary forces were used as an adjunct to warfare between conventional armies, while in yet others an asymmetric contest between guerrilla and regular forces could lead the latter to use auxiliaries to deal with a covert enemy in violation of the conventions of war. This was the case in trans-Caucasia after 1920, discussed in chapter ten by Uğor Ümit Üngör, where the Bolsheviks faced extreme difficulties in 'pacifying' local populations which fought amongst themselves over border territories and engaged in ethnic cleansing, with Armenian paramilitaries being particularly active and violent.[34] It was equally the role played by the British Black and Tans and their police Auxiliaries used in the Irish War of Independence, discussed by Anne Dolan in chapter twelve.[35] In yet other cases, the struggle to frame the nation and achieve independence incorporated a strong ideological component (most notably in the Finnish Civil War and the Baltic states). Indeed, in the case of Finland discussed by Pertti Haapala and Marko Tikka in chapter five, a civil war between two sides whose differences were relatively small (reformist socialists and moderate democrats) saw a brief but intense incidence of brutality as two versions of the newly independent state were

---

[34] Jörg Baberowski, *Der Feind ist überall: Stalinismus im Kaukasus* (Munich, 2003).
[35] See, too: David Leeson, *The Black and Tans: British Police and Auxiliaries in the Irish War of Independence, 1920–21* (Oxford, 2001).

polarized and magnified in their opposition to each other by the proxy influence of Russian Communist and counter-revolutionary German forces.[36]

The question in each of these instances is not only the type, scale and ferocity of paramilitary violence but also its impact on the causes in whose name it was deployed. There was nothing intrinsic in the 'nation' (variously defined) that made self-constituted paramilitaries a source of legitimacy, though they may have generated potent memories or even provided founding myths. However, where a putative or actual nation state found itself separated by postwar frontiers from communities deemed to belong to it, or invested by remnants of the former state or social elites that were now held to have no place in the new state, irredentist violence was possible, whether in 'defence' of vulnerable members or for communal violence against the perceived anti-bodies so as to assert the new national community. Both dynamics were in evidence in the wars between Poland and the Ukraine and Poland and Lithuania in 1918–19. Paramilitary forces sought to mark out and intimidate or expel the other ethnicity in broad swathes of the contested frontier territories of Eastern Poland.[37] Tomas Balkelis shows in the case of the Baltic states, in chapter eight, how paramilitary formations that mobilized against both Bolshevism and the new army of neighbouring Poland became the nucleus for the project of independent Lithuanian, Latvian and Estonian statehood, remaining a touchstone of popular mobilization up to the absorbtion of the Baltic states by Stalin's Russia in 1939–40. Likewise, the violence in Ireland was at its most bitter where the logic of exclusion resulted in paramilitary brutality being used against civilians of the other community, as in mixed areas of Ulster or on the part of the Irish Republican Army (IRA) in some regions of the south. Julia Eichenberg's chapter explores this logic of paramilitary exclusion and violence in Ireland and Poland.[38]

Where national aspirations continued to be threatened or unsatisfied in the longer term, there remained the potential for paramilitary violence (like terror) to short-circuit revolutionary or democratic self-affirmation and supply a legitimating claim to act for the nation in a more durable manner. This is precisely is what the IRA did during the Irish Civil War of 1922–23 and subsequently, when it repudiated the Anglo-Irish Treaty establishing the Free State (despite this having been approved by the underground Irish parliament, or Dáil) in the name of the integral but unrealized 32-county Republic. Likewise, the Internal Macedonian Revolutionary Organization (IMRO) asserted the indefeasible right to independence or association with Bulgaria of those parts of Thrace and Macedonia held by Bulgaria briefly in 1912–13 and during the Great War without any popular

---

[36] On Finland, see Heikki Ylikangas, *Der Weg nach Tampere. Die Niederlage der Roten im finnischen Bürgerkrieg 1918* (Berlin, 2002).

[37] Julia Eichenberg, 'The Dark Side of Independence: Paramilitary Violence in Ireland and Poland after the First World War', *Contemporary European History* 19 (2010), 231–48.

[38] Peter Hart, *The IRA at War, 1916–1923* (Oxford, 2003); Timothy Wilson, *Frontiers of Violence. Conflict and Identity in Ulster and Upper Silesia, 1918–1922* (Oxford, 2010).

endorsement. The very act of terror and paramilitary activity became a surrogate act of national sovereignty.[39]

The contrasting fates of Balkan national projects during this time (victory for the Little Entente states—Czechoslovakia, Romania, and Yugoslavia—especially for Serbian maximalism, a 'national catastrophe' for Bulgaria) provided the geopolitical setting in which the 'defeated' could stake their claim to sovereignty or to an irredentist version of the nation through paramilitary violence and terror over the longer term. Conversely, as John Paul Newman explores in his chapter on postwar paramilitary violence in Yugoslavia, the 'victors' also used paramilitary violence in order to entrench the new order, as with the Serbian and pro-Yugoslav paramilitary groups in Macedonia and Kosovo, where settlers protected by paramilitary forces sought to create ethnically and culturally homogenous zones via a programme of national consolidation which was supported in principle (if not always in execution) by the government and described euphemistically as 'pacification'. This in turn encouraged the IMRO and the pro-Albanian Kačak movement between 1918 and 1923 to forge links with other revisionist paramilitary groups active in Croatia, Italy, Austria, and Hungary, links which were sometimes dormant but always present in the interwar period. Whilst the ebbing away of paramilitary activity and violence in the region after 1923 was linked to the stabilization taking place throughout Europe, the people and networks involved in violent inter-ethnic conflict became absorbed into postwar political culture throughout the Balkans. Their paramilitary violence has to be understood as part of nation-building in South-Eastern Europe and, more immediately, as a response to the Wilsonian programme of self-determination throughout the region.[40]

LEGACIES

By late 1923, paramilitary violence seemed to have largely disappeared from European politics even if some of the most intractable disputes continued to provide fertile soil for paramilitary and terrorist organizations such as the IMRO and the IRA.[41] After the end of the Franco-Belgian occupation of the Ruhr, the termination of the Russian and Irish Civil Wars and the conclusion of the Lausanne Treaty (establishing the new Turkish Republic) which specifically aimed 'to bring

[39] Duncan Perry, *The Politics of Terror: The Macedonian Liberation Movements, 1893–1903* (Durham, 1988); Stefan Troebst, *Mussolini, Makedonien, und die Mächte 1922–1930* (Cologne, 1987); Andrew Rossos, 'Macedonianism and Macedonian Nationalism on the Left', in: Ivo Banac and Catherine Verdery (eds.), *National Character and Ideology in Interwar Eastern Europe* (New Haven and London, 1995); Ivo Banac, *The National Question in Yugoslavia: Origins, History, Politics* (Ithaca, 1984), 307–28.

[40] John Paul Newman, 'Post-imperial and Post-war Violence in the South Slav Lands, 1917–1923', *Contemporary European History* 19 (2010), 249–65.

[41] Brian Hanley, *The IRA, 1926–1936* (Dublin, 2002); Banac, *National Question*; Perry, *Politics of Terror*.

to a final close the state of war which has existed in the East since 1914',[42] Europe experienced a period of tentative political and economic stability that would last until the Great Depression.

Yet four qualifications must be made to this general truth. First, certain areas of Europe had remained virtually exempt from domestic paramilitary violence since the war. By and large they coincided with the victorious powers for whom the integrity of national frontiers, the authority of the state and the power and prestige of the army had all been enhanced. Britain, France, Belgium and even the newly established Czechoslovakia experienced little or no paramilitarism on their own soil. Since they had all been centrally involved in the war, they act as counter-examples that highlight the factors which determined paramilitarism elsewhere. John Horne makes this case for France in chapter thirteen.

The second qualification to the argument that paramilitary violence declined in Europe after 1923 is that the wider culture of violent rhetoric, uniformed politics and street fighting that had characterized so much of Central and Eastern Europe struck root beneath the apparent quiescence and return to the norms of peaceful politics. Paramilitarism remained a central feature of interwar European political cultures and it included movements as diverse as the German stormtroopers, the Italian squadristi, the legionaries of the Romanian Iron Guard, the Hungarian Arrow Cross, the Croation Ustasha, or Léon Degrelle's Rexist movement in Belgium and the Croix de Feu in France (founded at the end of the 1920s). While new developments, notably the Great Depression, contributed powerfully to many of these movements, their roots frequently lay in the upheavals of the immediate postwar period. Where those upheavals had been the most subject to the ideological counter-revolution, the raw violence of the paramilitaries was most likely to be translated into symbolic and organizational principles that helped structure mass movements and even new state forms. In the case of Italian fascism and German national socialism, the culture of 'paramilitarism' played a crucial role in enabling such movements to come to power. For although in both Italy and Germany electoral politics were also important, paramilitary intimidation influenced them—if only by display. Furthermore, the postwar experience supplied the cultural basis (whether directly experienced or not) for a form of para-military organization that could be applied internally in class warfare and against the liberal state or externally in irredentist struggles in ethnic 'shatter zones'.

Even in the case of the French Third Republic, which had emerged reinforced from its military victory in the First World War, the paramilitary response by the extreme right to both democratic politics and the Communist Party in 1924–26 has been labelled by one historian as the 'first wave' of French fascism, which was succeeded by a much more substantial 'second wave' under the impact of the economic crisis and faltering democratic politics in the 1930s.[43] A small scale

[42] The Treaty of Lausanne, in John A.S. Grenville and Bernhard Wasserstein (eds.), *The Major International Treaties of the Twentieth Century* (3rd edn., London, 2001), 123ff.

[43] Robert J. Soucy, *French Fascism: the First Wave* (London and New Haven, 1986); idem, *French Fascism: the Second Wave* (London and New Haven, 1995). See also Zeev Sternhell, *Neither Right nor Left: Fascist Ideology in France* (Berkeley, Ca., 1986).

organization of British fascists emerged in the same years (1923–26) in reaction against the formation of the Communist Party of Great Britain and the 'loss' of Southern Ireland, and in response to the industrial tension that culminated in the General Strike of 1926. While the later and more successful British Union of Fascists led by Oswald Mosley was a direct response to the political crisis of Labour and the social dislocation caused by the Depression, its paramilitarism also drew on the idealized experience and sacrifice of the Great War.[44]

A third durable legacy of this period was the perceived need to cleanse communities of their alien elements before a utopian new society could emerge, to root out those who were perceived to be harmful to the balance of the community. This belief constituted a powerful component of the common currency of radical politics and action in Europe between 1917 and the later 1940s.[45] Whatever its manifold political expressions, this politics of the purified community was a prominent element of peasant dreams, workers' ambitions and bureaucratic models of a People's Community. As such, it provides an important key for understanding the cycles of violence that characterized so many revolutionary upheavals in Europe after 1917. In Spain, for example, the dynamics of revolutionary and counter-revolutionary violence during the 1930s were driven forward by the way in which both sides, Nationalist and Republican, saw themselves as engaged in campaigns of purification: they were seeking to rid the body politic through actual or symbolic violence of those who, as a consequence of their ideological views, their social origins or their individual character, were prejudicial to the wider health of the community.[46] It was, however, indisputably in the ethnically diverse states of Central and Eastern Europe in the decades between the collapse of the pre-First World War empires and the enforced pacification of the early Cold War that these notions of the health of the community reached their fullest expression.[47] The ways by which these notions of purification and of purging were carried through by paramilitary movements owed much to the context within which they operated, and more especially to the crises of state authority and the exacerbation of inter-community relations by military conflicts and economic change.

Finally, paramilitary violence had ramifications in the colonial world as well, not least because it, too, was subject to the force-field of ideological conflict. Whereas nascent anti-colonial movements took inspiration from the Wilsonian discourse on democratic national self-determination at the Paris Peace Conference, the Communist (Third) International at its second congress in August 1920 sought to link colonial struggles against 'imperialism' with class war against the capitalist

[44] Martin Pugh, *Hurrah for the Blackshirts! Fascists and Fascism in Britain between the Wars* (London, 2005), 126–55 (though in Mosley's case, as with many fascists, preserving the victory of the war meant avoiding future war with ideologically sympathetic regimes such as Nazi Germany and Fascist Italy).

[45] Mann, *Dark Side*; Bloxham, *Final Solution*; Gerwarth and Conway, *Revolution*.

[46] Michael Richards, *A Time of Silence. Civil War and the Culture of Repression in Franco's Spain, 1936–1945* (Cambridge, 1998).

[47] Norman Naimark, *Fires of Hatred. Ethnic Cleansing in Twentieth Century Europe* (Cambridge, Ma., 2001).

world.[48] The fear of nationalist and communist revolt in the colonies began to reshape the relations of the British and French with their empires. While this led to reform as well as repression, the immediate result was violence against new colonial demands that often entailed the use of paramilitary forces. In Egypt, India and Iraq as well as in Afghanistan and Burma, Britain responded to demands and unrest by the colonized with armed police and paramilitary units as well as the military.[49] The Black and Tans travelled from Ireland to other colonial trouble spots, including Palestine.[50] Comparable use of paramilitary violence by the French occurred in Algeria, Syria and Indo-China. These conflicts and their long-term impact on the wars of decolonization after 1945 are remarkably understudied and will be the subject of a separate volume.

[48] Manela, *Wilsonian Moment*.

[49] Important studies on these conflicts include David M. Anderson and David Killingray, (eds.), *Policing and Decolonisation: Politics, Nationalism, and the Police, 1917–65* (Manchester, 1992); Thomas R. Mockaitis, *British Counterinsurgency, 1919–60* (Basingstoke, 1990); Kevin Grant, *A Civilised Savagery: Britain and the New Slaveries in Africa, 1884–1926* (London, 2005); Peter Sluget, *Britain in Iraq: Contriving King and Country* (2nd rev. edn., London, 2007), 61 and 91; Derek Sayer, 'British Reaction to the Amritsar Massacre 1919–1920', *Past and Present*, 131 (1991), 130–64.

[50] Charles Townshend, *Britain's Civil Wars: Counterinsurgency in the Twentieth Century* (London, Faber, 1986), 191–2; Bernard Wasserstein, *The British in Palestine: The Mandatory Government and the Arab-Jewish Conflict* (London, 1978).

PART I

REVOLUTION AND
COUNTER-REVOLUTION

2

Paramilitary Violence in Russia's Civil Wars, 1918–1920[1]

William G. Rosenberg

I THE QUESTION OF VIOLENCE IN REVOLUTIONARY RUSSIA

Despite the vast literature on revolutionary Russia, the issue of violence in this prolonged period of collective and individual trauma still warrants scholarly attention. As Peter Holquist has suggested, a 'syndrome' of violence emerged in all of its fury as a result of the close interplay between circumstance, ideology, and the political uses of force on both sides of the Bolshevik-anti-Bolshevik divide.[2] The interactions between thinking, behaviour and context differed with the times and regions in which the civil wars were fought in the vast expanse of the collapsed imperial Russian state, but the nature and forms of the violence itself did not. Everywhere in territories Red, White, Green, Black, and several shades in between, it was unimaginably brutal, merciless, devoid of normative moral restraints, and 'atrocious' in the fundamental meaning of atrocity. The rare oases of calm between 1918 and 1921, such as the so-called Crimean Republic in late 1918 and 1919, were themselves bounded by horrors inflicted before and afterwards by rampaging Bolshevized sailors, vengeful Tatars, and raging White 'interventionists,' once the foreign protection dissolved.[3] Unrestrained violence penetrated every boundary and border in this region between 1918 and 1920: personal, collective, social, cultural, and political. The Russian word for what many regarded as this Hobbesian chaos was *smuta*, which adds the connotations of chaos, brutality, and terror

---

[1] Some arguments presented here first appeared in my article 'Beheading the Revolution: Arno Mayer's "Furies"', *Journal of Modern History* 73 (2001), 908–30.

[2] See especially Peter Holquist, 'Reflections on the Russian Civil War' and Peter Gatrell, 'The Russian Revolution and Europe: 1917–1923', papers presented to the conference on Paramilitary Violence after the Great War, 1918–1923: Towards a Global Perspective, Clinton Institute, University College Dublin, 5–6 December 2008. See also Peter Holquist, 'Violent Russia, Deadly Marxism? Russia in the Epoch of Violence, 1905–21', *Kritika* 4 (2003), 627–52.

[3] See the discussion of these tensions in my *Liberals in the Russian Revolution: The Constitutional Democratic Party 1917–1921* (Princeton, 1974), ch. 12. Although this study is now quite dated, to my knowledge there is still no more recent discussion of the 'Crimean republic' in the literature.

Fig. 1. Red Army soldiers in front of the headquarter building at the Voronezh front in 1918.

to the meanings of 'violent socio-political disorder', and has no clear equivalents in Western European languages.[4]

Part of the reason for this brutality was that Russia's civil wars themselves transcended all of the imperial order's social, cultural, and national boundaries.[5] Fighting took place between (and among) Bolsheviks, other militant radicals, anti-Bolsheviks, local nationalists, anarchists, peasants and other groups, and in some places especially between different religious and ethnic groups in the Baltic states, Finland, Poland, Ukraine, Georgia, Armenia, Azerbaijan, and the ethno-political regions of Central Asia, Siberia, and the Far East. In part, the violence was caused by full independence (Poland, Finland) or claims to full independence (Ukraine, the Caucasus) throughout virtually all the ethnically delimited territories of the former tsarist Empire. This was true even within Russia proper, where local figures in ethic 'islands' like Tatarstan struggled for regional autonomy or to otherwise escape subordination to Moscow. In a larger measure, however, the transnational quality of Russia's civil conflicts challenged the very concept of national boundaries and everything they implied. The origins, rationalizations, and aims of the Great

---

[4] See, e.g., Vladimir Buldakov's magisterial 900-page volume *Krasnaia Smuta: Priroda i posledstviia revoliutsionnogo nasiliia* (Moscow, 2010).

[5] For convenience, I will use 'Russia' as a shorthand for the territory of the former Russian Empire throughout this essay.

War were all related to the need to defend these boundaries, justifying the war's unprecedented military horrors. Coming to power in what had been geographically the largest imperial European state, Bolshevik internationalism directly challenged the very political foundations of the entire European order.

So did the Bolshevik Party's unrestrained embrace of class warfare, its militant suppression of the church, and what, to many in Europe, was its surprising ability to remobilize war weary soldiers, workers and other supporters into large scale military forces capable of defending, if not advancing, its goals and interests. In all of this the early Bolshevik regime was not in any traditional sense 'Russian'. The diversities of language, ethnicity, and territorial location were fully subordinated to the ideological internationalism of a 'transnational' Soviet state, in which the distinctions that dominated European politics and culture for more than a century would be dissolved. Was this danger also a key aspect of violence in Russia itself at this time?

Even after nearly a century, and in a post-Soviet perspective, the violent aftermath of Russia's revolution is still seen in much of the literature as testimony to the inherent destructiveness of a utopian internationalism as well as of Lenin's personal lust for power. Understanding Russian violence in terms of competing ideological systems has appealed strongly as a means of discrediting *all* socialist thought as utopian and contrary to current neo-capitalism. The same is true of radical politics, now often conflated with 'terrorism' in virtually all of its forms.

The crucial question in the context of this book is whether the violence described thus far was in any meaningful sense paramilitary. Or was its real significance in that context rather that it served as an ideological excuse for different, counter-revolutionary forms of paramilitary organization elsewhere in Europe? This chapter suggests three important determinants of the violence in question. The first involves the wrenching scarcity and material deprivation which beset virtually the entire imperial Russian population from late 1915 until well into the 1920s, and which became especially severe during and immediately after the civil wars themselves. The second is the closely related indignity and humiliation that accompanied multiple kinds of loss as instability degenerated into a raw struggle for collective and individual survival. From these arise the third explanation, namely the role of what I would call 'functionality' as an element of political legitimacy. In this period it was increasingly difficult to make basic processes of production and distribution function effectively or even at all. While various ideologies and forms of political will clearly underlay the emergence of the Red and White Terror and help explain their ferocity, and while it is obviously true that after the Bolsheviks claimed power in October 1917 their rule involved an extremely violent socio-political dialectic, the broader syndrome of violence in Russia's civil wars is better explained by how these underlying currents and processes related to each other than by more conventional categories of political and ideological struggle.

This also has the benefit of reducing the role of both February and October 1917 as turning points. Each successive political regime faced the same range of fundamental problems, whether it assumed a large-scale 'imperial' or 'democratic' mandate or the narrowest ambitions of territorial control. The issue of power and control in this sense was subordinate to the tasks that scarcity and deprivation created, and which necessarily raised questions of purpose and competency. In dealing with the issue of purpose, meaning had to be given to increasingly horrific losses first of the World War, and then of the brutalities that followed. Explanations had to be found for the value of sacrifice. Death itself, not to say the ruination of millions of lives, demanded redemption and for many, cried for revenge. Solutions had to be found for material needs that escalated into sheer desperation, and mechanisms devised to cope with the psychological and social insecurities that attended them. The imperatives of governance became fraught with risk, encouraging stringent forms of social control. Scarcity and loss thus proved a perilous combination for individuals and collectivities alike.

II THE CENTRALITY OF SCARCITY AND LOSS

Scarcity as a root of paramilitary violence in revolutionary Russia was set in the problems of production and distribution that refracted almost every dimension of Russia's politics after 1914 and contextualized all possible outcomes after the collapse of the imperial regime. Chronic shortages in all sorts of essential goods rippled through the economy well before February 1917, and escalated catastrophically between 1918 and 1922. This was so for a variety of familiar reasons: the exigencies of a war unprecedented in scale and scope for which Russia was particularly ill-prepared; the depletion of reserve stores to assuage pressing military and civilian demands; the breakdown of transport; disruptions in industrial production caused by strike waves, lockouts, distribution problems and the absence of raw materials; the depopulation of able-bodied men from the countryside; restraints on pricing; accelerating practices of grain and goods requisition begun without adequate planning in 1915; an inflationary spiral that encouraged hoarding; the contraction and ultimate collapse of credit and investment capital as the political and economic climate soured; increasing difficulties in meeting wage demands and capitalizing new production; and finally, but not least, the inevitable spread of black and grey markets, which fed on themselves, involved their own violent practices, and accelerated disruption everywhere when authorities lacked the means to control them.[6]

Between 1914 and the end of 1916, these problems had ramifications not only in the familiar terms of tsarist political legitimacy, but in the mentalities and proclivities of many soldiers, peasants, industrial workers, and their families. Peasants and workers entered the war compelled to defend a regime that had wreaked its own violent fury on industrial neighbourhoods and the countryside in 1905 and 1906. Where else in Europe was a major industrial neighborhood bombarded by government cannon in the immediate aftermath of a manifesto guaranteeing basic civil rights, as occurred in Moscow in 1905, or were unruly peasants hanged in

---

[6] See the thorough discussion by Peter Gatrell in *Russia's First World War: A Social and Economic History* (London, 2005).

large numbers without civilian trials by the country's 'last great statesman', Petr Stolypin? When production and transport problems left tens of thousands without adequate arms and ammunition in 1915, and deadly assaults were made on enemy positions by troops ill-equipped to succeed, rage built against the 'aristocrat' officers who ordered them as well as, more abstractly, the regime, its systems, and its values. By August 1915, as much as 30 per cent of Russian front line troops were without arms.[7] Explanations for shortages were easily imagined in venality and profiteering, some of them true. When inadequate transport left thousands of badly wounded men lying unfed and uncared for on litters for days in 1915, the anger expressed in their officers' communications surely reflected even deeper passions among rank and file.[8]

Among its other effects, Russia's wartime experience thus proved to be one of near constant humiliation and socio-psychological dislocation for those closest to its horrors: raw recruits, experienced soldiers, and field officers alike. Suffice it here simply to point out that already by the end of 1915, almost 1.5 million men had returned from the front seriously wounded, inadequately cared for, and deprived of livelihoods as well as limbs. Some 1.54 million were missing or Prisoners of War.[9] More than 3 million civilians had become refugees—a 'whole empire walking' as Peter Gatrell portrays in his superb study, including between a half million and a million Jews forced out of their homes by the military, and mutilated physically and psychologically by the wanton confiscation of their personal belongings and 'gratuitous' pogroms.[10] By all accounts these were often viciously inflicted by local peasants whose own goods had been requisitioned and who themselves had suffered awful losses.[11] Like the spirals of scarcity and deprivation, those of humiliation and dislocation also rippled through Russian communities once violence was inflicted on its members. By the end of 1917, partly as a result of Kerensky's disastrous June offensive, military casualties alone, including those who had died as military prisoners or were still held by the Germans, were officially recorded at more than 7 million.[12]

Whatever the figure, the language of 'loss' itself camouflages a brutal fact: these casualties were the result of violence initiated by political regimes that left individuals and communities acutely scared in physical, psychological, and social terms—a whole nation brutalized, to paraphrase Gatrell. Yet one cannot really describe this as a 'culture of defeat' as the concept has been used to explain some paramilitary violence elsewhere in Europe after the war, since revolutionary Russia

[7] Irina Davidian, 'The Russian Soldier's Morale from the Evidence of Tsarist Military Censorship', in: *Facing Armageddon: The First World War Experienced* (London, 1996), 428–9.

[8] Russian State Historical Archive [RGIA], f.651, op. 1, del. 1029, ll. 2ff.

[9] *Rossiia v mirovoi voine 1914–1918 goda (v tsifrakh)* (Moscow, 1925), 30 (data of the Central Statistical Administration).

[10] Peter Gatrell, *A Whole Empire Walking. Refugees in Russia During World War I* (Bloomington, IN., 1999), 3.

[11] See the discussion in Eric Lohr, 'The Russian Army and the Jews: Mass Deportation, Hostages, and Violence during World War I', *Russian Review* 60 (2001), esp. 404–6, 414–17; Gatrell, *Russia's First World War*, 30–1, 178–83.

[12] *Rossiia v mirovoi voine*, 31.

essentially gave up the war on its own terms, at least until the Bolsheviks signed the Treaty of Brest Litovsk.[13] What it largely reflected instead was a very different 'culture of betrayal': the strong feelings that military censors reported welling up within army ranks already during the disastrous retreats of 1915 towards officers and state officials who treated them harshly and seemed totally uninterested in their welfare; the belief that high ranking officials and those around them, including the Minister of War, Sukhomlinov and even the empress herself, were sympathetic to Germany; the conviction especially among Russia's leading Duma figures that the regime's own incompetence and malfeasance were betraying Russia's national interests and leading the country toward disaster. A famous metaphor of the day described the country as an automobile careening down a mountain road with no one behind the wheel.

Even before the February revolution, moreover, the mentalities of betrayal were linked to the problems of scarcity through closely tied expectations and demands for reform. Among the upper reaches of society, as we know, the demand for 'responsible' leaders was coupled with the expectation that shifting authority from an isolated and overly centralized autocratic regime to knowledgeable and competent local figures would prevent further economic, and hence military collapse. Among 'ordinary' people, demands and expectations were even more succinct. Peasant-soldiers expected they would be given land as a reward for service. Workers expected a change in regimes would result in higher wages and the end of food lines. The strident call of their delegates to the Central War Industries Committee in January clearly echoed very broad sentiments—and led to their arrest.[14]

III PARAMILITARISM AND THE HOPES AND CHALLENGES OF REVOLUTIONARY DEMOCRACY

Although it was almost certainly unavoidable, the February revolution quickly brought the problems of scarcity and the mentalities of betrayal together in a risky and volatile mix. This occurred not so much in the rhetoric of the moment (although there, too) but in the complementary set of measures the new liberal provisional government and the more radical Petrograd Soviet both adopted to address them. Their goal was precisely to empower those directly involved in production, distribution, and the situation at the front to address pressing concerns at a local level, and thus be able to implement effective solutions. The army's loyalty to the revolution had to be assured, along with its ability to defend it. Production had to be increased, especially of military supplies and foodstuffs. Improving supply and distribution systems was urgent. In organizational terms, these measures involved the sanctioning of (and helping to create) elected worker committees in major state and private industrial plants; a radical reorganization of railroad administration that empowered local and central 'line committees;' legislation to allow

---

[13] See the discussion in Gerwarth and Horne, above.
[14] RGIA, f. 32, op. 1, del. 2123.

the formation of district Dumas in Russian cities and new, elected, town and city governments; the formation of 'land committees' in the countryside to address the problems of agrarian production and land use; legislation establishing district (volost') zemstvos to govern rural localities and granting new powers to the zemstvo and urban unions; and most demonstrative of all, the sanctioning of elected local worker and peasant soviets as well as broader district, city, and 'All Russian' committees, elected by those they represented. And with the notable exception of the Soviet's famous 'Order Number One', which sanctioned soldiers' committees in the army to end abuse and defend against counterrevolution, all of these measures initially had broad support across the 'dual power' divide. Albeit with varying degrees of enthusiasm, provisional government and Soviet leaders both saw them as a fundamental part of the devolution of power needed for economic as well as political reasons.[15]

So were efforts to strengthen the state's 'non-partisan' (in Russian, *nad-partiinyi*) role in the areas of regulation and industrial capitalization. Suffice it to note that it was a leading liberal, Andrei Shingarev, who drafted the provisional government's new law on the state's grain monopoly, designed legislation to supply peasants with needed commodities at fixed prices, helped prepare decrees that forbade the sale of grain except at fixed prices through newly created food supply organs, and compelled all surpluses to be delivered to state procurement agents rather than sold on open markets. Soviet and state figures cooperated to fix prices as well on 'articles of primary need', and both were determined to make these available to the population 'at the lowest possible prices'.[16] A new state monopoly over fuel was created, building on the preparatory work of the tsarist 'special councils', while in the textile and leather markets, the Central Cotton and Wool Committees 'practically eliminated all existing private commercial machinery', according to a liberal participant.[17] Meanwhile the Ministry of War, first under the conservative liberal Guchkov and then, after May, one of the country's best known socialists, Alexander Kerensky, further engaged local War Industries Committees and 'Zemgor' groups to help meet its needs.

For our purposes, one can see in all of this not simply the enormous hopes and challenges facing the democratic revolutionary state, but also what one might call the ideal foundation for the formation of paramilitarism: local groups sanctioned or tolerated by the state and charged with implementing what were broadly regarded as urgent reforms, but without access to any of effective state power that would ordinarily be available to enforce them. In comparative terms, these institutional foundations for paramilitary violence emerging in Russia were fundamentally different from those that soon developed anywhere else in Europe, since they reflected a broadly shared understanding of how the new revolutionary state could

---

[15] See my article, 'The Democratization of Russia's Railroads in 1917', *American Historical Review*, 86 (1981), 983–1008.

[16] See, e.g., *Vestnik vremennago pravitel'stva*, 28 March 1917. There is an excellent discussion of the food supply question throughout this period in Lars Lih, *Bread and Authority in Russia 1914–1921* (Berkeley and Los Angeles, 1990).

[17] S.O. Zagorsky, *State Control of Industry During the War* (New Haven, 1928), 224.

best resolve the pressing problems of scarcity and distribution and, it was hoped, constructively channel popular discontent. Russia's successful transformation into a democratic state would justify the war's horrific losses.

This was so because democratization in these and other terms was such a broadly shared goal in the first months of the revolution, and because the hopes placed in the committee structure seemed initially to be warranted. New quantities of food-stuffs were soon being distributed from government stocks. New wage agreements and the involvement of worker committees in addressing the problems of trans-port and production brought immediate improvement in the distribution of goods. Issues of dignity and social humiliation were also addressed in this way. As we know, soldiers' soviets altered forms of address in the army even in units where discipline remained. The ritualized humiliation of military flogging was aban-doned. Streetcars were 'liberated' from 'bourgeois' restrictions on their use by 'lower elements'. New forms of polite address and 'dignified' treatment were pres-sured into use through legal and orderly strikes. In Petrograd, café and restaurant workers even won a strike to *end* tipping, gaining the dignity of salaries instead.[18] It is true, of course, that in the process, retributive humiliations were also some-times visited on real and imagined 'oppressors': officers lynched and mutilated; factory managers tarred and run out of their plants in wheelbarrows; estates burned and their owners brutalized when peasants began to seize the property that they thought was 'rightfully' theirs. But initially, at least, these were excesses that were widely seen inside the committee structure and out as threatening to shared values, not tactics or behaviours that served partisan political ends. The revolution as a whole was almost universally welcomed.

Already by the spring of 1917, however, ominous developments were altering this 'normative' understanding of how local soviets and other committees should function. Most familiar was the rapid radicalization of political discourse that Len-in's *April Theses* did so much to encourage upon his return to Russia, and which accelerated so greatly as Kerensky initiated the ill-fated June offensive. While the increasing brutalization of politics and social relations may be partly explained in these terms, the more important issues have to do with why Lenin's voice gained such rapid purchase in industrial centres like Petrograd and at the front, and why the actions of local committees and soviets found increasingly violent paramilitary expression.

First and foremost, in my view, was the renewal of Russia's economic deterior-ation in the late spring of Russia's economy, and the increasing inability of the revo-lutionary regime itself, including soviet organizations still largely dominated by moderate socialists, to mitigate the effects of continued deprivation and loss. Even before the June offensive, the role of the war in all of this was problematic; with its collapse, and the subsequent desertion of tens of thousands of angry soldiers from the front, Bolshevik opposition even to 'revolutionary defencism' provided not so much a persuasive 'utopian' vision but a coherent, if inaccurate, explanation of

---

[18] See the extended discussion of this and other labour conflicts in Diane Koenker and William G. Rosenberg, *Strikes and Revolution in Russia* (Princeton, 1989).

what was going wrong, and why. State intervention, mediation and sanctioned forms of labour protest like strikes were proving ineffective because the 'bourgeoisie' was defending its interests and hoarding goods. Rising prices meant higher profits. The private ownership of landed estates perpetuated the injustices of capitalism. Continuing the murderous war instead of suing for peace protected imperial ambitions and war profits. The 'minister-capitalists' and their socialist 'lackeys' were at fault because 'their' 'bourgeois' state lacked both the will and power to intervene to protect the wellbeing of ordinary workers, peasants, and soldiers. Revolutionary Russia's 'democracy' was thus fully justified in using the committee structures it now had readily at hand to defend itself aggressively against continued 'bourgeois-capitalist' subjugation.

The essential element here, in other words, was not located in ideology or the discursive shift of 'democracy' from practices to people, but in the clearly increasing inability of the coalition regime to function effectively even after socialists took control in July. For many on the right, resistant to national elections, the government now lacked legitimacy because it was illegally violating the authority still formally vested in the State Duma and its laws. For others, legitimacy required the popular mandate of a constituent assembly and new constitution. Among the broadest strata of the population, however, as evidenced by speeches, protests, and a near constant process of committee, soviet, and Duma elections at the local level, legitimacy was most closely tied simply to the ability to get things done. If the regime and the soviets could not adequately solve Russia's problems with their current forms and methods, others were 'justified' and had to be put in place.

The revolutionary Russian state had thus unwittingly provided the perfect incubator for popular violence that was paramilitary in precisely the sense formulated by Robert Gerwarth and John Horne: as 'military or quasi-military organizations and practices that either expanded or replaced the activities of conventional military formations.' The more dire Russia's economic condition, and the more ineffective the revolutionary state appeared in its efforts to assure popular well-being, the more democratic practices radicalized all sorts of local committees. The 'Red Guards' that were organized in great numbers in the summer and fall, especially after the Kornilov rebellion, were far better armed than they were disciplined. Hungry bands of deserters, some as large as 6,000, increasingly terrorized the countryside, fortifying the brutality of their erstwhile peasant comrades.[19] By October, as the economic situation deteriorated beyond any obvious repair, more than 8,000 state engraving workers were turning out some 30 million new paper rubles a day, an amount still insufficient to meet the state's wage and purchasing requirements. Socialist and liberal officials alike had come to the conclusion that the chances of meeting urban needs in the coming winter were slim, even if the coalition regime could use force.[20]

In retrospect, the unintended consequences of this seem fully predictable, if equally unavoidable. For both government officials and soviet leaders alike, taking

[19] See Sanborn, *Drafting the Russian Nation,* 173.
[20] Shingarev, *Finansovoe polozhenie,* 11.

responsibility for solving insoluble problems at both the local and state level, whether formally or informally, meant becoming the object of anger and new charges of 'betrayal' when situations did not improve, articulated by increasingly radical committee proclamations and actions. Officials on local food supply committees were now openly attacked, in some instances paraded around provincial towns with their hands tied behind them. As strikes resulted increasingly in lockouts or closures rather than higher wages, committee decisions to seize enterprises as a 'solution' to the problem of maintaining production and wages became more 'legitimate' and more common. By the autumn, 'formal' protests within the context of even of a poorly functioning democratic system reached the limit of their effectiveness.[21]

In the process, the bases for political legitimacy understandably shifted on all sides to evaluations of function, from commitment to relatively complex and contested notions of legality and constitutionality to simplistic and contested promises of what would work, whether imposed by force or not. Until the Bolsheviks themselves seized responsibility for solving these problems in October, brought to power by their own 'military revolutionary committees', ideology trumped circumstance only as a promise for betterment, not as a formalized system of rule. 'All Power to the Soviets' and 'Bread, Land, and Peace' were slogans that resonated with fear, loss, insecurity and popular demands, but they were not a system of governance. The same was true of 'Defend the Constituent Assembly' and 'Russia, One and Indivisible', the emerging rallying cries of the anti-Bolshevik centre and right. The impossible hopes they all reflected set the stage for the particularities of Russian violence in the awful years of civil war that followed.

IV ESCALATING AFTER OCTOBER: "LIFE IN CATASTROPHE"

It is hardly surprising that the October revolution involved a radical extension of the methods of regulation, requisition, and brutal confiscation that had become both formal and informal ways of coping with Russia's social and political economies of need and want. In its economic abstraction, 'scarcity' is the foundation of market as well as regulated systems of exchange; it relates to the ethical as well as practical issues involved in the social distribution of goods. Unabstracted, the need for food and other basic goods cuts to the heart of everyday subjectivities: the anxieties, fears, worries, angers, and, especially, propensities toward violence that affect perspectives and behaviours in profound if immeasurable ways. For Lenin and his supporters, who readily conflated all sources of deprivation and loss to a capitalist enemy in the broadest sense, and who legitimized violent 'solutions' by demonizing the individual faces of Russia's putative bourgeoisie, scarcity could only reinforce

---

[21] Diane Koenker and Wm. G. Rosenberg, 'The Limits of Formal Protest: Worker Activism and Social Polarization in Petrograd and Moscow, 1917', *American Historical Review*, 92 (1987), 296–326.

the redemptive urgency of their self-styled mission. The violent reform of Russia's social, economic, cultural and political order would finally bring an end to want for all who supported it. Here was the brutal core of Bolshevik politics that all historical actors, and especially the Bolsheviks themselves, understood as presaging class and civil war.

The rapid escalation of all types of violence after October has to be understood largely in these terms. Already in early 1918, well before formal Red and White armies 'legitimized' horrific treatments of their enemies, the struggle for foodstuffs and other goods throughout Russia's urban and rural spaces brought a new flood of 'informal' violence of near comparable brutality, if not yet comparable scale. Well-armed delegations of factory workers, many from factories that were 'nationalized' from below, were soon in the countryside demanding grain. And well before the Bolsheviks could organize their own paramilitary 'Committees of the Poor', peasant soviets and other rural groups themselves escalated their seizures of estates, sometimes destroying livestock and burning supply depots in a self-destructive rage. Some of the more horrendous acts of violence also took place in the North Caucasus and in the areas of Central Asia, where Kirghiz and others had risen up against the Russians when the tsarist regime tried to draft them in 1916.[22]

The difficulties of documenting all these encounters even in the heartland of the new Bolshevik state should not obscure the conflagration that raged throughout many parts of Russia during the winter of 1917–18. Paramilitarism was still rooted in the complementary conditions of material need and the subjectivities of loss and deprivation, and implemented through local councils and committees that tried with increasingly less success to meet the needs and impulses of their constituents. In these circumstances there was no possibility whatsoever that once in power, Lenin and his party, beleaguered on all sides by hostile forces and convictions, could bring any modicum of material or social security even to their most ardent supporters. Violence first had to be monopolized under Bolshevik control, a primary task of the Cheka. Red Guards had to be mobilized into something formally resembling an army, even if to show their ostensible revolutionary commitments, its commanders did not wear epaulettes. While Brest Litovsk may have provided an urgent breathing space for the Bolsheviks to consolidate power within the truncated territory now under their control, its devastating economic implications in terms of access to raw materials and grain production in German occupied Ukraine also set the brutal terms of isolation in which urgent need readily merged with Lenin's new 'nationalistic internationalism', based on transnational military and revolutionary forces. Defending Bolshevik Russia now meant defending world revolution. Spontaneous acts of violence even by those supportive of many Bolshevik goals were 'counterrevolutionary'.

But directing force inward to establish some semblance of order was an urgent need in non-Bolshevik areas as well, since foodstuffs and other essential goods were only relatively more abundant away from Bolshevik areas of control. Here, too, a

---

[22] See I. Borisenko, *Sovetskie respubliki na Severnom Kavkaze v 1918 g.* (Rostov na Donu, 1930).

spiral of violence was rooted fundamentally in the impossible task of restoring control over production and distribution in ways that met material and emotional needs while also assuring a modicum of security. For a while, as we know, the Allied powers managed to provide essential military goods to both the South Russian and Siberian movements. The German occupation of Ukraine also helped temporarily spare this region from some degree of excess. By 1919, however, the Bolshevik conviction that capitalism everywhere was the source of all misery and loss was balanced by the equally formulaic condemnation of every form of 'Bolshevism' as the cause of catastrophe even in areas of the former Empire that were not formally Russian like the Baltic region and Transcaucasia.

For many now caught in the unrestrained violence of civil war, however, the inability of *any* regime to bring security and well-being only escalated brutal forms of resistance and intensified cultures of betrayal. Once they were formed, Red and White armies both suffered massive desertions, especially in 1919 and 1920. Further breakdowns of transport and industry followed one after another like a crumbling sea wall within and along shifting civil war boundaries. So did brutal searches for hoarded goods, equipment, and residual supplies, wherever they were imagined or could be found. As the Bolsheviks moved towards elements of a natural economy whose wisdom was fiercely debated but which made some sense in terms of the urgencies of order, supply, and control, the expanding apparatus governing production and exchange became itself a fierce network of both formal and informal aggression and resistance. And as the Whites forcefully mobilized reluctant peasants into their ranks, especially in South Russia and the Ukraine after the German withdrawal, temporary victories on the battlefield were subverted by popular resistance and increasing brutality behind the lines. Although it maintained its own fierce security detachments, the Armed Forces of South Russia under General Denikin literally melted away as they got within striking distance of Moscow in 1919, their rank and file pillaging their way home in a rampage.

For ordinary men and women still literally bearing the scars of the World War, these new battles were also again about how they were still being 'betrayed', this time by *all* formal political powers and regimes; how the end of the war was bringing only new misfortune; how Bolshevized trade unions, factory committees, and especially Red Guards and White Guards were reducing ordinary people everywhere to destitution; and how the burgeoning anti-Bolshevik movements in 1919 and 1920 were betraying the purposes and hopes that overthrew the Tsar. In the process, paramilitary violence wreaked by formations that expanded or replaced conventional military forms increasingly imbricated the behaviours of more conventional armies and detachments. In Red Russia, violent clashes between the first Red Guard units of Trotsky's new Bolshevik Army and those whose interests they supposedly reflected spread widely already between March and the end of June, 1918, well before the White armies were a serious threat: at major industrial plants in Petrograd, Moscow, Tula, Kostroma; along the railroads; and into villages whose resources were still being plundered by every imaginable kind of armed delegation. At meetings held in June in connection with new Petrograd soviet elections, Bolshevik speakers could not make themselves heard even in the party's Vyborg stronghold. In White Russia, meanwhile, the occupation of 'Bolshevik' villages and towns led to paroxysms of violent rage, especially towards the 'Bolshevik Jews'. Everywhere, moreover, it was the need for 'extraordinary' measures of every kind to control how and which goods were produced and distributed, and to whom, that sanctioned the lynching of 'speculators', 'deserters', 'hoarders' and other subversives, as well as black and grey marketeers. While the spreading 'formal' wars between Reds, Whites, Greens, and others escalated violence exponentially, its roots still lay in the antagonistic and repressive necessities of individual and collective survival. Indeed, as we know, the final emblematic horrors of the Kronstadt rebellion in 1921 came after Denikin, Kolchak, Wrangel, and the furies of war against the Whites and Allies were extinguished. This last horrific effect of seven years of loss and deprivation awaited only the Bolsheviks' *relaxation* of control.[23] And then, after most of the awful varieties of man-made violence ended temporarily in 1921, the agonies of starvation, disease, and sheer despair were left to wipe out several additional millions. According to the best estimates, some 16 million deaths were directly attributable to the violence and deprivations of the 1914–22 period.[24] 'Life in catastrophe', as it has been described in a fine recent study, characterized the effects of scarcity, deprivation, and loss in virtually every part for the Russian world.[25]

V WAS VIOLENCE "PARAMILITARY" IN THE RUSSIAN CIVIL WARS?

Understanding the Russian case in these terms allows us to treat carefully some of the basic questions about paramilitary violence with which this volume is concerned: in its relationship to more conventional military forces; in its relation to ethnicity; as an effect of the brutalization of social relations throughout this region; as a force that affected the outcome of the civil war itself; and in its relationship to the dangers Bolshevism represented as a threat to the established European social order, political institutions, and value systems. Finally, this should enable us to take up the question of whether and how 'paramilitary' itself is an appropriate designation for much of the violence that occurred in this region, and how its various forms were brought to bear on issues of political legitimacy, especially for the Bolshevik state that alone managed to survive the maelstrom.

One has to recognize first, that with more than 30 different governments claiming the right to control various parts of the former Russian Empire, between 1918

---

[23] See V.P. Kozlov et al., *Kronshtadtskaia tragediia 1921 goda. Dokumenty v dvukh knigakh* (Moscow, 1999).

[24] Frank Lorimer, *The Population of the Soviet Union: History and Prospects* (Geneva, 1946), 29–43; E.Z. Volkov, *Dinamika naseleniia SSSR za vosem'desiat let* (Moscow, 1930), 262; L.I. Lubny-Gertsyk, *Dvizhenie naseleniia na territorii SSSR za vremia mirovoi voiny i revoliutsii* (Moscow, 1926), esp. 22; and the data of the Central Statistical Administration published in *Rossiia v mirovoi voine*, 30–42.

[25] Igor Narskii, *Zhizn' v katastrofe. Budni naseleniia Urala v 1917–1922 gg.* (Moscow, 2001).

and 1921, violence of any sort was not far removed from some organized political structure and ambition. The major claimants to power may have set familiar patterns of Red and White terror, but the forces of lesser claimants, like Nestor Makhno in the Ukraine or Alexander Antonov in Tambov, acted in similar ways, as did the formal armies themselves. General Denikin's troops took few if any prisoners during the formative period of the Armed Forces of South Russia. The expansion of his armies and power into the Ukraine after the withdrawal of the Germans allowed an unprecedented mass murder of Jews between June and December 1919, with casualties as high as 100,000.[26]

Why this occurred has several explanations. According to a leading historian of Denikin's movement, the Volunteer Army 'succeeded in murdering as many Jews as all other armies put together, because they were the best organized, carried out like military operations, and the most ideologically motivated.'[27] Jews in small Ukrainian villages bore the murderous hatred of anti-Bolshevism, however, for reasons that extend well beyond ideology. Already by 1915, Jews were being victimized by the Imperial Russian army in Galicia and Poland as sympathetic to the Germans, 'enemy' elements who betrayed Russian positions. As much as the sanctions of Denikin's commanders, paramilitary violence against the 'Jewish enemy' everywhere in White Russia was thus a pre-emptive action against future 'betrayal' as well as retribution for the dangers, humiliations, and betrayals their 'Jewish Bolshevik allies' had already wrought, as it was soon to be in Europe as well.

More prosaically, anti-Semitic violence in Ukraine was also simply the most extreme means of confiscation for troops extended without adequate lines of supply. Here its forms reflected those of other confiscatory military detachments in regions where there were no Jews. In Siberia, the Supreme Ruler Admiral Kolchak categorized all resistance as 'bolshevik' and resisters themselves as 'enemies of the people', mimicking Leninist discourse. As many as 2,500 such 'enemies' may have been executed in Omsk itself, Kolchak's capital, as the new government violently overthrew a regime legitimized by the 1918 Constituent Assembly, Russia's last gasp attempt at democratic governance. Kolchak's new 'all-Russian' state formally sanctioned summary executions especially of 'traitors' hoarding goods. It confiscated property, condoned mass floggings, and moved brutally to crush all real and imagined forms of 'bolshevik criminality'.[28] Indeed, as the Red Army itself expanded rapidly over the winter of 1918–19, and especially during the time of Denikin's and then Kolchak's advances in 1919 and 1920, the need for food was so widespread and urgent, especially in the cities, that armed and hungry workers and soldiers still took what they could from urban

---

[26] See Peter Kenez, 'Pogroms and White Ideology in the Russian Civil War', in: John Klier and Shlomo Lambroza (eds.), *Pogroms: Anti-Jewish Violence in Modern Russian History* (Cambridge, 1992), 302, citing among others Elias Heifetz, *The Slaughter of the Jews in the Ukraine in 1919* (New York, 1921), 72–3 and S.I. Gusev-Orenburgskii, *Bagrovaia kniga. Pogromy 1919–1920 gg. na Ukraine* (Harbin, 1922), 15; N.I. Shtif, 'Dobrovol'tsy i evreiskie pogromy', in: *Revoliutsiia i Grazhdanskaia voina v opisaniakh belogvardeitsev: Denikin, Iudenich, Vrangel* (Moscow, 1991); Oleg Budnitzkij, *Russian Jews between Reds and Whites, 1917–20* (Philadelphia, 2011).

[27] Kenez, 'Pogroms,' 302.

[28] Rosenberg, *Liberals*, ch. 13; V. Zh. Tsvetkov, *Beloe delo v Rossii, 1917–1918* (Moscow, 2008); A. Litvin, *Krasnyi i belyi terror, 1918–1922* (Moscow, 2004).

stores as well as the countryside regardless of severe penalties. 'We must protest against the center's policies', workers describing themselves as 'conscious' and 'patiently starving revolutionaries' telegraphed from Ivanovo-Voznesensk late in 1918, for example. 'Everything is taken from us, nothing is provided...We have not a pound of reserves...We can accept no responsibility for what happens if our needs are not met.'[29]

In many places 'requisition' simply became chaotic and violent confiscation.[30] On 2 April 1919, the Bolsheviks organized a special armed division to conduct 'flying inspections' of warehouses and other storage facilities. Within six months, more than 250 raids took place, uncovering malfeasance of every sort—and very few stores of goods.[31] From Kaluga province, not far from Moscow, inspectors attributed this to local Bolshevik authorities themselves illegally confiscating and distributing property and supplies, and protecting themselves with wanton force, illegal arrests, and acting as a state unto themselves.[32] Similar kinds of reports were filed from scores of other places by the Bolsheviks' Commissariat of State Control, and in South Russia and the Ukraine, by Denikin's own counterintelligence units, the 'Osvag'.[33]

At the same time, comparable forms of violence were also occurring everywhere in areas not formally under Red or White control in this period, or otherwise associated with more or less conventional military forces and formal political claims. These, too, reflect the centrality of scarcity, dysfunctional government, and both material and emotional deprivation in structuring its extent and nature. Here the brutalization of social relations wrought by the revolution itself seems to have played a determinant role, since the most pervasive form was the reciprocal and localized brutalities in which ordinary people engaged, whether or not it was done in the name of any higher purpose. As Igor Narskii and others have shown, violence here was 'small scale' in the sense of the numbers involved in given instances but hardly so in the aggregate or in terms of the havoc they wrought. Theft, loss of livelihood, and violent retribution for real and imagined offences forced many from their towns and villages in Red and White areas alike, often after the murders or maiming of loved ones and friends.[34] Displaced legions then formed their own, autonomous 'partisan' detachments, fighting 'against all'. In towns and settlements throughout the Urals, people leaving home in the morning searching for something to eat were not sure they would return. Many joined together instead in armed local bands with no political goals besides protecting themselves and driving away the 'outsiders'.[35]

[29] *Ekonomicheskaia Zhizn'*, 16 November 1918.

[30] See, e.g., Narskii, *Zhizn' v katastrofe*, 231ff.

[31] RGASPI, f. 5, op.1. del. 2660, ll.45ff; GARF, f. 4085, op.22, del. 269.

[32] RGASPI, f. 5, op. 1, del 2660, l.51.

[33] Ibid. GARF, f. 4085, op. 22, del. 269.

[34] See the documents in *Zelenaia Kniga: Istoriia krest'ianskago dvizheniia v chernomorskoi gubernii* (Prague, 1921).

[35] Narskii, *Zhizn' v katastrofe*, 225.

The emergence of Makhno's 'Black' anarchist movement in Ukraine and Antonov's 'Greens' in the Tambov region in 1919 and 1920 reflected the condensation of these diverse bands into huge marauding armies, ones again without any functional regimes or achievable political ambitions. The notorious suppression of Antonov by Mikhail Tukhachevskii was every bit as horrific, and perhaps even more so if that is possible, as the brutalities that accompanied the defeat of the Whites.[36] Although somewhat different in its particulars, especially in its brutality towards Jews (and despite its well-known defence by Voline, himself of Jewish origin), Makhno's anarchist movement in Ukraine was essentially a similar phenomenon.[37]

Here the pattern of violence also suggests how conditions of scarcity and loss also created as well as exacerbated ethnic tensions throughout the region, as it did in the murder of the Jews. While most combatant groups were partly mixed in ethnic terms, a logical consequence of the diversity of the failed Empire itself, plunder and retribution were always more easily directed against real or imagined 'others', as indeed they still are. It may well be that ethnic violence in places like Transcaucasia would have occurred with the Empire's collapse even in a time of material abundance, as with the recent Balkan wars. But scarcities always seem easier to manage if 'others' can be driven from their properties and goods, especially if they can be blamed for deprivation and loss, as in the case of 'Bolshevik Jews'.

In this we can also identify an additional kind of informal violence in the Russian region at this time, one that might be called 'reciprocal' or 'emulatory'. Violence of this type was experienced especially along the railroads in virtually all parts of the former Empire in 1918 and 1919, perhaps epitomized in the well-known experience of the Czech legion as it battled its way out of Russia along the length of the trans-Siberian line. The Czechs (and others) brutally seized the stores they needed from nearby villages as they moved east, only to find themselves under equally brutal retaliatory attacks by those they had looted. The situation became much worse everywhere in the region in 1919 and 1920, well after the Czechs were gone. Trains carrying goods also carried armoured cars and their own informal militias with no particular political loyalties. In Soviet and White Russia alike, local railroad committees, the remnants of early provisional government reform, were authorities unto themselves, squeezed between the threat of harsh discipline and arguments 'settled with revolvers', as the journal *Zheleznyi Put'* put it. At all levels of service railroad workers and administrators sought to conceal information, hide equipment and goods, and lied about available supplies. When loading

[36] See the rather romanticized discussion by Oliver Radkey, *The Unknown Civil War in Soviet Russia: A Study of the Green Movement in the Tambov Region 1920–21* (Stanford, 1976). Radkey says virtually nothing about the forms and extent of the *Antonovshchina's* own violence. A full collection of documents and memoirs has recently been published. See L. G. Protasov and V. P. Danilov (eds.), *Antonovshchina: Krestianskoe vosstanie v Tambovskoi gub. v 1920–21 gg: Dokumenty, materialy, vospominaniia* (Tambov, 2007). Tukhachevskii himself was a product of the tsarist Imperial General Staff.
[37] A good recent study is A. Shubin, *Anarkhii-mat' poriadka: Mezhdu krasnymi I belymi. Nestor Makhno kak zerkalo Rossiiskoi revoliutsii* (Moscow, 2005). See also V. F. Verstiuk, *Makhnovshchina: selianskyi povstanskii rukh na Ukraini 1918–1921* (Kyiv, 1991) and Voline, *The Unknown Revolution* (New York, 1974).

goods meant armed clashes, they found it easier to cooperate with black market-eers; if unloading freight wagons meant risking armed conflict, it was easier not to unload the goods at all, and hide the wagons on guarded sidings. Well before the defeat of the Whites and Trotsky's decision to combat these problems by militariz-ing lines under Bolshevik control, railroaders everywhere felt themselves under siege, and reacted accordingly to all claimants to power.[38]

Other kinds of assaults by marauding bands also became common. In Siberia and South Russia, self-styled 'atamans' like Semenov and Ungern-Sternberg led 'Cossacks' of various provenance in all sorts of brutal raids. Although sanctioned by Denikin's and Kolchak's armies, these bands were only loosely affiliated with their regimes, and essentially as a matter of licence. Their 'Whiteness' came from the fact that they were fiercely 'anti-Red,' a colour that now covered a broad spec-trum of victims and justified rather than explained their brutality. Throughout the region, in one description, 'the rural localities turned into a sea of literally inde-pendent "rural-republics" [*dereven-respubliki*]' with their own conscripts, 'punitive detachments', and fierce codes of 'retribution' against all suspected 'traitors' and 'enemies'.[39]

Paramilitary violence here clearly grew on itself, with each successive incident emulating and reciprocating what preceded it. Bands of Cossacks nominally under Denikin's control in South Russia repeatedly taught 'regular' soldiers how to sack Jewish settlements and maim or murder women and children along with the men. The writings of Denikin and his advisers reflect their concerns with this, as well as their inability to control it.[40] Here and elsewhere, 'commissars' burned or boiled alive seared callousness into even reluctant participants, much as rape became, as it always does in these circumstances, a 'proof of manhood' strengthening group 'solidarity' as well as an act of violent horror. In this and other ways throughout all of civil war Russia the 'unspeakable' thus became 'spoken', easing, facilitating, and encouraging even more of these most awful acts.

One can also argue that all of this unleashed less complicated sadistic impulses, even if a larger question is why the psychopathology of sadism itself found such wide resonance during the Russian civil wars. The most likely answer is that most of those engaged in atrocities had themselves experienced some deeply humiliating experience during these awful years in a context where scarcity and loss built on the accumulated indignities of recent and more distant pasts. Humiliation also allows little formal historical evidence, but the context itself bears ample testimony. Demobilization and desertion allowed for few heroes. Women begging for food and their children's lives represented the ultimate forms of human weakness. Those maimed or wounded had little hope for survival, and many undoubtedly acted brutally themselves out of pain and desperation. Photographs of the 'bourgeois'

---

[38] See the discussion in Wm. G. Rosenberg, 'The Social Background to Tsektran', in: Diane P. Koenker, William G. Rosenberg, and Ronald G. Suny (eds.), *Party, State, and Society in the Russian Civil war: Explorations in Social History* (Bloomington, IN., 1989), 349–73.

[39] Ibid., 264.

[40] See Kenez, 'Pogroms'; E. Giatsintov, *Zapiski belogo ofitsera* (St Petersburg, 1992).

women selling intimate household goods readily suggest scarred psyches, as do the famous pictures of peasants marketing human flesh. For many, violent and sadistic retribution almost certainly 'compensated' for humiliation and loss in some immeasurable way.

VI AUTHORITY, LEGITIMACY, AND PARAMILITARY VIOLENCE IN REVOLUTIONARY RUSSIA

Finally, how did paramilitary violence in all of these forms affect the outcome of civil war in Russia? What does all of this suggest about the relation of violence and processes of political authority and legitimacy, and what does it mean for the value of 'paramilitary' as a way of understanding postwar violence generally in this region? If we conflate authority with simple force, the militarized movements and would-be governments covering these territories obviously commanded the authority of coercion in varying degrees and extents throughout Russia's modern 'time of troubles'. If we understand authority more usefully in terms of political legitimacy, the question becomes one of how the use of force did or did not effectively engage the crushing problems of scarcity and loss.

Fundamental to the role of paramilitary violence here in my view is that the collapse of the tsarist system meant, in effect, the collapse of the Russian state's legitimizing ideologies and socio-political institutions. Without any institutionalized foundation for legitimacy besides the often unstructured processes of popular election, the concept of legitimacy itself shifted rapidly from traditional views and beliefs to those of effectiveness and function. Initially popular Soviet leaders and provisional government officials both lost their legitimacy as they failed to cope with deteriorating economic and social conditions in 1917, replaced sequentially by more and more radical figures in the false hope that they might do better. And we now understand that while the Bolsheviks came to power 'legitimized' by a radically ideologized conception of universal and ineluctable historical processes that 'explained' deprivation and loss, it was the *promise* of function, not simply force, that underlay much of that regime's initial purchase. When, predictably, Lenin and his party fared even worse than their predecessors in addressing these critical problems, the claims of ideology were pressed ever more forcefully in literal as well as symbolic terms to legitimize what proved to be the bigger battalions.

If we return to the definition of paramilitary offered by Robert Gerwarth and John Horne as 'military or quasi-military organizations and practices that either expanded or replaced the activities of conventional military formations', we have to say that civil war on the territories of the former tsarist Empire everywhere involved overlapping patterns of paramilitary as well as conventional military formations, often with no clear distinction between them. Even the notion of 'conventional' needs some modification here. Formations like the Volunteer Army, the Armed Forces of South Russia, the White regimes in North Russia and Murmansk, and the legions of civil war Russia's self-styled 'Supreme Leader', Admiral Kolchak, all behaved in what were hitherto quite unconventional ways in their associations and engagements with local paramilitary groups. One can perhaps most usefully say that paramilitary has particular meaning in describing and understanding Russian violence in this period precisely in the ways that it distorted and corrupted the 'conventional', although these distortions were themselves rooted in the ways the Bolshevik revolution threatened to bring convention in postwar Europe to an end.

In the awful circumstances of Russia's civil wars, moreover, paramilitary violence in this sense most likely worked to the Bolsheviks' advantage. The relative coherence of Bolshevik ideology still explained, justified, and rationalized its use, reducing what for many were inexplicable sufferings to the simplicities of 'imperialism', 'tsarism', 'capitalism', and the avarice of 'exploiters'. When Commissars flashed their credentials and their armed Red Guard or Cheka escorts brutally carried out the party's orders, their purpose was still set in the higher struggle for 'land', 'bread', and the end of capitalism and its imperial effects, however distorted these concepts had become. Those who struggled against them could make little or no such claim. While Bolsheviks and others also became 'Jews' in areas under White and Green control, and their murder 'justified' on the grounds of 'betrayal', little if anything in the Whites' purpose, ideology, or mentality convincingly brought or promised relief. Scarcity, deprivation, and loss only swept further along with their military advances and retreats.

At the same time, while the more conventional Red and White armies each suffered massive desertions in 1919 and 1920, controlling their effects was almost certainly easier in territories where local Bolshevized Soviets had paramilitary forces at their disposal. This was true as well with efforts to control lines of supply and distribution. At least for a time in 1920, Trotsky's militarization of labour and the railroads was rationalized as well by the urgent need to increase production, improve and safeguard the transport of goods, combat desertion, and, not least, impose order, despite its own brutalities.

In this regard as well as others, we can therefore fairly conclude that the syndrome of violence characterizing Russia's civil wars was, indeed, unparallelled in form or content anywhere else in Europe after 1918, at least until the Nazis formally came to power. Although civil war Russia was a rationalizing touchstone for paramilitary movements in many others places in the postwar world, as other essays in this volume describe, in no other place were all forms of violence so closely related to near universal deprivations of scarcity and loss, and the ways civil and political lives and cultures were so thoroughly brutalized for so long.

3

Bolshevism as Fantasy: Fear of Revolution and Counter-Revolutionary Violence, 1917–1923

Robert Gerwarth and John Horne

In 1924, John Buchan published the fourth of his five thrillers about Richard Hannay, the upper class hero who protects Britain, the Empire and the English class system from the underhand enemies who menace it on every side. Whereas the threat in the three previous novels had been the evil Hun, the villain of *The Three Hostages* was Dominick Medina, the very picture of the urbane English conservative politician but who, as his name hinted, had a suspicious touch of the exotic about him and was actually *déraciné* Irish 'with a far-away streak of Latin...and that never makes a good cross.' Medina stood for the nihilism that seemed to encircle the established order after the upheaval of the war. 'He declared that behind all the world's creeds...lay an ancient devil-worship and that it was raising its head again. Bolshevism, he said, was a form of it....'[1] As Buchan's page-turner suggested, the threat of revolution was the stuff of myth and fantasy. The question is what role such fantasy played in inspiring conservative and counter-revolutionary politics and the paramilitary responses that they generated across Europe.

The theme of revolutionary menace was nothing new. In response to the French Revolution and subsequent insurrectionary episodes in the nineteenth century, conservatives and counter-revolutionaries elaborated a demonology of threat to the established order. This took the imagined form of the violent and often faceless crowd that assaulted bourgeois notions of class, property—and gender. Part of the shock of the June Days in 1848 in Paris came from the role of women on the barricades, while the *pétroleuses* who torched Paris in defence of the Commune were one of the enduring myths bequeathed by that episode. But counter-revolutionary mythology also drew on older, religious fears of subversion and covert conversion that emphasized conspiracy and occult influences. Black legends of the Jesuits and the Free Masons circulated in pre-Revolutionary France before helping to structure stereotypes of counter-revolutionary and revolutionary conspiracies respectively throughout the nineteenth century.[2] Fear of mass society and urban breakdown

---

[1] John Buchan, *The Three Hostages* (London, 1924, new edn., 1995), 118, 199.
[2] Geoffrey Cubitt, *The Jesuit Myth: Conspiracy, Theory and Politics in Nineteenth Century France* (Oxford, 1993).

was a powerful stimulus to crowd theories in the 1890s as it was to new theories of inherited criminality.[3] But individual acts of terror, such as those that produced a wave of political assassinations in the 30 years from the killing of Alexander II in 1881 to that of Archduke Franz Ferdinand in June 1914, heightened anxieties about the conspiracies underlying modern politics. Just as much as riots and strikes did, they fuelled or justified draconian security measures in a number of states including the French Third Republic.[4]

In Germany, the apparent threat of revolution had long found its embodiment in the Social Democratic Party (SPD), the largest German party in the Reichstag on the eve of the Great War and a party which (at least in theory) remained committed to a revolutionary overthrow of capitalism and the established political structures. In reality, of course, the Social Democratic leadership had long parted with the revolutionary aims still inscribed in their party programme. Only outsiders on the margins of the SPD favoured radical revolution—most importantly, of course, Karl Liebknecht, the son of the founder of the SPD who had famously voted against the war credits in 1914 and was imprisoned in 1916 for giving an anti-war speech on Potsdamer Platz. Fear of revolution was deeply embedded in the minds of Germany's liberal and conservative elites, but after 1914 and as a result of the *Burgfrieden*, the threat seemed less acute than it had ever been since the emergence of the organized labour movement in the second half of the nineteenth century.

However, by the time Liebknecht was freed from prison in the final months of the war, the situation had changed: the Bolshevik takeover in Russia made 'world revolution' a seemingly plausible threat and in Germany, Liebknecht became the personification of that threat. He played the role well: within hours of his release from prison, Liebknecht led a procession of anti-war socialists who joyfully welcomed the return of their leader with a parade through central Berlin. He returned to Potsdamer Platz where he spoke publicly for the first time in almost two and a half years. From there, the procession made its way to the Russian Embassy—a highly symbolic gesture that was swiftly interpreted by the political establishment as proof of Liebknecht's 'Bolshevist ambitions'.[5] Liebknecht captured the imagination of the elites so powerfully because for them, he represented a dangerous alliance of threats. Allegedly a Jew (untrue), he stood for everything the middle and upper classes feared: an urban proletariat that had forgotten its place, criminals recently dismissed from prison; disorder and 'world revolution'.

Such fears could only become as strong as they did because with the Bolshevik Revolution an entire state once more embodied the violence of revolution (as it had in the 1790s) and the attempt to extend it to the rest of the world. Whether by mass uprising, conspiracy or a combination of the two, revolution was again

---

[3] Susannah Barrows, *Distorting Mirrors: Visions of the Crowd in Late 19th Century France* (New Haven, 1981).

[4] John Merriman, *The Dynamite Club: How a Bombing in Fin-de-Siècle Paris Ignited the Age of Terror* (Boston, 2009).

[5] Annalies Laschitza and Elke Keller, *Karl Liebknecht: Eine Biographie in Dokumenten* (Berlin, 1982), 374.

part of the state system as Soviet Russia gave it an apparent reach and force that it had not known for over a century. This was all the more so after 1920 when the split in socialist and trade union movements prompted by Moscow resulted in the Third International and the formation of communist parties loyal to Soviet Russia in many countries. All of this took place at a time when the disintegration of the pre-war state and the challenge to the social order in many countries cut political authority itself adrift, resulting in a crisis of legitimacy and a ferment of violence that lent itself to apocalyptic visions.

News about Bolshevik atrocities, many of them real, others exaggerated, spread quickly in Western Europe. In February 1918, for example, one German newspaper published a lengthy report on the Bolsheviks' 'unlimited terrorism' against everyone and everything considered 'middle class'. The apocalypse suddenly had a new name—'Russian conditions'—and it was defined as the negation of all values of Western (and in this particular case: German) civilization (or *Kultur*).[6] In July 1918, the worst fears of Bolshevik brutality seemed to be confirmed when the German ambassador to Moscow, Count Mirbach, was murdered inside the German Embassy. The shock extended to the social democratic press, which also reported on the murder in considerable detail.[7] Soon after, Germans learnt that the ex-Tsar had been executed.[8] Tension was increased further when on 1 November 1918 Germans learnt that Hungarian revolutionaries had killed Count Tisza, the Liberal Prime Minister in wartime Hungary.[9] In Munich, the Nobel Laureate Thomas Mann, normally not an alarmist, feared that a Communist coup d'état in Berlin was imminent.[10] Mann was also concerned by the news coming from Austria. In the wake of Tisza's murder, Mann wrote that the revolution in Vienna threatened to 'become anarchy and Bolshevism', and noted that it included ' "Red Guards" under the command of a Galician Jew who was once mentally ill.'[11] Even if the actual threat of a Bolshevik revolution in Germany was minimal, the perception was very different indeed. It was further increased when it was widely publicized that there were more than 1.4 million Russian prisoners of war in camps across Germany. Their very presence was perceived as a major threat as it was generally assumed that, once released, they would form a revolutionary army dedicated to the aim of spreading world revolution all the way to the Rhine.[12]

Fertile terrain thus emerged for new forms of power that bid for popular allegiance in the wake of mass political mobilization in the Great War.[13] In the *Three*

[6] *Beilage zum Staats-Anzeiger für Württemberg*, 22 February 1918, as quoted in Mark William Jones, 'Violence and Politics in the German Revolution 1918–19', unpublished PhD thesis, EUI, 89. See, too Russland *Deutscher Reichsanzeiger*, 7 February 1918.

[7] 'Revolver und Handgranate', *Volksstimme*, 9 July 1918.

[8] 'Nikolaus Romanow erschossen', *Volkstimme*, 23 July 1918.

[9] Jones, 'Violence', 92.

[10] Thomas Mann, *Tagebücher 1918–1921*, edited by Jens Inge and Peter de Mendelson (Frankfurt/M., 2003), entry of 1 November 1918, 52.

[11] Mann, *Tagebücher*, 1 November 1918, 53.

[12] Jones, 'Violence', 96.

[13] John Horne (ed.), *State, Society and Mobilization in Europe during the First World War* (Cambridge, 1997).

Hostages, Dominick Medina had studied mysticism and used hypnosis as a weapon, hinting at the potential of populist ideologies to command unquestioning allegiance in a world in which old forms of political legitimacy had been destroyed and new forces of revolution and counter-revolution vied with each other for supremacy. Moving in the world of clubs and ministries that he simultaneously planned to destroy, Medina also suggested the distinction that Max Weber continued to draw in the postwar period between charismatic and bureaucratic authority, though Weber died in 1920 before the full clash between left and right wing charismatic movements had become apparent.[14] Fear of revolution resulted in authoritarian measures, from strengthened policing to laws of exception, but also in a right-wing counter-mobilization that bred charismatic leaders and apocalyptic visions of its own. Bolshevism as imagined by its international opponents (few of whom had diplomatic relations with the new state or accurate knowledge of it in the immediate postwar period) fuelled the counter-revolutionary responses.

The precise role of anti-Bolshevik mythology varied with its political setting, which in turn was shaped by the fundamental distinction between victorious and defeated powers after the Great War. When the British delegation at the Paris Peace Conference modified its stance with regard to Germany in late March 1919 and urged the French to adopt a more conciliatory line, Lloyd George justified this by arguing that Germany (which had stabilized its postwar upheaval with a new centre-left government and was gradually isolating the more radical Workers and Soldiers' Councils) needed to become a bulwark against Bolshevism. 'The greatest danger', Lloyd George told Clemenceau and Wilson, 'is no longer Germany but Bolshevism, which could invade [Europe] after having conquered Russia.'[15] While continuing to stress Germany's responsibility for the war and the continued danger it posed to Europe, Clemenceau shared Lloyd George's concern enough to propose a 'cordon sanitaire' of new states that would isolate Germany from the east and protect all Europe from the Bolshevik virus.

In the French case, the revolutionary threat was added to the German threat, rather than replacing it as for the British, and the link was reinforced by the verbal similarity of *boche* and *bolchévique*. The main French propaganda effort responsible for re-mobilizing the home front during the last two years of the war, the *Union des Grandes Associations contre la Propagande Ennemie* (UGACPE), seamlessly expanded its target to include the Bolshevik revolution, which was seen as no less 'barbaric' than the *Boche* war effort. Culminating in the general election of November 1919 and the wave of industrial unrest that led to a short-lived general strike in May 1920, a flood of propaganda denounced the political tyranny and social ruin brought by Bolshevism to Russia, warning that it now threatened to spread to France in a new version of continental tyranny. The role played by the German Supreme Command in returning Lenin to Russia in 1917 in the notorious sealed

---

[14] Wolfgang J. Mommsen, *Max Weber and German Politics, 1959 and 1974*; translated from German, (Chicago and London, 1984), 421–4.

[15] H. Mordacq, *Le Ministère Clemenceau. Journal d'un témoin*, vol. 3, *novembre 1918–juin 1919* (Paris, 1933), 189.

train, not to mention the threat proffered by German generals and nationalist politicians as they played the 'catastrophist' card after the war (by which they threatened revolutionary chaos if the Allies imposed harsh peace terms), lent some force to fervid French images of Bolshevism as a German plot. French police and military authorities in Alsace-Lorraine and the Rhineland feared that contact between French soldiers and German revolutionaries or shady international go-betweens might let the bacillus of revolution into France.[16]

In Germany, by contrast, the anti-Bolshevik 'fear'—as well as supplying a tool of deliberate exaggeration in the diplomatic trial of strength with the western powers over the terms of the peace settlement—also provided a dramatic caricature of the threat or reality of social upheaval as the German revolution unfolded.[17] Yet, the fear of a Bolshevik revolution should not be underestimated as a mobilizing factor, even if a revolution of the kind that engulfed Russia was never likely in Germany, nor in Austria or Hungary either, where a more fundamental disintegration of the pre-war regime than in Germany was counter-balanced by a less industrialized and urbanized society, with fewer centres of proletarian power. The rapid rise and fall of Béla Kun's revolutionary star in Budapest, compared to the real class warfare that characterized the battles in the Ruhr between *Freikorps* and Red Guards in 1920, illustrates the point. But there was no close correlation between the actual size of the revolutionary threat and the fear of Bolshevism any more than there was a clear understanding of what the Bolshevik revolution actually consisted of by those who opposed it abroad. Anarchism, the Worker and Soldier Council movement (in its different manifestations), working class crowds taking over the streets in noisy demonstrations, strident feminists and revolutionary confusion such as that which engulfed Munich in early 1919 under Kurt Eisner and Ernst Toller, might all be seen as 'Bolshevism' by those for whom any threat to the social order or established authority turned the world upside down. In that sense, Bolshevism became the dark shadow behind defeat just as it threatened to undermine 'victory' for those who felt they had won the war.

Both points were true of Italy's profoundly ambiguous postwar situation—which was seen as both victory and defeat. Conservatives and emergent fascist groups discerned the long hand of Bolshevism in the worker occupation of the engineering factories in North-Western Italy in September 1920 as the great postwar trial of strength between industrialists and the trade unions came to a head. When the Italian General Confederation of Labour put the question of revolution to a vote in September 1920, it had in effect already decided against it.[18] But this was by no means obvious to those who opposed the strikers, and who saw the mere possibility of turning the factory occupations into class revolution as the shadow of

---

[16] Serge Berstein and Jean-Jacques Becker (eds.), *Histoire de l'anticommunisme en France*, vol. 1, *1917–1940* (Paris, 1987), 29–62.

[17] Robert Gerwarth, 'The Central European Counter-Revolution: Paramilitary Violence in Germany, Austria and Hungary after the Great War', *Past and Present*, 200 (2008), 175–209. See, too Richard Bessel, *Germany after the First World War* (Oxford, 1993).

[18] Gwyn Williams, *Proletarian Order. Antonio Gramsci and the Origins of Communism in Italy, 1011–1921* (London, 1975), 260–1.

Bolshevism hanging over all Italy. The prefects in Northern and Central Italy continued to use 'Bolshevism' as a catchall term for the multiple threats that they faced, and the emergent fascist *squadristi* who increasingly took the lead in responding to those threats also perceived the 'Bolsheviks' to be their principal opponent. So much did the counter-revolution require its opposite to exist at least in symbolic or imaginary form that waning socialist and trade union strength in Italy in the early 1920s did nothing to reduce fascist fear-mongering about the Bolshevik threat.[19] If fascism was indeed a 'civic religion,' then like many religions it had to stage a Manichaean struggle against its own antithesis.[20]

Granted that fear of Bolshevism had as much to do with those who experienced and indulged it as it did with the realities of Soviet Russia, what forms did it take? Were there generic myths or features in different settings that help explain its role as stimulus to conservative and paramilitary reaction? However imperfect the intelligence on conditions in Russia, the violence of the Civil War and extreme dislocation of everyday life were of course known, including the 1921 famine in whose relief the Save Children Fund became involved.[21] But it was the link between such chaos and the overthrow of the social system through collectivization and the confiscation of wealth that made Bolshevism the awful confirmation of half a century of counter-revolutionary warning that socialism meant the destruction of the economy and civilization itself. In a pamphlet of the UGACPE published in 1919, a Frenchman who had spent the winter of 1917 and much of 1918 in Petrograd related the extreme difficulty of simply surviving and the violence of everyday life ('often bandits shot with rifles and pistols the people they were robbing') and concluded:

> Bolshevism, which is the immediate and complete application of the principles of Marxist socialism—class struggle, socialization of the means of production and [the introduction of] communism by the suppression of private property—has been the subject in Russia for the first time in the history of the world of a striking experiment. The result can be seen by everyone, and no witness in good faith could deny it: **Bolshevism = ruin.**[22]

Such impressions were graphically displayed in poster and film. The poster used by French industrialists in an anti-Bolshevik campaign in 1920 shows the 'three elements of production—labour, capital and competence' literally exploding under the torch of a Bolshevik saboteur, demonstrating that 'France would decline into wretchedness if it allowed Bolshevism to enter' (fig. 2). Films portrayed famine and violence as the key experiences in Bolshevik Russia, as suggested by a German poster in 1921 advertising 'Soviet Russia and the Hunger Catastrophe in Film' (fig. 3). Among the most remarkable films made on the subject was the documentary

[19] Adrian Lyttelton, *The Seizure of Power. Fascism in Italy, 1919–1929* (1973; new edn., London, 2004), 53, 157.

[20] Emilio Gentile, *Fascismo. Storia e interpretazione* (Bari, 2002), 206–34 (civic religion).

[21] Stephen Wheatcroft and Robert W. Davies, 'Population,' in: Robert W. Davies, Mark Harrison and Stephen Wheatcroft, *The Economic Transformation of the Soviet Union, 1913–45* (Cambridge, 1994).

[22] Claude Anet, *Le Bolchevisme tel que je l'ai vu* (Paris, 1919), 15.

Fig. 2. 'France would decline if it allowed Bolshevism to enter'. Poster used during a French industrialists' campaign against Bolshevism, 1920.

of the 1921 famine by the Save the Children Fund as a means of raising voluntary aid. No less striking is a lengthy drama about the destruction of the class system and wilful ruining of the Russian economy, entitled *Bolshevism* and made in Leipzig in 1920 by White Russian émigrés. It tells the story of a group of anti-Bolsheviks class refugees who at the end of the film manage to flee to safety.[23]

Bolshevism, then, stood for the negation of ordered society and civilization—and as such was personified by the figure of death or criminality. Different versions of this latter figure, a bloody dagger clutched between his teeth, appeared at the same moment in France and Germany. The French version was entitled 'L'Homme avec le couteau aux dents' (The Man with the Dagger between his Teeth) and was published by a Paris business group for the November 1919 general election (which returned a centre-right majority), while in Germany, Rudi Feld published 'Die Gefahr des Bolschewismus' (The Danger of Bolshevism) (fig. 4). Both posters drew on images that were omnipresent further east, notably in Poland and Hungary since 1918. Russian émigré anti-Bolsheviks played a key role in exporting such

---

[23] William Karsiol, *Der Todesreigen* (Problem Film, Germany, 1922).

Fig. 3. 'Soviet Russia and the Hunger Catastrophe', German poster of 1921 portrays famine as a key experience of Bolshevism.

images to the west, which reinforced older western stereotypes of the uncivilized 'Slavic East'.[24]

Protection against Bolshevism meant eternal vigilance. But it also meant that the well-rehearsed responses to the revolutionary conspiracy familiar from nineteenth-century demonology could be pressed into service. A brief glance at the measures envisaged by the French in 1918–21 illustrates the point. From the start the security forces tried to track 'Bolshevik gold' which they assumed was being smuggled into the country to corrupt and undermine workers and the labour movement. In this regard, Bolshevism slotted directly into the concern during the war that 'German gold' funded espionage and served to subvert the press, and indeed the link between the two informed the suspicion that Germans playing the 'catastrophist' card were using the Bolsheviks to try and overturn France as they had Russia in 1917. French military and civilian security agents warned constantly from the end of the war that Russian subsidies were funding home grown radicalism.

---

[24] Michael Kellogg, *The Russian Roots of Nazism: White Russians and the Making of National Socialism, 1917–1945* (New York, 2005).

Fig. 4. Poster of Rudi Feld: 'The Danger of Bolshevism', 1919.

In December 1918, for example, they declared that the leading French and Italian socialist papers, *L'Humanité* and *Avanti!*, neither of which supported Bolshevism, were being funded from Moscow.[25] The Independent Social Democratic Party in Germany likewise had to defend itself against the charge of Bolshevik subvention.[26] To the objection that many countries in the west seemed impervious to Bolshevism, the conspiracy theory responded that precisely the minority and clandestine nature of Bolshevism before the revolution meant that sleeping cells and covert organizations would bide their time, awaiting a moment of crisis or internal weakness. A French security report in November 1920 traced 'Bolshevik gold' through a network of agents in Scandinavia (Holland and Switzerland—also former neutral countries—were likewise considered weak spots). Faced with the evidence that Sweden was an 'essentially bourgeois' country, it concluded that:

[25] Archives Nationales (AN), Paris, F7 13506, report on 'Propagande bolchéviste', 3 December 1918.
[26] Alexander Gallus (ed.), *Die vergessene Revolution von 1918/19* (Göttingen, 2010).

'Bolshevik activity in Sweden seems to have renounced brusque methods in order to concentrate on a long-term underground propaganda campaign.'[27]

Yet the French security response also hints at other, older conspiracy myths. The fact that one of the most notorious French Bolshevik sympathisers, Jacques Sadoul, who as naval officer had taken part in a mutiny aboard a French battleship of the Black Sea Fleet against Allied intervention in Russia, was also a Freemason, led to accusations that the Grand Orient of France was sympathetic at least to the aspirations of Bolshevism, if not to all its methods.[28] More significantly, the French police noted the number of real or alleged Bolshevik supporters from the former Russian Empire now in France who were Jewish—with one French agent confidently asserting from Geneva in November 1918 that: 'It is a fact that the majority of Bolshevik leaders are of Jewish religion and Germanic origin.'[29] They also picked up what was to prove one of the fundamental mutations in anti-Bolshevik mythology when White Russian émigrés grafted their long history of endogenous anti-Semitism onto the visceral hatred of the revolution that had expelled them from their homeland. One police agent noted that conservative Russian émigré circles in Paris believed that the 'international revolutionary movement which is tending to take over the whole world is driven by an international plot organized by the Free Masons and directed by the Jews with their money'.[30]

The comparatively strong Jewish representation in the Russian 'Populist' movement and its successor, the Socialist Revolutionary Party, in the socialist Jewish workers' organization the 'Bund', and in the ranks and leadership of the Russian Social Democratic Party that spawned both Bolsheviks and Mensheviks, encouraged the association of Jews with revolutionary tendencies.[31] It was used for propaganda purposes by the 'White' Russian forces as they tried to orchestrate resistance against the revolutionaries who otherwise had much more to offer to new recruits: land, bread, 'liberation'.[32] The anti-Judeo-Bolshevik card gave the 'Whites' at least something popular to be identified with. In Western Russia, General Anton Denikin's 'Volunteer Army' reserved its greatest atrocities for the Jewish populations of the western and southwestern territories in which they had their support base. Ukrainian and Polish nationalist forces and various peasant factions also participated in the slaughter of Jews, for whom the overall death toll reached possibly 50,000. Though a (relatively small) number of Jews were murdered by communists, this did not undermine the conviction of the nationalists and counterrevolutionaries about Judeo-Bolshevism, which was intertwined with accusations that the Jews were German agents. There were elements of pogrom here, if on a

---

[27] AN F7 13506, 'Renseignements de Suède et Norvège, 1er novembre 1920'.

[28] AN F7 13506, 'Franc-Maçonnerie et Bolshévisme', dossier 1919–20.

[29] AN F7 13506, report of 19 November 1918 (by 'V').

[30] AN F7 13506, 'Les Monarchistes russes et l'influence de la maçonnerie', 17 January 1920.

[31] John D. Klier, 'Russian Jewry as the "Little Nation" of the Russian Revolution', in: Yaacov Ro'i (ed.), *Jews and Jewish Life in Russia and the Soviet Union* (London, 1995), 146–56.

[32] Norman Cohn, *Warrant for Genocide: The Jewish World Conspiracy and the Protocols of the Elders of Zion* (London, 1996).

massive scale, but beyond its intrinsic significance, the often systematic murder of
Jews in 1917–19 is noteworthy because the primary agents were now official mili-
taries and organized militias.[33]

It did not take long before such images spread beyond the Russian borders. In
February 1918, Kaiser Wilhelm II of Germany declared that 'the Russian people
are at the mercy of the revenge of the Jews, who are allied with all the Jews of the
world.'[34] The fact that a relatively high proportion of Jews played prominent roles
in the subsequent Central European revolutions—Rosa Luxemburg in Berlin,
Kurt Eisner in Bavaria, and Béla Kun in Hungary—seemed to make such accusations plausible, even for observers further west. Many contemporary French
newspapers, for instance, attributed the Bolshevik revolution to Jewish influence.[35]
And in Britain, Winston Churchill, who was not in any sense a generic anti-Semite,
nonetheless reinforced the connection of Jews and Bolshevism in his infamous
1920 article:

> From the days of Spartacus-Weishaupt to those of Karl Marx, and down to Trotsky
> (Russia), Bela Kun (Hungary), Rosa Luxemburg (Germany), and Emma Goldman
> (United States), this world-wide revolutionary conspiracy for the overthrow of civil-
> ization and for the reconstitution of society on the basis of arrested development, of
> envious malevolence, and impossible equality, has been steadily growing....It has
> been the mainspring of every subversive movement during the nineteenth century;
> and now at last this band of extraordinary personalities from the underworlds of the
> great cities of Europe and America have gripped the Russian people by the hair of their
> heads and have become practically the undisputed masters of the enormous Empire.
>
> There is no need to exaggerate the part played in the creating of Bolshevism and in
> the actual bringing about of the Russian Revolution by these international and for the
> most part atheistic Jews. It is certainly the very great one; it probably outweighs all
> others.[36]

Such views were further fuelled by the broad international circulation of the
forged *Protocols of the Elders of Zion*. This was an invention of the pre-war tsarist
police that was translated into Western European languages from 1919 onwards.
Its exposure as a forgery in 1921 did not reverse its enormous impact on the
counter-revolutionary imagination. Yet, the unholy marriage of anti-Semitism
and anti-Bolshevism produced very different results in different European settings. East of the river Rhine (and more dramatically east of the river Elbe), anti-
'Judeo-bolshevism' would fuel the pogroms and mass murders of Jews that became
such a stark and gruesome feature of European history between the 1920s and
1945. This was largely the case because in the shatter zones of East-Central Europe
'defeat' was also blamed on the Jews, as was the collapse of the state.

---

[33] Henry Abrahamson, *Prayer for the Government: Ukrainians and Jews in Revolutionary Times,
1917–1920* (Cambridge, MA, 1999); David Vital, *A People Apart: The Jews in Europe, 1789–1939*
(Oxford, 1999), 724–6.
[34] Holger Herwig, 'Tunes of Glory at the Twilight Stage: The Bad-Homburg Crown Council and
the Evolution of German Statecraft 1917/1918', *German Studies Review* 6 (1983), 475–94.
[35] Léon Poliakov, *The History of Anti-Semitism. Vol. IV* (Philadelphia, 2003), 274–6.
[36] Winston Churchill, 'Zionism versus Bolshevism', *Illustrated Sunday Herald*, 8 February 1920.

In Western Europe, by contrast, for all the strident accusations made by the conservative press and right-wing organizations in France and Britain about the Bolshevik conspiracy (which the *Morning Post* believed to lie behind the strike by the Triple Alliance in 1920 just as right-wing French papers saw it at work in the general strike of the same year), governments took a calmer view and distinguished carefully between home-grown labour militancy and native socialism on the one hand, and the actual threat from Russian communism on the other. In the zones of overt ideological conflict and civil war in Central Europe and Northern Italy, however, the anti-Bolshevik myths had much greater influence precisely because they served to stigmatize as foreign, and therefore totally unacceptable, the multiple opponents that arose locally and regionally from different processes of change and breakdown which in reality were very different to those in Russia.

CONCLUSION

The largely fantastic fear of a Bolshevik takeover of the entire old world exerted a powerful influence on the political imagination of Europeans after Lenin came to power in Russia. Partly propaganda and partly a genuine concern for those who had more to lose than their chains, Bolshevism quickly became synonymous with the elusive threats and underhand enemies that menaced European post-war societies. The morbid fantasy of encirclement by nihilistic forces of disorder inspired conservative and counter-revolutionary politics across Europe, but it played out in different ways. Where victory in the Great War had strengthened the state and its institutions, anti-Bolshevik mythology also served to stabilize the existing system by rallying those prepared to defend it against 'chaos'. In the loser states of Europe, anti-Bolshevism helped to explain why the war had been lost, the old regimes disappeared and why chaos ruled over much of Eastern and Central Europe. Anti-Bolshevism—usually coupled with anti-Semitism—gave paramilitary responses a direction and a goal; it helped to make the illusive enemy identifiable, drew on familiar resentments against the urban poor, the Jews and disorder more generally. The precise role of anti-Bolshevism thus varied depending on the space and political context in which it occurred. It found its most violent expressions in Central and Eastern European both between 1918 and 1923 and then—even more dramatically—in the 1930s and during the Second World War.[37] The Western European variant, although much less violent in nature, proved to be more enduring and long-lived as it was remobilized for propaganda against the Soviet Union between 1945 and the end of the Cold War.

[37] Kellogg, *The Russian Roots of Nazism.*

4

Fighting the Red Beast: Counter-Revolutionary Violence in the Defeated States of Central Europe

Robert Gerwarth

INTRODUCTION

When Lieutenant Theodor Lohse returned to Berlin from the Western Front in November 1918 he encountered an alienating world of revolutionary upheaval: 'They had destroyed the army, they had taken over the State . . . the Kaiser had been betrayed, the Republic was a Jewish conspiracy.' Forced to earn a meagre living as a private tutor in the household of a wealthy Jewish businessman, Lohse soon despaired over his loss of professional prestige, the perceived national humiliation caused by military collapse, and the hostility with which his own family greeted his return from the battlefields of the Great War: 'They couldn't forgive Theodor for having failed—he who had twice been mentioned in despatches—to die a hero's death as a lieutenant. A dead son would have been the pride of the family. A demobilised lieutenant, a victim of the revolution, was a burden to his womenfolk. . . . He could have told his sisters that he was not responsible for his own misfortune; that he cursed the revolution and was gnawed by hatred for the socialists and the Jews; that he bore each day like a yoke across his bowed neck and felt himself trapped in his epoch as in some sunless prison.'[1]

The only escape route from the 'sunless prison' of an invalidated existence presented itself in the form of paramilitary activity—an activity that offered structure and purpose when it was most needed. Lohse joined one of the many ultra-right-wing paramilitary organizations that mushroomed in the defeated states of Central Europe immediately after the war. Here he encountered like-minded ex-officers from the former imperial armies of Germany, Austria and Hungary, murdered alleged traitors within the organization's ranks and battled with Communists on the streets of Berlin and rebellious Polish land labourers on Germany's new Eastern border.

---

[1] Joseph Roth, *The Spider's Web* (New York, 2003), 4–6.

The fictional life of Theodor Lohse, eternalized in Joseph Roth's remarkably perceptive novel *The Spider's Web* (1923), encapsulates the subject of this chapter: the emergence of a violent counter-revolutionary subculture in the defeated states of Central Europe, where the transition from war to 'peace' was fraught with a whole range of seemingly unresolvable problems, notably the demobilization of some sixteen million defeated soldiers who had fought (and survived) the Great War; the collapse of traditional political authority; and the territorial amputation (or complete disintegration) of the former Central European Empires. The perceived threat posed by these developments triggered the emergence of a transnational right-wing milieu of revisionist militants in Central Europe, paramilitaries determined to violently suppress those internal and external enemies held responsible for defeat, territorial disintegration and revolutionary upheaval. In this respect, this chapter critically engages with George Mosse's 'brutalization thesis' by suggesting that it was not the war itself, but the postwar experiences of defeat, revolution, and territorial amputation that left a range of devastating legacies in Central European history.[2]

Some qualifications to this general argument are necessary. What Benjamin Ziemann called the 'transfiguration' of wartime experiences into peacetime society could take different forms: from conscious abstinence form the world of politics to pacifist activism or a violent refusal to accept the new realities in postwar Central Europe's 'cultures of defeat'.[3] While the vast majority of the German, Austrian, and Hungarian soldiers who survived the Great War returned to 'normal' civilian lives in November 1918, hundreds of thousands of ex-servicemen did not. In Germany alone, estimates range from 250,000 to 400,000 men organized in roughly 120 *Freikorps*, whereas the combined membership in Austrian and Hungarian paramilitary organizations of the right amounted to less than half.[4]

Despite these quantitative differences, paramilitary subcultures in Germany, Austria, and Hungary shared important characteristics. In all three countries, the leading figures involved in setting up and running paramilitary organizations of the right were junior ex-officers (mostly lieutenants and captains, occasionally colonels) from middle- or upper-class backgrounds such as Hanns Albin Rauter, Ernst Rüdiger Starhemberg, Eduard Baar von Baarenfels, Beppo Römer, Gerhard Roßbach, Franz von Epp, István Hejjas, Pál Prónay, and Gyula Osztenburg, who

---

[2] George Mosse, *Fallen Soldiers: Reshaping the Memory of the World Wars* (Oxford,1990).

[3] On the 'transfigurations' in postwar Germany, see Benjamin Ziemann, *War Experiences in Rural Germany 1914–1923* (Oxford and New York, 2007), 214ff. On the 'cultures of defeat' concept, see Wolfgang Schivelbusch, *The* Culture of Defeat: *On National Trauma, Mourning, and Recovery* (New York, 2003); John Horne, 'Defeat and Memory since the French Revolution: Some Reflections', in: Jenny Macleod (ed.), *Defeat and Memory. Cultural Histories of Military Defeat since 1815* (London, 2008), 11–29.

[4] Bernhard Sauer, 'Freikorps und Antisemtismus in der Frühzeit der Weimarer Republik', *Zeitschrift für Geschichtswissenschaft* 56 (2008); Robert Gerwarth, 'The Central European Counter-Revolution: Paramilitary Violence in Germany, Austria and Hungary after the Great War', *Past & Present* 200 (2008), 175–209.

had been educated and trained in the military academies of the late Habsburg and Hohenzollern Empires.[5] In Hungary, it was not only Gyula Gömbös's powerful veterans' organization *MOVE* (Hungarian National Defence Union) or the Union of Awakening Hungarians, but also the much more sizeable Hungarian National Army that was dominated by former combat officers. Of the 6,568 volunteers who followed Horthy's initial recruitment call of 5 June 1919 for the formation of the counterrevolutionary National Army, almost 3,000 were former army and cavalry officers and an additional 800 men were officers from the semi-military border guards, the *Gendarmerie*. Many of the activists in all three countries came from rural backgrounds and notably from the border regions where notions of embattled ethnicity were much more real than they were in larger cities such as Budapest, Vienna or Berlin. In the case of Hungary, the large influx of refugees from Transylvania further contributed to the radicalization of the atmosphere in Budapest, a capital city already militarized by the experiences of revolution and temporary occupation by Romanian forces.[6]

Paramilitary violence in the defeated states of Central Europe was generally most marked along the new German frontier with Poland and the Baltic states as well as in the ethnically diverse 'shatter zones' of the Habsburg Empire where irregular Austrian, Hungarian, Polish, Ukranian, Lithuanian, and Slovenian militias, 'nationalized' through imperial implosion and newly imposed border changes, fought against both internal and external enemies for territorial control, material gain, or ideological fulfilment.[7] In these contested borderlands, military conflict continued unabated, often taking a more unconventional (and sometimes even more brutal) form than during the Great War because the activists were no longer 'restrained' by traditional military discipline.

It is this wave of postwar paramilitary violence in post-imperial Germany, Austria and Hungary, its origins, manifestations, and legacies, which this chapter seeks to explore.[8] More specifically, the purpose of this essay is to analyse the ways in which German, Austrian and Hungarian veterans and members of the so-called 'war youth generation' made the painful transition from war to peace, and how their search for a postwar project to justify their wartime sacrifices found its

---

[5] See, too, the very detailed autobiographical account of this education in Ernst Heydendorff, 'Kriegsschule 1912–1914', in: Heydendorff papers, in: Österreichisches Staatsarchiv, Vienna, B 844/74.

[6] Béla Kelemen, *Adatok a szegedi ellenforradalom és a szegedi kormány történetéhez* (Szeged, 1923), 495–6. For Austria, see Walter Wiltschegg, *Die Heimwehr: Eine unwiderstehliche Volksbewegung?* (Munich, 1985), 274–80. For Germany, see Gerwarth, 'Counterrevolution'. See, too, Ernst Heydendorff, 'Kriegsschule 1912–1914', in: Heydendorff papers, in: Österreichisches Staatsarchiv, Vienna, B 844/74.

[7] On the shatter zones, see: Donald Bloxham, *The Final Solution: A Genocide* (Oxford, 2009), 84f; Alexander V. Prusin, *The Lands Between: Conflict in the East European Borderlands, 1870–1992* (Oxford, 2010), 73ff.

[8] The subject has received remarkably little attention since the 1970s and transnational or comparative studies are altogether absent. For 'classic' studies, see Hagen Schulze, *Freikorps und Republik 1918–1920* (Boppard, 1969); Robert G. L. Waite, *Vanguard of Nazism. The Free Corps Movement in Postwar Germany 1918–23* (Cambridge, MA, 1952); Gerhard Botz, *Gewalt in der Politik: Attentate, Zusammenstöße, Putschversuche, Unruhen in Österreich 1918 bis 1938* (2nd edn., Munich, 1983).

expression in the attempted 'cleansing of the nation' of social elements perceived to be obstacles to a 'national rebirth'. It will do so by investigating nationalist perceptions of defeat and revolution and by explaining how these perceptions and memories served as a source of mobilization in the emergence of right-wing paramilitary groups in the defeated states of Central Europe.

BRUTALIZATION THROUGH DEFEAT, REVOLUTION, AND TERRITORIAL AMPUTATION

In explaining their refusal to demobilize and their determination to continue their soldierly existence after November 1918, paramilitary activists across Central Europe frequently invoked the horrors of returning from the front in 1918 to an entirely hostile world of upheaval, a perception triggered by both the temporary collapse of military hierarchies and public order.[9]

The prominent Carinthian *Heimwehr* activist, Hanns Albin Rauter, who returned to Graz at the end of the war, emphasized his first contact with the 'red mob' as an 'eye-opener': 'When I finally arrived in Graz, I found that the Communists had taken the streets.' Confronted by a group of Communist soldiers, 'I pulled my gun and I was arrested. This was how the *Heimat* welcomed me.' Being arrested by soldiers of lower rank reinforced Rauter's perception of having returned to a 'world turned upside down', a revolutionary world in which hitherto unquestionable norms and values, social hierarchies, institutions, and authorities had suddenly become obsolete.[10]

Experiences in Budapest and Munich were not dissimilar. Upon arrival in Hungary from the front in the late autumn of 1918, the Hussar officer Miklós Kozma was one of many war veterans 'welcomed' by disorderly crowds shouting abuse at the returning troops as well as by ordinary soldiers physically attacking their officers. In Kozma's account, revolutionary activists always appeared as an effeminate 'dirty crowd', a crowd 'that has not washed in weeks and has not changed their clothes in months; the smell of clothes and shoes rotting on their bodies is unbearable.'[11] Ex-officers in neighbouring Bavaria echoed such impressions. The future Austrian

---

[9] On the deterioration of the relationship between home front and war front in the later stages of the war, see Richard G. Plaschka, et al. (eds.), *Innere Front: Militärassistenz, Widerstand und Umsturz in der Donaumonarchie 1918*, 2 vols. (Munich, 1974); Mark Cornwall, *The Undermining of Austria-Hungary: The Battle for Hearts and Minds* (New York, 2000); Manfred Rauchensteiner, *Der Tod des Doppeladlers: Österreich-Ungarn und der Erste Weltkrieg* (Graz, 1993). That the revolution was brought about by men who had not served at the front was a common accusation made by right-wing veterans. See, e.g., Ernst Rüdiger Starhemberg, 'Aufzeichnungen', 21. On Germany, see Richard Bessel, *Germany after the First World War* (Oxford, 1993); on Munich in particular, see Adam R. Seipp, *The Ordeal of Peace: Demobilization and the Urban Experience in Britain and Germany, 1917–1921* (Farnham, 2009), 91–130.

[10] Rauter Papers, NIOD (Amsterdam), Doc I 1380, H, 2. On the 'world turned upside down', see Martin H. Geyer, *Verkehrte Welt: Revolution, Inflation und Moderne. München, 1914–1924* (Göttingen, 1998).

[11] Miklós Kozma, *Makensens Ungarische Husaren: Tagebuch eines Frontoffiziers, 1914–1918* (Berlin and Vienna, 1933), 459.

Vice-Chancellor and *Heimwehr* activist, Eduard Baar von Baarenfels, for example, reported back to Austria from revolutionary Munich how he had witnessed jewellery shops being plundered, and officers being disarmed and insulted. The revolution, Baarenfels insisted, had 'washed up the worst scum from the deepest depths of hell'—people who were now freely roaming the streets of Central European capital cities.[12]

What Baarenfels, Kozma, and many others described was a nightmare that had haunted Europe's conservative establishment since the French Revolution, a nightmare that—ever since the Bolshevik takeover in Russia in 1917—appeared to have become a reality: the triumph of a faceless revolutionary crowd over the forces of law and order. The image they invoked was partly influenced by a vulgarized understanding of Gustave Le Bon's *Psychologie des foules* (1895), whose ideas were widely discussed in right-wing circles across Europe from the turn of the century. Le Bon's juxtaposition of the 'barbarian' masses and the 'civilized' individual was also reflected in the ways in which many Austrian and Hungarian ex-officers described the humiliating experiences of being stripped of their military decorations by agitated crowds or lower-ranked soldiers.[13] They refused to accept that military defeat had caused the collapse of the Central European Empires and regarded the revolutions in Berlin, Vienna, and Budapest as an intolerable insult to their honour as 'militarily undefeated' officers. As the war veteran and infamous *Freikorps* leader, Manfred von Killinger, expressed in a letter to his family: 'I have made a promise to myself, Father. Without armed struggle, I have handed over my torpedo boat to the enemies and watched my flag go down. I have sworn to take revenge against those who are responsible for this.'[14] Confronted with public unrest and personal insults, the future *Heimwehr* leader, Ernst Rüdiger Starhemberg came to a similar conclusion when he expressed his 'burning desire to return to my soldier's existence as soon as possible, to stand up for the humiliated Fatherland.' Only then, 'the shame of a gloomy present' could be forgotten.[15]

Equally important for the remobilization of German, Austrian and Hungarian veterans was the experience of territorial disintegration. While the German cessation of Alsace-Lorraine in the Treaty of Versailles did not come as a surprise to most contemporary observers, German politicians of left and right vehemently rejected Polish territorial ambitions in West Prussia, Upper Silesia, and the Posen region. In the Treaty of St Germain, the German-Austrian rump state was forced to cede South Tyrol to Italy, Southern Styria to the Kingdom of Serbs, Croats, and Slovenes, Feldsberg and Böhmzell to Czechoslovakia whilst also being denied the *Anschluss* with the German Reich—a ruling rightfully interpreted by politicians of

---

[12] Eduard Baar von Baarenfels, 'Erinnerungen (1947)', Österreichisches Staatsarchiv, MS B/120:1, here 10–13. See, too Anita Korp, 'Der Aufstieg vom Soldaten zum Vizekanzler im Dienste der Heimwehr: Eduard Baar von Baarenfels', MA thesis (Vienna, 1998).

[13] Starhemberg, 'Aufzeichnungen', 16–17. See, too Emil Fey, *Schwertbrüder des Deutschen Ordens* (Vienna, 1937), 218–20.

[14] Manfred von Killinger, *Der Klabautermann. Eine Lebensgeschichte* (3rd edn., Munich, 1936), 263.

[15] Starhemberg, 'Aufzeichnungen', 20–2.

the moderate left and right alike as a flagrant violation of the Wilsonian principle of national self-determination. Hungary was hit even harder by the peace provisions: it lost two-thirds of its pre-war territory and one-third of its population according to the Treaty of Trianon.[16]

Yet as long as the Paris Peace Conference had not made a final decision on the redrawing of European borders, veterans across Central Europe tried to create new territorial realities through (para-) military action, 'realities' which they believed the peacemakers in Paris could not ignore. Since the armistice between the Allied Powers and Germany of 11 November 1918 did not specify the exact extent of territorial losses, German, Polish, and Baltic paramilitaries were quick to undertake violent attempts to redraw the borders in their favour (see Map 1). In December 1918, the First Polish Uprising triggered a wave of often vicious fighting between Polish insurgents and German *Freikorps* in Upper Silesia and West Prussia, while up to 100,000 German volunteers fought in the Baltic region in 1919 to secure the 'German cities' of Riga and Vilnius.[17] Simultaneously, from November 1918 onwards, Austrian volunteers were militarily engaged with Yugoslav troops in Carinthia.[18] As 'victories in defeat', the violent clashes between Yugoslav troops and Austrian volunteers in Carinthia and the victory of German *Freikorps* over Polish insurgents in the 1921 'Battle of Annaberg' soon played a crucial role in paramilitary memory culture, because they testified to the activists' unbroken spirit of defiance against both external enemies and the 'weak' central governments. 'Carinthia' and 'Annaberg' became synonymous with the paramilitaries' alleged military superiority over the 'Slav enemy'. A popular poem of 2 May 1919, the day of the 'liberation' of the Carinthian village of Völkermarkt, celebrated the Carinthian 'freedom' from 'the Slav yoke' by emphasizing that 'the freedom fighters triumphed over treason... You, Slav, should remember the important lesson that Carinthian fists are hard as iron'.[19]

The interconnected experiences of defeat, revolution, and territorial disintegration also contributed to the mobilization and radicalization of the so-called 'war youth generation', those teenage boys who had been too young to serve in the war and who were to gain their first combat experiences on the postwar battlefields of the Burgenland, Styria, Carinthia, or Upper Silesia. The unofficial chronicler of that younger generation of paramilitaries became Ernst von Salomon, a former officer cadet during the Great War who participated in the 1922 assassination of German Foreign Minister Walther Rathenau before publishing a widely read autobiographical trilogy on his postwar experiences: *The Outlaws*, *The City*, and *The*

---

[16] For a general account of the effects of St Germain and Trianon, see Robert Evans, 'The Successor States', in: Robert Gerwarth (ed.), *Twisted Paths: Europe 1914–45* (Oxford, 2007), 210–36.

[17] Bernhard Sauer, 'Vom "Mythos des ewigen Soldatentum": der Feldzug deutscher Soldaten im Baltikum im Jahre 1919', *ZfG* 43 (1993); Tim Wilson, *Frontiers of Violence: Conflict and Identity in Ulster and Upper Silesia, 1918–1922* (Oxford, 2010).

[18] On Carinthia see *Darstellungen aus den Nachkriegskämpfen deutscher Truppen und Freikorps*, vols. 7 and 8 (Berlin, 1941–42) and the autobiographical account by Jaromir Diakow, in: Österreichisches Staatsarchiv, Diakow Papers, B727. See, too Walter Blasi, 'Erlebte österreichische Geschichte am Beispiel des Jaromir Diakow', MA thesis (Vienna, 1995).

[19] On Carinthia and a reprint of the poem, see the anonymous text 'Der Sturm auf Völkermarkt am 2. Mai 1919', in: Knaus Papers, Kriegsarchiv Vienna, B 694, 31.

Cadets. Whilst walking through the streets of Berlin in his officer cadet uniform in November 1918, the 16-year-old von Salomon had an encounter he would subsequently describe as his 'political awakening':

> I felt how I turned pale, I pulled myself together and said to myself 'stand to attention' ....I sensed chaos and turmoil. A huge flag was carried in front of a long procession of people, and the flag was red....I stood still and watched. Following the flag, tired crowds surged in a disorderly fashion. Women marched in front. They proceeded in their wide skirts, the grey skin of their sharp bony faces was wrinkled....Covered in dark, ragged cloths they were singing a song which was out of tune with the hesitant heaviness of their march....Here they were: the champions of the revolution. So this was the dark crowd from which the glowing flame [of revolution] was to emerge, the crowd set out to realise the dream of blood and barricades. It was impossible to capitulate to them. I sneered at their claims which knew no pride, no confidence in victory...I stood straight and watched and thought 'cowards' and 'scum' and 'mob' and I...watched these hollow, dissolute figures; they are just like rats, I thought, grey and with red-framed eyes, carrying the dust of the streets on their backs.[20]

For many of young officer cadets such as Ernst von Salomon, who had grown up on tales of heroic bloodshed but had missed out on their first-hand experience of the 'storms of steel', the militias offered a welcome opportunity to live their fantasies of a romanticized warrior existence. As Ernst Rüdiger Starhemberg correctly observed, many members of the war youth generation tried to compensate for their lack of combat experience through 'rough militarist behaviour' which was 'nurtured as a virtue in large parts of the post-war youth' and which deeply affected the general tone and atmosphere within paramilitary organizations after 1918.[21]

What motivated these younger paramilitaries, who under different circumstances are likely to have lived 'normal' peaceful existences, was both a violent rejection of an unexpected defeat and revolutionary unrest, and a strong desire to prove themselves in battle. Austrian and Hungarian officer cadets, in particular, who had been mentally and physically prepared for a heroic death on the battlefield, felt a deep sense of betrayal when the war ended abruptly in 1918. Once they had joined paramilitary units dominated by former shock-troop officers, they were keen to prove their worthiness within a community of often highly decorated warriors and 'war heroes', a community that offered them the opportunity to act upon their adolescent power fantasies and to live up to the idealized image of militarized masculinity promoted in wartime propaganda.[22]

However, romanticized fantasies about warriordom were not the only reasons for joining a paramilitary formation. In addition, and this applied primarily to

---

[20] Ernst von Salomon, *Die Geächteten* (Berlin, 1930), 10–11 (English trans., *The Outlaws*, London, 1931).

[21] Starhemberg, 'Aufzeichnungen', 26. On the German war youth generation, see Michael Wildt, *Generation des Unbedingten* (Hamburg, 2000), and Andrew Donson, *Youth in the Fatherless Land: War Pedagogy, Nationalism, and Authority in Germany, 1914–1918* (Cambridge, MA, 2010). For Austria and Hungary, no comparable studies on the war youth generation exist to date. Older studies suggest, however, that the percentage of teenage volunteers may have been as high as 50%. On Hungary, see Kelemen, *Adatok*, 495f. On Austria, see Walter Wiltschegg, *Die Heimwehr. Eine unwiderstehliche Volksbewegung?* (Munich, 1985), 274–80.

[22] Gerwarth, 'Central European Counter-Revolution', 175ff.

Hungary and the embattled German borderlands, large numbers of landless labourers were attracted by the prospect of theft, plunder, rape, extortion, or simply by the opportunity to settle scores with neighbours of different ethnicity without fear of state reprisals. In addition, local paramilitary groups were often formed out of fears of disbanded and impoverished soldiers rather than with a clearly defined political aim.[23]

Together, the veterans and members of the war youth generation formed explosive subcultures of ultra-militant masculinity in which violence was not merely perceived as a politically necessary act of self-defence in order to suppress the communist revolts of Central Europe, but also as a positive value in itself, as a morally correct expression of youthful virility that distinguished the activists from the 'indifferent' majority of bourgeois society unwilling to rise in the face of revolution and defeat. In marked contrast to the upheaval that surrounded them, the militias offered clearly defined hierarchies and a familiar sense of belonging and purpose. The paramilitary groups were fortresses of soldierly camaraderie and 'order' in what the activists perceived as a hostile world of democratic egalitarianism and communist internationalism. It was this spirit of defiance, coupled with the desire to be part of a postwar project that would imbue meaning to an otherwise pointless experience of mass death during the Great War, devalued by defeat, that held these groups together. They perceived themselves to be the nucleus of a 'new society' of warriors, representing both the eternal values of the nation and new authoritarian concepts for a state in which that nation could thrive.[24]

The paramilitaries' inclination to use extreme violence against their enemies was further exacerbated by fear of world revolution and stories (some true, some exaggerated or imagined) about communist atrocities both inside and outside their respective national communities. Although the actual number of casualties inflicted during the 'Red Terror' of 1919 was relatively low, accounts of mass murder, rape, corpses' mutilations, and prisoners' castrations by revolutionary 'savages' in Russia and Central Europe featured very prominently in conservative newspapers and paramilitaries' autobiographies where they served the purpose of legitimizing the use of violence against de-humanized internal and external enemies accused of pursuing a policy of total annihilation.[25]

MANIFESTATIONS OF VIOLENCE

The actual levels of physical violence differed remarkably in the three defeated states of Central Europe. The situation in post-revolutionary Hungary and Germany was far more extreme than in Austria. In the revolutionary 'hotspots' of

---

[23] Béla Bodó, 'Militia Violence and State Power in Hungary, 1919–1922', *Hungarian Studies Review* 33 (2006), 121–67, particularly 131–2. Ziemann, *War Experiences*, 227ff.

[24] Jürgen Reulecke, '*Ich möchte einer werden so wie die…*': *Männerbünde im 20. Jahrhundert* (Frankfurt, 2001), 89ff.

[25] See, e.g., 'Revolution überall', *Innsbrucker Nachrichten*, 12 November 1918, 2; 'Bestialische Ermordung von Geiseln' by Bavarian Communists, *Innsbrucker Nachrichten*, 3 May 1919, 2.

Munich, Berlin and the industrial areas along the Ruhr and Saale rivers, the violent clashes between left and right left thousands of people dead. In Hungary alone, between 1,500 and 4,000 people died in 1919–20. By contrast, the vast majority of the 859 political murders in interwar Austria occurred in the early 1930s, not in the immediate postwar period.[26]

In order to explain the relative salience of the Austrian right in the years immediately after 1918, two factors need to be taken into consideration.[27] First, the apparently limited activism of the Austrian right (limited when compared to the situation in Hungary and further East), owed much to the existence of a strong militarized left, most notably the *Volkswehr* and the socialist party guard, the *Schutzbund*.[28] In Tyrol, for example, 12,000 *Heimwehr* men, two-thirds of them armed, faced roughly 7,500 *Schutzbund* members in 1922.[29] Both sides kept each other in check and their self-limitation was, in many ways, a strategy for survival since victory in a potential civil war was anything but a foregone conclusion.[30] Hence, throughout the 1920s, both sides largely confined themselves to symbolically charged gestures of military strength such as the largely non-violent *Heimwehr* and *Schutzbund* marches through 'enemy territory'.[31]

Secondly, and this is frequently ignored in historical analyses of interwar Austria, many of the most violent activists of the right spent much of the period 1918–21 *outside* Austria. Austrian members of the infamous *Freikorps* Oberland, for example, including the future *Heimwehr* leader, Ernst Rüdiger Starhemberg, helped to crush the Munich Councils' Republic in 1919. During the third Polish Uprising of 1921, to name another example, student volunteers from Innsbruck University joined the Upper Silesian *Selbstschutz* in its struggle against Polish insurgents. Both examples testify to the transnational dynamic of counter-revolutionary and ethnic violence in postwar Central Europe, a dynamic that facilitated concrete cooperation and

[26] The exact number of deaths inflicted by postwar paramilitary violence is still disputed. On Germany and the borderlands, see Hagen Schultze, *Freikorps und Republik, 1918–1920* (Boppard, 1968); Bernhard Sauer, 'Vom "Mythos des ewigen Soldatentum": der Feldzug deutscher Soldaten im Baltikum im Jahre 1919', *ZfG* 43 (1993); Wilson, *Frontiers of Violence*. For Hungary, a member of the 1918 Károlyi government, Oszkár Jászi, estimated that the counterrevolution claimed the lives of at least 4,000 victims, but this figure has recently been revised downwards to 1,500. See Oszkár Jászi, *Revolution and Counter-Revolution in Hungary* (London, 1924), 120; Béla Bodo, 'Paramilitary Violence in Hungary after the First World War', *East European Quarterly* 38 (2004), 129–72, here 167. For Austria, Gerhard Botz has established the relatively low figure of 859 victims of political violence during the first Austrian Republic (12 November 1918–11 February 1934), but this figure does not account for the murders committed by the numerous Austrian volunteers who fought in German *Freikorps*. Botz, *Gewalt*, 237.

[27] On the salience of the Austrian revolution, see John W. Boyer, 'Silent War and Bitter Peace: The Revolution of 1918 in Austria', *Austrian History Yearbook* 34 (2003), 1–56.

[28] On this, with particular reference to the Tyrol, see Richard Schober, 'Die paramilitärischen Verbände in Tirol 1918–1927', in: Thomas Albrich et al. (eds.), *Tirol und der Anschluß: Voraussetzungen, Entwicklungen, Rahmenbedingungen 1918–1938* (Innsbruck, 1988), 113–41.

[29] Verena Lösch, 'Die Geschichte der Tiroler Heimatwehr von ihren Anfängen bis zum Korneuburger Eid' (1920–1930), PhD thesis (Innsbruck, 1986), 162.

[30] Gerhard Botz, 'Handlungsspielräume der Sozialdemokratie während der "Österreichischen Revolution"', in: Rudolf Altmüller et al. (eds.), *Festschrift Mélanges Felix Kreissler* (Vienna, 1985), 16.

[31] See Alfred Krauss, 'Revolution 1918?', in: Krauss papers, Kriegsarchiv Vienna, B 60, 5e, 1.

Fig. 5. After the fall of the Munich Councils Republic in 1919, Freikorps soldiers march off arrested revolutionaries through the streets of Munich.

exchanges between German, Finnish, Russian, Hungarian, Austrian, and Italian opponents of the 'Bolshevization' and 'Balkanization' of Europe.[32] Local newspapers in Austria frequently offered detailed reports about violent developments in Italy, Finland, Russia, Ukraine, Hungary, and Bavaria which profoundly affected the way in which counterrevolutionary activists in Austria perceived their own situation.[33] The revolutions in Munich and Budapest in particular featured prominently in the minds of Austrian paramilitary activists (if only as a scenario they desperately wanted to prevent repeating itself in Austria) and many of the atrocities attributed to the revolutionary left were a direct reflection of the horror stories about the 'Red Terror' that raged in Austria's border-states. In addition, some *Heimwehr* activists felt inspired by the example of Hungarian or German militias who fought in the

[32] Michael Gehler, 'Studentischer Wehrverband im Grenzlandkampf: Exemplarische Studie zum "Sturmzug Tirol" in Oberschlesien 1921', *Oberschlesisches Jahrbuch* 5 (1989), 33–63; idem, *Studenten und Politik: Der Kampf um die Vorherrschaft an der Universität Innsbruck 1918–1938* (Innsbruck, 1990); Sabine Falch, 'Zwischen Heimatwehr und Nationalsozialismus: Der "Bund Oberland" in Tirol', *Geschichte und Region* 6 (1997), 51–86. Finally, see Hans Steinacher, *Oberschlesien* (Berlin, 1927).

[33] See, e.g., the following articles in the *Innsbrucker Nachrichten*: 'Der Krieg im Frieden' (25 May 1919), 'Gegen den Bolschewismus' (17 November 1918), 'Die Sowjetherrschaft in Ungarn' (26 March 1919), 'Die Verhältnisse in Bayern' (10 April 1919) and 'Bayern als Räterepublik' (8 April 1919).

borderlands or against communist insurgents, defying the pacifist majority in their countries. 'Full of envy' Starhemberg recalled, 'we fantasised about participating in the struggles of our German comrades who overthrew the Councils' Republic after Eisner's assassination, or the actions of the Hungarian volunteer army which restored Hungary's honour under Horthy's leadership.'[34]

In Hungary, where the Red Terror of 1919 claimed the lives of between 400 and 500 victims, violent fantasies of retribution were based on much more tangible first-hand experiences. The atrocities committed by the so-called 'Lenin Boys' under the leadership of József Cserny in particular spurred the imagination of nationalist activists. After the fall of the Béla Kun regime, the time had come to 'avenge' these crimes. The Hungarian ex-officer, Miklós Kozma, wrote in early August 1919: 'We shall see to it... that the flame of nationalism leaps high... We shall also punish. Those who for months have committed heinous crimes must receive their punishment. It is predictable... that the compromisers and those with weak stomachs will moan and groan when we line up a few red rogues and terrorists against the wall. The false slogans of humanism and other "isms" have helped to drive the country into ruin before. This second time they will wail in vain.'[35]

Kozma's reasoning was taken to its extreme in the Hungarian Plain and, even more dramatically, in the Baltic *Freikorps* campaign where previously disciplined troops transformed into marauding mercenaries reminiscent of those of the Thirty Years' War, modern warlords who plundered and murdered their way across the countryside, transforming it into a landscape of destruction.[36] Still in 1946–47, whilst waiting for his execution in a Polish prison, the former Camp Commander of Auschwitz, Rudolf Höß, recalled the Baltic campaign as a manifestation of previously unseen violence: 'The fighting in the Baltics was of a wildness and grimness which I neither experienced during the Great War nor in any of the subsequent struggles of the *Freikorps*. There was no proper front, the enemy was everywhere. Whenever there was a clash, it turned into pure slaughter to the point of complete annihilation.... Countless times I saw the horrifying images of burned-out huts and charred or rotten bodies of women and children....Back then I believed that there could be no intensification of this destructive madness!'[37]

Less intense, but new in terms of quality, was the simultaneous internalization of conflict, the identification and persecution of 'community aliens' who had to be rooted out before a national rebirth could occur. In Germany prominent republi-

---

[34] Starhemberg, 'Aufzeichnungen', 23. On the transnational context, see Gerwarth, 'Central European Counter-Revolution', 175–209. See, too Bruno Thoss, *Der Ludendorff-Kreis: München als Zentrum der mitteleuropäischen Gegenrevolution zwischen Revolution und Hitler-Putsch* (Munich, 1978); Lajos Kerekes, 'Die "weiße" Allianz: Bayerisch-österreichisch-ungarische Projekte gegen die Regierung Renner im Jahre 1920', *Österreichische Osthefte* 7 (1965), 353–66; Ludger Rape, *Die österreichischen Heimwehren und die bayerische Rechte 1920–1923* (Vienna, 1977); Horst G. Nusser, *Konservative Wehrverbände in Bayern, Preussen und Österreich* (Munich, 1973).

[35] Miklós Kozma, *Az összeomlás 1918–1919* (Budapest, 1935), 380. On Kozma's war experience, see Kozma, *Tagebuch eines Frontoffiziers 1914–1918*.

[36] Vejas Gabriel Liulevicius, *War Land on the Eastern Front: Culture, National Identity and German Occupation in World War I* (Cambridge, 2000), 233ff.

[37] Rudolf Höß, *Kommandant in Auschwitz. Autobiographische Aufzeichnungen*, introduced and commented by Martin Broszat (Stuttgart, 1958), 34f.

can politicians such as Walther Rathenau and Matthias Erzberger were assassinated by right-wing extremists. In Hungary, prominent intellectual critics of the Hungarian White Terror such as the journalist Béla Bacsó and the editor of the socialist democratic daily *Népszava*, Béla Somogyi were abducted and murdered by members of the infamous Prónay battalion.[38] A further 75,000 individuals were imprisoned, and 100,000 went into exile, many of them to Soviet Russia where Stalin eventually killed those who had escaped Horthy's death squads. Given that many leaders of the Hungarian revolution, including Béla Kun, managed to escape before they could be arrested, others had to pay for their 'treason'.[39]

Socialists, Jews, and trade unionists, when caught, were dragged into the barracks and beaten unconscious. 'On these occasions', the Hungarian militia leader and temporary head of Horthy's bodyguard, Pál Prónay, recalled, 'I ordered an additional fifty strokes with the rod for these fanatic human animals, whose heads were drunk with the twisted ideology of Marx.'[40] For Prónay and many others, the de-humanized ('human animal') and de-nationalized (Bolshevik) enemy could be tortured and killed without remorse, because these acts were legitimized and necessitated by the holiness of the cause: the salvation of the nation threatened by a socialist abyss and territorial amputation. Against the background of civil war and revolution, the activists were convinced that they lived in an age of unfettered violence, in which the internal enemy, who had broken the rules of 'civilized' military conduct, could only be stopped through the use of the same kind of extreme violence which their opponents were—rightly or wrongly—believed to have employed during the brief 'Red Terror' in Bavaria and Hungary.

Younger paramilitaries who had not served in the Great War often proved particularly violent. In Germany, one of the most widely discussed cases of paramilitary atrocity involved a number of fraternity students from Marburg who had shot more than a dozen previously imprisoned 'Spartakists' in Thuringia.[41] On another occasion, during the Communist uprising in the Ruhr in 1920, a young student volunteer joyfully reported in a letter to his parents: 'No pardon is given. We shoot even the wounded. The enthusiasm is tremendous—unbelievable. Our battalion has had two deaths, the Reds two or three hundred. Anyone who falls into our hands gets the rifle butt and is then finished off with a bullet.'[42] And even the Hungarian militia leader, Pál Prónay, infamous for ruthlessly torturing and burning his victims alive, was positively surprised by the 'overly ambitious and highly motivated new recruits' who tried to impress him by 'beating up Jews outside the gate of the barracks or by bringing them in where they can give them a real thrashing.'[43]

[38] On the assassination of Somogyi and Bacsó, see Ernő Gergely and Pál Schönwald, *A Somogyi-Bacsó-Gyilkosság* (Budapest, 1978).
[39] Rudolf Tokes, *Béla Kun and the Hungarian Soviet Republic: the Origins and Role of the Communist Party of Hungary in the Revolutions of 1918–1919* (New York and Stanford, 1967), 159. See, too Gyorgy Borsanyi, *The Life of a Communist Revolutionary: Béla Kun* (New York, 1993).
[40] Pál Prónay, *A határban a halál kaszál: fejezetek Prónay Pál feljegyzéseiből*, edited by Ágnes Szabó and Ervin Pamlényi (Budapest, 1963), 90.
[41] See *Der Marburger Studentenprozeß* (Leipzig and Berlin, 1921) as well as Michael Lemling, 'Das "Studentenkorps Marburg" und die "Tragödie von Mechterstädt"', in: Peter Krüger and Anne C. Nagel (eds.), *Mechterstädt—25.3.1920. Skandal und Krise in der Frühphase der Weimarer Republik* (Münster, 1996), 44–88.
[42] Max Zeller, as quoted in Jones, *Hitler's Heralds*, 50.   [43] Prónay, *A határban*, 41.

Fig. 6. Hungarian White militias hang a revolutionary, 1919.

The postwar project of 'cleansing' the nation of its internal enemies was viewed by most paramilitary activists as a necessary precondition for a 'national rebirth', a form of violent regeneration that would justify the sacrifices of the war despite defeat and revolution. In some ways, this abstract hope for national 'rebirth' out of the ruins of empire was the only thing that held the highly heterogeneous paramilitary groups in Germany, Austria, and Hungary together. Altogether, the paramilitary upsurge of the months after November 1918 looked more like an attack on the new political establishments and the territorial amputations imposed by the Western Allies, than a coordinated attempt to create any particular form of authoritarian new order. For despite their common opposition to revolution and the common hope for national revival, the activists involved in right-wing paramilitary action did not necessarily share the same ideological aims and ambitions. Quite the opposite: paramilitary activists of the political right in Central Europe were in fact deeply divided by their divergent visions of the future form of state: there were strong legitimist forces, particularly in the Hungarian community in Vienna, from where two attempts were undertaken to restore the last Habsburg King Charles to the throne of St Stephen, but also proto-fascist activists who despised the monarchy nearly as much as they loathed communism. Some royalist paramilitaries in Austria, too, demanded a restoration of the Habsburg monarchy (though not necessarily under the old Kaiser) and found themselves in direct confrontation with those in favour of a syndicalist form of independent Austrian government. Others, notably those organized in the Austro-Bavarian 'Oberland League', a radical minority of some 1,000 men, favoured unification with the German Reich.[44] For the *großdeutsch* right in Austria, defeat and imperial dissolution thus offered another postwar project whose fulfilment would justify the wartime sacrifices: the creation of a Greater German Reich. General Alfred Krauss, for example, who in 1914 had interpreted the Great War itself as a unique opportunity to 're-negotiate' the power structure within the Habsburg Empire in favour of its German citizens saw the collapse of the multi-ethnic Habsburg Empire as an opportunity for the ethnic 'unmixing of peoples'.[45] 'Great is the time in which we live', Krauss noted in a somewhat deluded essay of 1920, for *großdeutsch* 'unification can no longer be hindered.'[46]

Furthermore, as the 'Oberland League' phrased it in its pamphlet *The Policy of German Resistance*, a national 'rebirth' was only possible through a thoroughly critical engagement with the 'ideas of 1789', driven by the traditions of the enlightenment and humanism. 'The ideas of 1789 are manifest in modern individualism, bourgeois views on the word and economy, parliamentarianism, and modern democracy.... We members of the Oberland League will continue on our path, marked out by the blood of the German martyrs who have died for the future Reich, and we will continue, then as now, to be the shock troops of the German resistance movement.'[47]

Despite the widespread urge to 'redeem' themselves in the face of a double humiliation by military defeat and revolution, it would therefore be wrong to suggest that all paramilitaries in Central Europe shared the same motivations for getting involved in counterrevolutionary activities. Catchphrases such as the '*Freikorps* spirit' in Germany, the 'Szeged Idea' in Hungary (Szeged being the headquarters of Horthy's counter-revolutionary National Army in 1919), or the ideas underpinning the 'Korneuburger Oath' of the Austrian *Heimwehr* movement, are clearly suggesting a unity of political aims and motivations that never existed. They were retrospective constructions of unity that were intended to give meaning to violent actions that were usually carried out without a univocal political agenda. Yet, as long as the perceived threats of 'international Bolshevism', 'international Jewry', and 'international feminism', as well as a fear of national decay and territorial disintegration persisted, there was a clear common goal that temporarily seemed more important than disagreements about the future form of government. Still, in 1931 the German-born assassin

---

[44] See Hans Jürgen Kuron, 'Freikorps und Bund Oberland', PhD thesis (Munich 1960), 134; Falch, "Bund Oberland", 51; Verena Lösch, 'Die Geschichte der Tiroler Heimatwehr von ihren Anfängen bis zum Korneuburger Eid (1920–1930)', PhD thesis (Innsbruck, 1986), 162.

[45] Alfred Krauss, 'Schaffen wir ein neues, starkes Österreich!' (1914), in: Krauss papers, Österreichisches Staatsarchiv, Vienna, B60.

[46] Alfred Krauss, *Unser Deutschtum!* (Salzburg, 1920), 8–9.

[47] 'Die Politik des deutschen Widerstands' (1931), Österreichisches Staatsarchiv Vienna, B 1477.

of Rosa Luxemburg and subsequent military organizer of the Austrian *Heimwehr*, Waldemar Pabst, wrote a political programme for a White International, his 'favorite child of the future', in which he articulated a 'minimal consensus' for counter-revolutionary movements across Europe: 'The path towards a new Europe lies in the … replacement of the old Trinity of the French Revolution [*liberté, egalité, fraternité*] which has proven to be false, sterile, and destructive with a new Trinity: authority, order, justice. … Only on the basis of this spirit can a new Europe be built, a Europe that is currently torn up by class war and suffocated with hypocrisy.'[48]

The pamphlets published by right-wing militants in the 1920s demonstrate quite clearly that the paramilitary world of postwar Central Europe was a world of action, not ideas. Against whom these actions should be directed was consequently one of the most widely discussed themes in paramilitary circles. For the former infantry general and commander-in-chief of the Habsburg Empire's Eastern Armies, Alfred Krauss, the 'enemies of the German people' included 'the French, the English, the Czechs, the Italians'—a clear indication of the continuity of wartime propaganda after 1918. More dangerous than the nationalist ambitions of other countries, however, were the internationalist enemies: 'the Red International', the 'Black International' (political Catholicism), and, 'above all', the 'Jewish people, which aims at mastery of the Germans'. All other enemies, Krauss was certain, stood in the paid service of the latter.[49]

Unsurprisingly, given such widespread sentiments, the Jews, although a small minority of no more than 5 per cent of the Austrian and Hungarian populations, suffered most from right-wing paramilitary violence after the Great War. As Jakob Krausz, a Jewish refugee from the Hungarian White Terror, observed in 1922, 'anti-Semitism did not lose its intensity during the war. Quite the opposite: it unfolded in a more beastly way. This war has only made the anti-Semites more brutal. … The trenches were flooded with anti-Semitic pamphlets, particularly those of the Central Powers. The more their situation deteriorated, the more intense and blood-thirsty the anti-Semitic propaganda became. The post-war pogroms in Hungary, Poland, and the Ukraine, as well as the anti-Semitic campaigns in Germany and Austria were prepared in the trenches.'[50] As Krausz correctly observed, one of the main reasons for the violent anti-Semitism in Central Europe after 1918 was that the Jews became the projection screen for everything the paramilitary right despised. Paradoxically, they could simultaneously be portrayed as the embodiment of a pan-Slavic revolutionary menace from 'the East' that threatened the traditional order of Christian Central Europe, as 'red agents' of Moscow, and as representatives of an obscure 'Golden International' and western democratization.

[48] Pabst Papers, Bundesarchiv (Berlin), NY4035/6, 37–9.   [49] Krauss, *Unser Deutschtum!*, 7–13.
[50] Jakob Krausz (ed.), *Martyrium: ein jüdisches Jahrbuch* (Vienna, 1922), 17. See, too Frank M. Schuster, *Zwischen allen Fronten: Osteuropäische Juden während des Ersten Weltkriegs (1914–1919)*, (Cologne, 2004).

In Hungary, by contrast to Germany and Austria, anti-Semitic violence was tolerated by the state authorities and at times applauded by the nationalist press.[51] A report on anti-Semitic violence published by Vienna's Jewish community in 1922 reported that 'more than 3000 Jews were murdered in Transdanubia', the broad region of Hungary west of the Danube.[52] Although these figures are probably exaggerated, there can be no doubt that the White Terror specifically targeted Jews in substantial numbers. A typical case of anti-Semitic violence in Hungary was reported to the police by Ignaz Bing from Bőhőnye in October 1919: 'During the night before 1 October, a group of sixty White Guards came to our community and ordered that every Jewish man had to appear immediately on the market square.' The Jewish men, seventeen altogether, who were entirely innocent of Communist activity, followed the order. When they had assembled, 'they were beaten and tortured and—without any interrogation— they [the soldiers] started hanging them'—an act of violence that served the dual purpose of eliminating the 'source of Bolshevism' and giving a public demonstration of what would happen to an enemy who fell into their hands.[53]

In Austria and Germany, anti-Semitism was equally widespread even though it never assumed an even remotely similar violent character prior to 1933–38. Before 1914, anti-Semitism in Austria had been common currency among right-wing politicians who bitterly complained about the high numbers of Jews from Galicia and the Bukovina who had migrated to Vienna. When in 1918 Galicia fell to Poland and the Bukovina to Romania, the number of Jewish migrants further increased, accelerated by large-scale pogroms in Galicia and Ukraine. In 1918, 125,000 Jews lived in Vienna, although German-Austrian nationalists maintained that the number was as high as 450,000.[54] The postwar influx of 'Eastern Jews' fanned anti-Semitic feelings in Vienna which— since the days of Karl Lueger and Georg von Schönerer—were never far from the surface and which had been reinforced by the popular wartime stereotype of the 'Jewish profiteer'.[55]

[51] On Hungarian anti-Semitism after 1918, see: Robert M. Bigler, 'Heil Hitler and Heil Horthy! The nature of Hungarian racist nationalism and its impact on German-Hungarian relations 1919–1945', *East European Quarterly* 8 (1974), 251–72; Béla Bodo, ' "White Terror", Newspapers and the Evolution of Hungarian Anti-Semitism after World War I', *Yad Vashem Studies* 34 (2006); Nathaniel Katzburg, *Hungary and the Jews: Policy and Legislation, 1920–1943* (Ramat-Gan, 1981); and Rolf Fischer, *Entwicklungsstufen des Antisemitismus in Ungarn, 1867–1939: Die Zerstörung der magyarisch-jüdischen Symbiose* (Munich, 1998).

[52] Josef Halmi, 'Akten über die Pogrome in Ungarn', in: Krausz, *Martyrium*, 59. See also Oskar Jászi, *Magyariens Schuld: Ungarns Sühne* (Munich, 1923), 168–79. Josef Pogány, *Der Weiße Terror in Ungarn* (Vienna, 1920). British Joint Labour Delegation to Hungary: *The White Terror in Hungary. Report of the British Joint Labour Delegation to Hungary* (London, 1920) and *The Jews in Hungary: Correspondence with His Majesty's Government, presented to the Jewish Board of Deputies and the Council of the Anglo-Jewish Association, October 1920*, TNA, FO 371/3558, 206720.

[53] Halmi, 'Pogrome', 64.

[54] See Bruce F. Pauley, 'Politischer Antisemitismus im Wien der Zwischenkriegszeit', in: Gerhard Botz et al. (eds.), *Eine zerstörte Kultur: Jüdisches Leben und Antisemitismus in Wien seit dem 19. Jahrhundert* (Buchloe, 1990), 221–3.

[55] On the history of anti-Semitism up to the Great War, see Peter Pulzer, *The Rise of Political Anti-Semitism in Germany and Austria* (2nd rev. edn., Cambridge, MA, 1988); and John W. Boyer, 'Karl Lueger and the Viennese Jews', *Yearbook of the Leo Baeck Institute*, xxvi (1981), 125–44. On the image of the 'Jewish profiteer' in wartime Vienna, see Maureen Healy, *Vienna and the Fall of the Habsburg Empire: Total War and Everyday Life in World War I* (Cambridge, 2004). On anti-Semitism in Austrian universities, see Michael Gehler, *Studenten und Politik: Der Kampf um die Vorherrschaft an der Universität Innsbruck 1919–1938* (Innsbruck, 1990), 93–8.

After 1918, right-wing veterans maintained, 'the Jew' had become the 'slaveholder' of a defenceless German people, determined 'to exploit our peril in order to make good business…and to squeeze out our last drop of blood'.[56] The identification of 'the Jewish people' as the 'wire-pullers' behind revolution and imperial collapse was generally linked to the hope that 'the German giant will rise again one day' and that then, 'the day of reckoning must come for all the treason, hypocrisy and barbarism, for all their crimes against the German people and against humanity.'[57]

Similar to Hungary, anti-Semites in Austria usually appealed to Christian principles and linked the notion of Jewish responsibility for the military collapse to older Christian stereotypes of 'Jewish treason'.[58] In consequence, Christian Social politicians such as the Tyrolese *Heimwehr* leader, Richard Steidle, suggested that 'only a thorough reckoning with the spirit of Jewry and its helpers can save the German Alpine lands'.[59] Anti-Semitism after 1918 was further exacerbated by the widespread perception that a 'Jewish conspiracy' was at the heart of the revolutions of 1918–19. The fact that the intellectual leader of the Red Guards, Leo Rothziegel, and prominent members of the Social Democratic Party such as Victor Adler and Otto Bauer were Jewish was referred to constantly.

Although physical violence against German or Austrian Jews remained the exception, the language of violence used by German and Austrian paramilitaries certainly foreshadowed the infinitely more dramatic wave of anti-Jewish violence of the late 1930s and 1940s. Whether Hanns Albin Rauter expressed his aim to 'get rid of the Jews as soon as possible' as a student leader in Graz or Starhemberg attacked the 'Jewish war profiteers' as 'parasites', the rhetoric of violent anti-Semitism constituted a tradition on which radical nationalists would build in subsequent decades.[60]

LEGACIES

Crude notions of violently 'un-mixing' the ethnic complexity of the new German, Austrian and Hungarian borderlands, coupled with militant anti-Bolshevism and radicalized anti-Semitism directed against the 'enemy within' created fateful legacies for all three societies. The Hungarian White Terror revealed much of the later chauvinist and racist mood in the country, notably through its sudden and sanguinary animus against the Jews. It was revived with added fury (and on a broader popular

---

[56] Krauss, *Unser Deutschtum!*, 20.

[57] Krauss, *Unser Deutschtum!*, 16–17.

[58] See, e.g., the article series on 'The Racial-Political Causes of the Collapse', *Neue Tiroler Stimmen*, 9, 10 and 30 December 1918 and 2 January 1919 as quoted in Carr, *Revolution*, 261. See, too *Innsbrucker Nachrichten*, 8 April 1919. On the broader context: Paul Rena, *Der christlichsoziale Antisemitismus in Wien 1848–1938* (unpublished thesis, Vienna, 1991) and Christine Sagoschen, *Judenbilder im Wandel der Zeit: die Entwicklung des katholischen Antisemitismus am Beispiel jüdischer Stereotypen unter besonderer Berücksichtigung der Entwicklung in der ersten Republik,* PhD thesis (Vienna, 1998).

[59] *Tagespost,* 27 May 1919.

[60] Rauter Papers, NIOD (Amsterdam), Doc I-1380 Pr 6-12-97, 46–7. Starhemberg, 'Meine Stellungnahme zur Judenfrage', Starhemberg Papers, OÖLA.

basis) in the 1930s, exacerbated by the frustrations caused by the Great Depression. In Austria and Germany, too, anti-Semitism and anti-Slavic sentiments would resurface with renewed intensity after the brief moment of political stabilization in the mid-1920s gave way to economic depression and political turmoil. For many Austrian, German, and Hungarian fascists of the 1930s, the experiences of 1918–19 provided a decisive catalyst for political radicalization and a catalogue of political agendas whose implementation was merely postponed during the years of relative stability between 1923 and 1929. Some of the most prominent paramilitary activists of the immediate postwar period would resurface in the central European dictatorships of the right. In Hungary, Ferenc Szálasi and many other Arrow Cross members of the 1940s, including the infamous militia leader Pál Prónay, repeatedly pointed to the period between November 1918 and the signing of the Trianon Treaty as the moment of their political awakening. In Austria and Germany, too, personal continuities between the immediate postwar period and the Nazi dictatorship are easy to identify. Robert Ritter von Greim, leader of the Tyrolese branch of the 'Oberland League' after 1922, became Göring's successor as commander of the German Luftwaffe in 1945; Hanns Albin Rauter, who had contributed decisively to the radicalization of the *großdeutsch* wing of the Styrian Heimwehr, became Higher SS and Police Chief in the Nazi-occupied Netherlands, whilst his compatriot and friend, Ernst Kaltenbrunner, succeeded Reinhard Heydrich as head of the Nazis' Reich Security Main Office in 1943. For all of these men, the fascist dictatorships of Central Europe provided an opportunity to settle old scores and to 'solve' some of the issues, which the inglorious defeat of 1918 and the subsequent revolution had raised.

Yet, whereas in Italy—as Emilio Gentile points out in his contribution to this volume—paramilitary violence provided a key source of legitimacy for Mussolini's totalitarian regime and a model for violent practices against opponents of the fascist state, the relationship between post-1918 paramilitarism and the fascist dictatorships of Central Europe in the 1930s was more complicated. Many of the most prominent paramilitaries of the immediate postwar period—including Ludendorff, Horthy and Starhemberg—were dedicated anti-Bolsheviks and committed anti-Semites in 1918, but their conservatism and regional loyalties made them suspicious in the eyes of the Nazis. Starhemberg, who had entertained close personal relations with Hitler until 1923 (and indeed participated in the unsuccessful Munich putsch of 9 November 1923), began to oppose the Austrian Nazi movement in the 1930s, rejected his own postwar anti-Semitism as 'nonsense', insisted on Austrian independence in 1938, and even served in the British and Free French forces during the Second World War.[61] Starhemberg was not the only prominent paramilitary whose vision for a national Austrian 'rebirth' was incompatible with that of Nazism. Captain Karl Burian, founder and head of the monarchist combat organization Ostara after the end of the Great War, paid for his continued royalist beliefs in the 1930s with his arrest by the Gestapo and his execution in 1944.[62] Not

---

[61] In the 1930s, Starhemberg rejected the myth of a Jewish world conspiracy as 'nonsense' and 'scientific' racism as a propagandistic 'lie', See Starhemberg, 'Meine Stellungnahme zur Judenfrage', Starhemberg Papers, OÖLA.

[62] See the Gestapo file on Burian in: Burian papers, Österreichisches Staatsarchiv, Vienna B 1394.

entirely dissimilar to the situation in Germany, where the direct personal continuities between the *Freikorps* and the Third Reich ended with the Night of the Long
Knives in the summer of 1934, Austrian paramilitary veterans had to come to the
realization that Nazism was not always compatible with the ideas for which they
had fought in 1918.

The fact that the Nazis themselves ended many personal continuities between
the postwar paramilitary conflicts and the emerging Third Reich by decapitating
the SA in 1934 and murdering many Heimwehr activists after the *Anschluss* of
1938 did not prevent them from celebrating the '*Freikorps* spirit' as one of the key
inspirations for and forerunners of the Nazi movement. It was no coincidence that
the largest memorial ever to be built in Nazi Germany was the Annaberg monument which commemorated the joint German-Austrian effort to 'liberate' Upper
Silesia during the Third Polish Uprising of 1921.[63] What mattered far more than
the largely invented tradition of personal continuities was that the Nazis set out to
violently resolve the issues that had been raised but not settled during the turbulent period between 1917 and 1923.

CONCLUSIONS

Post-imperial Central Europe witnessed the emergence of a sizeable paramilitary
subculture, one that was shaped by the successive traumatizing experiences of war,
defeat, revolution, and territorial disintegration. Those members of the male wartime generation active in this subculture fed on a doctrine of hyper-nationalism
and shared a determination to use violence in order to suppress a (real or alleged)
revolutionary threat and to avenge their perceived humiliations at the hands of
external and internal enemies.

If the war had laid the foundation for the creation of a violent subculture of
demobilized officers, defeat and revolution significantly contributed to the radicalization and enlargement of this paramilitary milieu. Ex-officers brutalized by
the war and infuriated by its *outcome* joined forces with, and transmitted their
'values' to, members of a younger generation, who compensated for their lack of
combat experience by often surpassing the war veterans in terms of radicalism,
activism, and brutality. Together the veterans and members of the war youth generation formed an ultra-militant masculine subculture that differed from the 'community of the trenches' in its social make-up, its 'liberation' from the constraints
of military discipline, and its self-imposed postwar mission of destroying both the
external and internal enemy in order to pave the way for a national rebirth.

Everywhere in the region, anti-Bolshevism, anti-Semitism, and anti-Slavism—
often amalgamated into a single enemy image of 'Jewish-Slav Bolshevism'—oper-

[63] James Bjork and Robert Gerwarth, 'The Annaberg as a German-Polish Lieu de Memoire',
German History 25 (2007), 372–400.

ated as touchstones for paramilitary movements. Unlike during the Great War, violence was primarily directed against civilians and more specifically against those perceived to be 'community aliens' who had to be 'removed' in one way or another before a new utopian society could emerge from the debris caused by defeat and revolution. The desire to 'cleanse' their new nation-states from these broadly defined enemies went hand in hand with a fundamental distrust of the democratic, capitalist 'West' whose promises of national self-determination clashed violently with postwar realities in Austria, Hungary, and the German borderlands. If, however, paramilitaries in all three countries shared similar fantasies of violence, they differed in their ability to live out these fantasies. Whereas in post-revolutionary Hungary and the ethnically contested borderlands in the German East, fantasies turned into reality on a large scale, Austrian paramilitaries at home either had to 'confine' themselves to small-scale fighting in the Austrian borderlands with Yugoslav troops or they had to join forces with German *Freikorps* in Munich or Upper Silesia where violent action against a common enemy was possible.

Although in a small minority everywhere in the former Habsburg and Hohenzollern Empires, paramilitary activists managed to overcome their marginality within the majority of veterans by creating parallel universes of tightly-knit veteran communities with few ties to mainstream society and by linking their postwar fate to similar paramilitary groups in the other defeated states of Central Europe who shared their determination to challenge the moral and political authority of the Wilsonian postwar European order.

These international ties with other revisionist forces in Central Europe were one of the lasting legacies of the immediate transitional period from war to 'peace'. Perhaps more importantly, the men who continued their military careers well into the postwar period, created a language and practices of violent exclusion of all those they perceived as obstacles to a future national rebirth which alone could justify the sacrifices made during the war. More than direct personal continuities between the postwar period and the fascist dictatorships of the 1930s and 1940s, it was this legacy of national redemption through violent exclusion that proved to be of fatal significance for Central Europe during the Second World War.

5

Revolution, Civil War, and Terror in Finland in 1918

Pertti Haapala and Marko Tikka

INTRODUCTION

The Finnish Civil War in the winter months of 1918 was part of a wider process of political and social disintegration of the great European land empires at the end of the First World War. When the Russian Empire collapsed, Finland, like other western territories and autonomous parts of Russia such as the Baltic states and Ukraine, declared independence but remained in a state of political turmoil as the imperial forces—Russian or German—left the country.[1] At the same time, the subsequent civil war in Finland was also exceptional, notably with respect to its extraordinarily high death toll of over 36,000 people within six months.[2] Alongside the Spanish and Russian civil wars, the Finnish Civil War was one of the deadliest internal conflicts in Europe in the twentieth century in terms of the rate of fatalities. Over 1 per cent of the population was killed in the conflict.

Two further aspects stand out: first, one third of the Civil War's victims died in the so-called Red or White Terrors outside battle, and these murders were carried out not by regular armies but by paramilitary groups and extralegal courts martial.[3] This dimension of the conflict, which set it apart from 'normal' warfare, profoundly marked both contemporary understanding of the Civil War and its place in Finnish

---

[1] On the Finnish Civil War in English: Anthony Upton, *The Finnish Revolution* (Minnesota, 1980); Risto Alapuro, *State and Revolution in Finland* (California, 1988); Tuomas Hoppu and Pertti Haapala (eds.), *Tampere 1918: A Town in the Civil War* (Tampere, 2010); Jason Lavery, 'Finland 1917–19: Three Conflicts, One Country', *Scandinavian Review* 94 (2006); C. Jay Smith, *Finland and The Russian Revolution* (Atlanta, Georgia, 1958); Richard Luckett, *The White Generals. An Account of the White Movement and the Russian Civil War* (London, 1971), 131–53; Evan Mawdsley, *The Russian Civil War* (London, 2000), 27–9. In Finnish language the war was not called a civil war in 1918 but a 'Revolution', 'Revolt', 'Mutiny', 'Freedom Battle' or 'Liberation War', which became the official name in independent Finland in the 1920s. About the history of naming the war, see articles by Pertti Haapala et al., *Historiallinen Aikakauskirja* no. 2/1993. A recent general account in Finnish is Pertti Haapala and Tuomas Hoppu (eds.), *Sisällissodan pikkujättiläinen* (Helsinki, 2009).

[2] See Lars Westerlund (ed.), *Sotaoloissa vuosina 1914–1922 surmansa saaneet. Tilastoraportti* (Helsinki, 2004).

[3] Aapo Roselius, *Amatöörien sota* (Helsinki, 2006).

Fig. 7. Finnish Red Guards and a Russian sailor pose before the Battle of Pekkala in February 1918.

popular memory ever since. Secondly, prior to the Civil War, Finland had enjoyed an extraordinarily long period of peace since 1809. Finland was not directly involved in the Great War, and had no army of its own. There was no mandatory military service for Finns in the Russian army and few men had gone through any military training. It is true that there was a long tradition of Finnish noble sons entering the Russian army and hundreds of them served as officers during the Great War.[4] Also, about 1,500 young men volunteered for the German and Russian armies in 1914 and 1915.[5] But the vast majority of the roughly 200,000 men who fought in the two armies of the Finnish Civil War, the Whites and the Reds, had no previous experience in fighting, raising the question of where the brutality of the civil war came from. This chapter will try to answer that question and also to account for the often unpredictable and irrational nature of the violence during the Civil War.[6]

[4] John. E. O. Screen, *The Entry of Finnish Officers into Russian Military Service 1809–1917* (Ph.D thesis, University of London, 1976); Pertti Luntinen, 'Imperial Russian Army and Navy in Finland, 1809–1918', in: *Studia Historica* 56 (Helsinki, 1996).
[5] Tuomas Hoppu, *Historian unohtamat: Suomalaiset vapaaehtoiset Venäjän armeijassa 1. maailmansodassa 1914–1918* (SKS, 2005); Matti Lackman, *Suomen vai Saksan puolesta? Jääkäreiden tuntematon historia* (Helsinki, 2000).
[6] Ulla-Maija Peltonen, 'Civil war victims and the ways of mourning in Finland in 1918', in: Kenneth Christie and Robert Cribb (eds.), *Historical Injustice and Democratic Transition in Eastern Asia and Northern Europe* (London: 2002), 184–97; Pertti Haapala, 'The Many Truths of 1918', in: *Tampere 1918*, 185–92.

THE CAUSES AND COURSE OF THE WAR

Since 1918, Finnish historiography—itself deeply politicized by the conflict—has offered a number of explanations for the particular brutality of the Civil War. If conservative historians, the state authorities, right-wing parties, and the church have long interpreted the Civil War as a war of liberation that freed Finland of the Bolshevik threat and secured national independence, historians of the political left always viewed the conflict as a classic example of a class war. In recent decades, a more differentiated picture has emerged, often emphasizing a combination of several of the following factors: the social conditions of Finland's working classes, socialist and nationalist ideologies, the alleged injustices and oppression of the pre-war political system, a violent rejection of the (largely imagined) attempts at the 'Russification' of Finland, German and Russian involvement in the Civil War, or long-standing communal tensions.[7]

In explaining Finland's violent trajectory of 1918, contemporaries—and generations of historians after them—have frequently pointed to the fact that Finland was then a part of the Russian Empire, and directly affected by the Russian revolutions as well. During the Civil War the Finnish Whites declared that they were fighting against the Bolsheviks and not against their fellow citizens. This contemporary perspective, which informed White propaganda, remained a major popular explanation of the war for decades.[8] In fact the war in Finland was a genuine civil war, a conflict between opposed and armed Finnish civilians, and not a war against an external state involving regular armies and soldiers. On the other hand the Civil War in Finland cannot be conceived without its connection to the Russian Revolution and the Russian Civil War. The 'Russian connection' does not explain the eruption of violence in Finland, but it was among the key factors that shaped its particular nature and timing.

The key question in defining the 'Russian connection', true or imagined, is the role of the Finnish socialists, who were accused of having betrayed their country by staging a 'Bolshevik revolution'. It is a fact that the socialists carried out a coup d'état on 28 January 1918 in Helsinki and other major localities in Southern Finland. They called it a revolution and in their first declarations the Reds said that they had started a 'war of liberation' against their oppressors and against capitalism in general.[9]

---

[7] Various explanations have been analysed in Risto Alapuro, 'The Finnish Civil War: Politics, and Microhistory', in: Anna-Maija Castren, Markku Lonkila and Matti Peltronen (eds), *Between Sociology and History* (Helsinki, 2004), 130–47; Pertti Haapala, *Kun yhteiskunta hajosi. Suomi 1914–1920* (Helsinki, 1995); Ilkka Herlin, *Valkoista ja punaista hulluutta: Historiantutkijan muotokuva* (Helsinki, 1997); Juha Siltala, 'National Rebirth out of Young Blood. Sacrificial fantasies in the Finnish Civil War, 1917–1918', *Scandinavian Journal of History*, vol. 31, 290–307; Juha Siltala, *Sisällissodan psykohistoria* (Helsinki, 2009).

[8] On the role of Russians in the white discource, see Turo Manninen, *Vapaustaistelu, kansalaissota ja kapina*. Historica Jyväkyläensia 24, Jyväskylä 1982; Ylikangas, Heikki, *Der Weg nach Tampere. Die Niederlage der Roten im finnischen Bürgerkrieg 1918* (Berlin, 2002).

[9] This appears clearly in official documents of the Reds, in local documents and in the newspapers of the time.

In defending the cause of workers and all oppressed people, the Finnish socialists used classic Marxist rhetoric which they had adopted from Germany, not from the Russian revolutionaries. The political mobilization of Finnish workers followed the German model; they were highly organized in trade unions and the Social Democratic Party (the so-called Workers' Party), which held a majority of seats in the Finnish parliament until autumn 1917. But while no revolutionary councils of soldiers or workers were set up in Finland during the Russian Revolution, Finnish socialists maintained close contacts with leading Russian revolutionaries, especially with Lenin, contacts which they had cultivated since the revolution of 1905. The common enemy was Russian autocracy. When the war broke out in 1914 Finns remained loyal to Russia, however, and many were serving in the Russian army, especially senior officers, but also soldiers. Unlike the Russians, Finnish workers benefited economically from the war until the summer of 1917.

Finnish-Russian relations changed radically with the fall of the Tsar in March 1917. Though state power in Finland was in the hands of the Finns themselves, the overall situation in the Baltic area was tense, due to the German military presence. The Russian provisional government was afraid of Finnish separatism, which was supported by the Bolsheviks. For them Finland, with 100,000 demoralized Russian soldiers, was an important support base for the revolution. Above all, the Bolsheviks had a political ally in Finland, the Social Democratic Party, which opposed the provisional government, which, in turn, fraternized with Finnish centre-right parties in order to contain the socialists' influence. In July 1917 the Finnish parliament led by the Social Democrats passed a law of supreme power by which the parliament denied the rule of the Russian provisional government in Finland. The reaction was harsh: the parliament was dissolved by Russian soldiers and the Social Democrats lost their majority in the next general election.[10]

The events of 1917 and the worsening economic condition of Finland created a political crisis in which the struggles for state power in Russia and in Finland were closely intertwined. The Finns were not passive partners in the crisis but actively helped to bring it about. When the opposing political parties in Finland could not compromise, they all began seeking support from Russia (and later from Germany). In this process the socialists became allies of the Bolsheviks as did the conservatives of the German military and of emerging counter-revolutionary forces. Even though the socialists refused to obey Lenin and Stalin, and neglected the best chance for takeover in November, they trusted in Lenin's promises of national independence, and became dependent on the Bolsheviks' military help when they finally made the revolution in order to create their ideal state. In the eyes of the Finnish middle classes the socialists were undoubtedly serving the enemy's cause, and there is no doubt that some socialists did indeed view the October Revolution as an inspirational model.[11]

---

[10] On the heated months and deepening crises in the autumn of 1917, see Upton, 1982; Haapala, 1995; Ketola, Eino, *Kansalliseen kansanvaltaan. Suomen itsenäisyys, sosiaalidemokraatit ja Venäjän vallankumous 1917* (Helsinki, 1987); Seikko Eskola, *Suomen hurja vuosi 1917 Ruotsin peilissä* (Helsinki, 2010); Juha Siltala, *Sisällissodan psykohistoria* (Helsinki, 2009).

[11] The connections between Finnish socialists and Russians have been documented carefully by Ketola, ibid.

The actual coup d'état of January 1918 was carried out by the radicalized Red Guards, but the Social Democrats immediately assumed the leadership in organizing the revolution. Within a few weeks, the Reds succeeded in occupying major cities and held most of Southern Finland. There was no active resistance and it seemed likely that they would be able to co-opt the state administration.[12] The Reds produced a new constitution and began to introduce elements of direct democracy.[13] The intention of the Finnish revolutionaries was not to establish Finland as a Soviet Republic or to become a constituent part of Lenin's Russia but to build an independent democratic nation-state whose constitutional model was Switzerland. For their political opponents, however, it seemed clear that Finland was to become a Bolshevik state.[14] In reality, the direct Russian involvement in the Finnish Civil War was at best marginal. Russian volunteers made up 5–10 per cent of active soldiers on the Red side and many of those captured were summarily executed by the Whites after the end of the Civil War. A minimum number of officers was vital for the amateur Red Army, which also could not fight without Lenin's rifles and cannons. But Bolshevik support did not go beyond that and Russian forces were actually withdrawn from Finland during the months of the Civil War.[15]

An alternative, and more traditional, view of the origins of the Civil War has been to trace these back to the structures of the pre-war society. In this interpretation, the political crisis of 1917–18 only made visible the deeper frictions in Finnish society. It is certainly true that deep class divisions existed in early twentieth century Finnish society: Finland was partly urbanized but mostly agrarian and hence a great majority of its working class were living off agriculture and forestry. Urban and industrial workers had been highly organized since 1905. Strong unions and the support of the rural workers in Southern Finland made the Social Democrats the largest party in the parliament after universal suffrage was introduced in 1907.[16]

The principal divisions in Finnish society were based on work and land ownership. Wage-earning manual labourers made up 60 per cent of the population, with small scale independent farmers accounting for 25 per cent and most of the remaining 15 per cent comprising the lower middle class. The upper middle class and the educated elite were numerically small but influential, especially as civil servants. The elite was divided into two mutually hostile sections: nationally minded

---

[12] Juhani Piilonen, *Vallankumous kunnallishallinnossa. Punaisen Suomen historia 1918* (Helsinki, 1982); Osmo Rinta-Tassi, *Kansanvaltuuskunta Punaisen Suomen hallituksena. Punaisen Suomen historia 1918* (Helsinki, 1986).

[13] Rinta-Tassi, ibid; Maurice Carrez, *La fabrique d'un révolutionnaire: O. W. Kuusinen (1881–1918)*, II (Toulouse, 2008). Kuusinen was the leading ideologist of the revolutionary government and claimed afterwards that they were not 'real revolutionaries', see O.W. Kuusinen, *The Finnish Revolution: a Self-Criticism* (London, 1919).

[14] On the Swedish party and their role in peace-making in Finland, see Eskola, ibid.

[15] Aatos Tanskanen, *Venäläiset Suomen sisällissodassa 1918*. Acta universitatis tamperensis, 1978 (Summary: The Russians in the Finnish Civil War); Tuomas Hoppu, 'The Fate of Russian Officers', in: *Tampere 1918* (2010), 152–3.

[16] Haapala, 1995.

Fennomen (Finnish speakers) and *Svekomen* (Swedish speakers) who were themselves divided into conservative and liberal fractions. There were two dominant political cultures with real capacities for popular mobilization—(Finnish) nationalism and socialism, both of which emphasized the need for social cohesion and a politically unified independent nation-state.[17]

Working-class resentment towards 'the rich' was certainly exploited by socialist agitation and may well be one explanation for the violence of the Civil War.[18] The social divisions were amplified when a severe economic crisis hit Finland in the summer and autumn of 1917 after a long war boom. Unemployment, inflation and food shortages in the cities increased by the end of 1917, but serious difficulties were experienced only during and after the Civil War in 1918.[19]

However, it would be simplistic to focus solely on the long-term structural faultlines in Finnish society as an explanation of the Civil War. Social mobility was fairly high compared to most European societies. The middle class was mixed by origin and the small aristocracy no longer had any special privileges. Compared to Russia's other autonomous territories Finland looked like a relatively egalitarian society with equal political rights, a comparatively high level of education and opportunities for upward social mobility. The complexity of the social context of the Civil War is indicated by the fact that the Reds dominated the wealthier parts of the country in Southern Finland but were defeated by an army made of farmers from the poorer North, but led by upper class officers trained in Russia.

The political crisis that was the immediate cause of the Civil War went back as far as 1899, when the Russian government sought to introduce military service in Finland, thus de facto undermining Finnish autonomy within the Russian Empire. The plan resulted in protests, conscription strikes and even political murders. Military service was withdrawn after the 1905 revolution, accompanied by a national strike in Finland, but the limits of the political and administrative autonomy of Finland remained unclear.[20]

When the Great War broke out in August 1914, the situation in Finland remained stable. The war seemed to be far away even though St Petersburg, the capital of the Russian Empire, was at the Finnish border and Helsinki was a major naval base of the Russian Baltic Fleet. Despite the approximately 100,000 Russian troops stationed in Finland, the first years of war were peaceful and many Finns actually benefited a good deal from providing military supplies to the Russian army.[21]

[17] Ibid.

[18] Jari Ehrnrooth, *Sanan vallassa, vihan voimalla. Sosialistiset vallankumousopit ja niiden vaikutus Suomen työväenliikkeessä 1905–1914* (Helsinki, 1992).

[19] Haapala, 1995, 155–217; Leo Harmaja, *Effects of the War on Economic and Social Life in Finland* (New Haven, 1933).

[20] Osmo Jussila, *Suomen suuriruhtinaskunta 1809–1917* (Helsinki, 2004); Pertti Haapala et al (eds.), *Kansa kaikkivaltias. Suurlakko Suomessa 1905* (Helsinki, 2008); Marko Tikka, *Kun kansa leikki kuningasta. Suomen suuri lakko 1905* (Helsinki, 2009).

[21] For a description of the social conditions in 1914–20, see Haapala, 1995.

After the March Revolution of 1917 Finland became practically independent. A coalition government was formed under the Social Democrat, Oskari Tokoi, whose party had won the majority of seats in the Finnish parliament in 1916. However, the new coalition government did not last long and collapsed in 1917. This is a tragic example of political failure at a critical moment. During the most severe disorder and confusion—from late July to early November 1917—Finland had no working government and no military or police to maintain public order as the latter had gone on strike to secure their pay. The members of the senate resigned one by one, because they were criticized by the people and the press—and not supported by their parties. With the political crisis, popular distrust of politics had become widespread by the end of the year. There was much violence in the streets, rumours of murders and fears of a German invasion. In the parliament two major political forces, the bourgeois coalition and the socialists, argued about the foundations of political authority, accusing each other of planning a coup.[22]

Under these circumstances rival political groups began to develop their own bands of security guards to protect their property and defend their rival political agendas.[23] Street violence peaked during the general strike at the beginning of November 1917, when over 30 people were killed in rioting. At the same time there were clashes between Workers' Guards and bourgeois Protection Guards. Both were armed with the ammunition they appropriated from the retreating Imperial Russian Army.[24]

The political crisis and violence escalated further in January 1918 when the socialists, after seizing power in Helsinki, went on to occupy much of Southern Finland, prompting the Whites to occupy the north of the country. An unofficial front divided Finland from Pori in the west to Viipuri in the East. The Civil War in Finland, as in Russia, was a railway war: both sides tried to control the east-west railway lines in order to move troops and armaments.[25] There were tens of thousands of Russian soldiers still in Finland, but they stayed mostly passive and were withdrawn between late January and May 1918. German troops, instead, landed in Southern Finland at the beginning of April—at the same time that the Whites engaged in bitter fighting in Tampere. The fall of 'Red Tampere', the major industrial centre in Finland, marked the beginning of the end of Red rule in Southern Finland. This was the first urban battle in Scandinavia, and it was particularly brutal. One third of the total of 1,200 Reds who died were summarily executed, and after the capitulation of the city, courts martials condemned to death nearly 300 out of over 11,000 Red Prisoners of War (POWs).[26]

---

[22] For a summary of the deepening crises of 1917, see Pertti Haapala, 'Vuoden 1917 kriisi', in: Haapala and Hoppu 2008, 58–91.

[23] For a detailed history of the guards, see Turo Manninen, 'Kaartit vastakkain', in: *Itsenäistymisen vuodet. Suomi 1917–1920*, vol. 2, (Helsinki, 1992), 246–396. For a sociological analysis of mobilization, see Alapuro, 1988, chs. 7–9.

[24] Manninen, 1992.

[25] Evan Mawdsley, *The Russian Civil War* (London, 2000), 16–30.

[26] The battle in Tampere is described in *Tampere 1918* (2010), 44–147; Aapo Roselius and Marko Tikka, *Taistelujen jälkeen välittömästi paikalla ammutut* (Westerlund, 2004), 107–14.

After the fall of Tampere, the Civil War assumed an even more violent character. First the Reds killed their white hostages; over a fourth of the victims of the Red Terror—640 people—were killed as the Reds retreated.[27] The Red massacres were followed by White reprisals. Within a few weeks after the Reds' capitulation, over 4,500 Reds were shot.[28] In addition, over 68,000 prisoners were sentenced by special courts, mostly to two or three years' imprisonment.[29]

During and after the Finnish Civil War, both sides tried to legitimize their use of violence against unarmed enemies, often denying the important fact that terror was a key strategy employed by both sides.[30] A comparison between the ways in which both sides used this strategy reveals some structural similarities.

TERROR AS A STRATEGY IN THE CIVIL WAR

In Southern Finland the revolutionaries built up their own provisional administration whose authority rested on the Red Guards, a locally organized paramilitary force of between 90,000 and 100,000 men. The Red Guard supported the local red power, and a small part of the guard was on active service. Their rank-and-file was relatively young (the average age of those Red Guards killed in action being 27 years), and largely composed of factory and farm workers.[31]

The Reds used terror for two principal reasons. First, it was a means to repress counter-revolutionary forces in the occupied areas, a strategy adopted from the Russian Civil War.[32] Secondly, the use of terror was also ideologically motivated. The Finnish Revolution was—at least for a small part of the Finnish revolutionaries—a class war designed to destroy class enemies. Rank-and-file men in the Red Guard usually had no idea of these ideological aspects, but the revolutionary leaders did. In some areas—especially in Kymi industrial area and in Toijala near Tampere— they were also active in terror.[33] Where revolutionary activists reinforced the military volunteers, a threshold was crossed in the political use of military violence, which now became a means of eliminating the enemy as part of a class that was condemned by history to disappear.

[27] Jaakko Paavolainen, *Poliittiset väkivaltaisuudet Suomessa 1918 I: Punainen terrori* (Helsinki, 1966), 113.

[28] Marko Tikka, 'Teloitetut, ammutut, murhatut', in: Westerlund, 2004, 105.

[29] On the prison camps, see Jaakko Paavolainen, *Vankileirit Suomessa 1918* (Helsinki, 1971); Pentti Mäkelä, *Vuosien 1917–19 Kulkutaudit, espanjantauti ja vankileirikatastrofi* (Helsinki, 2007), (Summary: Communicable diseases, pandemic flu and the aftermath of civil war. High mortality in Finland at the end of 1910s).

[30] Paavolainen, 1966, and Jaakko Paavolainen, *Poliittiset väkivaltaisuudet Suomessa 1918 II: Valkoinen terrori* (Helsinki, 1967).

[31] Aapo Roselius, *Amatöörien sota. Rintamataisteluiden henkilötappiot Suomen sisällissodassa 1918* (Helsinki, 2006), 23–5.

[32] Tikka, 2004, 96–108 and 112–13; George Leggett, *The Cheka: Lenin's Political Police* (Oxford, 1981), 55, 150–1 and W. Bruce Lincoln, *Passage Trough Armageddon. The Russians in War and Revolution 1914–1918* (Oxford, 1994), 50.

[33] Tikka, 2004, 96–108.

Finally, individuals used the red terror for a range of personal motives, from revenge to looting. In Finnish historiography, this aspect of civil war violence has been exaggerated, because it provides a consensual explanation that avoids the need to confront the deeper dynamics of violence at work in the conflict. In reality, however, only a small part of the terror was individually motivated in this way. Even so, the Finnish Revolution was gentle rather than furious. Although the Reds took control of the most populated areas in Finland, in three months of occupation they committed some 1,600 acts of terror, mostly at the beginning and at the end of the war.[34]

The Red terror worked in two ways. Military courts operated near the front. Behind the lines the terror was in the hands of the Red investigative organs. On the battlefield, or after the occupation of an area, the staff of the local Red Guard formed a court from its own officers and tried counter-revolutionaries. Usually this meant shooting on the spot. When an occupied area was controlled for weeks, even months, the local Red staff handed the investigation of counter-revolutionary activities over to an investigative unit, usually called a 'flying patrol'.[35]

There was no official guideline on terror, and in many ways it depended on local initiative. Every Red Guard Staff had a chief of reconnaissance who was responsible for coordinating the activities of his rank-and-file men, who were usually young factory or farm workers and who were occasionally supported by skilled labourers such as tailors, craftsmen, blacksmiths, machinists, and upholsterers. Most of them had no criminal record before the Civil War; yet these ordinary men took part in the random killings and executions of White POWs and 'class enemies'.

Not entirely dissimilar to the Red troops, the White army consisted of local paramilitary groups, the so-called Protection Guards. The bourgeois Senate in January 1918 nominated local Protection Guards to be the troops of the government. Similar to the Finnish Red Army, officers of the White Army were mainly ex-officers from the Imperial Russian Army while the rank-and-file solders of the White Army were young men without any previous war experience. The average age of those killed in action was 23 years.[36] The White Army consisted of landowners and their sons, students and other middle-class volunteers.

In justifying their violent suppression of Red resistance, the White Army drew on the legacy of repressive legislation from the tsarist regime. In 1909 Nicholas II had introduced a set of special laws strengthening military law in time of war.[37] These enabled the state to declare local or regional states of war in order to repress strikes and political agitation, powers the regime had long used in Russia itself. Although this legislation was criticized in Finland during the war, it was pressed into service by the White Guards (despite the fall of the regime on whose authority it depended) in order to deal with the Reds during the Civil War. It meant that all crimes, including fighting against the White army, would be judged by courts martial under Russian military law.[38] In addition, on 25 February, the commander

---

[34] Paavolainen, 1966, 92–6.   [35] Tikka, 2004, 85–6, 112–13.
[36] Hoppu, 2005, 314; Roselius, 2006, 24–5.   [37] Tikka, 2004, 149–55.
[38] See Richard Pipes, *The Russian Revolution 1899–1919* (London, 1997), 170–1.

of the White Army, General C. G. E. Mannerheim, issued his infamous 'shoot on the spot' order, which sanctioned summary execution of even unarmed opponents in the name of 'self-defence'.[39]

After the fall of Tampere, the White Army took over 11,000 men and women as POWs. Here and in other newly-occupied towns in Southern Finland, the power to organize the court martials was now in the hands of the local Commandant of the White Army. The Commandant's office arranged the interrogations of the prisoners of war. All POWs were put into military courts after the capitulation.[40] Commandants set up three-man courts to conduct the investigations and divide the prisoners into three groups: first, the suspected Red Guard leaders, war criminals, murderers, looters and the main leaders of the revolutionary civil commissions, all of whom were to suffer capital punishment; secondly all other members and supporters of the Red Guards who were imprisoned in POW camps; and third, the 'innocent' people who were to be set free. While the courts handed down their sentences, the White Army patrols or local Protection Guard patrols conducted the executions or moved imprisoned persons to POW camps.[41]

Central to the White's system of oppression were a number of special units organized and commanded by White Army headquarters to eliminate the enemy from newly 'liberated' areas. In General Mannerheim's office there was a 'Desk for Securing Occupied Areas' (*Valloitettujen Alueiden Turvaamis Osasto*) that organized such purges. The special paramilitary units consisted of remarkably young volunteers, sometimes even 12–15-year-old schoolboys and their teachers. These units hunted, arrested, guarded, sentenced, and executed POWs. One of these units that operated in the southern part of Tampere shot over 900 Reds and arrested more than 4,000 political opponents in the space of a few weeks.[42] After this extremely violent wave of repression, all remaining resistance died down.

After the first wave of purges the local White Guard established their local rule while continuing to carry out arrests. Between May and June 1918 the local guards identified and arrested all Reds and their supporters who had escaped the first purges. In cooperation with the central White authorities the local guards started official investigations and committed the Reds to detention camps. This was a demanding undertaking for the local guards, because it involved hundreds of investigations and detentions in every 'liberated' district.[43]

The White Guards thus performed para-state functions in the absence of a working executive. During the Civil War the local police force had virtually ceased to operate after the majority of its members had been dismissed and many of them killed during the conflict. The local police was too weak and dispersed to take control over any of the contested areas in the spring of 1918.

In this situation the White Guards de facto adopted the role of a state institution, a role that was legalized in August 1918, when a new law made the White

[39] Paavolainen, 1967, 58–70.   [40] Tikka, 2004, 188–92.   [41] Tikka, 2004, 214–17.
[42] Marko Tikka, 'Field Courts Martial in Tampere', in: *Tampere 1918*, 148–59.
[43] Ibid, 148–60; Tikka, 2004, 114–48; Marko Tikka, *Valkoisen hämärän maa? Suojeluskunnat, virkavalta ja kansa 1918–1921* (Helsinki 2006), 31–6.

Guards an official adjunct of the police.[44] Although officially under the command of the police, local guards continued to act independently. In the summer of 1918, they also acted as an adjunct to the new secret police (EK) and the White Army's internal intelligence in supervising the release of Red prisoners from the detention camps.[45]

Paradoxically, the release of many Red prisoners in the summer of 1918 strengthened their role further. Many conservatives believed that their release was premature and when the Finnish Communist Party was founded in Moscow in August 1918 by Finnish communists who had fled the country, their fears of a second attempt at revolution in Finland intensified.

The tense atmosphere in post-civil-war Finland continued to translate into acts of violence for years to come. Between 1918 and 1921, 326 serious violent incidents occurred, in which 226 people were killed. The victims of these acts of violence can be divided in to three groups; 45 per cent of them were ex-Reds, 27.5 per cent were ex-Whites or members of the Civil Guard and 27.5 per cent were bystanders.[46] The continued violence that overwhelmingly targeted activists of the political left mirrored a broader pattern in post-revolutionary Europe, be it in Germany, Austria or Italy between 1918 and 1922.[47] The White Guards were heavily involved in the killings of real or alleged 'Reds'. Yet—again following a broader European pattern—the excessive violence used by counter-revolutionary forces increasingly weakened their position. As in Germany or Hungary, public opinion began to turn against the role of the White Guards as an official part of the executive, leading to their withdrawal from active police service in 1921.[48]

CONCLUSION

The Finnish Civil War was a paramilitary conflict in several ways: in the absence of a national army, the two sides in the Civil War largely relied on militarily inexperienced volunteers who collectively sought to act as surrogates of the defunct state agencies normally charged with upholding public order: notably the police and the non-existing national army. On both sides of the conflict, however, those in charge proved unable to fully control their troops which contributed to a spiralling escalation of violence. Yet, as long as the outcome of the war was uncertain, both sides actively supported this escalation as long as it helped their cause, and both sides used special forces that adopted terror as a tactic to win the conflict. Because of the political nature of the conflict there was a strong justification for the terror and illegal

---

[44] Kari Selén, *Sarkatakkien maa. Suojeluskuntajärjestö ja yhteiskunta 1918–1944* (Helsinki, 2001), 40–5.

[45] Tikka, 2006, 31–43.

[46] Tikka, 2006, 173–214.

[47] Gerhard Botz, 'Political Violence, its Forms and Strategies in the First Austrian Rebuplic', in: Wolfgang J. Mommsen and Gerhard Hirschfeld (eds.), *Social Protest, Violence & Terror in Nineteenth-&Twentieth-Century Europe* (Hong Kong, 1982), 300–5; Jens Petersen, 'Violence in Italian Fascism, 1919–1925', ibid, 275–99.

[48] Tikka, 2006, 219–21.

executions. There were over 1,600 victims of the Red Terror and more than five times as many died during the White Terror, which was most often presented as a just punishment of the Red violence. Given the 'total' nature of the conflict, it is unsurprising that the end of the Civil War did not immediately lead to a period of peace and reconciliation, even if the new democratic constitution introduced in 1919 was intended as a compromise to heal the wounds inflicted by the war. Between 1919 and 1921, there occurred over 300 politically motivated acts of violence leading to 226 deaths. The first years of the democratic republic were thus characterized by an enduring culture of officially endorsed paramilitarism as the White Protection Guards acted as state-supported local militias.

Paramilitary activists such as the members of the Protection Guards were also instrumental in the post-civil-war trials against those accused of fighting or supporting the 'Reds', trials, which were not based on normal legal processes. Local Protection Guards carried out the 'criminal investigations' and often initiated man hunts that ended in the death of a fugitive Red guard leader or Red war criminal.

The paramilitary nature of the conflict helps to explain the peculiar nature of its violence which was unrestrained by international norms of warfare. The use of extreme violence on both sides was justified by the violence of the enemy, which was heavily exaggerated in the media and in contemporary political discourse. It has taken decades for Finnish historians and the public at large to come to terms with the apparent 'mystery' of the Civil War's particular brutality and to dismiss politically charged mono-causal explanations such as the Soviet 'infection' of Finnish politics or class struggle as simplistic. What made violence *possible* was the gradual process of state collapse in 1917 and the government's loss of control over

Fig. 8. Victorious White Guards after the end of the Battle of Tampere.

the monopoly of force, a process that soon began to affect civil society, the economy, and everyday life, and which eroded the belief in common values and norms. In that situation the step to violence was surprisingly short: the same young people, who a year previously had been enthusiastically founding reading clubs, choirs, and dance groups, were now organizing small armed groups willing to annihilate the enemy. The sudden mobilization of loosely connected local paramilitary groups was possible due to the high level of political organization, but that does not in itself explain why this political and organizational mobilization produced particularly brutal forms of violence. While ideology and political ambitions of the armies' leadership certainly contributed to it, the peculiar psychological dynamics of a civil war fought between inhabitants of the same villages and towns also account for the bloodiness of the conflict.

What makes the Finnish case peculiar in the context of other case studies discussed in the volume is not the use of paramilitarism in the absence of a functioning state authority, but the rapid escalation of extreme violence in a country with strong civic institutions that had not participated in the Great War or any other military conflict since the early nineteenth century. The Finnish case therefore illustrates that the 'brutalization' of politics in interwar Europe was not dependent on without participation in the Great War and that the emergence of a new kind of ideologically driven paramilitarism was possible even without 'brutalized' ex-servicemen.

6

Paramilitary Violence in Italy: The Rationale of Fascism and the Origins of Totalitarianism

Emilio Gentile

In the preface to the volume published by the Fascist Party in 1927, *The Grand Council in the First Five Years of the Fascist Era*, Mussolini wrote that the destruction of the liberal state had been started immediately after the 'March on Rome', when the Fascist Grand Council, which had only just been established, decided on the night of 12 January 1923 to establish the Voluntary Militia for National Security (Milizia Volontaria per la Sicurezza Nazionale—MVSN), which provided a legal basis for the military organization of the Fascist Party. 'The creation of the Militia,' wrote Mussolini, 'was the fundamental, irreplaceable act that put the government on a different plane to all its predecessors and made it into a regime. The armed party led to the regime. That night in January 1923, when the Militia was created, signed the death warrant of the old democratic-liberal state... From that point, the old democratic-liberal state simply awaited its own burial, which took place with full honours on the 3rd of January 1925.'[1] At least on this occasion, the Duce was right.

Fascism was the first organized military party to take power in a liberal state in Western Europe and in so doing it gave birth to a new type of regime founded on the rule of a single party. Fascism thus became a model for other European nationalist paramilitary movements that aimed to destroy democratically elected governments. As regards the origins of fascism, one might well say that: 'In the beginning there was violence'. By this I mean that paramilitary violence was a fundamental feature of the collective identity of fascism as an organisation, as a mentality, as a political culture and as a style of life and struggle, to say nothing of the fact that it was the main reason for its triumph. Let us now examine the most important aspects of the relationship between paramilitary violence and fascism.

To deal with fascist paramilitary violence in Italy between 1919 and 1923 is, by definition, to investigate the origins of the Fascist Militia Party and of the new type of dictatorial rule that fascism implemented after its rise to power on 30 October 1922. In order to provide a conceptual understanding of this form of political

---

[1] Partito Nazionale Fascista, *Il Gran Consiglio nei primi cinque anni dell'Era Fascista* (Rome, 1927), xi.

Fig. 9. On the eve of the March on Rome Mussolini and his followers in Naples in October 1922

authority, a number of anti-fascists coined the terms 'totalitarian' and 'totalitarianism' in 1923.[2]

My contribution will cover the main stages in the process I have just described. I shall endeavour to show why I believe that the practice and culture of paramilitary violence were what I call 'the rationale of fascism', or, in other words, the essential conditions for the emergence, expansion and success of fascism and, consequently, for the laying of the foundations of a new type of political regime in Italy that opened the way to the rise of totalitarianism in Western Europe.

Fascist paramilitary violence was for the most part the consequence of combat experience in the Great War, but it was also the cause of the collapse of any hope of creating a safer world for democracy. The First World War concluded with the triumph of democratic governments in Europe.[3] The collapse of German militarism, the break-up of the centuries-old autocratic Empires, the emergence of new republican states and a greater role for parliament in the new constitutions, were the key features of political democratization in Europe in 1919. Democratic governments and especially the newly constituted parliamentary regimes were characterized by a 'process of the rationalization of power', as the Russian jurist Boris Mirkine-Guétzevitch, defined it, meaning the 'tendency to submit the totality of collective life to legal norms.'[4] This expressed in full the constitutional principle of

[2] See Abbot Gleason, *Totalitarianism. The Inner History of the Cold War* (New York and Oxford, 1995), 13–15; Emilio Gentile, 'Fascism in Power: the Totalitarian Experiment', in: *Adrian Lyttelton* (ed.), *Liberal and Fascist Italy 1900–1945* (Oxford, 2002), 139–42.

[3] See Georges Guy-Grand, *La Démocratie et l'après-guerre* (Paris, 1922).

[4] Boris Mirkine-Guerzévitch, *Les constitutions de l'Europe nouvelle* (Paris, 1930), 11.

popular sovereignty and of parliamentary government in a state based on law. 'There is not and cannot be any form of state other than democracy that realizes the supremacy of the law; hence general constitutional law consists of all the juridical forms of democracy, of the state based on law.'[5]

However, expectations of a long-lasting peace were rapidly thwarted by the outbreak of paramilitary violence in many European countries. Political violence spread due to the Bolshevik revolution in Russia and also on account of the sense of humiliation felt by nationalist movements either because of defeat in the war or by virtue of what was seen, in Italy in particular, as a 'mutilated victory'. From that point on, paramilitary violence became a permanent condition on the European continent down to the outbreak of the Second World War. All of this lent an air of civil war to the social and political battles that arose out of the 1914–18 conflict, and this was particularly true of the Italian case.

Italy emerged victorious from the Great War and thus passed the most tragic test to which it had been put since national unification 60 years before. The dissolution of the Austro-Hungarian Empire, the expansion of Italy's borders to the Brennero Pass and Istria, the incorporation into Italy of Italian speaking minorities of the Habsburg Empire and, finally, a place at the negotiating table as one of the four great powers, could be deemed by many Italians as fitting compensation for the sacrifice of half-a-million lives and millions of wounded. Furthermore, an important electoral reform in 1919 led to the democratic transformation of the liberal regime and, indeed, the parliamentary majority was now made up of mass political parties, such as the Socialist Party and the newly founded Catholic Popular Party. These represented broad sectors of the Italian population that to this point in time had been excluded from parliamentary politics on account of the restricted electoral suffrage. Despite this, however, Italy was the first country to succumb to paramilitary violence and to experience the collapse of its democratic regime. Moreover, this occurred following a period in which violence had taken a rapid upturn: for example, deaths by suicide numbered 938 in 1918 and rose to 1,633 in 1919, to 2,661 in 1920 and to 2,750 in 1921; incidents of grievous bodily harm increased from 58,148 in 1918 to 108,208 in 1922; finally, breaches of the peace went up from 766 in 1918 to 1,004 in 1919, and again from 1,785 in 1920 to 2,458 in 1921.[6]

Moreover, Italy was the only one of the victorious states that underwent a process of the 'brutalization of politics', notably owing to the use of paramilitary violence. In this it was comparable to what happened in Germany and the countries of Eastern Europe—only with this difference that in the Italian case the system that was 'brutalized' was a liberal one, which, since the beginning of the century, had been in the process of becoming a democracy.[7]

---

[5] Ibid, 15.

[6] See Emilio Gentile, *Storia del partito fascista. 1919–1922. Movimento e milizia* (Rome and Bari, 1989), 741. Many of the more than 700 pages of this volume contain a detailed analysis of the various practices of fascist paramilitary violence in the period from 1919 to 1922. However, Emilio Traverso's assertion that my interpretation of the violence of fascism is only symbolic could not be further from the truth (E. Traverso, 'Interpreting Fascism', *Constellations*, September 2008, 302–19).

[7] George L. Mosse, *Fallen Soldiers. Reshaping the Memory of the World Wars* (New York and Oxford 1990), ch. 8.

Paramilitary violence was introduced into Italy by new organizations made up of ex-combatants, such as the *Arditi* (shock troops), the *Fasci di combattimento* founded by Mussolini in March 1919 and the armed movement led by the poet Gabriele D'Annunzio in the occupation of Fiume in September 1919.[8] Brandishing the slogan of the 'mutilated victory', these movements spread the conviction that, having won against its enemies on the battlefield, Italy had then been betrayed at the peace conference by its own allies, who had refused to grant full recognition of Italy's territorial claims as compensation for its contribution to the war effort. However, the paramilitary violence of the nationalists was just one of the various forms of political violence manifest in Italy.

These became widespread both on account of the serious economic and social crisis produced by the Great War and because of the political extremism of the socialists. During its national congress of October 1919, the Socialist Party, at that time dominated by the maximalist current, openly adopted a programme of social revolution along Bolshevik lines. The party's new constitution proclaimed that: 'the violent seizure of power on the part of the workers must mark the passage to . . . the transitional regime of the dictatorship of the proletariat.'[9]

Between 1919 and 1920, in most of Northern and Central Italy, the class struggles were led by the Socialist Party and workers' organizations, while in Southern Italy the traditional liberal and democratic parties, formed of local clientele groups, held sway. When, in the autumn and early winter of 1919, the Socialist Party became the largest party in parliament and obtained control over the majority of local councils and provincial governments in many regions of Central Italy and in the Po Valley, socialists announced their intention to use violence to overthrow the institutions of the bourgeois state.[10]

Moreover, in the main rural areas of Northern Italy where they had most influence, socialists exercised widespread control over economic and social activity, imposing their terms and conditions on property owners as a prelude to the imminent revolution and the abolition of private property. 'Red baronies' was the term used by communist Palmiro Togliatti to describe the system of rule by socialist maximalists.[11]

Violent class struggle, including continuous strikes in the state and private sectors, reached its apex in the autumn of 1920 with the occupation of the factories, and this gave the impression that Italy was prey to anarchy and on the brink of social revolution and civil war. The dramatic situation created by the political violence in those years was described by socialist Anna Kuliscioff in a letter of 4 May 1920 to her companion Filippo Turati, himself one of the founders of the Socialist Party and the main exponent of its reformist current:

> I have just been reading this morning's newspapers, and it all felt like a red nightmare on account of the civil war taking shape all over Italy. Socialists are killing Catholics,

---

[8] See Michael Ledeen, *The First Duce: D'Annunzio at Fiume* (Baltimore, 1977).
[9] See Emilio Gentile, *Fascismo e antifascismo. I partiti italiani fra le due guerre* (Milan, 2000), 40–6.
[10] *Cf.* Gentile, *Storia del partito fascista*, 146–7.
[11] Palmiro Togliatti, 'Baronie rosse', *Ordine Nuovo*, 5 June 1921.

in Romagna fisticuffs break out between socialists and republicans, in Liguria socialists and anarchists come to blows, and everywhere people die or are injured in bloody battles with police and *carabinieri*... The fact of the matter is that we're heading towards a major cataclysm... The contest with the communists exceeds everything we could have predicted, as each side attempts to undo the other's unity.[12]

It is interesting to note how in this letter Kuliscioff makes no reference to fascism and to fascist violence. But it needs to be remembered that in the spring of 1920 fascism was still a marginal movement in Italian politics. At the end of 1919, seven months after the founding of Mussolini's *Fasci di combattimento*, there were only 37 *fasci* in Italy, with a total of 800 members. In November of the following year, by which time the violent actions of fascist squads had commenced, there were 88 *fasci* with 20,615 members. Fascism's violent anti-proletarian offensive, which was encouraged and supported by the bourgeoisie and the middle classes, began at the end of 1920 in the regions of the Po Valley dominated by the Socialist Party.[13]

The identification of fascism with paramilitary violence was present from fascism's very inception. On 19 November 1918, just a fortnight after the end of the war with Austria, police reports noted 'revolutionary movements in Milan and Turin' and 'riotous movements' goaded by Mussolini and the *Arditi*, and referred to these as 'the first signs of an imminent revolution'. The reports in question added that Mussolini 'creates disorder everywhere. He speaks without mincing his words and is accompanied wherever he goes by his followers: disabled ex-servicemen, soldiers from every corps, officers and shock troops' who 'use daggers to threaten anyone they deem to be internal enemies of the nation. With this pretext of high patriotism they perpetrate acts of violence of every sort in Milan... chanting "We control the streets, Italy is ours and we'll do whatever we like with it." '[14]

The first public manifestation of fascist violence was on 15 April 1919 in Milan, when armed fascists attacked and destroyed the offices of *Avanti!*, the official daily newspaper of the Socialist Party. Mussolini's *Fasci di combattimento* defined fascism as war against adversaries using the methods of paramilitary violence that the fascists (for the most part ex-servicemen) had inherited directly from their experience of combat during the Great War.[15]

A paramilitary organization set up specifically for the practice of political violence was present in fascism from the very outset. A police report stated that it had existed in the *Fasci di combattimento* in Milan since 1919, and that it had been established 'not only to fight against the laws of the state, and not only with the

[12] Filippo Turati-Anna Kuliscioff, *Carteggio*, (ed. by F. Pedone), vol. V (Turin, 1977), 469–70.
[13] See Alberto Aquarone, 'Violenza e consenso nel fascismo italianao', *Storia contemporanea*, February 1979, 145–55; Adrian Lyttelton, 'Fascismo e violenza: conflitto sociale e azione politica in Italia nel primo dopoguerra'; Jens Petersen, 'Il problema della violenza nel fascismo italiano'; and Paolo Nello, 'La rivoluzione fascista ovvero dello squadrismo nazionalrivoluzionario', *Storia contemporanea*, December 1982.
[14] Archivio Centrale dello Stato, Ministero del'Interiore, Direzione generale di Pubblica sicurezza, Affari generali e riservati, categoria C2, 'Movimento sovversivo. Milano', cit. in Gentile, *Storia del partito fascista*, 20.
[15] *Cf.* Michael Ledeen, 'Italy. War as a Style of Life', in: Stephen Ward (ed.), *The War Generation. Veterans of the First World War* (Port Washington (NY) and London, 1975), 104–34.

intention of usurping police powers, but with the deliberate purpose of committing crimes against persons, against police officers and against the peace, all for political and electoral ends and in pursuance of a premeditated plan'. The report went on to say that there was 'a down and out military hierarchy of armed officers and privates, many of whom wear uniforms. They are divided up into squads, each of which is under a single commander'. In some cases 'they were paid and received precise instructions regarding the methods with which they were to achieve the tasks assigned to them'. These early squads were armed with pistols, daggers and hand bombs and were paid 25 lire a day to protect fascist premises. The police report continued by noting that 'The intention of the armed units—independent of any secondary incidents that spill over into even more serious crimes—is precisely that of achieving their predetermined, fixed and very often publicly announced goals, which are to be achieved using any methods deemed suitable, including illegal ones, and by resorting to the use of arms in a manner that is out of all proportion to the provocation to which they react. All of this has the deliberate goal of inflicting personal injury and committing murder to overcome any obstacles to their desired ends. It takes the form of excessive reactions and violence even as a response to a simple verbal insult on the part of socialists'.[16]

On 16 October 1920, hence on the eve of the offensive of the fascist squads against the working class, the official fascist daily openly pronounced its declaration of civil war against socialism: 'If civil war is unavoidable, then let it be!' It incited fascists to gear up for 'an ever more resolute armed struggle to the death' and to be ready for 'increasingly violent combat, with no scruples and no limits'. Between November and December 1920, the killing of several fascists by socialists provided the catalyst for the fascist onslaught. From that moment on, paramilitary violence was adopted by fascist squads in a systematic campaign of destruction against the political organizations and trade unions of the working class.[17] A police report of June 1921 gave a useful description of the ensuing fascist paramilitary violence:

Incursions are made on lorries by armed fascists to destroy workers clubs, leagues and cooperatives, to kidnap and intimidate people and commit acts of violence, above all against opponent leaders. Their only intention is to punish the socialist, communist or catholic perpetrators of real or presumed insults or unjust acts... The worst thing is that this same tactic is then adopted against the cooperatives which were founded for the most part by socialists and which have had a positive impact on the national economy.[18]

---

[16] Archivio Centrale dello Stato, Ministero del'Interiore, Direzione generale di Pubblica sicurezza, Affari generali e riservati, categoria E1, 'Elezioni politiche. Milano' report of the Milan police commissioner, 21 November 1919, cit. in Gentile, *Storia del partito fascista*, 477.

[17] See Gentile, *Storia del partito fascista*, 149–62. On the organization, methods and culture of squadrism, see Gentile, *Storia del partito fascista*, ch. 7; Roberta Suzzi Valli, 'The Myth of Squadrismo in the Fascist Regime', *Journal of Contemporary History*, April 2000, 131–50; Sven Reichardt, *Faschistische Kampfbünde. Gewalt und Gemeinschaft im Italienischen Squadrismus und in der deutschen SA* (Cologne, 2002); M. Franzinelli, *Squadristi. Protagonisti e tecniche della violenza squadrista 1919–1922* (Milan, 2003). On the rites and symbols of squadrism, see Emilio Gentile, *The Sacralization of Politics in Fascist Italy* (Cambridge MA, 1996), ch. 1.

[18] Ibid., 152–3.

Table 1: Fascist Party membership, December 1920-May 1921.

Month (end of)	Sections	Members
December 1920	88	20,165
March 1921	317	80,476
April 1921	471	98,298
May 1921	1,001	187,588

If, in the six months between the end of 1920 and the beginning of 1921, the fascists, having effectively reduced the opposition parties to a state of impotence, emerged as the strongest party in Italy, this was due mainly to the use of paramilitary violence. Table 1 (Fascist Party membership, Dec 1920–May 1921) illustrates the rapid expansion of fascism in this period, with an increase in membership that was nearly ten-fold.

Table 2 demonstrates that at the end of the period (May 1921), over half the fascist membership was in northern Italy and nearly 30 per cent was in the south, whereas merely 15 per cent of the movement's activists were from central Italy. In the meantime, 38 fascist candidates had been elected to the Chamber of Deputies (though four were not approved as they were under the minimum age limit of 30 years).[19]

As for the social composition of fascism, at the end of 1921, the middle and lower middle classes predominated amongst the leaders of the *squadristi*. Of 127 national and provincial leaders, 77 per cent belonged to the middle classes, 4 per cent to the bourgeoisie and only one was a worker. The best-represented professions were lawyers (35 per cent), journalists (22 per cent), teachers (6 per cent), employees (5 per cent), engineers (4.7 per cent), officials (4.7 per cent), insurance agents (3 per cent) and landlords (3 per cent), with 16.6 per cent in other categories. Of 192 leaders of local *fasci* (fascist groups which were more broadly-based than the paramilitary squads), fully 80 per cent belonged to the middle and lower middle classes, with 10.5 per cent from the bourgoisie and 5 per cent from the proletariat.[20] Students played a disproportionately important part in the squads; whereas they made up 13 per cent of party members in 1921, they constituted a

Table 2: Regional distribution of Fascist Party membership, May 1921.

Region	Membership	Percentage
North	114,487	56%
Centre	28,704	15%
South	44,397	29%
Total	187,588	100%

[19] Ibid., 205–6.   [20] Ibid., 364–6, 556–8.

much higher percentage of the squadristi, reaching 42.7 per cent in the case of Bologna.[21]

It should be noted that fascists rationalized their paramilitary violence as a response to socialist aggression. In reality, however, even if socialist supremacy was in many respects high-handed, spilling over into episodes of violence against people and property, the Socialist Party did not resort to systematic paramilitary violence in order to eliminate its political adversaries. As a Republican review observed, there was no comparison between socialist and fascist violence because 'burning down of buildings, devastating local centres, destroying documents and personal membership cards, and gunning down a citizen simply as an act of reprisal were all a quintessentially fascist method. And this method, which the socialists had not yet taken up—it is a truth that has to be admitted—has now been adopted as a general method of political struggle, completely disregarding the consequences for parties, men and ideas.'[22]

Figures for political violence issued by the Ministry of the Interior in 1920 and 1921 showed that the main victims of political violence were in fact socialists and militants of non-fascist parties. In 1920, 172 socialists were killed, as were 10 members of the Catholic Popular Party, 4 fascists, 51 innocent bystanders and 51 law enforcement officers; 578 socialists were wounded, as were 99 *popolari*, 57 fascists, 305 bystanders and 437 law enforcement officers.[23] Between 1 January and 7 April 1921, socialist deaths totalled 41, while the number of fascists killed was 25; 41 bystanders and 20 law enforcement officers also lost their lives, while 123 socialists, 108 fascists, 107 bystanders and 50 law enforcement officers were injured. Between 16 and 31 May that same year, 31 socialists, 16 fascists, 20 bystanders and 4 law enforcement officers were killed, whereas 78 socialists, 63 fascists, 56 bystanders and 19 law enforcement agents were injured. The greatest number of victims was registered during the elections of 1921: on election day alone (15 May), there were 28 deaths, of which 10 were fascists, 7 socialists, and 11 bystanders and law enforcement officers; that same day, 104 people were injured, of whom 37 were fascists, 38 bystanders, 26 socialists and 3 law enforcement officers. The following day, 10 socialists were killed, as were 2 fascists, 2 innocent bystanders and 1 law enforcement officer, whereas 34 socialists, 14 fascists, 16 bystanders and 4 law enforcement officers were wounded.[24]

When the fascist movement became a party in 1921, it was the strongest in Italy and ruled without opposition in many regions of the north and centre of the peninsula, having destroyed most of the opposition's organizations. In the period during which they imposed their authoritarian control over political, economic and social life, fascists accounted for most of the political violence that took place in Italian society. In July 1921, anti-fascists tried to react to fascist violence by setting up their own paramilitary organization. Groups known as the *Arditi del popolo* were formed

[21] See Suzzi Valli, *The Myth*, 35.
[22] 'La natura del fascismo', *La critica politica*, 16 November 1921.
[23] Statistics according to Gentile, *Storia del partito fascista*, 472–5.
[24] See ibid., cit., 202.

in Milan, Rome and other cities. These were composed of anarchists, republicans, socialists and communists joining together to defend workers' organizations from violent fascist assaults. However, the subsequent withdrawal of socialists and communists from the movement meant that the *Arditi del popolo* could not develop into a paramilitary organization capable of countering fascist violence.[25]

It is important to note that, after 1921, fascist paramilitary violence no longer had any type of pretext, not even as a reaction against the threat of a Bolshevik revolution in Italy. Assuming that such a threat ever really existed, by that time it had vanished, for a number of reasons. First among these was the violent reaction of fascism itself, which had reduced its adversaries to impotence. Secondly, the workers' movement was weakened even further by its own internal conflicts that led to the founding of the Communist Party and to further splits in the Socialist Party. But the most important factor to make any threat of a socialist revolution unthinkable in Italy was the failure of the Russian Bolsheviks to export the revolution to Europe. Mussolini himself declared in 1921 that to speak of a Bolshevik threat in Italy was absurd. Indeed, in the spring of 1922 it was none other than Italy that played host to an international conference in Genoa in which the Bolshevik government participated. The meeting concluded with the signing of a treaty between Germany and Russia that put an end to the diplomatic isolation of the first communist state in history.

In this situation, any fascist pretext to rationalize its violence and paramilitary organization as a response to the threat of a Bolshevik revolution was so much hot air. After 1921, even the bourgeoisie, which up to that point in time had supported fascism and fascist violence, began to request an end to the actions of the paramilitary squads and the dismantling of the fascist paramilitary organization. In reality, however, none of these requests were realistic and in fact only served as a further pretext for the fascists to bolster the paramilitary organization and unleash a new wave of violence, this time against the parties of the bourgeoisie itself.

This occurred most clearly during the grave internal crisis that fascism underwent in the summer of 1921, when the leaders of *squadrismo* engineered the failure of Mussolini's attempt to realize a peace agreement with the Socialist Party and to transform the fascist movement into a kind of labour party for the lower middle classes. Mussolini held that it was possible to dissociate the local fascist bosses from the party activists, to distinguish between the 'warriors' and the 'politicals', and so to dismantle or at least to reorder the paramilitary organization by subordinating the activities of the 'warriors' to the authority of the 'politicals'.[26] In reality, a large proportion of the main political leaders were also 'warriors'. The most important provincial fascist bosses, Roberto Farinacci, Dino Grandi, Italo Balbo, Renato Ricci, Dino Perrone Compagni, were all 'warriors' and they refused to disarm fascism so as to transform it into a parliamentary party as Mussolini wished.

[25] Eros Francescangeli, *Arditi del popolo. Argo Secondari e la prima organizzazione antifascista (1917–1922)* (Rome, 2000).
[26] The distinction between 'warriors' and 'politicals' is not an expression of Mussolini but one that the author introduced into the analysis of fascism. See Gentile, *Storia del partito fascista*, 215 *et seq.*

The mass of the *squadristi* rebelled against Mussolini calling him a traitor, and in the end they forced him to accept the identification of the new national Fascist Party, founded in November 1921, with its own paramilitary organization. This was the price of his continued recognition as the *duce* of fascism. Mussolini's attempt to dissociate 'politicals' from 'warriors' and to consider violence a purely transitory phase of fascism was definitively buried by the formal link between the political and armed organizations that was institutionalized in the statutes of the National Fascist Party.[27]

In the end, the *squadristi* forced Mussolini to accept that the identity of the new Fascist National Party should be conflated with that of its paramilitary organization and that Mussolini himself should be recognized as undisputed *duce*. In the programme, it was stated quite clearly that 'the Fascist National Party forms an inseparable whole with the squads, the voluntary militia at the service of the nation and the state and the living force in which fascist Italy is embodied and with which it defends itself'.[28]

Thus was born what I have defined as the 'Militia Party', the first mass party in contemporary European history to institutionalize the militarization of politics in its own organization, modes of action, style of behaviour and in the way it waged the struggle against its political adversaries, who were treated as 'the enemy within' to be annihilated.[29] It should be stressed that I have adopted this definition not because the Fascist Party had a paramilitary apparatus but because the party as a whole identified itself with the paramilitary organization and considered violence, that is to say the use for terrorist purposes of the paramilitary organization, as a founding element of its means of action in relation to its enemies. The definitive militarization of the politics of the Fascist Party was confirmed in the regulations for the Fascist Militia published by *Il Popolo d'Italia* on 8 October 1922, which stated that the Fascist Party 'is still a militia' and that 'all party members must abide by the Fascist Militia's special laws of honour and military discipline, which are firmly founded on the [authority of] the hierarchy.'[30]

The praxis of violence expressed through its own paramilitary organization was certainly not the sole origin of fascism as a mass movement, but it was the element around which fascism defined its identity of origin and elaborated its political culture.

All the founders of fascism came from a background of violence that had germin-ated even before the Great War in the ambit of socialism, revolutionary syndical-ism, radical nationalism and the futurist avant-garde. By the end of 1918, these had fused into a political party that subsequently took part in the founding of fas-cism. The myth of violence theorized by Georges Sorel as a catalyst for regener-ation was the point of departure for a variety of groups that in 1914–15 merged in revolutionary nationalist interventionism, the immediate precursor of fascism. The experience of interventionism and war added new myths to the nationalist culture of violence. Primary among these was the exaltation of combatants as the militant avant-garde of the new Italians, men whose task it was to unseat the old political

[27] Ibid., 397 *et seq.*   [28] Ibid., 392.   [29] Ibid., ch. 7.   [30] Quoted in ibid., 537.

rulers of liberal and bourgeois Italy and, in so doing, to regenerate the nation and make it greater and more powerful. Fascism, as Mussolini openly declared, was born of action and went forward on the basis of myths and ideals adopted as dogmas of one's politics, which in turn was conceived as combat against the nation's 'internal enemies'. In an article of 20 November 1920, the official newspaper of the fascist movement theorised the primacy of violence in the following manner:

> The fist is the synthesis of theory...It represents the impossibility of achieving one's aims with mere words. Thus the fascist smashes the socialist's head in and thereby inserts his ideas into the latter's skull. It's a guaranteed time-saving device, with all the virtues of a finely tuned and penetrating synthesis [that] acts directly on the opponent's body both rapidly and definitively...And what could be more of a synthesis than the shot of a pistol? It gets to its destination with an initial speed of 300 metres per second and finishes the job immediately and professionally...Its efficiency lies in the fact that, with maximum economy and speed, it prevents debates from ever opening up again...And then there's the synthesis of all syntheses and hence the favourite of fascists: the bomb. The fascist loves this weapon, which is more powerful than some unknown divinity or some woman one knows only too well. The bomb is adorably divine, and the fascist divinely adores it.[31]

Paramilitary violence permeated every element of fascism. Out of the original nucleus of the culture of violence there arose the entire apparatus of myths, rituals and symbols that fascism invented during the period of its armed reaction against the organizations of the working class. The destruction of workers' organizations was represented as a crusade for liberation, purification and regeneration of the areas and populations influenced by the Socialist Party. These were re-baptized into the cult of the nation by means of fascist rituals. The nation, sacralized as the secular divinity of fascism, had its foundation in violence because this served to legitimate the fascist monopoly over patriotism and hence the persecution of anyone, including non socialists, who did not yield to fascist rule. Such people would be assaulted, humiliated or banished from their own homes. In this way, the sacralization of the nation became the sacralization of fascism, represented as a lay religion.

This in turn served to bestow on the paramilitary organization the halo of a 'holy militia', as the press of the *squadristi* defined it, whose every violent act was permissible. The cult of the fascist fallen, now consecrated as martyrs, drew its origin from the culture of violence celebrated as a noble and heroic virtue of national regeneration paid for with one's life. Moreover, for the fascist squads, paramilitary violence constituted the very basis of their union: complicity in criminal actions fuelled by nationalist fanaticism contributed towards cementing their comradeship, inciting them to terrorist action as a periodical ritual to reinforce their communion. Finally, the violence exhibited by the fascists in their rituals and symbols played an important propagandistic role, inasmuch as it attracted young people to fascism, especially those who were too young to have taken part in the Great War.

---

[31] Luigi Freddi, 'Sintesi', *Il Fascio*, 20 November 1920.

The fascists explicitly professed Sorel's understanding of the role of the myth. 'We have created our own myth,' Mussolini claimed on 3 October 1922. 'This myth is a question of faith, or passion. It does not have to be a reality. It is real by virtue of the fact that it is a spur to action, a matter of hope, faith and courage. Our myth is the nation and the greatness of the nation. Everything else comes second to this myth, this greatness, which we want to transform into complete reality.'[32] With ideology thus condensed into myth, belonging to fascism was identified as an act of faith. The acceptance of fascist myths was a matter of obedience to dogma and political activism became a total dedication to the cause with exalted feelings that fascism guided and stimulated through the powerful fascination exercised by collective symbols and rites. Around the original nucleus of the culture of violence and the myth of the nation, the fascists forged an apparatus of rites and symbols during the period of armed aggression against the organized proletariat. 'A few simple teachings are worth more than wordy dissertations,' explained the official review *Gerarchia* (Hierarchy). 'And choreographed displays, ceremonials and rites are more effective than any teaching in exalting feelings. Pennants waving in the wind, black shirts, helmets, anthems, the *alalà* (fascist war cry), the *fasci* (bundles of bound sticks, symbol of fascism), the Roman salute, the invocation of the dead, popular festivals (*sagre*), solemn oaths, military parades with the goose-step (*passo militare)*, and the entire collection of rituals that shake the "superior" men of the old bourgoisie to the roots also demonstrate how the original instincts of the race are undergoing a powerful resurrection.'[33]

This largely spontaneous elaboration of a fascist liturgy incorporated the older ritual traditions and symbolism of Mazzinian Republicans and the legionaries of D'Annunzio. But the fascists considered it to be the expression of a renaissance of the founding qualities of the Italian race—a renewal that was expressed by the use of violence.

From 1921 onwards the Fascist Militia Party undermined the state's monopoly on force. The effects of this became tragically evident when, in 1922, fascism began to invade entire cities to remove prefects whom they considered antifascist simply because they had chosen to obey the law. Furthermore, in order to enforce the nationalization of ethnic minority populations, and to persecute anti-fascist parliamentarians with violent assaults and banishment from their cities, fascists also occupied the border regions that had just been annexed to Italy.

In 1922, fascist violence was also turned against the Catholics of the Popolari and the clergy. The priest and founder of the Popolari Party, Luigi Sturzo, protested to the prime minister many times about the continued fascist use of violence. He denounced the passivity of the forces of public order and the magistrates: 'In both towns and the countryside,' he wrote on 24 February 1922, 'the Popolari are repeatedly subjected to bribery, intimidation, reprisals, and violence on the part of the fascists with a ferocity that sometimes assumes exceptional proportions. All this

---

[32] B. Mussolini, *Opera Omnia* (ed. by E. and D. Susmel), 35 vol., Florence, 1951–63, vol. XVIIII, 457.
[33] G. Lumbroso, 'La genesi e i fini del fascismo', *Gerarchia*, October 1922.

takes place freely and without any restraint because the authorities charged with maintaining public order, the forces of the Regi Carabinieri [Royal Carabinieri—CB] for the most part limit their activity and display a calm indifference in the face these very serious actions when they ought to be anticipating and preventing them and imposing sanctions when they occur. I am told that the bulk of the proceedings initiated against the fascists are still on hold in preparatory hearings and in the law courts in the expectation that there will be some amnesty.'[34]

Fascist violence was facilitated by the acquiescence of many local authorities and by the weakness of central government. Between 1919 and 1922, a succession of five governments propped up by unsteady majorities exacerbated the crisis of the parliamentary regime, lent credit to fascist anti-democratic propaganda and confirmed the inability of the state to prevent, block or repress fascist violence. In order to carry out acts of violence in any given area, fascists adopted tactics consisting of rapid incursions of squads who had arrived from other provinces, in this way making it impossible, or at least very difficult, to identify those responsible for the aggression. Only in rare cases did the police or *carabinieri* manage to repress fascist violence, and in such instances the fascists invariably gave way. But in 1922, the situation had reached a point at which the state no longer had the political will or the ability to impose its authority on fascism. When the government threatened to dissolve the fascist squads, the fascist leaders retorted that *squadrismo* identified itself with the Fascist Party and tauntingly dared the state to ban an organization that had over 300,000 members and was already controlling many cities and provinces by violent means. Further confirmation of the government's powerlessness came at the beginning of August 1922, when the fascist squads forcefully put an end to a strike that had been called by anti-fascist parties to protest against fascist violence.

Having taken due note of the impotence of the state, the disintegration of the opposition parties, the resignation of the working class, the apathy of the majority of the population after the tragic experience of four years of war and another four of political violence, the Fascist Party decided that the time was ripe to make a bid for power. The party leadership declared publicly that it intended to conquer power and smash the liberal state: 'The century of democracy is over,' proclaimed Mussolini on the eve of the 'march on Rome' in October 1922. Anticipating the policies of the future fascist state, Mussolini added that fascism would deny all liberties to its adversaries: 'The Italians can be divided into three categories: the "indifferent", who will stay at home and wait; the "sympathisers", who can freely circulate; and, finally, the "enemies", who won't be allowed to circulate'.

The democratic newspaper *La Stampa*, owned by the industrialist Giovanni Agnelli, founder of FIAT, could forecast as much in July 1922:

Fascism is a movement that tends to adopt any means at its disposal to take over the state and society and to set up an absolute single party dictatorship. The essential means adopted are the programme, the resolve of the leaders and members, and the complete suppression of all constitutional public and private freedoms, which is to say

[34] See Gentile, *Storia del partito fascista*, 580–1.

the destruction of the Statute and the gains made by the liberals since the Italian Risorgimento.[35]

In 1922, very few people understood the danger of institutionalized paramilitary violence for the future of the parliamentary regime. The liberal bourgeoisie believed in the possibility of domesticating fascism by involving it in government, while the majority of anti-fascist parties were of the view that fascism was an ephemeral movement destined to fizzle out once it had fulfilled its function as the armed guard of the bourgeois state. These illusions prevailed even after the 'march on Rome' and facilitated the Fascist Party's destruction of the parliamentary regime.[36]

Fascism took power by menacing an armed insurrection against the state, a threat that forced the king to invite a young 39-year-old, who had no previous experience, to form a government. Mussolini had in fact been elected to the chamber of deputies only a year before and could count on the backing of just 30 fascist MPs. For the first time in the history of European parliamentary regimes, the government of a liberal state had, therefore, been handed over to the head of a militia party that had imposed its authority by means of paramilitary violence. There is no doubt that the military might of the state could easily have defeated the paramilitary force of fascism and nipped the fascist revolution in the bud. But neither the king nor the government had the political will or the moral courage to impart an order that might have saved the parliamentary regime. Rather, they feared that repression of the fascist onslaught would breathe new life into the socialist revolution and they nurtured the illusion that the responsibilities of government would suffice to convince fascists to renounce their violent paramilitary organization and buttress the foundations of the liberal state.

Once head of government, Mussolini did not consider ending fascist paramilitary violence but rather legalized it as an instrument of his personal power and removed it from under the control of local squadrist chiefs, known as the *ras*. But the MVSN did not prevent the *ras* from practising paramilitary violence to consolidate their local power bases. Mussolini may have promised normalization, pacification and the restoration of law and order in words, but in deeds he and others continued to use the paramilitary violence of the Militia, alongside the repressive forces of the state, to reduce opponents to even further impotence and extend the power of fascism throughout the entire country.

The armed force of the squads and paramilitary violence continued to guarantee the predominance of the Fascist Party in the country. In April 1923, in a public speech in Turin, Cesare Maria de Vecchi, who was the leader of Piedmontese fascism, one of the 'quadumvirate' of the March on Rome and a member of the government, declared that the fascist revolution was proceeding inexorably, 'with

[35] 'Il governo e la destra', *La Stampa*, 18 July 1922.

[36] On the March on Rome, still fundamental although some of its judgments are debatable, see Antonio Repaci, *La Marcia su Roma* (revd edn. with previously unpublished documents, Milan, 1972); Renzo De Felice, *Mussolini il fascista. La conquista del potere 1921–1925* (Turin, 1966), 282 *et seq.*; Gentile, *Storia del partito fascista*, ch. 8. The most recent study, with useful documentation though perhaps an excessive claim to original interpretations, is Giulia Albanese, *La marcia su Roma* (Roma-Bari, 2006).

or without the consensus [of all] but most certainly with the force of these 300,000 black shirts who are now incorporated into the MVSN....Today they carry car-bines and bayonets but in the future they will have canon and flame-throwers for the purpose of internal policing and in order to warn those outside Italy that they must respect us...If necessary, and I think it certainly will be in order to install the new order fully and to attain the supreme goal..., we shall know how to create a state of siege for half an hour and to open fire for a minute. I think that should do it.'[37] In December 1922, de Vecchi had sent a message of congratulation to the Turin *squadristi* who had assassinated 23 workers in response to the wounding of two fascists.

In his speeches Mussolini condemned illegal fascist activities and promised 'nor-malization', pacification and the restoration of the rule of law. On the basis of these promises he won the confidence of parliament and full powers to restore order and put the national finances on a sound footing. Moreover, his government had the support of the monarchy, the leading figures in the economy and the Church, and conservative public opinion both inside Italy and abroad. The constitutional par-ties proclaimed their faith in the new prime minister. Mussolini's enemies were powerless and internally divided. The working class felt abandoned and resigned to its fate; the bourgeoisie was reassured and satisfied; the lower middle classes approved the change in politics. A new electoral law was voted in 1923 with the support of conservatives and liberals, and it gave Mussolini a parliamentary major-ity such as no Italian prime minister had known before. Economic conditions were already improving before the March on Rome. Yet nothing seemed to stand in the way of the restoration of a parliamentary regime, as was happening in other coun-tries in Europe after the convulsion of the early postwar years.

Nothing stood in its way that is except the Fascist Party and the decision of its leader to consider his own arrival at the head of the government a definitive and irreversible fact. In one of the first meetings of the council of ministers, on 15 December 1922, Mussolini referred to the 'absolutely irrevocable nature of the change of regime in October.'[38] Four days later, he issued a warning to the effect that 'the fascist state is strong and committed to defending itself at all costs with cold, inexhaustible energy'.[39] On 10 February 1923, he declared to the Chamber of Deputies that: 'We shall last at least thirty years.'[40] On 8 June 1923, he admon-ished the Senate that 'there is a powerful army of volunteers ready to defend the nation and to defend this special form of political regime that is called fascism.'[41]

On taking over government of the parliamentary regime, fascism did not dis-mantle the paramilitary organization but transformed it into an institution of the state, the MVSN, under the command of Mussolini.[42] The new organ of the PNF,

[37] Quoted in *Il Mondo*, 26 April 1923.   [38] Mussolini, *Opera Omnia*, vol. XIX, 66.
[39] Ibid., 73.
[40] *Atti Parlamentari, Camera dei Deputati, XXVI Legislatura, 1a Sessione, 2a Tornata, 10 February 1923*, p. 8576.
[41] Mussolini, *Opera Omnia*, XIX, 256.
[42] There exists no full scientific study of the MVSN. For a general overview, albeit inadequate, especially as far as its historical analysis is concerned, see Albert Aquarone 'La Milizia volontaria per la

the fascist Grand Council, which Mussolini had created shortly after the March on Rome, took this decision at its first meeting, held on 12 January 1923. It declared that the action squads of the PNF were free to enter the MVSN and that they should preserve its 'essentially fascist [nature], which was to protect the inevitable and inexorable development of the October revolution, conserving its symbols, insignia and the names that consecrated its victorious battles and the blood that had been spilled for the cause.'[43] The function of a 'force for the purpose of the goals of the fascist revolution' was endorsed at the meeting of the Grand Council on 13 February, thereby confirming the paramilitary nature and aims of a body that considered itself beyond the existing constitutional order.[44] The association of fascism with the paramilitary dimension became obligatory the following April when the Grand Council ordained that all members of the Fascist Party were by that fact also members of the Militia, and in the following session the Council prescribed 'a rapid and diligent choice of the black shirt cadres'.[45]

Italo Balbo, a 'representative hero' of the party militia, was nominated the first commander in chief. He was 27 years old, a former officer in one of the elite alpine regiments during the Great War, when he had been much decorated, and an anti-clerical Republican who had become the leader of fascism in Ferrara. He was one of the most efficient organizers of *squadrismo* and was also one of the principal architects of the liturgy of fascism.[46]

After the institution of the MVSN, the most difficult problem that arose in the reorganization of fascist paramilitary forces, aside from the lack of discipline of the *squadristi*, the difficulty of selecting officers and the lukewarm attitude of the army, was the shortfall in arms. In 1923, the Militia numbered about 190,000 men but in August that year they possessed only 142,026 rifles and 151 machine guns.[47] Another very serious problem was the new conflict between 'warriors' and 'politicals' that resulted from the combination of the roles of political leader and *squadrista* in the same person. In a report made on the 15 June 1923 to Italo Balbo as commander of the MVSN, the deputy chief of the General Staff, Commandante Vittorio Verné, complained that: 'Another thing that really slows up the organization [of the armed forces] is political influence in military matters. Uniting military and political responsibilities in the same person is a real handicap; by doing too many things, everything is done badly.' Moreover, the rivalry between leaders led to 'a self-organization by clienteles in the militia around too many [leaders] who want to turn their position into a political platform or a

---

sicurezza nazionale', in: Alberto Aquarone and Maurizio Vernassa (eds.), *Il Regime fascista* (Bologna, 1974), 84–111; Eliza Valleri, 'Dal Partito armato al regime totalitario: la Milizia', *Italia contemporanea*, October–December 1980, 31–60.

[43] *Il Regime Fascista dopo la Marcia su Roma. Raccolta delle deliberazioni del Grand Consiglio con una premessa di Benito Mussolini* (provisional edn., Rome, 1924), 18.

[44] Ibid., 19.

[45] Ibid.

[46] See Sergio Panunzio, *Italo Balbo* (Milan, 1923), 34 et seq.; Giordano Bruno Guerri, *Italo Balbo* (Milan, 1984) 34 et seq; Giorgio Rochat, *Italo Balbo* (Turin, 1986); Claudio G. Segrè, *Italo Balbo. Aviazione e potere areo* (Rome, 1998), 13–48.

[47] Ibid., 145.

means of reaping private and personal gains.'[48] Consequently, Verné made a series
of proposals:

A. To remove the Militia as far as possible from political interference by establishing a
clear distinction between political and military responsibilities and stating the incom-
patibility between them, and by spelling out the relationship between the Militia and
the party.
B. To purge ruthlessly the officer cadres so that the commanders have full confidence in those who [remain and] are worthy and capable of such trust.
C. To maintain firm and iron discipline at all costs.
Acting in this manner, the Militia will really be the serious thing that the prime
minister [Mussolini] says it is, and it will serve not only to defend the regime and the
fascist revolution domestically and abroad but will also be able to take on other highly
important goals. It will prove the best school of the nation and maintain the offensive
spirit of the race.

Notwithstanding the difficulties of reorganization and the quarrels between 'soldier' and 'political' leaders—which did not however alter the equation of the 'warrior' and the 'political' in the person of the *ras* (the leaders of fascism in the
provinces)—paramilitary organization remained the principal means by which the
Fascist Party consolidated and extended its hold over the whole country. In fact, in
its July session in 1923, the Grand Council declared that fascism would keep its
'armed forces' until 'the state has become entirely fascist,' with the complete replacement of the ruling class, and 'until any faint revolt by anti-national elements is
irreversibly over'. The Militia would then become 'a great political police force'.[49]
    In the months that followed, the dualism of the Fascist Party and the nation-
state (which prompted the antifascists to coin the term 'totalitarian' in 1923)
spread to all state institutions, political and military, at the centre and on the
periphery of the country. It also became evident in the Militia. At the end of 1923,
Commandant Verné once more pointed out the dilemma that this posed in a
report on the 'State of mind and morale of the Militia regarding its functions, its
future and its relationships with the country and with the other armed organizations of the state.'

This is the dilemma.
    Today, the Militia, if it wishes to be solely the Militia of the Party, is too militarized;
it has lost all flexibility, has grown heavy and has deteriorated.
    If it wishes to be a National Militia with a military purpose, it is still too much the
militia of the party and has only a very limited military and combat capability.
    This equivocation must be ended and the future path [of its development] deci-
sively set out.

The solution that Verné proposed foreshadowed in late 1923 much of what the
MVSN would actually become after 1926 once the totalitarian regime with a single party had been installed, though his final point was to prove the exception.

---

[48] Balbo Archive, Rome. I would like to thank Mr Paolo Balbo for his generosity in letting me
consult his archive.
[49] Ibid.

[The Militia should have] clear, precise and unequivocal tasks, namely:

A. The defence of the fascist regime.

B. Pre-military instruction and the preparation of the young for the army.

C. Keeping the citizenry prepared for war, notably by means of post-military instruction.

D. [The Militia] should return to the army or navy in case of mobilization.

Verné pointed out that in its first year of existence, the Militia had fulfilled only the first of these functions. The points that he had made in relation to this role during the first year of fascist government were a realistic evaluation of the obstacles that still stood in the way of the fulfilment of the fascist revolution, but they also confirmed that for both the Party and the Militia the rise to power of fascism was an irreversible event. They were a regime, not just a government, and they had to consolidate their hold on power by politically eliminating all their opponents. According to Verné:

> Although the fascist regime has never been seriously threatened, it remains the case that the presence of this strongly motivated armed force [the Militia] has inspired a wise prudence in opponents of every stripe.
>
> This first task entrusted to the Militia proved to be of central importance in the period immediately following the revolution. It will gradually be extended as the regime consolidates and enlarges its base amongst the masses of the nation. Although the fascist revolution has not reached all its goals as quickly as was hoped, because it has no new ruling class with which to replace the old one, nonetheless there will come a moment, and we hope it will be soon, when the terminal weakness of the internal enemies [of the regime] will mean that we no longer need a special Militia but only an ordinary police force.[50]

The institutionalization of the paramilitary force of a political party was an entirely new development in the history of parliamentary democracies. The socialist deputy Giacomo Matteotti wrote that: 'Italy is the only civil country in which a party militia is armed and financed by the state against another part of the citizenry.'[51]

However, remarkably few anti-fascist politicians understood that a parliamentary regime could not survive rule by a party-militia that subjected the country to the arbitrary violence of its own soldiers, had the backing of the forces of order, and persecuted opponents as if they were to be eliminated as internal enemies of the nation.

In April 1923, the anti-fascist liberal Giovanni Amendola coined the term 'totalitarian' to define the methods adopted by the Fascist Party to destroy the opposition and impose its power on the state. Fascism, wrote Amendola, 'has not so much aimed at governing Italy as monopolizing control over the minds of all Italians. Power is not enough for it...It wants the conversion of the Italians...Fascism has the pretence of a religion...and the supreme ambitions and inhumane intransigency of a religious crusade.'[52] In the same month, Luigi Salvatorelli, a democratic anti-fascist, observed that fascism intended to implement 'the total

---

[50] Ibid.   [51] G. Matteotti, *Scritti sul fascismo* (ed. by S. Caretti) (Pisa, 1983), 122.

[52] In *Il Mondo*, 1 April 1923.

dictatorship of a single party, the suppression of all other parties, hence the end of political activity as it has been conceived in Europe for the past 100 years.'[53] Three days later, the communist, Palmiro Togliatti, commented ironically on

> the obstinacy with which liberals, democrats and the Popolari continue to hope that fascism may be contained by the constitution. Right up to the present moment they continue to believe that the fascist dictatorship will be short-lived and that it will progressively enter into a state of legality. The constitution of the national Militia has been unable to shake these hopes.[54]

After a year of fascist government, Matteotti used clear documentary evidence to denounce the continued use of violence by the fascists in order to impose their domination on the state and society, both symbolically and in reality. Only the fascists, wrote Matteotti, 'can carry revolvers and other arms. Possession of a party card is a virtual requirement if one wants to remain in public employment without being harassed. Many state employees—teachers, magistrates, workers—have been dispensed with or dismissed solely because they did not meet with the approval of the Fascist Party.' Overall, Matteotti concluded, 'being fascist has become a second and more important form of Italian citizenship without which it is not possible to enjoy civil rights or the freedom to vote, to choose where to live, to circulate, to meet, to work, to speak or even to think.'[55]

Amendola, Salvatorelli, Togliatti and Matteotti were not prophets. But they were astute enough to understand before many others that a party founded on paramilitary violence and on the pretence of imposing its own ideology as a religion was killing the parliamentary regime, to say nothing of the freedom and dignity of those who did not submit to the fascist monopoly of politics. Matteotti himself was murdered in June 1924 on the orders of Mussolini's closest associates, if not of Mussolini himself. This was clearly no isolated incident but rather the consequence of the totalitarian method with which fascism had been governing Italy for the previous year.

Hence paramilitary violence constituted the 'rationale of fascism'. It was the embryo from which the totalitarian regime came into being over the following years. As we have seen, from the outset the notion of 'totalitarianism' encapsulated the terrorist methods used by the Fascist Party to conquer power. After 1924, the same methods were adopted by the state under the rule of a single party and a police regime. Together with the militarization of society, the cult of the *duce* and imperialist wars this produced a novel system of dictatorial rule. Many European anti-democratic nationalists were subsequently to embark on the trail that had been blazed between 1919 and 1923 by the paramilitary violence of Italian fascism.

---

[53] 'Secondo tempo', *La Stampa*, 25 April 1923.
[54] P. Togliatti, 'Sviluppi inesorabili,' *Il Lavoratore*, 28 April 1923.
[55] Matteotti, *Scritti sul fascismo*, 124–5.

PART II

NATIONS, BORDERLANDS AND ETHNIC VIOLENCE

7

Bands of Nation Builders?

Insurgency and Ideology in the Ukrainian Civil War

Serhy Yekelchyk

In Ukrainian history the experience of the First World War, significant and trau-
matic as it was, is usually overshadowed by the discussion of subsequent and somewhat contemporaneous events—in particular, the emergence of the Ukrainian
People's Republic. Carried away by their nation-building narratives, modern
Ukrainian historians tend to forget that this polity claimed full independence in
January 1918 precisely in order to be among the signatories of the Brest-Litovsk
peace treaty, which ended the war on the Eastern Front. The war's role in the shap-
ing of twentieth-century Ukraine becomes greater still if one includes the notions
of mass mobilization in the name of a nation, and ethnicity as a marker of
loyalty—both of which were introduced in this region during the First World War.
In this sense, it is misleading to frame the turbulent years 1917–20 as the 'Ukrainian Revolution,' as is common in the domestic and Western historiography of
Ukraine.[1] The Great War provided the participants in the myriad conflicts, large
and small, playing out in the Ukrainian territory with their arms, training, culture
of violence, and potent new vocabulary of nationalism. The war also led to the collapse of the Russian and Austro-Hungarian Empires, allowing, for the first time in
history, for a brief union of Eastern and Western Ukraine.

However, the chaotic events of 1917–20 are best understood not as the struggle
of the united Ukrainian people for independence but as a gamut of complex ideological conflicts and local violence unleashed by the collapse of the old dynastic
empires. At once a nationalistic movement and a socialist revolution, the Civil
War in Ukraine did not mean a clear-cut fight between socialists and nationalists—they were often the same people—but involved a confusing struggle between
Ukrainian patriots of different stripes, as well as among the many varieties of local
conservatives and socialists, who joined the forces of the Russian Red or White
armies, the Ukrainian republican or monarchist troops, or the bands led by local
warlords. If anything, the Ukrainian case helps problematize our notions of 'revolutionary', 'counter-revolutionary', and 'ethnic' violence by demonstrating a

---

[1] For an interesting attempt to go beyond the traditional historiographical models and chart out a
new research agenda, see Mark von Hagen, 'The Dilemmas of Ukrainian Independence and Statehood, 1917–1921', *The Harriman Institute Forum* 7 (1994), 7–11.

Fig. 10. Otaman Yukhym Bozhko (centre left) with his officers, and the writer Osyn Makovei (centre right) April 1919.

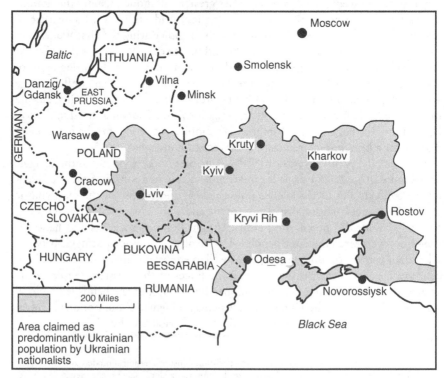

Map 2. Ukraine as imagined by Ukrainian nationalists.

common culture of violence shared by all sides and often perpetuated by the same soldiers conscripted over and over again into different armies marching through the land.

To be sure, the Ukrainian Civil War shared some basic characteristics with other instances of paramilitary violence developing in the wake of the Great War that are discussed in this volume. Former Russian Ukraine in particular was a classic 'shatter zone', where efficient state institutions were absent from the time the Russian monarchy fell in March 1917 until the decisive Bolshevik victory late in 1920. The collapse of civic order in the Ukrainian provinces was closely linked to the disintegration of the Russian army in the late summer and autumn of 1917, when retreating troops and masses of deserters brutalized the civilian population. As in other European countries, disillusioned veterans brought back both their arms and their frustrations, mostly over the scarcity of land but also over greater political issues of the day. As in other places, theirs was the political culture of defeat and a multilayered one to boot—the Russian army's perceived defeat in the Great War, unfulfilled promises of a democratic revolution, and the repeated failures of Ukrainian governments in the conflicts of 1918–20. Like elsewhere, the core group of the paramilitaries were young war veterans struggling with adjustment to civilian life.

However, the peculiarities of the Ukrainian case appear to be more important for its outcome than the characteristics it shared with the German case, for instance. Ukrainian paramilitaries were usually organized in peasant militia units or gangs operating in the countryside, neither having any clear political programme. The structures of contemporary peasant society translated into the prominence, among paramilitaries, of older men and the acceptance of women, even if most guerrilla leaders were former tsarist junior officers. The peasant-based nature of the Ukrainian paramilitary movement also meant the lack of a strong national framework because the members preferred operating in or near their home villages. They could be conscripted into any army passing through an area, but they usually joined as a unit and deserted together once the army moved away. This explains the wild fluctuation of numbers found in the sources—from over 600,000 soldiers of the Russian army declaring allegiance to the Ukrainian People's Republic to 8,000 being considered an effective fighting force and an army of 50,000—a strong army. Peasants could swell the ranks of any military force, but they were unlikely to stay.

Nor does the Ukrainian case—with the exception of the Ukrainian-Polish conflict in the former Austrian province of Galicia—fit easily in the cluster of 'ethnic' conflicts in Eastern and South-Eastern Europe. In most of Russian Ukraine, ethnicity remained fluid and nationalist organizations were weak. The peasants brought into the culture of the Civil War their traditional distrust of outsiders and willingness to loot the clearly identifiable 'other' (Jews and Mennonites, in particular), and their sentiments were refracted in a peculiar way through the prism of modern ideologies (Jews being allegedly pro-Bolshevik, and Mennonites wealthy exploiters). In the end, though, the Reds won the Civil War by placating the Ukrainian peasantry with promises regarding the issue that mattered most to them: land.

THE EASTERN FRONT DISINTEGRATES

The First World War did not just lead to the collapse of multinational empires, which offered Ukrainian patriots a chance to build their state. Rather, imperial belligerents themselves prepared the ground for the future European order by promoting ethnic solidarity as a means of destroying each other. Both the Russian and Austro-Hungarian Empires tried to undermine each other by flaunting the notion of an autonomous and united postwar Poland, but it did not occur to the imperial bureaucrats that the future Polish state would be independent and not part of their empires. The Ukrainian case was more complex. The tsarist government wanted to reclaim Austria's Ukrainian lands on the basis of ethnic criteria, but as 'Russian' ethnic territories, while the Central Powers wanted a puppet Ukrainian state carved out of the Russian Empire, but not including Austria's own Ukrainian lands. What both sides achieved in their conflicting efforts was, in Mark von Hagen's words, the 'militarization of the empires' nationality problem' in general and the Ukrainian problem in particular.[2] Ethnicity became a mobilization tool, and the notion that peasants on both sides of the Russo-Austrian border belonged to the same nationality—whether defined as Ukrainian or as a 'Little Russian tribe'—became common currency. These were the ideological foundations of modern Ukraine.

The Habsburgs went farther than the Romanovs by allowing, early in the war, the creation of an ethnic Ukrainian volunteer military unit, the 2,500-strong Ukrainian Sich Riflemen, but military fortune initially favoured the Russian side. By early September 1914 the Russian army captured the two main Ukrainian-populated territories of Austria-Hungary, Eastern Galicia and Bukovyna, and controlled much of the region until the summer of 1915. The tsarist authorities had no clear plan of how to incorporate these lands into the empire, but the Tsar's nationalistic governor, Count Georgii Bobrinsky, promptly shut down Ukrainian periodicals, cultural organizations and cooperatives, while also attempting to replace Ukrainian with Russian as the language of school instruction.[3] At the same time, Austria-Hungary sought to exploit the potential of Ukrainian nationalism against the Russian Empire when it allowed a group of socialist émigrés from Russian-ruled Ukraine, the Union for the Liberation of Ukraine, to propagate the idea of independent statehood among Russian POWs of Ukrainian ethnicity. With official support, the group set up a publishing venture in Vienna and dispatched its emissaries to a number of countries.

The war brought terrible destruction, human loss, and dislocation to Austrian Ukraine, particularly to Eastern Galicia and Bukovyna, where much of the fighting on the Eastern Front took place. On a more general scale, the colossal war effort

---

[2] Mark von Hagen, *War in a European Borderland: Occupations and Occupation Plans in Galicia and Ukraine, 1914–1918*, Donald W. Treadgold Studies on Russia, East Europe, and Central Asia (Seattle: The Herbert J. Ellison Center for Russian, East European, and Central Asian Studies, University of Washington, 2007), 14.

[3] See the excellent Russian study of tsarist policies in occupied eastern Galicia: A. I. Bakhturina, *Politika Rossiiskoi Imperii v Vostochnoi Galitsii v gody Pervoi mirovoi voiny* (Moscow, 2000).

caused extensive administrative and economic failures in the Russian and Austro-Hungarian Empires. As the social and ethnic imperial order disintegrated, widespread resentment in both states grew against the central authority. With ethnicity emerging as the new focus of popular loyalties in the borderlands, the age of multinational dynastic Empires was rapidly coming to a close.

The imperial collapse in Russia, however, started right in the imperial capital, where the Volhynian regiment, composed mainly of Ukrainians, was the first to take sides with the crowds of protesters in March 1917. Like elsewhere in the former Empire, two parallel power structures emerged in Ukraine: the Soviets (councils) of Workers' and Soldiers' Deputies and the Provisional Government's commissars. Yet far more dynamic in the early days of the revolution was a third claimant for power, a coordinating body of Ukrainian activists known as the Central Rada (Ukrainian for 'Council'), which was established in Kyiv on 17 March 1917. Originally a self-appointed group of Ukrainian public figures, the Rada soon came to be dominated by the Ukrainian Socialist Revolutionary Party and the Ukrainian Social Democratic Workers' Party. Its leaders were not right-wing nationalists obsessed with the purity of their nation, but leftists demanding merely territorial autonomy within a federal Russian republic.

In the heady days of spring 1917, however, a national programme seemed the best political medium in which to encapsulate the variety of social demands that made many Ukrainian activists believe in their ability to 'awaken' the masses. Indeed, for a while the nationalist patriotic message seems to have found an enthusiastic response. On 1 April 1917 an estimated 100,000 people marched in Kyiv under Ukrainian blue-and-yellow flags in support of autonomy for Ukraine. One should keep in mind, however, that the masses may have been attracted by the Central Rada's combination of a nationalist patriotic message with slogans of land reform and universal peace.[4]

This factor explains why the so-called 'Ukrainization' of the Russian army's units met with such an overwhelming response from the soldiers. From its very beginnings in the spring of 1917, this process was driven from below rather than from above. The Central Rada had no plans to create a Ukrainian army. Its leaders shared the contemporary socialist vision of regular armies as instruments of social and national oppression; they believed that a volunteer people's militia would replace both the army and the police. Nevertheless, following the example of the Poles, who had had their ethnic-based division in the Russian army and in the spring of 1917 received permission to create additional national units, soldiers of other nationalities began pushing for their transfer to ethnic-based units—a process that involved reorganization and a longer stay in the rear, or even a withdrawal from the front. The Bohdan Khmelnytsky First Cossack Regiment was formed in Kyiv in March 1917 without permission from the Russian army's command or the

---

[4] For decades this number (the 100,000 manifestation participants) passed from one history survey to another as proof of the popular support for the Central Rada. It is refreshing to see a present-day Ukrainian historian interpret this number as a reflection of wider social and national upheavals of 1917 that was *construed* by contemporaries as a sign of mass support for the Central Rada. See V. F. Soldatenko, *Ukrainska revoliutsiia: istorychnyi narys* (Kyiv, 1999), 139 and 292.

Central Rada. The initiative of some nationalistic patriotic officers resonated well with the soldiers of local reserve units, who dreaded the prospect of being sent to the trenches. The Central Rada also realized the benefits of having a 'Ukrainian' military unit in the city and supported the soldiers' initiative. By May the Russian military command finally recognized the first Ukrainian regiment, but on the condition that it departed immediately to the front. In the end, only one unit of this 'regiment', which in its entirety never had more than 3,000 bayonets, left with great fanfare for the South-Western Front, where it soon disintegrated.[5] Yet, a precedent had been established.

To strengthen its legitimacy and build popular support, the Central Rada organized a series of congresses in Kyiv in the spring and summer 1917, all of which delegated representatives to join the Rada: the National Congress, the Military Congress, the Peasant Congress, and the Workers' Congress. In May 1,000 delegates representing approximately 1 million Ukrainian soldiers in the Russian army (of the estimated total of 3.5 million Ukrainians constituting approximately 40 per cent in the Russian army in 1917) gathered in Kyiv for the First Ukrainian Military Congress. Embroiled as it was in a power struggle with Russia's provisional government, the Central Rada allowed the passage of resolutions about the mass 'Ukrainianization' of army units in the Russian army and the creation of the Ukrainian General Military Committee (UGMC)—an embryonic war ministry headed by the Ukrainian Social Democrat and accountant by profession, Symon Petliura, although the congress also affirmed the socialist line on the eventual replacement of the army with a 'people's militia'.[6]

By the summer of 1917 unauthorized Ukrainianization of army units became widespread. The 39th Army Corps, which was stationed in Volhynia and had a majority of ethnic Ukrainians in its ranks, possibly as high as 80 per cent, was the first to declare itself 'Ukrainian'. Reserve units assuming a Ukrainian designation often refused transfers to the front without the permission of the UGMC, while some frontline units withdrew from the front without permission in order to return to Ukraine, ostensibly for reorganization.[7] The head of the Central Rada, the historian Mykhailo Hrushevsky, later recalled a curious episode: a regiment on its way to the front from Saratov in Russia attempted, during a brief stop in Kyiv, to declare itself a Ukrainian regiment named after Hrushevsky. The historian agreed to the renaming and showed up to receive the regiment's parade, but politely suggested that the soldiers would have to proceed to the front in any case. The Mykhailo Hrushevsky Ukrainian Regiment from Saratov on the Volga was apparently never heard from again.[8]

While the Central Rada generally welcomed declarations by the military of loyalty to it and to the UGMC, it was also locked in a complex power struggle with the Russian Provisional Government, which required at least a formal commitment to a

[5] Viktor Holubko, *Armiia Ukrainskoi Narodnoi Respubliky 1917–1918: Utvorennia ta borotba za derzhavu* (Lviv, 1997), 44–8.

[6] Holubko, *Armiia*, 51–2.

[7] Ibid., 67–8.　　　[8] M. Hrushevsky, 'Spomyny,' *Kyiv* 10 (1989), 146.

joint war effort in the immediate future. In early July 1917 the Ukrainian government's procrastination on the issues of peace and the national army resulted in a mutiny that nearly succeeded in toppling the Rada. Some 5,000 new conscripts and soldiers awaiting reassignment in a transfer camp near Kyiv refused to go to the front, demanding that all of them be included in a new Ukrainian regiment named after Pavlo Polubotok (the Cossack leader from the early eighteenth century). Apparently with some guidance from the same nationalistic junior officers, who earlier had helped to establish the Bohdan Khmelnytsky Regiment, the soldiers declared their desire to remain near Kyiv in order 'to protect Ukraine's freedom'. They refused the UGMC's order to depart for the front and booed the high-profile delegation from the Rada headed by Volodymyr Vynnychenko and Petliura. On 5 July they captured the weapons of another reserve unit and marched on Kyiv, where they easily took the police HQ and military warehouses, and nearly captured the Central Bank before being finally rebuffed and disarmed (and eventually forcibly dispatched to the front) by the units still loyal to the Russian Provisional Government—not the Central Rada in Kyiv. The declaration issued by the rebels proclaimed their intention as 'Ukrainian Cossacks' to 'establish order in Ukraine' and 'remove all Russians and [Ukrainian] renegades' from the position of power.[9]

In late July the Russian army command finally embraced Ukrainianization as one of a very few remaining means to keep the units from deserting en masse and to secure the arrival of new conscripts from Ukraine. The new commander-in-chief, General Lavr Kornilov, signed an order authorizing the Ukrainization of 10 divisions, although given the increasing chaos and desertion, the only success story among them was that of the 34th (or 1st Ukrainian) Army Corps under the command of General Pavlo Skoropadsky, a Russian aristocrat of distant Ukrainian Cossack lineage. One reason for this was that the divisions of the 34th Corps were withdrawn from the front for reorganization and then stationed in Ukraine; Ukrainianization also did not work elsewhere in the frontline units, either because of the commanders' reluctance or high desertion rates, and the remaining soldiers still willing to participate often ended up being transferred to the 34th Corps, which soon grew to 40,000 soldiers. In contrast, the Ukrainianization of reserve units in the rear proved a success, with the participation by the autumn of 1917 of some 120,000 soldiers in 130 units. Other statistical data put the grand total of soldiers in Ukrainized detachments at as high as 637,000.[10]

Yet one should not make too much of the 1 million Ukrainian soldiers represented by a thousand delegates at a military congress or the hundreds of thousands in the formally 'Ukrainianized' units. As Hrushevsky himself was painfully aware, masses of soldiers 'responded enthusiastically to revolutionary slogans, which promised to remove [them] from the front, but responded weakly to appeals for fighting against any side.' Another prominent Ukrainian activist, Dmytro Doroshenko, was in agreement: 'When the Bolsheviks appeared in the autumn [of 1917]

---

[9] V. F. Soldatenko, 'Tsentralna Rada ta ukrainizatsiia armii,' *Ukrainskyi istorychnyi zhurnal*, no. 6 (1992), 28–9.
[10] Holubko, *Armiia*, 78–90, 149.

and offered the soldier masses slogans [that were] more basic and more attractive than those of the Ukrainian and Russian Socialist Revolutionaries, this million disappeared instantly.'[11]

As we have seen, beginning in the spring of 1917, soldiers from the Russian army played a major role in Ukrainian politics. Regular units stationed in the capital supported the Provisional Government, while other reserve and frontline troops vacillated between the Bolsheviks and the Ukrainian authorities—the former offering a more radical social programme and the latter, a more realistic chance of returning home. At the same time, the proximity of the frontline meant that thousands of often armed deserters introduced into the daily life of Ukrainian towns and villages a culture of violence and the right of the strong.

Most soldiers were peasants in uniform, and the Central Rada procrastinated with satisfying the peasants' principal demand: the redistribution of land. By early autumn 1917, with an ever-increasing number of deserters and disabled veterans back in their villages, the peasants took matters into their own hands and began mass, violent seizures of land belonging to the nobility or the crown. The Ukrainian government was losing both the trust of its main constituency—the peasantry—and control over the countryside. Like many socialists of the time, the head of the General Secretariat, Vynnychenko, and other Ukrainian leaders believed in the imminent 'withering away' of the bourgeois state apparatus, standing armies, and the police. Blinded by this unrealistic dream, they did not create any institutions capable of maintaining public order, and neither did they develop any functioning bureaucracy. With civic order collapsing, local soviets in the cities and ad hoc self-defence bodies in the countryside paid less and less attention to the proclamations issuing from Kyiv.

THE EMERGENCE OF THE 'FREE COSSACKS'

The growing chaos and lawlessness in the countryside led to the development of an impressive peasant self-defence movement, which assumed the historical name of the Cossacks. The last remnants of the Cossack state and territorial regimental structure disappeared in Ukraine by the early nineteenth century, but the memory of the Cossack past lived on in popular legends, in part because for enserfed and impoverished peasants as well as for patriotic writers it functioned as a myth of past freedom and prosperity.[12] (The coveted status of the Cossack indeed conferred personal freedom from the fifteenth century to the late eighteenth.) During the Crimean War masses of peasant serfs in Kyiv province declared themselves 'Cossacks' in 1855 in the hope that the government would accept them for military

---

[11] M. Hrushevsky, 'Spomyny,' *Kyiv*, no. 10 (1989), 124; D. Doroshenko, 'Voina i revoliutsiia na Ukraine,' in *Revoliutsiia na Ukraine po memuaram belykh* (ed. by N. N. Popov), 2nd edn. (Kyiv, 1990), 71.

[12] On the Cossack myth in 19th-century Ukrainian literature, see George G. Grabowicz, 'Three Perspectives on the Cossack Past: Gogol', Ševčenko, Kuliš,' *Harvard Ukrainian Studies* 5 (1981), 135–70.

service and thus grant freedom to them. It is not surprising, then, that the volunteer militia spontaneously emerging in the Ukrainian countryside during 1917 assumed the name of 'Free Cossacks'.

As is usually the case with other 'invented traditions' consciously mobilizing the past to develop a new legitimacy, a closer look at the origins of the 'Free Cossacks' shows that patriotic intellectuals helped shape the new institution. Although contemporary reports credit Nykodym Smoktii, a wealthy peasant of Cossack lineage, with founding the first group of 'Free Cossacks' in Zvenyhorodka county of Kyiv province in April 1917, he was apparently assisted by two nationalistic students from the Kyiv Commercial College, V. Kovtunenko and H. Pyshchalenko, who had returned to their native county to create a new revolutionary administration.[13] Until the summer very few people in Ukraine knew about this local initiative of protecting public order while wearing baggy trousers and embroidered shirts, and armed with sabres. Yet in early June two representatives of the Zvenyhorodka Free Cossacks made an appearance in their colourful, archaic dress at the Second Ukrainian Military Congress, causing a sensation. Since the creation of local self-defence units was by then a widely perceived need, their patriotic incarnation was all the more appealing. After the newspapers got involved in the discussion of this 'popular initiative', companies of the Free Cossacks sprang up during the summer throughout Ukraine, particularly in the Kyiv, Poltava, Chernihiv, and Katerynoslav provinces. Both the central and local authorities insisted that only males unfit for army service be allowed to enrol; for as long as this requirement could be realistically enforced, the Free Cossacks consisted mainly of peasants over the age of 43 and those under 18. There are, however, reports of women being accepted in some places and of a formal declaration of Ukrainian identity required in others. By October 1917 there were 72 documented companies of the Free Cossacks with 15,586 members and an estimated 300 companies that never registered with the UMGC, but numbered another 40,000, according to contemporary estimates.[14]

The Central Rada, however, remained cautious toward the now popular movement. It continued to put off developing its statute and never convened the planned congress of the Free Cossacks. In fact, the socialist leaders of the Rada worried that the institution of Free Cossackdom would provide wealthy peasants with a political and military arm, possibly with dire implications for national politics. In October the conference of the Rada's county commissars voted to ban the Free Cossacks, but in the same month a congress of Free Cossacks took place without official approval in the town of Chyhyryn, some distance from the capital. With very limited representation from local companies, the organizers managed to push through the proposal to elect as the *nakaznyi otaman,* or temporary Cossack leader, the same General Skoropadsky who had distinguished himself while Ukrainizing his 34th Army Corps. Since the leftist politicians of the Rada distrusted Skoropadsky on all three counts—as a Russian aristocrat, a large landowner, and a tsarist general—this act only confirmed their worst fears of the Free Cossacks becoming a vehicle for a conservative Bonapartist coup. Skoropadsky's election was never recognized by the UGMC; instead, in early November, when the Rada finally came up with the statute for the Free Cossacks, they were formally subordinated to a minister of internal affairs or deputy. At the same time the Rada attempted to capture the HQ of the Free Cossacks in the town of Bila Tserkva, just south of Kyiv, but its troops were rebuffed and the Cossack leadership threatened to march on Kyiv should an attempt to dissolve and disarm the Free Cossacks be repeated.[15]

By the autumn of 1917, national politics in Ukraine were becoming increasingly dependent on the strength of paramilitary units supporting various political forces. During the Bolshevik coup in Petrograd in November 1917, fighting broke out in Kyiv between the regular troops loyal to the Provisional Government and the paramilitary detachments of the Bolsheviks and the Central Rada, respectively. The latter two sided with each other in ousting the old authorities, but by the end of December they were at war with each other for control over Ukraine. As soon as the Bolsheviks proclaimed Ukraine a Soviet republic at the congress of Soviets held in the eastern city of Kharkiv on 25 December 1917, Bolshevik detachments arriving from Russia together with the local Red Guards began advancing on Kyiv.

The war against the Bolsheviks turned out to be a disaster for the Ukrainian republic. Most of the soldiers at the Eastern Front who had previously pledged loyalty to the Central Rada had returned to their villages. In fact, on 4 January 1918 the Ukrainian ministry of war issued an order demobilizing all soldiers in 'Ukrainianized' units of the former Russian army, because most of these units were by now either nonexistent or hostile to the Rada. However, attempts to create a new Ukrainianian army brought little success. In desperation, the government turned to the mercenary principle, offering large sums of money to warlords who promised to organize military detachments.[16] Ironically, the Free Cossacks were among the very few military groups willing to support the Ukrainian government, which only recently had tried to dissolve them. The standing Ukrainian army under Minister of War Symon Petliura consisted of 15,000 irregular 'Free Cossacks' and volunteers, who, however, remained an organized force only for as long as they operated near their home counties. In what was in fact a civil war, morale mattered more than numbers, and the overall combat performance of the Ukrainian troops was disappointing. According to Ukrainian historians, the Bolsheviks began their offensive with a force numbering no more than 8,000.[17] Yet, they were a better organized side, with superior propagandists, and they offered the frustrated masses the more radical social programme. The campaign was won by persuasion rather than by force, as soldiers of the Ukrainian volunteer regiments defected to the Bolsheviks en masse or just went home to their villages. A knowledgeable memoirist reveals that the Ukrainian military command actually suppressed the news of its

---

[15] Holubko, *Armiia*, 123.   [16] Holubko, *Armiia*, 163.
[17] I. L. Hoshuliak, 'Pro prychyny porazky Tsentralnoi Rady,' *Ukrainskyi istorychnyo zhurnal*, no. 1 (1994), 36.

first, embarrassing, attempt in December 1917 to send an army against the Bolsheviks: 'When, just before Christmas, an army was sent against the Bolsheviks, who by then had captured Kharkiv, almost all the soldiers in the army, including the Bohdan Khmelnytsky Regiment, deserted to their villages, taking with them their arms and horses. The military leadership made a great secret out of this because it was still hoping that the Cossacks would return to their detachments after the holidays, but those hopes were in vain—the Cossacks were happy to reach home at last.'[18]

With the Red Army advancing from the North, pro-Bolshevik workers in some Ukrainian cities also staged uprisings, most famously in Kyiv, where in January 1918 troops loyal to the Central Rada managed to suppress, only with great difficulty (and with extreme brutality, by executing some 300 workers), the rebellion led by the workers of the Arsenal, later depicted in Alexander Dovzhenko's famous film *Arsenal*. One week later the Ukrainian government was forced to abandon the capital; the only reliable military detachment selected to protect the republic's leadership actually consisted of former Austrian POWs of Galician-Ukrainian background, rather than Eastern Ukrainians.[19] On one of the final days of the capital's defence, 29 January 1918, the Bolshevik forces at Kruty encircled and slaughtered a unit consisting of some 300 Ukrainian schoolboys and student volunteers—the victims becoming national martyrs for anti-Soviet Ukrainians in the same way that the executed workers of the Arsenal became Soviet heroes. Having taken Kyiv, the Bolshevik troops, led by the brutal Mikhail Muravev, reportedly executed between 2,000 and 5,000 'class enemies' there,[20] but their control over the capital lasted only three weeks. It would be a mistake, however, to imagine the Red Army soldiers entering the capital as disciplined Bolshevik fanatics armed with murderous ideology. In fact, most of them were irregulars feeling strong allegiance only to their band leaders. As a contemporary Ukrainian Bolshevik functionary, H. Lapchynsky, recalled: 'They were strangely dressed, totally undisciplined people covered from head to toe with every imaginable type of weapon, from rifles to sabres to handguns of all makes, and grenades. Arguments and fights constantly flared up among their commanders.'[21]

Just a few days before the capture of Kyiv the Central Rada signed a separate peace treaty with the Central Powers on behalf of the Ukrainian People's Republic—an entity existing autonomously within Russia since the previous November, but which was proclaimed independent on 25 January 1918 precisely in order to become a legitimate signatory of international treaties. Based on the Treaty of Brest-Litovsk, a German and Austrian army of 450,000 bayonets marched into Ukraine, forcing the Bolsheviks to flee. Uncomfortable with the left-leaning Rada, by late April the Germans engineered a conservative coup that brought to power General Skoropadsky as the monarch of Ukraine, or *hetman*—the title traditionally

---

[18] Chykalenko, *Uryvok z moikh spomyniv za 1917 r.* (Prague, 1932), 28.
[19] Holubko, *Armiia*, 168.
[20] V. A. Smolii (ed.), *Istoriia Ukrainy* (Kyiv, 1997), 230.
[21] H. Lapchynsky, 'Borotba za Kyiv. Sichen 1918 r.,' *Litopys revoliutsii*, no. 2 (1928), 212.

used by Cossack leaders. Yet a conservative regime stood little chance of survival. German punitive expeditions to quell peasant looters and the forced collection of grain from the peasantry soon provoked unprecedented unrest in the countryside. With the withdrawal of the Central Powers soon after their capitulation in November 1918, two prominent socialist ministers of the General Secretariat, Volodymyr Vynnychenko and Symon Petliura, created a five-person committee named the Directory (after the French revolutionary government of 1795–99) to coordinate a rebellion against the monarchy. Tens of thousands of peasants—many of them probably former Free Cossacks—flocked to the Directory's headquarters in Bila Tserkva near Kyiv, and most of the *hetman*'s small army defected to their side.

THE FAILURE OF STATE BUILDING

If the developments in Russian Ukraine seemed just as chaotic and confusing for contemporaries as they are for later scholars, the revolutionary events in Austrian Ukraine appeared to be a clear-cut struggle against a clearly defined ethnic enemy. With the collapse of the Austro-Hungarian Empire in November 1918, two new states claimed authority over Eastern Galicia: the reconstituted Poland and the newly proclaimed Western Ukrainian People's Republic. At first, a group of young Ukrainian officers in the Austrian army easily took power in the province's capital of Lviv (Lemberg, Lwów), but street fighting with local Poles ensued and by the end of the month a Polish uprising forced the Ukrainians out of their new capital. The conflict between the two new states then developed into a fully-fledged Ukrainian-Polish war, in which the belligerent forces were clearly divided along ethnic lines—in contrast to the relative unimportance of ethnicity and fluid manpower in Russian Ukraine (see chapter 11 below).

Also unlike in the East, the Western Ukrainian People's Republic benefited from a long tradition of Ukrainian political and communal life in Austria-Hungary. The new state managed to set up an effective administrative apparatus and preserve civic order in the territories it controlled.[22] There was no spontaneous peasant insurgency in Galicia, and Ukrainian-Jewish relations remained relatively amicable throughout the republic's existence. What clearly did not work out, however, was the long-dreamed-of reunification of the two Ukraines. Solemnly proclaimed in Kyiv on 22 January 1919, it was never implemented. Moderate Western Ukrainian politicians could not find a common language with the socialist Easterners, and each side was embroiled in its own civil war with very different aims and enemies. While the Westerners focused on fighting against Poland, to the Easterners Poland seemed a natural ally against their own enemies—the Bolsheviks and the Russian Whites. Likewise, the Galicians did not mind allying themselves with the Russian Whites against Poland. As the two sides were soon to discover, however, befriending each other's enemy was not the best recipe for winning.

---

[22] See S. A. Makarchuk, *Ukrainska respublika halychan* (Lviv, 1997).

Because of their long tradition of communal organization, Ukrainians in Eastern Galicia were able to create something Kyiv never had: a reliable regular army, the so-called Ukrainian Galician Army (UGA). If it were not for its gruelling fighting against the much stronger Poles, the Galicians could have made a difference during the Civil War in Eastern Ukraine. Although short on senior officers, the army had many German and Austrian majors and colonels, and the two successive commanders-in-chief were former Russian generals, Mykhailo Omelianovych-Pavlenko and Oleksandr Hrekov. The army's greatest assets were its privates and junior officers: up to 60,000 conscientious and disciplined Ukrainian peasants and townspeople from Eastern Galicia.[23] The Ukrainian army began a counter-offensive in February 1919 and soon had Lviv encircled, but the arrival of major forces from Poland proper decided the outcome of the struggle in Galicia. Eager to create out of independent Poland a counterweight both to Germany and to Bolshevik Russia, the Allied negotiators at the Paris Peace Conference abandoned the Wilsonian principle of self-determination with regard to Eastern Galicia. They allowed the transfer there of the 100,000-strong Polish army of General Józef Haller, which was trained and equipped in France. At the same time, escalating social tensions undermined the textbook image of Western Ukrainians united in defence of their nation. Peasants protested the Ukrainian government's failure to enact a land reform, and a pro-Bolshevik workers' rebellion took place in the region's only industrial centre, Drohobych. Before internal problems had time to escalate, however, the Western Ukrainians lost the war to the Poles. On 16 July 1919 what remained of the UGA and the republic's administration crossed the Zbruch River into the former Russian Ukraine. At the same time the Allies agreed to the 'temporary' Polish occupation of Eastern Galicia, which became permanent after 1923.

Having crossed into Eastern Ukraine, the well-organized and nationalistic Galicians became just one of the many small armies wandering the land and constantly changing allegiance. But the last word belonged not to them, and not even to the mighty Russian Red and White armies fighting each other on Ukrainian territory (each including a significant share of ethnic Ukrainians), but to the Ukrainian peasantry on the ground.

The military situation of the Ukrainian government (now the Directory) worsened almost immediately after it took power in the wake of the German evacuation in December 1918. Some 60,000 French troops landed in Odessa and other Southern cities to support the Whites, who promised the restoration of a united anti-Bolshevik state. At the same time, the Bolsheviks began another invasion from the North. Vynnychenko, who was head of the Directory, felt that the only way of securing popular allegiances would be to match the Bolsheviks' radical social programme. He even spoke about Ukraine's entry into a revolutionary war of Soviet republics (including Russia and Hungary, where a communist rebellion was then underway) against the European reaction.[24] But his negotiations with the Bolsheviks were in vain, as their troops—once again swollen with Ukrainian volunteers

---

[23] See M. R. Lytvyn and K. Ie. Naumenko, *Istoriia halytskoho striletstva*, 2nd edn. (Lviv, 1991), 97.
[24] Volodymyr Vynnychenko, *Vidrodzhennia natsii*, reprint edn (Kyiv, 1990), vol. 3, 322–3.

and conscripts—were fast advancing toward Kyiv. Peasants who had supported the Directory against Skoropadsky returned to their villages, and the Ukrainian government was again struggling to raise an army. In any case, the Bolshevik military action against the Directory was marginal compared to Ukraine's becoming a battlefield in the Russian Civil War between the Reds and the Whites. But these events may also be characterized as a Ukrainian civil war inasmuch as ethnic Ukrainians who were serving in the Directory's, Bolshevik, and White armies were killing each other for the victory of their respective vision of 'Ukraine.'

Escaping from the Bolsheviks, the Directory retreated from Kyiv westward, from Vinnytsia to Rivne to Kamianets-Podilsky. In July 1919 the Galicians joined the struggling Directory on a tiny stretch of territory it still controlled, with its centre in Kamianets-Podilsky. By then Vynnychenko had resigned, because his radical socialist views prevented any possible dealings with the Allies, and was replaced by the more nationalistic Symon Petliura. Meanwhile, the Bolsheviks controlled most Ukrainian urban centres, but only managed to further antagonize the peasantry by sending out armed detachments to requisition grain. Instead of distributing land to the peasants, the new authorities preferred reorganizing the confiscated large estates into state farms.

THE RULE OF THE *OTAMANS*

Such policies only fanned the flames of the peasant rebellion, which was often aimed at all outsiders. The whole countryside became a sea of anarchy divided up and controlled by local peasant chieftains: the so-called *otamans*. Some of them led peasant armies of many thousands of men and could thus influence national politics.[25] Among the most famous were *otaman* Matvii Hryhoriiv, a former tsarist officer and Left Socialist Revolutionary, who in the spring of 1919 drove the French expedition corps out of Odessa but later turned against the Bolsheviks, and Nestor Makhno, the peasant anarchist, who concentrated his 40,000-strong army in the Southern steppes, supporting in turn the Bolsheviks, the Directory, and finally, the idea of a peasant anarchist republic. Other colourful personalities whose memories survive in folklore include no fewer than three different female *otamanshas*, all named Marusia (a diminutive for Maria).

The fact that one weak government was replacing another in Kyiv in 1919 had no impact on the countryside. The First World War and the ensuing collapse of local institutions left the Ukrainian peasantry heavily armed, experienced in fighting, and more self-confident than ever. Although local peasant bands switched their allegiance often, sometimes fighting under the slogans of socialist revolution or an independent Ukraine, their main interest was in survival, securing arable land,

---

[25] For an overall survey of peasant insurgency in Ukraine during 1918–20, see O. I. Hanzha, *Opir selian stanovlenniu totalitarnoho rezhymu v USRR* (Kyiv, 1996). Another good account with an emphasis on Soviet counter-measures is Andrea Graziosi, *The Great Soviet Peasant War: Bolsheviks and Peasants, 1917–1933* (Cambridge, MA, 1996), 11–37.

and looting. The revival of the term *otaman* suggested a spontaneous return to Cossack traditions, but the rebels were not conscious Ukrainian nationalists. Rather, they were motivated by local concerns, prejudices, and naive anarchism.

In fact, it would be a mistake to imagine the soldier deserters and Free Cossacks of 1917 as different people from the eager peasant looters and reluctant conscripts of 1918–19. They were probably very often the same people carrying the same rifles, even if they had changed uniforms when a new conscripting army had them. Reports of the collapse of civic order and warlordism are common in newspapers and memoirs beginning in the autumn of 1917. On 4 October 1917 the influential *Nova Rada* editorialized:

> From all parts of the country, but most of all from the right bank of the Dnieper, from the provinces of Podillia, Volhynia, and Kyiv, desperate telegrams arrive at the General Secretariat about the terrible anarchy, robbery, destruction of public property, and killings. Even pogromist excesses have returned, as was the case under the old regime, with attacks on the property and life of the Jewish people. In general, the attacks on private property, individuals, and groups have become common, whereby the criminals are emboldened by the realization of the lack of punishment for their evil deeds. It is not just bands of deserters that commit violations of public order, robberies, and violence, but also regular army units stationed in Ukraine, proceeding to the front, or being withdrawn from the front. Fields, houses, grain, and any property, even human life, are destroyed because of the lack of state representatives with strong authority and local support.[26]

Official reports about the retreat of the 2nd Guards Corps and various groups of deserters through the province of Volhynia in October 1917 compared the soldiers' actions to a sixteenth-century Tatar raid: 'Everything in the county has been destroyed: seeds, cattle, chickens, ponds emptied of water; soldiers were raping women; in the villages through which the army marched only fire-blackened walls have been left standing.'[27]

If peasants in army overcoats behaved this way, there is little reason to expect that other peasants dressed as Free Cossacks would refrain from looting and violence. They surely protected their own communities or at least those within their villages who were seen as insiders, but from the very first days of the Free Cossacks' existence in Zvenyhorod County reports surfaced about their 'lawless actions'. By the autumn of 1917 the Free Cossacks were conducting searches and confiscations in nearby towns, which sparked energetic protests from the local authorities, looting large estates, and arresting people at will. According to Skoropadsky himself, the General Staff of Free Cossacks had procured its operational funds by imposing a levy on the local Jews.[28] By February 1918 the distinction between local peasant bands engaged in looting and the Free Cossacks supposedly protecting public order in the countryside became so blurred that the Cossack leadership attempted to reregister all their manpower and issue the registered Cossacks permission to carry arms, which would distinguish them from the bandits. But this enterprise was abandoned amidst the

---

[26] *Nova Rada*, 4 October 1917, 1.   [27] Cited in Verstiuk, 'Vilne kozatstvo,' 449.
[28] Verstiuk, 'Vilne kozatstvo,' 430, 451, 453.

increasing chaos. In late March 1918, having lost all control over peasant rebels styling themselves as Cossacks, the Directory dissolved the Free Cossacks. Their leadership then came out in support of Skoropadsky's regime, but the companies on the ground increasingly led their own existence as peasant bands.[29] The end of the Cossack General Staff was telling: in January 1918 it was dispersed by some pro-Bolshevik military car-repair unit passing through the town of Bila Tserkva. The members of the elite Cossack Guards Company attached to the General Staff deserted, taking horses with them, but not before they joined forces with local peasant looters in pillaging and burning the nearby historic Branicki Palace.[30]

The violent Jewish pogroms that claimed more than 30,000 lives were perhaps the most tragic consequence of the chaos in Ukraine during 1917–20, but especially in 1919. All sides in the Civil War carried out pogroms: the Whites, the Directory troops, the independent *otamans*, and the Red Army. With the exception of some ideologically motivated White pogroms, the anti-Jewish violence was usually carried out by drunken mobs of anti-Semitic freebooters against the authorities' orders. The troops subordinated to the Directory committed 40 per cent of recorded pogroms—more than any other side, resulting in their commander-in-chief, Symon Petliura, being branded in the West as a violent anti-Semite. Despite this localized violence against Jews, on a national level the Ukrainian People's Republic had a good record of treating its national minorities. It was the first modern state to establish a ministry of Jewish affairs and guarantee the rights of the Jewish culture. Yet, it lacked authority. The government issued well-intentioned orders condemning pogroms and attempted to investigate them. In the meantime, marauding bands, often nominally considered to be part of the Ukrainian, Red, or White armies, simply moved on to the next village to perpetrate violence.

As the incomplete statistical data available indicate, there were approximately 60 anti-Jewish pogroms in Ukraine in 1917 and 80 in 1918, but a total of 934 were recorded in 1919 and 178 in 1920. These data also indicate that anti-Semitic beliefs of individual warlords played a major role in determining the level of violence. The average number of murdered Jews per pogrom was far and away the highest in the 52 pogroms committed by the troops of *Otaman* Hryhoriiv—67 per event, followed by the average of 34 for the Directory troops and 25 for the White Army, 15 for 'miscellaneous bands,' and 7 for the Red Army.[31] Ideologically, only the White Army embraced the pogroms to some degree, but Hryhoriiv's personal anti-Semitism is well-known, and other such *otamans* were more numerous among the irregular troops associated with the Directory than they were in the Red Army. At the same time, 'miscellaneous bands' were probably comprised of locals more interested in looting than in taking lives for ideological reasons.

This is probably even more true of the lesser-known simultaneous pogroms of Mennonite settlements in southern Ukraine. Like Jews, the Mennonites represented

[29] Holubko, *Armiia*, 183, 195–6.   [30] Verstiuk, 'Vilne kozatstvo,' 453–4.

[31] Henry Abramson, 'Jewish Representation in the Independent Ukrainian Governments of 1917–1920,' *Slavic Review* 50 3 (1991), 547–8.

an identifiable 'other' in the Ukrainian countryside, but they also usually lived in compact settlements perceived by the locals as being 'well-off'. Although most attacks on Mennonite villages were for the sake of pure looting, at least in the case of the powerful local warlord, Nestor Makhno, they were sanctified by the egalitarian rhetoric of redistributing wealth, which, of course, did not explain the brutal killings of Mennonite civilians.[32]

Like the Directory before them, the Bolsheviks in 1919 found governing Ukraine an almost impossible task. They barely had enough time to identify the problems before a well-organized White army, equipped by the Allies, moved in from the Don region, in Russia's South-East, in June. In July Petliura's detachments, reinforced by the UGA, started advancing from the West. This time, peasant conscripts abandoned the Reds en masse to join the stronger side. Beaten by both the Whites and the Directory, the Bolsheviks retired to Russia in late August, with the White general, Anton Denikin, in hot pursuit. Yet the friendly neutrality between the Ukrainians and the Whites did not last long, and soon the Whites forced the Ukrainian units out of Kyiv. They also proceeded with their plans of re-establishing the pre-revolutionary social order by restoring land to large landowners and banning the Ukrainian language. Amid the growing popular discontent against the Whites, the Directory finally declared war on them in late September.

However, military engagements with the mighty White army brought the Ukrainian troops no success. In October a typhus epidemic struck at a time when medical supplies were blocked by the Allies, killing about 70 per cent of manpower. Defeated and decimated by the epidemic, the Ukrainians finally gave up. The Galicians entered into secret negotiations with the Whites, which ended in the UGA's subordination to Denikin on 6 November. At the same time, Petliura reached an agreement with the Galicians' sworn enemy, Poland. The rupture between the two Ukrainian armies was now complete, and military catastrophe assured. The Polish army then moved into the Western provinces of Volhynia and Podillia, where Petliura and his government were travelling in several railroad cars. What remained of the Directory was attacked by local peasant bands; the state treasury was stolen, and the staff of the war ministry was left behind.[33] On 15 November Petliura was officially proclaimed a dictator and he fled to Warsaw soon afterward.

As these events were unfolding near the Polish border, in Ukraine's central provinces the Reds were beating back the Whites. In December 1919 the Bolsheviks took Kyiv for the third time, and on this occasion they seriously evaluated their Ukrainian policy. The Kremlin allowed the formal independence of Soviet Ukraine (in federation with Soviet Russia), official recognition of the Ukrainian language, and a more careful agrarian policy. To placate the countryside, in the spring of

---

[32] See John B. Toews, 'The Origins and Activities of the Mennonite "Selbstschutz" in the Ukraine (1918–1919),' *Mennonite Quarterly Review* 46 (1972), 5–40 and Toews, 'No Songs Were Sung at the Graveside: The Blumenort (Russia) Massacre (10–12 November 1919),' *Journal of Mennonite Studies* 13 (1995), 51–70.

[33] Isak Mazepa, *Ukraina v ohni i buri revoliutsii: 1917–1922* (Kyiv, 2003), 317–24.

1920 the Bolsheviks terminated the creation of state farms and communes, opting instead for a massive distribution of confiscated land to the peasantry.[34] This measure secured popular support for them at a decisive moment of the Civil War. By the autumn of 1920 forced requisitioning of grain from the peasants destroyed this effect and led to new peasant revolts, but the Bolsheviks' overall victory was by then ensured.

The two final conflicts of the Russian Civil War also took place on Ukrainian territory, although they were really more of a postscript to the titanic clash between the Reds and the Whites of the previous year. Between April and October 1920 a quick Polish-Soviet war played out in Ukraine, in the end curbing the expansionist ambitions of both young states. At first, the Poles took Kyiv and installed Petliura as their puppet Ukrainian ruler, but then only the 'miracle on the Vistula' helped them stop the Red cavalry on the outskirts of Warsaw. In November 1920 the Reds also stormed the last White stronghold in the Ukrainian South, the Crimea, and brutally executed thousands of officers and 'class aliens' who did not manage to escape by sea to Turkey (and eventually resettle all over the world). The Bolsheviks still required considerable time and effort to suppress peasant insurgents of various political stripes, but their victory was no longer in question.

CONCLUSIONS

If the brief Polish-Ukrainian war in the former Austro-Hungarian Empire fits well the model of an 'Eastern European' ethnic conflict, the civil war in the much larger former Russian Ukraine challenges this model as well as the traditional understanding of paramilitary violence. With ethnic identities in flux and social issues predominant, a multi-faceted conflict developed, a conflict in which fighters could switch their allegiances depending on which of the strongest armies currently fighting each other in Ukraine had an agenda that resonated best with this person's views on Ukraine's future. For the majority of Ukrainians, however, ideology mattered only in its application to the issues of survival and local concerns. Peasant bands, often posing as militia units, ruled the countryside; and, although people could be conscripted into any army passing through the region, local warlordism became a central factor in the Ukrainian Civil War. Ideologies did play a role— after all, the conflict between the Reds and Whites was intensely ideological, and all the Ukrainian governments tried to establish their nation's separate existence— but this role was often that of a prism refracting the dreams and phobias of mostly illiterate peasant rebels through the vocabulary of modern socialism or nationalism. In the end, the programme of land distribution was a crucial factor in the Bolshevik victory in Ukraine, although the socialist dream might attract some, with the early assimilationist measures repelling others.

[34] O. S. Rublov and O. P. Reient, *Ukrainski vyzvolni zmahannia 1917–1921 rr.* (Kyiv, 1999), 228.

It is tempting to trace the violence of the Stalinist collectivization of agriculture back to the Civil War, especially because so many Bolshevik activists and collective farm chairmen were Red Army veterans. Yet, it was very clearly state-sponsored and centrally coordinated violence based on Soviet ideology, notably the dual aim to eliminate private property on the land and to destroy the *kulaks* who were conceptualized as class enemies. This violence was related to the events of the previous decade only insofar as the entire political culture of the Bolshevik regime was shaped by the Civil War, a point often made by students of Stalinism.[35] Perhaps a better connection to paramilitarism can be seen in the development of the underground 'Organization of Ukrainian Nationalists' in the Western Ukrainian provinces under Polish rule. There, membership consisted largely of veterans of the Great War, who were usually also veterans of the Ukrainian-Polish war, and who often took part in fighting against the Bolsheviks in Central Ukraine. A culture of defeat, virulent nationalism, and the ready use of force stress its generic similarity to other right-wing paramilitary organizations in interwar Europe.

[35] See, e.g., Sheila Fitzpatrick, *The Russian Revolution*, 2nd edn. (New York, 1994), 87–92.

8

Turning Citizens into Soldiers: Baltic Paramilitary Movements after the Great War

Tomas Balkelis

INTRODUCTION: WAR, PARAMILITARISM AND NATION-MAKING IN THE BALTIC STATES

After the First World War, Lithuania, Latvia, Estonia, Finland and Poland became post-imperial 'shatter zones' par excellence. Throughout 1918–20 a new military action swept the North-Western borderlands of the former Russian Empire in a wave of bloodshed. The Soviets, Whites, Germans, Lithuanians, Latvians, Estonians, Finns and Poles fought each other with ferocity that often matched the belligerency of 1914–15. In contrast to the warfare of the Great War, this postwar violence was more low-scale, irregular and volatile. Yet it was more ideologically and ethnically motivated and involved a greater variety of combatants: not only conventional armies, but also civilian self-defence bands, partisans and voluntary paramilitary formations. Various nationalist and counter-revolutionary aspirations clashed with each other and with the Bolshevik revolutionary vision, all claiming parts of the region as part of their 'new orders'. For some Western observers, none more prominent than Winston Churchill, these violent clashes seemed nothing more than 'wars of pygmies', but for the locals their significance could not be overestimated.[1] Indeed, one of the unique features of this region today is that, unlike in Western Europe, the memory of the Great War was completely overwhelmed by the memory of this post-First World War conflict. Its legacy is alive in local national mythologies and contemporary politics.[2]

As the new armies had been hurriedly assembled from the veterans of old imperial troops and fresh recruits, the distinction between 'paramilitarism' and 'militarism' became blurred. The postwar years were 'the golden era' for paramilitaries as they emerged all over Central and Eastern Europe and beyond.[3] Along with the

---

[1] Adrian Hyde-Price, *Germany and European Order* (Manchester, 2001), 75.

[2] Vėjas G. Liulevičius, 'Building Nationalism: Monuments, Museums, and the Politics of War Memory in Inter-War Lithuania', *Nord-Ost Archiv*, 27 (2008), 230–4.

[3] A new comparative approach to European paramilitary movements was proposed by Robert Gerwarth, 'The Central European Counter-Revolution: Paramilitary Violence in Germany, Austria and Hungary after the Great War', *Past & Present* 200 (2008), 175–209. For a recent account, see, too Alexander V. Prusin, *The Lands Between: Conflict in the East European Borderlands, 1870–1992* (Oxford, 2010), particularly ch. 3.

conventional national, revolutionary or counter-revolutionary armies, various para-military formations played prominent roles in this postwar conflict. In the newly created Lithuania, Latvia and Estonia the paramilitaries included Red and Green guerrillas, German and White Russian volunteers, and Polish, Lithuanian, Latvian and Estonian home guard movements.

This chapter will primarily focus on one of the least known of these paramilitary groups—the *Šauliai* (Lithuanian Riflemen's Union or LRU). It will also provide a comparative perspective on two other paramilitary formations that emerged in Latvia and Estonia: the Latvian *Aizsargi* (Home Guard) and the Estonian *Kaitseliit* (Defence League). All three were established in 1918–19 as self-defence citizen militias. By 1940 each grew to more than 60,000 members (the *Kaitseliit* to almost 100,000 with all auxiliaries). Yet by late 1940 they were dissolved by the Soviets as their leaders were arrested, imprisoned, deported or executed. I will explore their ideological roots, military activities, political aims and initiatives, as well as long-term legacies in order to explain their evolution into sizeable social movements with more similarities than differences between them.

The broader concern here is the relationship between paramilitarism and nation-making. Was this paramilitarism a consequence of the Great War or an outcome of the postwar conflict? What were the sources of its legitimacy? Was it a nation-making strategy? What are its long-term legacies?

Due to a belated and incomplete process of nation-making that was hindered by Russian imperialism and the Great War, in the Baltic the ensuing 'wars of

Fig. 11. A group of Lithuanian Riflemen posing in 1920.

liberation' (1918–20) produced a radical strategy of nation-making: national militarism.[4] This was a particular type of 'total mobilization' that required the call-up of entire populations. While its immediate causes were rooted in the post-First World War conflict, its ideological and psychological foundations were shaped by the experience of the Great War and the Russian Revolution. Most importantly, paramilitarism was a symptomatic outgrowth of this national militarism whose major concern was how to transform the civilian populations into citizen-soldiers.

Yet at its core, this paramilitarism was also an integration policy that called not only for more soldiers, but also strived to reshape local politics and identities. In this sense, it was both counter-revolutionary (defensive) and revolutionary (expansive). Thus the *Šauliai, Aizsargi* and *Kaitseliit* engaged simultaneously in military action, political and cultural activism, and nation-making. Although they never lost their paramilitary swagger, after the postwar conflict, they evolved into massive social and cultural movements. Their transformative character is one of the most overlooked and least understood aspects of their brief, yet dynamic, history. It was vividly captured in a remark made by one of the founders of the *Šauliai* Vladas Pūtvis-Putvinskis (1873–1929): 'Lithuania was ours, but we did not belong to ourselves'.[5] In other words, the new nation-state that had emerged from the cauldron of the Great War needed to be 'nationalized' to be a long-lasting political project.

Due to their radical calls for a populist national revolution, the *Šauliai*, the *Aizsargi* (and to a lesser extent the *Kaitseliit*) generated a great deal of tension between the nation and the state.[6] If the state was barely able to cope with a challenge of nation-building and survival under conditions of war, then the paramilitaries stepped in by calling for the political 'awakening' and militarization of all citizens. Yet by doing this, they claimed an autonomous status within the state. In 1919 Pūtvis referred to the *Šauliai* as 'a small version of a state'.[7] Certainly, similar claims generated suspicion among state bureaucrats (particularly within the army) who often saw the paramilitaries as their competitors. In Latvia the army tried to control the *Aizsargi*, as the president Karlis Ulmanis drew them closer as his personal armed political force.[8]

The connection between the citizens and their readiness to wage a war, of course, was reinforced by the dynamic course of military action. None of the newly created Baltic nation-states (all emerged in 1918) felt secure about their chances of survival in 1918–20. In the short period between December 1918 and December 1919,

---

[4] The argument of the belated nation-making was advanced by Miroslav Hroch. See Miroslav Hroch, *Social Preconditions of National Revival in Europe: A Comparative Analysis of the Social Composition of Patriotic Groups among the Smaller European Nations* (Cambridge, 1985), 86–8.

[5] Pūtvis, 'Memoirs', in: Aleksandras Marcinkevičius-Mantautas (ed.), *Vladas Putvinskis-Pūtvis: gyvenimas ir parinktieji raštai* (Chicago, 1973), vol. 1, 150.

[6] Liulevičius describes the dichotomy between the nation and the state as one of key features of interwar Lithuanian nationalism. See, Liulevičius, 'Building Nationalism', 235.

[7] Pūtvis, 'Memoirs', vol. 1, 150.

[8] Valdis O. Lumans, *Latvia in World War II* (Fordham, 2006), 27.

Lithuania, Latvia and Estonia had to turn back the advance of the Red Army, which occupied more than half of their territories. The situation in Latvia was even worse, as Latvians in June 1919 had to face not only the Reds but also Baltic Germans (*Landeswehr*) and German *Freikorps*. With the help of the Estonians, this German threat was eliminated in the battle of Wenden on 23 July 1919. In the battle combined forces of Latvians and Estonians defeated the Germans thus ending their domination in Latvia. To make things even more chaotic, between July and December 1919, Latvia and Lithuania also had to defend themselves against an invasion of the German-White Russian troops of General Pavel Bermondt-Avalov. Finally, in August 1920, the Poles, in pursuit of the retreating Red Army, launched an attack against Lithuania which led to their capture of Vilnius on 8 October. The respite for Estonians came only in December 1919, for Lithuanians in July 1920 and for Latvians in August 1920, after each signed separate peace treaties with Soviet Russia.[9]

Unsurprisingly, this expanding military action demanded the mobilization of all available economic and human resources. Yet the militarization of citizenries was also deeply immersed in the Great War experience of the Balts. The Baltic societies have been exposed to military mobilizations, marching armies, mass evacuations and military violence from 1914.[10] Overall, more than 64,000 Lithuanians and 100,000 Estonians were drafted into the Russian imperial army (of those 11,000 and 10,000 were killed in action).[11] The number of drafted Latvians was even higher reaching 130,000, as Russia mobilized Latvian riflemen to defend against the advancing Germans in 1915–17.[12] Moreover, Lithuania and almost half of Latvia spent most of the war under the German military occupation regime with its harsh policies of requisitions and economic exploitation. Germans captured the whole of Estonia only as late as February 1918.

The Bolshevik Revolution with its military slogans of the 'class war' came as another powerful source of military radicalism which found a particularly strong reception in Latvia. It was reflected in Soviet Russia's attempt to instil short-lived Bolshevik governments in each of the Baltic countries during 1918–19.[13] Meanwhile, between 1918 and 1921 the mass return of more than 200,000 First World War refugees from Russia to Lithuania and almost 400,000 from Russia to Latvia gave these nation-states an opportunity to tap their feelings of anxiety and political radicalism.[14]

[9] For a brief overview of the 1918–20 period of the history of the Baltic see Georg von Rauch, *The Baltic States: The Years of Independence: Estonia, Latvia, Lithuania, 1917–1940* (London, 1995).

[10] Military violence came to Estonia only in 1918.

[11] Vytautas Lesčius, *Lietuvos kariuomenė, 1918–1920* (Vilnius, 1998), 19.

[12] Andrew Parrott, 'The Baltic States from 1914 to 1923: The First World War and the Wars of Independence', *Baltic Defense Review* 8 (2002), 147.

[13] The Lithuanian-Belorussian Soviet Republic (LitBel) lasted from February to August 1919. The Latvian and Estonian Soviet republics survived until late 1919.

[14] On the impact of the refugee movement on the state-making processes in the former Russian Empire see, Nick Baron and Peter Gatrell (eds.), *Homelands: War, Population Displacement and Statehood in the East-West Borderlands, 1918–1924* (London, 2004), 74–98.

THE ORIGINS OF BALTIC PARAMILITARISM

The roots of the *Kaitseliit* in Estonia, the *Aizsargi* in Latvia, and the *Šauliai* in Lithuania, lay in the culture of the Great War. All of them emerged from the national militarism espoused by the newly created nation-states fighting for their survival during the chaotic postwar period. Thus contrary to the pre-First World War movements such as the Czech (and Polish) *Sokols* whom they ideologically followed (though the *Kaitseliit* was heavily influenced by the Finnish *Suojeluskunta*), the Baltic movements were more military. All three were created as civil 'self-defence' militias under conditions of war with an aim of providing internal security, but soon expanded into vast social movements. All three played prominent military roles alongside the regular armies between 1919 and 1920. Due to their quasi-independence, at least two of them (the LRU and the *Aizsargi*) also produced tensions and divisions within power structures of their states. Finally, all were gradually subsumed by the states as instruments of patriotic education and mobilization.

The *Šauliai* were assembled as a civilian self-defence force against the invading Bolsheviks in June 1919. Yet their ideological roots were formed in the course of the Great War. They can be traced back from the biography of one of their founders and ideological leaders Pūtvis.[15] Pūtvis was born into an old but poor Polish-speaking gentry family in 1873. He was one of the very few landowners from Lithuania who completely forsook his social and cultural ties with Poland. In 1896 he converted himself and his gentry wife into Lithuanian patriots.[16] In his mid-twenties Pūtvis reinvented himself by learning the Lithuanian language and making new friends among the Lithuanian-speaking intelligentsia of peasant origins. Most of his early life was spent working on his father's estate as an agriculturalist and trying to improve social conditions of peasant servants. Arrested twice in 1906 and 1914 for his pro-Lithuanian activities, during the Great War he was sent to exile in Central Russia. There he survived a painful incident when a mob of angry Russians wanted to kill him as a '*Germanec*'.

After his release from exile, in Novocherkask (Ukraine) in 1917 he became involved with a Ukrainian self-defence guard. In his memoirs Pūtvis claims that this experience as well as his pre-war studies of the Czech *Sokols* and the Swiss paramilitaries inspired him to create a paramilitary self-defence guard in Lithuania.[17] He also deeply admired the White Finnish militias (*Suojeluskunnat*) whom he considered an example of successful mobilization and patriotic education of the civilian population.[18] These were the key paramilitary movements that inspired him to pursue a similar path.

---

[15] The best source to study the history of the LRU and the biography of its leader is an edited volume of Pūtvis' writings: Aleksandras Marcinkevičius-Mantautas (ed.), *Vladas Putvinskis-Pūtvis: gyvenimas ir parinktieji raštai* (Chicago, 1973).

[16] Pūtvis, 'Memoirs', in ibid., vol. 1, 73.

[17] Pūtvis, 'Memoirs', in ibid., vol. 1, 169–70.   [18] Pūtvis, 'Memoirs', in ibid., vol. 1, 170.

In his writings Pūtvis openly acknowledged the transnational nature of 'the rifle-men's movement', as he called it. He traced its pre-modern roots and claimed 'it will live as long as the nation lives; it is forever destined to be a source of nation-hood and its defender.'[19] He became convinced that only those nations that are able to militarily mobilize their civilian populations in defence of their national homelands have a chance of survival and flourishing. Speaking of Lithuania he said that 'the riflemen's idea in our country is still weak, because the nation's conscious-ness, despite the existence of the state, is so far undeveloped.'[20]

Having returned to Lithuania in 1918, he started assembling his personal ar-senal of guns. Contemporaries recalled him always walking around with a pistol under his belt. His infatuation with guns was vividly described by his daughter Sofia who recalled that their estate was always filled with different types of arms owned by her father. One of his favourite pastimes was pulling out a revolver and taking a quick shot. Pūtvis light-heartedly used to call this exercise 'shooting a governor'.[21]

He established the LRU with a tiny group of like-minded intelligentsia as 'a non-partisan voluntary organisation' under the auspices of the Lithuanian Sport's Union with the key aim of 'protecting the independence of Lithuania'.[22] Besides military drilling, collection of arms and serving as a citizen militia, its other activ-ities included sport training, patriotic education and agitation. Initially, like the Czech *Sokols*, registered as a sport society, the LRU was made up only of a small band of intellectuals and state bureaucrats (about 30), mostly Pūtvis' relatives and acquaintances. The idea of arming state employees was approved of in government circles, since in May 1919 the Bolsheviks still threatened Lithuania. Every week 'the battalion of intellectuals' would gather in a local park to exercise and to learn a military drill.[23] Pūtvis described the high-spirit of these early meetings: 'we worked like amateurs but with the desire not for a salary or career but to help our state. This was the psychology of volunteer soldiers, not state bureaucrats.'[24]

The ideology of the *Šauliai* was based on Pūtvis' views on the incompatible relationship between the nation and the state. He claimed that 'the major problem of the national idea is the state; and the biggest mistake is that this idea is being expressed in all its forms only through the state.'[25] Although he believed 'a good state is necessary for the nation', he saw the state as a replaceable structure that can be lost and recreated anew. What could not be replaced was a national spirit, the will of the nation. In his view, the aim of the *Šauliai* was to protect and generate

---

[19] Pūtvis, 'Memoirs', in ibid., vol. 1, 170.

[20] Pūtvis, 'Istorinis žvilgsnis į šauliškumą' in ibid., vol. 2, 108.

[21] Memoir of Sofia Pūtvytė, in: Marcinkevičius-Mantautas (ed.), *Vladas Putvinskis-Pūtvis: gyveni-mas ir parinktieji raštai* (Chicago, 1973), vol. 1, 114.

[22] 'The Main Statute of the LRU' in Lithuanian Central State Archive, Fond 561, Section 2, File 2, 3.

[23] Besides this name, the early members also called it 'the Iron Battalion'. See Marcinkevičius-Mantautas (ed.), *Vladas Putvinskis-Pūtvis,* vol. 1, 141.

[24] Pūtvis, 'Memoirs', vol. 1, 150.

[25] Pūtvis, 'Idėjyno vieningumas', in: Marcinkevičius-Mantautas (ed.), *Vladas Putvinskis-Pūtvis,* vol. 2, 11.

this national spirit. His Herderian view of nationhood was also strengthened by the belief that the *Šauliai* should be a spiritual elite of the Lithuanian nation. He explained this by the fact that Lithuanians had lost their aristocracy to the Poles in the course of history. Overall, the elitism of this early circle reflected the situation in the countryside where state structures remained rather weak and the local population needed to be convinced to support the Kaunas government.[26]

Unlike the *Šauliai* who were born as a result of the private efforts of a small group of state clerks and intellectuals, the *Aizsargi* and the *Kaitseliit* were established as government-led initiatives. The *Aizsargi* came into being on 30 March 1919 on the order of the head of the Latvian provisional government, Karlis Ulmanis. The *Kaitseliit* were founded by the Estonian government on 11 November 1918 and made directly responsible to a minister of defence. The *Kaitseliit* emerged on the basis of the *Omakaitse* ('Home Guard'), the militia organization that was founded in 1917 to protect the Estonian population from the revolutionary disorder. In 1918 the German occupation authorities outlawed the *Omakaitse* due to its support of the Estonian independence which was proclaimed just before the German takeover in February 1918.

EXPANSION THROUGH WARFARE

It seemed that after the removal of the direct Bolshevik threat to Kaunas in late summer 1919 the *Šauliai* had lost their initial sense of purpose. At one point only Pūtvis and his three most devout followers gathered in the park for their usual military training.[27] Yet in August Pūtvis managed to reinvent the *Šauliai* by drafting an expanded version of their statute and by making a decision to transform them into an independent paramilitary organization with a central apparatus, permanent membership and regional branches. In October 1919 the defence minister Povilas Žadeikis confirmed their independent status and pledged the army's support. Soon the *Šauliai's* civilian clothing was replaced with military uniforms. Their arms were purchased from members' personal savings or secured from the army. Pūtvis rallied his supporters by calling for their spiritual reawakening and by urging to create 'a new type of defender of Lithuania, a citizen-soldier.'[28]

Another powerful impulse to renewal was an attempt of the Polish Military Organization (POW) to overthrow the Kaunas government on 28–29 August 1919. During these days the armed *Šauliai* took to the streets guarding government buildings and conducting searches of POW members. From now on an anti-Polish stance became one of the most visible features of their programme. Their anti-Bolshevism had been gradually replaced by their anti-Polish propaganda as

---

[26] This was reflected in the fact that a first military draft of all Lithuanian males on 13 February 1919 resulted in a high evasion rate: of 17,400 called to the service only 6,800 were enlisted and 4,800 did not show up at all. See Vytautas Lesčius, *Lietuvos Kariuomenė, 1918–1920* (Vilnius, 1998), 158.

[27] Jonas Matusas, *Lietuvos šaulių sąjungos istorija* (Vilnius, 1992), 12.

[28] Memoir of Mikas Mikelkevičius, in: Marcinkevičius-Mantautas (ed.), *Vladas Putvinskis-Pūtvis*, vol. 1, 157.

Lithuania successfully pushed back the invading Red troops and became involved in the military conflict with Poland. Thus in 1923 the key newspaper of the LRU *Trimitas* ('The Trumpet') rhetorically announced: 'Lithuanian, who is your greatest enemy? The Pole!'[29]

The invasion of Bermondt-Avalov into North Lithuania in July 1919 and the continuing presence of Bolsheviks (they still occupied Eastern Lithuania) ignited an armed resistance movement among the local Lithuanian peasantry. Starting from late summer of 1919 various partisan and self-defence units sprang up in Šiauliai, Panevėžys, Seda, Pasvalys, Joniškėlis and elsewhere. By the autumn there were about 30 partisan units in northern Lithuania alone.[30] Initially their ties with Kaunas were weak: most operated as independent groups trying to disrupt Bolshevik and German communications and to protect local peasants from requisitions and brigandage.[31]

The *Šauliai* stepped in as an umbrella organization for these units and as their self-proclaimed liaison with the government and the army. Individual members of the LRU were sent out to various towns to organize partisan activities, to gather military intelligence and to spread political propaganda among the population. Local cells established along a network of county administrations as citizen militias. By December 1919 the LRU already claimed to have 16 regional branches and 39 units.[32] The organizational structure of this resistance network remained loose and flexible: many of the partisans still acted as independent forces behind the enemy lines and kept only informal links with the LRU leadership based in Kaunas.

However, the military significance of these LRU partisan bands should not be underestimated. They actively fought the enemy along with the national army in operations such as the battle for the town of Šauliai in November 1919.[33] In the area of Raseiniai alone, Bermondt's troops lost 10 officers, 137 soldiers and 35 horses as a result of their activities.[34] The majority of the local population supported these bands since most of them were organized locally and were seen as self-defence forces against the marauding German and Russian soldiers. The *Šauliai* partisan bands were also active on the Polish-Lithuanian front. Starting from the summer of 1919 they became involved in sabotage and military intelligence in South-Eastern Lithuania. From the autumn of 1920 the Central Headquarters of the LRU supervised their paramilitary actions on the entire Polish-Lithuanian front.[35]

The Lithuanian army was able to use the expanding network of these paramilitary groups to its own advantage. From November 1920 the LRU established its special Information Bureau (*Žinių koncentracijos biuras*) to gather intelligence from

[29] 'Lietuvi, kas tavo didžiausias priešas?', *Trimitas*, 1923, no. 159, 3.
[30] Vytautas Lesčius, *Lietuvos kariuomenė nepriklausomybės kovose, 1918–1920* (Vilnius, 2004), 230.
[31] Lesčius, *Lietuvos kariuomenė*, 230.
[32] Marcinkevičius-Mantautas (ed.), *Vladas Putvinskis-Pūtvis*, vol. 1, 176.
[33] Lesčius, *Lietuvos kariuomenė*, 230–1.
[34] Ibid., 232.   [35] Marcinkevičius-Mantautas (ed.), *Vladas Putvinskis-Pūtvis*, vol. 1, 182.

various parts of Lithuania. The agency ran a network of more than 50 spies that supplied intelligence to the LRU, army and civilian authorities. According to one estimate, throughout 1919–22, it registered more than 1,300 'state enemies' and unmasked about 250 'anti-government activities'.[36] The main categories of 'enemies' included Bolshevik and Polish sympathisers, and saboteurs of government decrees.

If the *Šiauliai* were a voluntary organization, the *Aizsargi* and the *Kaitseliit*, at least initially, served as self-defence militias that compulsorily enrolled all males who were unfit to serve in the national armies. This strategy reflected a great shortage of military cadres that all the Baltic states faced in the early stage of their existence. It was also responsible for different rates of growth in their paramilitary memberships: in January 1919 the *Šauliai* had only 800 members, while the *Kaisteliit* enrolled more than 100,000 in November 1919 (of those 32,000 with military training).[37] During the last stages of the Baltic wars of independence, Latvian and Estonian paramilitaries equalled or even exceeded their respective national troops.[38] Their extraordinary growth came to a halt in 1922 in Latvia and in 1920 in Estonia when the majority of the compulsorily drafted males were relieved after the cessation of military action. After that the *Aizsargi* and the *Kaitseliit*, like the *Šauliai*, were turned into voluntary associations.

There is no clear-cut data on how many war veterans and soldiers joined the Baltic paramilitary formations. Yet there is little doubt that they played prominent roles in their histories (particularly in the early period of 1919–20). Since the *Kaitseliit* functioned as a military reserve for the army, most veterans of the War of Independence joined its ranks.[39] In Lithuania many local units of the *Šauliai* included ex-tsarist soldiers who provided leadership and their military expertise.[40] After the military reform of 1935, hundreds of the Lithuanian army reserve officers joined the LRU.[41] In Latvia, ex-soldiers made up more than 60 per cent of all the *Aizsargi* in 1929.[42] The presence of these war-hardened veterans made the paramilitary units a serious threat to the regular armies they fought against. In his memoir, a Major of the Polish army, S. Aleksandrowicz wrote: 'we suffered losses from their *Šauliai* partisans... captured and sentenced to be shot, they would not allow covering their eyes.'[43]

[36] Matusas, *Lietuvos šaulių sąjungos istorija*, 58.
[37] 'Defence League', in: Toivo Miljan, *Historical Dictionary of Estonia* (Lanham, 2004), 167. The number of the *Aizsargi* was in the ten thousands in 1920.
[38] The size of the Estonian army in January 1919 was about 13,000 soldiers. The Latvian army was 19,000 strong in the autumn of 1919. See Mati Laur (ed.), *History of Estonia* (Talinn, 2002), 214; Jürgen von Henn, (ed.), *Von den Baltischen Provincen zu den Baltischen Staaten* (Marburg, 1977), 367.
[39] Andres Kasekamp, *The Radical Right in Interwar Estonia* (New York, 2000), 96.
[40] Petronėlė Česnulevičiūtė, *Perloja 1378–1923* (Vilnius, 2008), 119.
[41] Stasys Raštikis, *Kovose dėl Lietuvos* (Vilnius, 1990), vol. 1, 403.
[42] 'Aizsargi', in: Arveds Švābe (ed.), *Latvju enciklopedija*, (Rīga, 2005), vol. 1, 29.
[43] Vygantas Vareikis, *Lietuvos šaulių sąjungos politinė ir karinė veikla (1919–1923)* (Kaunas, 1999), 62.

HOME FRONT: PROPAGANDA AND CULTURAL WORK

All three Baltic movements were founded as civil guards with the purpose of avert-
ing immediate foreign invasions and providing internal security and military support to the armies. All three claimed they were non-partisan. Yet all three clearly
served political aims of supporting their governments, conducting nationalist
propaganda and cultural agitation. Their memberships were given a new boost
after their revitalization as cultural and patriotic movements from the mid-1920s.
None of them lost their military colours (military drills, parades, guns and uniforms remained part of their identities), but their social and cultural activities
rapidly expanded in scope and ambition. As a result of this expansion, from the
late 1920s all three added massive women and youth sub-sections. In Lithuania
and Estonia in 1939–40 there were about 15,000–16,000 *Šauliai* and *Kaitseliit*
women and similar numbers of the youth.[44]

The transformative social character of all three movements was evident in their
ability to create massive social and cultural networks and, in particular, in their
efforts to infiltrate the young. After 1926, the *Šauliai* developed their youth association *Jaunoji Lietuva* ('Young Lithuania') whose key aim was patriotic training.
By 1940 it had almost 40,000 members. In 1939 the LRU sponsored 125 choirs,
400 drama companies, 4 theatres, 105 orchestras, 350 libraries, and 115 clubs.[45]
More than half of the teachers in Lithuania enrolled in the LRU in the 1930s. The
nation-building effort was also a key aim of the huge network of social and cultural
clubs and societies created by the *Aizsargi*. Two thirds of the registered sportsmen
belonged to *Aizsargi* clubs as well as 159 orchestras (with 2,000 members) and 229
choirs (7,800). Their Department of Propaganda held more than 10,000 lectures
between 1935 and 1939.[46] In Estonia the *Kaitseliit* was less prominent in social
and cultural affairs but more active in patriotic commemoration and in the field of
sports.[47]

By 1940 the *Kaitseliit* grew to more than 100,000 members (including women
and youth auxiliaries), while the *Aizsargi* had 68,000 and the *Šauliai* 62,000 members. Compared to the sizes of populations, this amounted to almost 9 per cent of
the whole population in Estonia, and roughly 3 per cent of populations in Latvia
and Lithuania. This seems to confirm the suggestion made by Ruutsoo that the
Kaitseliit was the strongest of these movements by its 'popular character' and had
the highest degree of social representation.[48]

[44] Vytautas Mankevičius, 'Historical Survey of Voluntary Non-Governmental Organizations in
Lithuania Before 1940', *Revue Baltique*, 15 (1999), 86; Kasekamp, *The Radical Right in Interwar
Estonia*, 95.

[45] 'Šaulių sąjunga', in: Vaclovas Biržiška (ed.), *Lietuvių enciklopedija* (Boston, 1963), vol. 29, 380.

[46] Ilvars Butulis, 'Autoritäre Ideologie und Praxis des Ulmanis-Regimes in Lettland, 1939–1940',
in: Erwin Oberländer (ed.), *Autoritäre Regime in Ostmittel und Südosteuropa 1919–1940* (Paderborn,
2001), 263, 274, 285.

[47] Rein Ruutsoo, 'European Traditions and the Development of Civic Society in the Baltic States:
1918–1940', in: Christiano Giordano (ed.), *Baltic States: Looking at Small Societies on Europe's Margin*
(Fribourg, 2003), 45.

[48] Ruutsoo, 'European Traditions', 44.

Differing social profiles of the movements were almost a direct reflection of the agrarian character of interwar Baltic societies. Their main support came from farmers: among the *Šauliai* they constituted at least 80 per cent in 1940.[49] In 1928 among the *Aizsargi* there were 95 per cent of peasants of whom 25 per cent were landless.[50] Only the *Kaitseliit* had a lower number of farm owners—34 per cent, while workers made up 12 per cent and state clerks 9 per cent of their membership. The intelligentsia constituted a meagre 6 per cent of the *Šauliai* in 1940.[51] If the *Kaitseliit* were quite popular among all key social categories of the Estonian population, the *Aizsargi* enjoyed the lowest legitimacy of all three movements among the working class. This was largely due to the fact that Latvia was politically most divided among the Baltics along the right-left political axis.[52]

All three movements were only partially dependent on the state's financial support, even if the degree of this dependence was variable. All three relied on the revenue collected from their membership fees and various social activities such as lotteries, fundraising events, clubs, concerts and charities. In addition, they also owned whole networks of 'Peoples' Houses', libraries and charitable institutions. Thus in 1939 the *Aizsargi* had 89 'People's Houses' in the countryside, and the *Šauliai* 72.[53] The most independent financially seemed to be the *Kaitseliit* who collected more than half of their budget from membership fees, lotteries and fundraising events.[54] In 1927 the *Aizsargi* collected one third of their budget from non-state sources which seemed to be an average for the most of the interwar period.[55] *Šauliai's* fortunes were more mixed: in 1930 they received from the state a huge amount of 650,000 litai, but in 1935 it shrank to only 350,000. Yet in 1940 more than two thirds of their budget was collected from membership fees, public activities and émigré charities.[56]

The socially transformative impact of paramilitarism can be observed in greater detail in the case of Lithuania. Despite its self-proclaimed non-partisan character, the LRU openly engaged in political propaganda and patriotic agitation among different groups of the population. In fact, its entire ideological vision was based on the notion of nationalist mobilization that would reshape local identities and would transform the citizens from passive observers into active participants in state and national affairs. The mobilization of the home front was seen as one of its key objectives that spared neither effort nor resources. Pūtvis urged, 'in the time of war we have to protect the rearguard of the army…we all have to work together. All institutions, all citizens: women, old people and children, they all have to work,

[49] Biržiška (ed.), *Lietuvių enciklopedija*, vol. 29, 381; Ruutsoo, 'European Traditions', 44.
[50] 'Švābe (ed.), *Latvju enciklopedija*, vol. 1, 29.
[51] This figure does not include students and teachers who were active in the LRU. See Biržiška (ed.), *Lietuvių enciklopedija*, vol. 29, 380.
[52] Ruutsoo, 'European Traditions', 44. Yet there were some exceptions to this, as in Ventspils, where the local *Aizsargi* unit included 26% of workers.
[53] Biržiška (ed.), *Lietuvių enciklopedija*, vol. 29, 380.
[54] Ruutsoo, 'European Traditions', 43.
[55] Švābe (ed.), *Latvju enciklopedija*, vol. 1, 30.
[56] Biržiška (ed.), *Lietuvių enciklopedija*, vol. 29, 380.

they all have to know their place'.[57] It was an open call for nationalization of the whole society, the goal that the pre-First World War Lithuanian intelligentsia had struggled to accomplish.[58]

To achieve their aims the *Šauliai* ran a large-scale propaganda campaign through their press and various types of publications. Their newly established 'Section for Propaganda and Culture' took care of the expanding agitation among the masses. Since May 1920 the LRU had been publishing its newspaper *Trimitas* ('The Trumpet') (reaching 30,000 copies), while its popular brochures such as 'A Guide for the *Šauliai*' and 'The Idea and Work' were printed in editions reaching 35,000 copies.[59] The pages of their newspaper were filled with patriotic calls to the home front, political news, poetry, fiction and accounts of the heroic struggle of the army and *Šauliai* units.

The propaganda campaign amounted to nothing less than a cultural change that aimed to transform the lives of ordinary citizens by lifting their sense of national consciousness and citizenship. In their meetings the *Šauliai* paid particular attention to the preservation and transmission of national traditions, family values, sense of duty, discipline and work ethic. Patriotic lectures and discussions, military parades, and collective celebrations of traditional holidays such as the Feast of St John became regular activities of their clubs that spread out all over Lithuania.[60]

The statute of the *Šauliai* allowed women and minors to join their ranks. From 1921 some local units started developing special groups of the *Vyčiai* (the Riders), the youth subdivision of the *Šauliai*, to attract youngsters between the ages of 15 and 17.[61] Soon the *Vyčiai* became so popular that they raised concerns of teachers and education bureaucrats who even tried to forbid them in 1930.[62] Meanwhile, women activists were involved with the LRU from as early as mid-1919, mostly in home front duties as clerks, nurses and teachers. In one of his propaganda articles 'The Gallantry of the *Šaulliai*', Pūtvis claimed that the primary task of the male *Šaulys* is to defend the chastity of Lithuanian women, while 'the women must preserve their female dignity'.[63]

The expansive reach of the campaign targeted even minor groups such as alcoholics. The LRU leadership publicly lambasted the drinking habits of society among its members. Pūtvis urged the alcoholics to help the *Šauliai* by joining them in 'national work'. Interestingly, he showed his sympathy in their 'difficult yet heroic struggle to overcome their illness' and his contempt towards 'those who drink in moderation...and ethically legalize the use of alcohol.'[64] The *Šauliai* also

---

[57] Pūtvis, 'Kaip atsirado Lietuvos Šauliai', in: Marcinkevičius-Mantautas (ed.), *Vladas Putvinskis-Pūtvis*, vol. 2, 113.

[58] For the difficulties of forming the mass support for the Lithuanian national movement, see Tomas Balkelis, *The Making of Modern Lithuania* (London, 2009).

[59] Marcinkevičius-Mantautas (ed.), *Vladas Putvinskis-Pūtvis*, vol. 1, 183.

[60] Ibid., vol. 1, 183.

[61] *Vytis* (Lith. 'a rider') is a symbol on the historical flag of the medieval Grand Duchy of Lithuania.

[62] Matusas, *Lietuvos šaulių sąjungos istorija*, 181.

[63] Pūtvis, 'Šaulių riteriškumas', in: Marcinkevičius-Mantautas (ed.), *Vladas Putvinskis-Pūtvis*, vol. 1, 186.

[64] Pūtvis, 'Broliai girtuokliai—alkoholikai', in: Marcinkevičius-Mantautas (ed.), *Vladas Putvinskis-Pūtvis*, vol. 2, 266.

actively participated in the policing of the illegal moonshine making and smuggling all over the country, essentially serving as 'the moral police'.

Although the campaign targeted largely ethnic Lithuanians, the LRU also made a great effort trying to secure support among the Jews. In 1919 it published an address to the Jews of Lithuania calling for their active participation in the defence of the state.[65] Pūtvis appealed to the democratic rights given to the Jews and their sense of citizenship.[66] Yet there is no evidence that they joined the ranks of the LRU in any significant numbers. Contrary to the LRU leadership, many of the rank-and-file were openly anti-Semitic. In 1923 in Kaunas, Šauliai and other towns, radical members of the LRU and students smashed windows of Jewish shops and painted over their Yiddish and Russian inscriptions.[67] Meanwhile, in 1922 *Trimitas* declared the Jews to be 'a non-producing and degenerating nation'.[68]

The massive expansion in the membership (by April 1922 the LRU had grown to more than 9,000) resulted in a need to tighten political and moral control within its ranks.[69] In 1922 Pūtvis launched an ambitious internal reform of the *Šauliai*. It had to reduce the numbers of unruly elements that joined their ranks in the course of the war and to raise the moral qualities of their leadership.[70] For this purpose he started establishing 'elite cells' as examples of discipline and dedication. The aim was a moral renewal of the *Šauliai*. Pūtvis wrote, 'our strategy is truly revolutionary, but not mutinous.... We want to make a moral change in our life itself'.[71]

RELATIONS WITH THE ARMY

By no means were the *Šauliai*, *Aizsargi* and *Kaitseliit* the only organizations that represented national militarism in the Baltic states. Their national armies served as the main pillars of this ideology. The armies were not only military defenders of the nation-states but also the political, social and cultural institutions that actively engaged in nation-making.[72] In them new peasant recruits were instilled with national and civil consciousness and learned crafts and various skills.[73]

Yet the early development of these armies also went through a paramilitary phase. In early 1919 their chains of commands were flexible and undeveloped, officers were more numerous than the rank-and-file, there was no specialization in categories of arms, their training was poor and the equipment was pitiable. No

[65] The appeal is published in *Pagrindiniai Lietuvos šaulių sąjungos įstatai* (Kaunas, 1919).

[66] Pūtvis, 'Lietuvos piliečiai žydai', in: Marcinkevičius-Mantautas (ed.), *Vladas Putvinskis-Pūtvis*, vol. 2, 236–7.

[67] Povilas Gaučys, *Tarp dviejų pasaulių* (Vilnius, 1992), 73.

[68] Jokūbas Blažiūnas, 'Žydai—mūsų bičiuliai', *Trimitas*, 48, 1922, 20.

[69] Sigitas Jegelevičius, *Nemunaitis ir jo parapija. II knyga* (Vilnius, 2002), 727.

[70] Marcinkevičius-Mantautas (ed.), *Vladas Putvinskis-Pūtvis*, vol. 1, 202.

[71] Pūtvis, 'Šauliai, ruoškim gyvenimo perversmą', *Trimitas*, 13, 1922, 4.

[72] Liulevičius, 'Building Nationalism', 234.

[73] Vytas S. Vardys and Judith B. Sedaitis, *Lithuania: The Rebel Nation* (Westview Press, 1997), 42.

wonder that during the early period of 'wars of independence', the newly created Baltic armies had to rely on foreign troops and military experts.[74]

The Lithuanian Volunteer Army, established on 23 November 1918, was initially conceived as a voluntary force. Due to the lack of manpower, it was rapidly turned into an army of recruits. The core of the army was made up of the junior ex-tsarist officers, Great War veterans, who returned to Lithuania from Russia between 1918 and 1920. In July 1920 the chief of the Lithuanian army was an ex-tsarist captain Konstantinas Žukas.[75] Yet by May 1919 the army was turned into an effective fighting force of about 11,000 soldiers.[76] In Estonia only three of 90 officers (most educated in Russia) who organized the Estonian armed forces had experience of serving at divisional command level, while 70 had only battalion command experience.[77]

The growing popularity of the *Šauliai* did not spare them from the suspicion of those army bureaucrats who saw them as a cover for various unruly elements. Some officers officially complained that the *Šauliai* conducted personal revenge acts against the civilians, that they were completely demoralized and were involved in illegal arrests, requisitions and robberies.[78] Their operational freedom alongside the forces of the police often caused confusion and protests among the local population. As a result of this pressure, in October 1920 the government had to issue an order that forbade the *Šauliai* to conduct any searches, arrests and requisitions without an official order of the chief of the army.[79]

The tense relationship between the *Šauliai* and the army was further damaged by a military incident that occurred during one of the LRU meetings near Kaunas on the Feast of St John on 23 June 1922. The celebration that involved about 100 *Šauliai* and almost 3,000 onlookers ended up in a scuffle between a crowd of half-drunk soldiers of a local garrison and the *Šauliai* who opened fire and wounded five soldiers.[80] The incident received negative coverage in the national press and damaged the LRU's reputation.[81] Pūtvis' attempt to defend the *Šauliai* in the press was censored by the military. Moreover, the event led to an official inquiry in parliament where the Deputy Minister of Defence accused the LRU of staging the unrest. Other public accusations soon followed including of the dominance of Pūtvis' relatives in the central bureau of the LRU, its lack of leadership and suspicions of financial fraud. Pūtvis took the accusations very personally and resigned as the chief of the LRU on 24 July 1922.

The army's leadership did not like the idea of sharing the monopoly of state-legalized violence with the paramilitaries who claimed to represent the nation's vanguard. On the ground, there were minor misunderstandings between the LRU

---

[74] Parrott, 'The Baltic States from 1914 to 1923', 156.

[75] Leščius, *Lietuvos kariuomenė*, 90.

[76] Ibid., 162.

[77] Miljan, *Historical Dictionary of Estonia*, 109.

[78] See the report of Mjr. Laurinaitis published in Vygantas Vareikis, *Lietuvos šaulių sąjungos politinė ir karinė veikla, 1919–1923* (Kaunas, 1999), 68.

[79] Ibid., 52.

[80] 'Baisus įvykis' in *Trimitas*, no. 25, 1922, 12–13.

[81] 'Steigiamasis Seimas', *Lietuvos žinios*, no. 105, 9 July 1922, 2.

and the army, usually when the *Šauliai* tried to claim their share of military booty captured in the battle.[82] The LRU also disliked (but had to obey) an army order 5 December 1919 to register all its firearms. Yet more serious tensions surfaced when high-ranking army bureaucrats tried to curtail its public character and autonomy. This was clearly reflected in the attempts to censor the LRU newspaper in mid-1922, to redraft its statute, and to install an army representative as the LRU's vice-chief in September 1922.[83] From now on the military side of the LRU was completely under the army's control, as it was allowed to retain autonomy only in its social and cultural activities. Finally, in 1935 a set of reforms within the LRU made it directly subordinate to the chief of the army turning the organization basically into the army's military reserve.

From the mid-1920s the Baltic governments (and particularly army leaderships) increased their efforts to integrate all three paramilitary movements into the official military structures. Usually this was achieved by subordinating their paramilitary leaders directly to the chiefs of the armies, appointing army officers to their headquarters, imposing greater controls on the use of weapons, and attaching local paramilitary units to county administrative structures. By the late 1920s all three organizations were divided territorially, each being attached to local regional administrations. For example, the *Aizsargi* were organized territorially with units in each township (*pagasts*), grouped in 19 regiments, one for each of Latvia's counties (*aprinkis*).[84] Overall, these changes reinforced their highly hierarchical organizational structures whose most prominent features were the presence of charismatic leaders (V. Putvis, A. Krėvė-Mickevičius, A. Berzins, J. Laidoner) and close ties with the military and ruling establishments.

Of all three Baltic movements, the *Šauliai* seemed to enjoy the longest spell of semi-independence. Between 1919 and 1921 they functioned largely as an independent body. From 1921 their military matters were controlled by the army, and only in 1935 did all its activities (including social and cultural) come under the complete supervision of the chief of the army. In Latvia the army competed with Ulmanis for the control of the *Aizsargi*: after the 1934 coup they were removed from the Ministry of the Interior and placed under the newly created Ministry of Public Works, run by the leader of the *Aizsargi* Alfreds Berzins, a close confidant of Ulmanis.[85] The Latvian dictator patronized the *Aizsargi* at the expense of the army which only increased the tension between them. By the late 1930s the Lithuanian and Latvian paramilitaries were transformed into military reserves for the standing armies. Meanwhile, the *Kaisteliit* were seen as the military reserve for the army from their inception: from December 1918 they were subordinated directly to the Commander-in-Chief of the Estonian army.

All three movements also developed some connections with each other and, particularly, with the Finnish movement. The *Šauliai* and the *Aizsargi* kept friendly organizational ties with the *Suojeluskunta*, exchanging occasional visits with each

[82] Matusas, *Lietuvos šaulių sąjungos istorija*, 182.
[83] Marcinkevičius-Mantautas (ed.), *Vladas Putvinskis-Pūtvis*, vol. 1, 225.
[84] Lumans, *Latvia in World War II*, 27.   [85] Ibid., 27, 45.

other.[86] In June 1939 the leader of the *Aizsargi* Kārlis Prauls was met with full military spectacle in Lithuania to celebrate the twentieth anniversary of the *Šauliai*.

LEGACIES

The mobilizing impact of the Baltic paramilitary movements was one of the key factors in the survival of the three Baltic nation-states in the post-First World War military cauldron. Yet the existence of the large and well-developed paramilitary organizations with expansive social networks exerted great pressure on interwar Baltic politics and contributed to the early downfall of the short-lived Baltic democracies. In this respect the Baltics followed the paramilitary tendencies that evolved in post-First World War Italy and Weimar Germany.

The right-wing anti-government putsches that installed the authoritarian regimes of Smetona, Ulmanis and Päts were engineered within the military circles with close ties to the armies and the paramilitaries. However, of all three Baltic movements, only the *Aizsargi* were directly involved in the presidential coup of 1934. After it they became virtually a personal guard of the Ulmanis' dictatorship. In Lithuania the 1926 putsch of Smetona was prepared within a small group of army officers. Yet after the coup, the *Šauliai* enthusiastically lent their support to the regime serving as its political police and an instrument of internal security. Only the Estonian dictator Päts could not rely on the highly populist and hetero-geneous *Kaitseliit*: after the 1934 putsch their ranks had to be purged of thousands of socialists and the right-wing Freedom Fighters.[87]

Even if all three Baltic paramilitary movements claimed to be non-partisan, in reality only the *Kaitseliit* came close to this. All putsch organizers insisted that they were saving their state on behalf of the nation either from communists or right-wing radicals. In reality, the threat of a left-wing revolution was quite exaggerated, since all three Baltic Communist parties were already outlawed, and trade unions were small and ineffective. Nevertheless, the authoritarian regimes successfully used the *Šauliai*, *Aizsargi* and *Kaitseliit* to contain the Baltic ultra-nationalist groups such as the *Geležinis vilkas* ('The Iron Wolf') in Lithuania, *Perkonkrusts* ('The Thundercross') in Latvia and *Vabadusojalased* ('The Freedom Fighters') in Estonia.

Yet the darkest page in the legacy of the Baltic paramilitaries remains their involvement in the Holocaust. Although the Soviets dissolved the *Šauliai*, *Aizsargi and Kaitseliit* in 1940, and their leaderships were destroyed, their informal social networks survived. The ex-*Šauliai* were among the most active groups who supported the provisional government of Lithuania (LLV) that tried to reinstitute independence before the Nazi takeover on 23 June 1941. This political experiment was short-lived as the Nazis did not allow it to last. Yet the new government

---

[86] Valters Šèerbinskis, 'Intentions and Reality: Latvian—Finnish Military Co-operation in the 1920s and 1930s', *Baltic Defence Review*, 1999, no. 2, 126.
[87] Kasekamp, *The Radical Right*, 96.

discredited themselves by their unofficial endorsement of the massacres of Jews by the bands of the armed 'Lithuanian partisans' and the Nazis during the first months of the German occupation. On 24 June 1941 an LLV representative issued an order to all ex-Šauliai to remobilize in Kaunas region.[88] Many of the former *Šauliai* were among the most active volunteers in these 'partisan bands' that took part in mass killings, round-ups and robbing of Jews all over Lithuania.[89] Some of the ex-*Šauliai* even served in the notorious killing *Ypatingasis būrys* ('The Special Squad') in Paneriai (Ponary) where more than 80,000 people, nearly all of them Jews, were executed.[90]

The war record of the former *Aizsargi* was quite similar: many joined various local 'self-defence groups' that independently or together with the Nazis participated in mass killings, arrests and deportations of the Jews in Riga, Liepaja, Daugavpils and many other places.[91] The vicious Arajs' commandos, made up largely of Latvian volunteers, included many former members of the *Aizsargi* and the *Perkonkrusts*.[92] In June 1943 the Nazis approved reconstitution of the *Aizsargi*, as a concession to Latvian self-administration. Meanwhile, the Estonians managed to re-establish their paramilitary organization under its old name the *Omakaitse* ('Home Guard') in the first days of July 1941.[93] Yet some of the *Omakaitse* units also took part in the round-up and killing of the Jews. Allegedly, of more than 30,000 members of this organization, between 1,000 and 1,200 men participated in the killings.[94] Overall, the Second World War legacies of the Baltic paramilitaries are still little discussed and remain one of the most painful episodes of their history.

During the interwar years the patriotic deeds of the *Šauliai*, *Aizsargi* and *Kaitseliit* quickly entered the canon of local national mythologies alongside the heroic military exploits of the Baltic national armies. Their legacies of 'wars of liberation' were enshrined and commemorated in numerous publications, official holidays,

---

[88] Order No. 1 of the 24 June 1941 by the Kaunas Military Commandant to the inhabitants of Kaunas City and District, in Lithuanian Central State Archive, Fond R-1444, Section 1, File 8, 7.

[89] e.g. former LRU members were actively involved in the annihilation of Jewish communities in Jieznas, Leipalingis, Babtai, Salantai, Kretinga, Skuodas and Eišiškės. See Arūnas Bubnys, 'Holocaust in Lithuanian Province in 1941', a report published by the International Commission for the Evaluation of the Crimes of the Nazi and Soviet Occupation Regimes in Lithuania, available at <http://www.komisija.lt>.

[90] Some of the squad's leaders such as Juozas Šidlauskas and Balys Norvaiša were former members of the LRU. See also Czesław Michalski, 'Ponary—the Golgoth of Wilno Region', *Konspekt: A Journal of the Academy of Pedagogy in Cracow* (2000–2001), 45; Kazimierz Sakowicz, *Ponary Diary 1941–1943: A Bystander's Account of a Mass Murder* (London and New Haven, 2005), 12.

[91] Lumans, *Latvia in World War II*, 242–3.

[92] The Araj's commandos was a unit of 200–300 Latvian volunteers formed around a former Latvian policeman Viktor Arajs in June 1941. It actively participated in mass killings of the Jews in Latvia and other countries.

[93] Peeter Kaasik, Mika Raudvassar, 'Estonia from June to October, 1941: Forest Brothers and Summer War', in: Toomas Hiio, Meelis Maripuu and Indrek Paavle, *Estonia 1940–1945: Reports of the Estonian International Commission for the Investigation of Crimes Against Humanity* (Tallinn, 2006), 495–517.

[94] 'Phase II: The German Occupation of Estonia in 1941–1944', a Report by the Estonian International Commission for the Investigation of Crimes against Humanity (Tallinn, 2006), 21.

history textbooks, folklore, military cemeteries, monuments and state museums. Today the Lithuanian army and the *Šauliai* enjoy their separate history museums in Central Kaunas, the former capital of interwar Lithuania. In Latvia the Brothers Cemetery and the Freedom Monument, built in 1935 and dedicated to the victims of the Latvian war of independence, remain symbolic sites of national significance. At the beginning of the new millennium the *Kaitseliit* prided themselves as the patriotic guard involving 15,000 men, 4,000 women and 4,600 children.[95] The revival and continuing existence of the Baltic paramilitary movements after 1989–90 speaks about the long-lasting legacy of paramilitarism in the history of nation-making in Lithuania, Latvia and Estonia. Although their heritage from the years of Nazi occupation remains questionable, they continue to enjoy their privileged position in the collective memories of the Baltic societies.

CONCLUSIONS

Writing about the emergence of early structures of civil society in the interwar Baltic states, Rein Ruutsoo suggested that a high degree of similarity existed between the Estonian, Latvian and Lithuanian paramilitary movements. He argues that 'without this kind of "organizational resources" the Baltic nations could have hardly spontaneously risen up against invaders'.[96] Yet besides being 'association movements' that strengthened, as Ruutsoo suggests, the social fabric of the Baltic states, the movements also developed massive paramilitary organizations. The political and cultural impact of these paramilitary formations on the interwar politics of the Baltic states is still poorly studied. Moreover, their Second World War legacies remain, to say the least, controversial due to their involvement in the Holocaust.

All three Baltic paramilitary movements were produced by the ideology of national militarism that emerged in the cauldron of the continuous war. In Lithuania and Latvia the war started in 1914–15, in Estonia in 1918. It did not end in 1918, as in the West, but continued until the early 1920s. The key aim of this ideology was to transform the Baltic civilian populations into potential soldier-patriots. This was to be achieved by well-organized military mobilizations, propaganda campaigns and by the use of the partisan groups that emerged during the 'wars of liberation'. Thus the convergence of the paramilitary structures and the spontaneous armed resistance movements was a typical, if not unique, feature of Baltic paramilitarism.

Despite minor variations, the early history of the *Šauliai* and the *Aizsargi* (the *Kaitseliit* seem to be an exception) showed an uneasy tension between the nation and the state that emerged as a result of their uneven development in the postwar years. Paramilitarism was both a source and a reaction to this process. The state was able to share its monopoly of legal violence with the paramilitaries as long as its

[95] Miljan, *Historical Dictionary of Estonia*, 168.   [96] Rein Ruutsoo, 'European Traditions', 43.

own survival required the mobilization of all economic and human resources for the war. Yet the development of large-scale social movements led by the paramilitary organizations that claimed their allegiance to the nation or to one of its leaders, rather than the state, generated the hostility of the state's military establishment who demanded their subordination. By the late 1930s the Lithuanian and Latvian movements had lost most of their autonomy to the state.

Paramilitarism was also seen as an effective nation-making strategy that strengthened citizens' political loyalty, sense of patriotism, duty, and their readiness to wage a war on behalf of their homeland. By the late 1920s political leaders in all three Baltics were perfectly aware of the transformative patriotic potential that lay in these paramilitary organizations. They all tried to use them as tools of national agitation and patriotic education. Their paramilitarism was justified as the defence of the nation-state and its land, the latter understood both as symbolic 'homeland', contested political space, and economic resource. It was also seen as the defence of the spiritual-cultural essence of the nation against foreign invaders. Thus the ideologies of the Baltic paramilitaries were unimaginable without the stereotypical negative images of the 'Bolshevik', 'German' or 'Pole'. The first Soviet occupation (1940–41) was a key factor that radicalized the paramilitary formations and reignited their military activities. Their social networks survived the formal closure of their organizations by the Soviets in 1940 and contributed to the armed Baltic resistance movements during and, in particular, after the Second World War.

Yet, in its different forms, the paramilitarism of the *Šauliai, Aizsargi* and *Kaitseliit* replicated the patterns of the revolutionary and Great War mobilizations. By their reformist zeal and organizational structures they were indebted to the Czech *Sokols*, the oldest and strongest of the paramilitary movements in Eastern Europe. Baltic paramilitary leaders such as Pūtvis and others repeatedly expressed their admiration and intellectual inspiration of the *Sokols*. Yet, by their militarism, the Baltic movements were more similar to paramilitary formations such as the White Finnish militias (*Suojeluskunnat*) and the *Polska Organizacja Wojskowa*, POW. As a rule, the veterans of ex-imperial armies played prominent roles in their ranks. Overall, the postwar conflict added a military swagger to all of them making them more violent, structured, hierarchical and politically radical. Today the paramilitary movements are more remembered for their military exploits than their social and cultural activism.

9

The Origins, Attributes, and Legacies of Paramilitary Violence in the Balkans

John Paul Newman

INTRODUCTION: PARAMILITARISM IN THE BALKANS

This chapter will trace the continuities and discontinuities of paramilitary violence in the Balkans from the beginning of the twentieth century onwards. The importation of nationalism to the region in the nineteenth century created violent rivalries between various state and nation building projects. As the history of the Balkan wars shows, these violent rivalries predated the European conflict of 1914–18; paramilitary violence in the Balkans was not a by-product of the violence of the First World War. Nevertheless, 1917–23 is a pivotal period because it opened up the region to numerous outside influences and altered the contours of existing struggles. Battles fought by pre-war paramilitary groups entered a new phase during 1917–23, as ethno-nationalist goals also became a matter of revising or protecting the postwar settlements, and were thus linked to larger forces throughout Europe. Pre-war programmes became overlaid by Wilsonian or Leninist ideologies, again linking local paramilitaries to larger transnational networks, creating new constellations, allies, and enemies. Importantly, the disintegration of Austria-Hungary and the creation of a large South Slav state in 1918 linked previously separated regions and actors, creating new and expanded 'zones of violence'.[1] Even if the immediate wave of postwar violence appeared to have subsided by 1923, transnational networks of paramilitary violence can be traced throughout the interwar period. They would play an important role for revisionist groups in the 1930s, and during the Second World War.

---

[1] The 'Zones of Violence' concept is taken from the important Oxford University Press series of that name, edited by Donald Bloxham and Mark Levene.

ANTECEDENTS: THE BALKAN REVOLUTIONARY TRADITION

In order to understand the context of violence in the region during 1917–23 it is necessary to look first at the cycle of national wars and revolutions which were an important part of the region's history from the beginning of the nineteenth century until the eve of the First World War. As Béla Király has noted in his introduction to an influential volume of essays on the two Balkan wars, this cycle began with the First Serbian Uprising of 1804, culminated with war in Bosnia (1876–78) and the signing of the Treaty of Berlin (1878), and ended with the Balkan wars (1912–13).[2]

In this respect, the various nations of the Balkan region were each part of the same historical process: the protracted and often violent transition out of the Otto-

Fig. 12. Jovan Babunski in full Četnik regalia. Babunski was responisble for several post-war atrocities in Albania and Macedonia.

[2] See Béla Király, 'East Central European Society and Warfare in the Era of the Balkan Wars', in: Béla Király and Dimitrije Đorđević, *East Central European Society and the Balkan Wars* (Boulder, 1987), 6.

man Empire and into nationhood. The timeline is a useful heuristic tool, but it must be remembered that the Balkan nations were awakening and developing each after their own fashion, with a great amount of overlap and conflict. If defined in 'maximalist' terms, every single programme of national integration overlapped at some point with at least one other, creating flashpoints or 'zones of conflict' throughout the region. Nowhere was this friction more apparent than in Macedonia,[3] the last region to be 'liberated' from the Ottomans. Here Serbian, Bulgarian, Greek, and Macedonian nationalists held competing territorial claims.

As Ottoman control in the Balkans weakened, each of these states was concerned with 'nationalizing' the region in its own image through propaganda, popular agitation, and violence. Bulgarian and Macedonian autonomist interests, often although not always coextensive at this time, were represented by a group that would become known as the Internal Macedonian Revolutionary Organization (IMRO), founded in Salonika in 1893.[4] Beginning in 1895 the IMRO used small units of armed men, known as *čete* (comprising *četnici,* known by the Ottomans as *komitadji*), to agitate amongst the population and carry out raids against Ottoman authorities. These were also the intentions of certain factions within the Kingdom of Serbia, who, in 1902, established a committee in Belgrade that sent Serbian *čete* into the Ottoman Balkans to promote (or perhaps to create) Serbian national sentiment. Like the IMRO, the mission of Serbian *četnici* was to 'nationalize' Ottoman lands and their Slav populations, to raise a still developing national consciousness amongst the population. Serbian *četnici* who were active in Macedonia both before and after 1918 were often referred to as 'national workers' (*nationalni radnici*), they used violence against the Ottomans and against rival *čete,* but they also tried to promote Serbian interests through propaganda in schools, churches, publishing, and so on.[5]

Unlike other European paramilitary bands such as the *Heimwehren* or the *Freikorps,* Balkan *čete* were not a by-product of the First World War, nor even of the

[3] 'Macedonia' is used here as an approximation. Until 1912, the region was divided between the Ottoman Vilayets of Kosovo, Monastir and Salonica. As Mark Mazower notes, under the Ottomans, 'Macedonia was a region with no clear borders and not even a formal existence as an administrative Ottoman entity', see Mark Mazower, *The Balkans: From the End of Byzantium to the Present Day* (London, 2000).

[4] The organization went by various names throughout the period covered in this chapter. See Duncan Perry, *The Politics of Terror: The Macedonian Revolutionary Movements 1893–1903* (London, 1988), 40–1. For more information on the organization from a range of perspectives, see John Swire, *Bulgarian Conspiracy* (London, 1939); Kosta Todoroff, 'The Macedonian Organization Yesterday and Today', *Foreign Affairs,* 6/3 (April 1928); Elizabeth Barker, *Macedonia: Its Place in Balkan Power Politics* (Westport, 1980); Ksente Bogoev, 'The Macedonian Revolutionary Liberation Organization (IMRO) in the Past Hundred Years', *Macedonian Review,* vol. XXIII, 2–3 (1993); Andrew Rossos, 'Macedonianism and Macedonian Nationalism on the Left', in: Ivo Banac and Katherine Verdery (eds.), *National Character and Ideology in Interwar Eastern Europe* (New Haven, 1995); James Pettifer (ed.), *The New Macedonian Question* (Basingstoke, 2001).

[5] On Serbian *Četnici* from 1903 onwards see 'Četnička akcija', in: *Narodna enciklopedija: srpsko-hrvatsko-slovenačka,* 4 vols. (Zagreb, 1925–1929); Jovan Hadži Vasiljević, *Četnička akcija u Staroj Srbiji i Maćedoniji* (Belgrade, 1928); Stanislav Krakov, *Plamen četništva* (Belgrade, 1930); Aleksa Jovanović (ed.), *Spomenica dvadesetpetgodišnjice oslobođenje južne Srbije 1912–1937* (Skopje, 1937); Stevan Simić, *Srpska revolucionarna organizacija: komitsko četovanje u staroj Srbiji i Makedoniji 1903–1912* (Belgrade, 1998); Vladimir Ilić, *Srpska četnička akcija 1903–1912* (Belgrade, 2006).

Balkan wars. A tradition of large, organized paramilitary bands with coherent
political goals and official support was established at the beginning of the twentieth century. These bands were concerned with imposing their own national programme on regions still under Ottoman control and were in conflict both with
imperial authorities *and* other like-minded national *čete*. This latter conflict would
continue after the expulsion of the Ottomans from the region.

THE BALKAN WARS 1912–1913

Paramilitary forces were used by both Serbia and Bulgaria as auxiliaries to regular
armies during the Balkan wars, providing knowledge of local conditions and circumstances that larger national armies lacked.[6] In the brief interlude between the
end of the Second Balkan War and the beginning of the First World War, Balkan
paramilitary groups were concerned with more than simply expelling the Ottomans from Europe. Serbian attempts to 'Serbianize' Macedonia involved terroriz-
ing the 'Bulgarophile' population using *čete* bands, and also attacking rival
paramilitary groups. These attempts were met in kind by the IMRO, which on the
eve of the First World War was in the process of being reformed by its new leaders
Aleksandar Protogerov and Todor Aleksandrov.[7] Consolidation of Serbia's victories
and territorial expansion also met with resistance in areas with significant Albanian
populations.[8] In Kosovo, for example, annexed by Serbia during the First Balkan
War, clan leaders such as Isa Boletini and Bajram Tsur called for armed action
against the Serbs in order to enlarge territories controlled by Albanian clans. Others, such as Esad Pasha, looked more favourably on Serbia, even providing the
Serbian army with information about operations planned against it.[9] Serbian
troops sometimes responded disproportionately to threats here, and their attempts
to disarm, win over, or otherwise 'pacify' Albanian populations in areas gained during the Balkan wars often intensified anti-Serbian sentiment.[10]

Aside from the expulsion of the Ottomans, very little in the Balkans had been
settled on the eve of the First World War. In fact, many new conflicts had been
created during 1912–13. Richard Crampton has described the Second Balkan War
as 'the most important turning point in modern Bulgarian history'.[11] The defeat of
1913 created a powerful revisionist impulse amongst many elements in Bulgaria
and Macedonia, including the IMRO, and seriously undermined good-neigh-
bourly relations with Serbia (and later Yugoslavia) and with Greece.

[6] A fact noted by Leon Trotsky in his reportage of the conflicts. See Leon Trotsky, *The War Correspondence of Leon Trotsky: The Balkan Wars 1912–1913* (New York, 2008), 161–2. See also Vladimir
Ilić, 'Učešće srpskih komita u kumanovskoj operaciji 1912. godine', *Vojnoistorijski glasnik*, year 43,
no. 1–3 (1992).
    [7] John Swire, *Bulgarian Conspiracy* (London, 1939), 129–30.
    [8] See Djordje Mikić, 'The Albanians and Serbia during the Balkan Wars', in: Király and Đorđević,
East-Central Europe. See also Dimitrije Bogdanović, *Knjiga o Kosovu* (Belgrade, 1985), 165–76.
    [9] Mikić, 190–1.
    [10] Bogdanović, 176.   [11] Richard Crampton, *Bulgaria* (Oxford, 2008), 204.

The Kingdom of Serbia, a clear winner in both Balkan wars, had acquired its maximalist territorial claims in the South, short of an outlet to the sea. All that remained 'unredeemed' in 1913 were the Habsburg South Slav territories of Bosnia and Herzegovina and, in the north, the lands of the Vojvodina. Whilst it is true that a long-term goal of Serbian nationalists was the recovery of Serb-populated Habsburg lands (and had been since the nineteenth century), Serbia after the Balkan wars was hardly in a position to launch yet another attack on a larger foe. The country was still coming to terms with the material and human cost of the two Balkan wars, its army was little more than 'a peasant mob',[12] and much official energy was absorbed in efforts to 'nationalize' newly-gained territory in the South, a process which would continue throughout the interwar period.

Nevertheless, there were factions inside and outside of Serbia that sought a more immediate reckoning with Austria-Hungary. The last two years before the beginning of the First World War were marked by a number of failed assassination attempts on Habsburg officials and dignitaries carried out by members of the revolutionary South Slav youth. The assassination of Franz Ferdinand by Bosnian Serb schoolboy Gavrilo Princip in June 1914 was very nearly yet another of these failed attempts. In the event, it began a new phase of conflict in the Balkans.

1914–1918: VICTORIES AND DEFEATS

If the First Balkan War was fought to complete the process of national emancipation from imperial rule, and the second was fought over competing programmes of national integration, the First World War was at once a continuation of the goals of 1912–13, redefined by the international situation and overlaid by the fates, fortunes, and war aims of the great powers. As Barbara and Charles Jelavich have noted, the Balkan nations during the First World War merely 'desired to complete the process of national unity'.[13] But this desire, or rather these desires, invariably became interlocked with either the cause of the Central Powers or that of the Allies. The events in Russia during 1917 added yet another dimension to the war and its violent aftermath in the region.

Serbia's alliance with the Allies in the First World War was determined by its opposition to Austria-Hungary, and the enmity between Serbia and Austria-Hungary underlined the anti-imperial tenor of Serbian nationalism. The war against the Habsburgs became a war for the 'liberation and unification' of all South Slavs into one state (that is to say, the inclusion of the Habsburg lands populated by South Slavs into one enlarged Serbian/Yugoslav state).[14] This goal became the ideological justification for war against the Habsburgs, linking the current war to the anti-Ottoman struggle of the nineteenth and early twentieth centuries. Serbia's

[12] See James M.B. Lyon ' "A Peasant Mob": The Serbian Army on the Eve of the Great War', *The Journal of Military History* (1997).
[13] Barbara and Charles Jelavich, *The Establishment of Balkan States 1834–1920* (Washington, 1977), 284.
[14] See Milorad Ekmečić, *Ratni ciljevi Srbije 1914* (Belgrade, 1973), 80–112.

unexpected initial victories against Austria-Hungary ensured its popularity as 'gallant little Serbia' and reinforced its affiliation with the Allies. However, the putative incorporation of Dalmatia into a large South Slav state made an enemy out of Italy, which had been promised territories here in exchange for fighting with the Allies.

Bulgaria, on the other hand, fought against the Allies not due to sympathy with the cause of the Central Powers, but in order to regain territory lost to it during the Second Balkan War. Its entrance into the war towards the end of 1915 contributed to the defeat and occupation of Serbia, and the annexation/unification of Macedonia with Bulgaria. In Macedonia, the IMRO 'identified completely with the Bulgarian cause'[15] serving as a kind of gendarmerie working hand in glove to 'Bulgarianize' the region. The IMRO's role in nationalizing wartime Macedonia and its actions against the non-Bulgarian population meant that many of its leaders, including Todor Aleksandrov and Aleksandar Protogerov, were branded war criminals by Yugoslav authorities after 1918.[16] But Bulgarian policy in Macedonia, including its paramilitary aspect, was almost identical in its intent and execution to the Serbian policy that preceded it and the Yugoslav policy that followed it. Violence here, and to a lesser extent in occupied Serbia, was motivated by what Alan Kramer has termed a 'dynamic of destruction',[17] a desire not just to defeat the enemy militarily, but also to erase all traces of its culture, to destroy any evidence that it had, in fact, ever been there at all.

Natalija Matić Zrnić, a Serbian woman who spent the years 1915–18 in the Bulgarian occupation zone of Serbia, experienced firsthand the suppression of national life and violence that attended this 'dynamic of destruction'. For example, occupation authorities, faced with the problem of anti-occupation *čete*, detained men between the ages of 17–50,[18] followed by more systematic and targeted internment of Serbian priests,[19] and the introduction of a Bulgarian curriculum in the schools.[20] This was what the 'desire to complete the process of national unity' entailed in many parts of the Balkans during and after the First World War: cultural and physical violence was part of a systematic programme of remaking the national composition and character of certain regions.

But under occupation (Bulgarian and Austro-Hungarian), Serbia could also draw on its own paramilitary expertise and traditions. The Serbian High Command at Salonika was able to assist when, in 1917, a large Serbian uprising broke out in the Bulgarian occupation zone following attempts by the Bulgarian army to

[15] Rossos, *Macedonia and the Macedonians: A History* (Stanford, 2008), 129.
[16] The South Slav delegates at the peace conferences in Paris submitted a list of 1,662 'war criminals' residing in Bulgaria, 216 of whom were leaders of the IMRO. See R.A. [Rodolphe Archibald] Reiss, *The Comitadji Question in Southern Serbia* (London, 1925), 41. Examples of the violent 'crimes' committed by 'Bulgarians' during the wartime occupations in the region were a constant concern of the Yugoslav press in the period immediately after the war, not least because such elements were still considered a threat to security after 1918. See, e.g., *Politika,* 3 September 1919, 20 November 1919, 18 October 1920.
[17] Alan Kramer, *Dynamic of Destruction: Culture and Mass Killing in the First World War* (Oxford, 2007), 1–2.
[18] Jill A. Irvine and Carol S. Lilly, *Natalija: Life in the Balkan Powder Keg 1880–1956* (Budapest, New York, 2008). See also Andrej Mitrović, *Serbia's Great War 1914–1918* (London, 2007), 221.
[19] Ibid., 223.   [20] Ibid., 235.

conscript Serbian men. The policy was identical to that previously pursued by the Serbian army, which had attempted to conscript Bulgarians at the beginning of 1914 in Macedonia. On that occasion, the IMRO had helped people avoid the Serbian call-up.[21] In 1917, Serbian *četnici* were led by guerrilla leaders Kosta Vojinović 'Kosovac' and Kosta Milovanović 'Pećanac', the latter having been flown into Serbia from Salonika for the purpose of directing the insurrection.[22] IMRO leader Aleskandar Protogerov was reassigned (from Macedonia) by the Bulgarian army to assist with the counter-insurgency operations, which were met with harsh reprisals throughout the country. Under the umbrella of a European conflict Bulgarians and Serbs were waging a more ferocious version of the war which had begun in *čete* skirmishes at the turn of the twentieth century, and would continue after 1918.

The First World War, then, did not create the conditions for paramilitary violence in the region after 1918. However, it did alter and expand the dimensions of pre-existing conflicts. As already noted, Serbia's anti-imperial war aims gave an ideological continuity to the national revolutionary struggle waged during the Balkan wars against the Ottomans and in the First World War against the Habsburgs. In contrast to victorious Serbia, Bulgaria was yet again on the losing side in 1918, experiencing its second 'national catastrophe' and once again forfeiting most of its territorial claims in Macedonia to Serbia/Yugoslavia. The shock of defeat would convulse Bulgaria into revolution, and eventually violent counter-revolution; paramilitary groups would play a role in both.

If Serbia and Bulgaria were at opposite ends of the spectrum of victory and defeat after 1918, other parts of the region fell somewhere between these two poles. There was Albania, for example, a state that collapsed in its infancy in 1914 and was dismembered and occupied by almost every single one of its neighbours, not regaining its sovereignty until the end of the war. During 1914–18, a coherent Albanian national sentiment all but disappeared beneath layers of clan and regional interests that fought both for and against the Central Powers and the Allies, as well as with each other.[23] Montenegro too was divided in 1918. It had been part of a military alliance with Serbia from the beginning of the war until its surrender to Austria-Hungary at the beginning of 1916. The tiny kingdom was famously the sole ally not to be represented at the peace conferences, symbolized by its 'empty chair' at Versailles. In fact, the pro-independence forces that wanted to fill that chair were marginal; the real battle after 1918 was fought between two factions, the 'Whites' who favoured unconditional unification with Serbia, and the 'Greens' who favoured a unification with Serbia in which Montenegrins retained some form of federal autonomy.[24] Habsburg South Slavs complicated the situation further.

---

[21] Swire, 130.

[22] For a full account of the insurrection and its aftermath see Mitrović, *Ustaničke borbe u Srbiji 1916–1918* (Belgrade, 1987).

[23] See Jelavich, 316.

[24] See Novica Raković, *Crna Gora u Prvom svetskom ratu 1914–1918* (Cetinje, 1969), 428–9; Srdja Pavlović, *Balkan Anschluss: The Annexation of Montenegro and the Creation of a Common South Slav State* (Purdue, 2008), 153.

Their attitudes towards the collapse of Austria-Hungary and the creation of the
South Slav state were mixed. Some (such as those who were associated with the
revolutionary youth movement) welcomed the creation of Yugoslavia[25] and some
were even prepared to resort to violence in order to protect it. Others, such as a
number of high-ranking Habsburg army officers of South Slav descent, experienced 1918 and the creation of Yugoslavia as a defeat. Between these two extremes
there were many South Slavs who had been lukewarm or indifferent to the
Habsburgs' war, or who were suspicious of both Habsburg and Yugoslav authority
during the transition from Empire into nation-state.

ZONES OF VIOLENCE POST-1918

Perhaps the most significant developments in the region after 1918 were the disintegration of Austria-Hungary and the creation of Yugoslavia. The first development linked the Balkans to the waves of violence that engulfed Central Europe
after the fall of Austria-Hungary, creating a new 'zone of violence'. The second
development drew Italy into Balkan affairs as a revisionist state and a powerful
sponsor and coordinator of paramilitary forces in the region. It is helpful, then, to
approach post-1918 waves of paramilitary violence via two 'zones'. The first zone
encompasses the southern Balkan regions: Macedonia, Kosovo, northern Albania,
and so on, regions which had been contested before 1914 by rival Balkan nationalisms and would continue to be contested after 1918. The second zone encompasses
the Adriatic littoral, the Italo-Yugoslav border and 'Central Europe': Croatia, Slavonia, Austria, and Hungary, that is to say, all those regions in which paramilitary
violence was either in part or in whole related to the disintegration of Austria-
Hungary.[26] There is, of course, a significant amount of overlap between these two
zones, and, as we shall see, they were linked to each other via transnational networks and ideologies prevalent throughout post-war Europe.

ZONE 1: 'THE CLASSICAL SOUTH'

Of all the Balkan States, Bulgaria underwent the most turbulent transition from
war to peace in 1918–19.[27] The upheaval caused by defeat produced new political
constellations and even new paramilitary formations, such as the 'Orange Guard',
the agrarian militia attached to Aleksandar Stamboliski's Bulgarian Agrarian

---

[25] In the first decade of its life, the South Slav state was known as the Kingdom of Serbs, Croats,
and Slovenes, becoming Yugoslavia in 1929. For sake of brevity, the state will be referred to hereafter
as Yugoslavia.

[26] See Robert Gerwarth, 'The Central European Counter-Revolution: Paramilitary Violence in
Germany, Austria, and Hungary after the Great War', *Past and Present*, 200 (2008).

[27] The events of this period are covered in M.A. Birman, *Revolutsionnaya situatsaya v Bolgarii v
1918–1919 g.* (Moscow, 1957).

National Union party.[28] The militarized atmosphere of politics within Bulgaria after 1918 was related to the instability caused by the end of the war, and in some respects violence here corresponds to violence seen in other defeated countries such as Germany, Austria, and Hungary.

These groups, however, were dwarfed in size and ambition by the IMRO, which would become the largest paramilitary force in the Balkans in the postwar period. The activities of the IMRO's *čete* had been in brief abeyance during 1918–20. But the severe terms of the Treaty of Neuilly, signed in November 1919 and confirming Bulgarian territorial losses, meant the organization entered a new phase of an ongoing conflict whose objective remained the forceful removal of foreign elements and control from Macedonia. Beginning in spring 1920, *čete* of the revived IMRO started to cross the border from Bulgaria into Yugoslavia for the sake of carrying out armed raids against Yugoslav gendarmes and civilians.[29] These attacks would continue, to a greater or lesser extent, throughout the 1920s.

From 1920 until 1923 the weakened Bulgarian state and its political leaders stood in the shadow of the IMRO. This relative strength of the IMRO against the Bulgarian state was sensationally and brutally demonstrated in June 1923, when the organization participated in a military coup that ousted Stamboliski as Bulgarian prime minister. For the IMRO, Stamboliski's gravest sin had been his attempt to reconcile Bulgaria with her neighbours and with the new European status quo by relinquishing territorial claims on Macedonia. The agrarian leader was kidnapped, tortured, and then murdered by the IMRO. The group would later boast of how its members 'cut off the hand' with which Stamboliski had signed a treaty over Macedonia with the Yugoslav government (they also sent his decapitated head to Sofia). The agrarian leader paid the price for trying to separate Bulgarian politics from its costly programme of national expansion and from its pre-war association with the IMRO.

In Serbia, now part of Yugoslavia, the nexus of weak state/strong paramilitary force was reversed. The Yugoslav army, the nucleus of which was provided by the pre-1918 army of the Kingdom of Serbian, was by far the strongest conventional military force in region after 1918.[30] One of its tasks was to secure the borders of newly-formed Yugoslavia and to 'pacify' restive regions within those borders. In the South, this involved taking on paramilitary forces such as the IMRO, but also Albanian guerrillas, Kaçaks, operating in Kosovo and Northern Albania. Initially, at least, Serbian paramilitary units operated as auxiliaries to the Serbian army in these 'Southern regions'. *Čete* such as the 'flying units' of Jovan Stojković 'Babunski', a guerrilla leader active in the Balkan wars and the First World War, and those

[28] See John D. Bell, *Peasants in Power: Alexander Stamboliski and the Bulgarian Agrarian National Union 1899–1923* (Princeton, 1977), 149.

[29] From April 1920, the Yugoslav Interior Ministry reported *čete* crossing the border and clashing with gendarmes in Bitolj, Štip, Kriva Palanka, Kratovo, and other towns and villages near the Bulgaro-Yugoslav border. The attacks continued into the summer, and local authorities asked Belgrade to increase the number of gendarmes in the affected areas. See Arhiv Jugoslavije (The Archive of Yugoslavia, hereafter AJ), fond 14 'MUP', fas. 28, jed. 76.

[30] The Yugoslav army comprised approximately 100,000 soldiers. Compare this to the Bulgarian army that, according to the terms of the Treaty of Neuilly, was reduced in size to 20,000 soldiers.

of Kosta Pečanac, also a *četnik* and one of the leaders of the anti-occupation uprising in 1917, were considered more suitable for an operation which the Serbian
High Command euphemistically called 'pacification'.[31] According to one *četnik*
who opted out of leading such flying units, 'pacification' meant a free hand to
'punish as you see fit those who undertake any anti-state activity'.[32]

Despite the creation of Yugoslavia, the 'Southern' regions of Kosovo and Macedonia remained essentially a Serbian—rather than a Yugoslav—concern. The regions
were known officially as 'Old Serbia' (Kosovo) and 'South Serbia' (Macedonia), and
a policy of cultural and national assimilation was set into motion almost immediately
after the end of the war. Serbian leaders continued to consider these regions as they
had before 1914, that is, as integral parts of the Serbian national body in which the
process of integration had not been completed, and in which they faced violent conflict with rival programmes of national integration/assimilation.

As part of this assimilation, the Slav population of the area was declared Serbian,
and Bulgarian cultural, religious, and educational institutions were closed down
(just as Serbian institutions had been during the war). In the longer term, Belgrade
authorities began a policy of colonization which, on paper at least, favoured veterans of the Serbian army. One of the intentions of this policy was to promote a
(Serbian) national spirit in the region.[33] The territories had already been established as important historical sites by national awakeners in the nineteenth century: Kosovo because it was the location of the Battle of Kosovo Field, 1389, and
Macedonia, because Skopje had been the capital of Dušan the Mighty's medieval
Serbian Empire. For Serbian patriots, these regions were known as the 'Classical
South',[34] and the task after 1918 was to make sure the present-day reality matched
the classical history.

The Balkan revolutionary tradition adapted to this civilizing mission accordingly. As early as summer 1919, the Serbian/Yugoslav authorities decided that
paramilitary auxiliaries such as those led by Kosta Pečanac and Jovan Babunski
were not furthering the state's aims in these regions.[35] The army was eventually
considered a more appropriate tool for maintaining order within the region, but
četnici still had a role to play. A number of former paramilitary activists took up the
government's offer, made during the war, of a parcel of free land in Kosovo or
Macedonia and resettled there after 1918. They had the right nationalist credentials since they had fought for Serbian interests in the South during 1912–18.
Some former soldiers, such as Kosta Pečanac, Ilija Trifunović 'Birčanin', Stevan

---

[31] Pečanac's units were also active in Kosovo, see Đorđe Borozan and Ljubodrag Dimić, *Jugoslovenksa država i Albanci*, vol. 1 (Belgrade, 1999), 125.

[32] Vasilije Trbić, *Memoari, knjiga 1: 1912–1918* (Belgrade, 1996), 146.

[33] Đorde Krstić, *Kolonizacija u južnoj Srbiji* (Sarajevo, 1928).

[34] The term can be found throughout the various newspapers and journals published in the region
to promote the process of 'nationalization' after 1918. Examples of these publications are *Južna Srbija,
Srpsko Kosovo, Južni pregled, Vardar*.

[35] See Vladan Jovanović, *Jugoslovenska država i južna Srbija 1918–1929* (Belgrade, 2002), 104–6,
and Dmitar Tasić, 'Između slave i optužbe: Kosta Milanović Pečanac 1919', *Istorija XX veka*, 2 (2007),
122.

Simić, Vasilije Trbić, Puniša Račić, and Aleksa Jovanović also contributed to the cultural life of the region as teachers, politicians, writers, and so on. They formed societies whose purpose was to raise monuments to Serbia's victories during 1912–18, or joined singing or philanthropic societies whose intention was to alter the cultural and physical landscape of the region.[36]

The lack of security in the region due to continued Kaçak or IMRO violence meant that many of these men were not entirely removed from their roles as paramilitary soldiers. Indeed, in the early stages of the colonization programme it was even suggested that loyal elements, former volunteers who fought in the Serbian army, should be moved as quickly as possible into restive regions such as Kosovo.[37] Exemplary of this interpretation of postwar paramilitaries as guardians of Serbian security in the south was the Štip-based 'Association against Bulgarian Bandits' who demanded assistance from the state (weapons) in order to defend themselves against anti-Serbian forces in the South.[38] Such demands were articulated with particular urgency following a massacre of twenty Serbians at the colony of Kadrifakovo (Ovče polje), Macedonia, in 1922.[39] Indeed, it was reported that the most frequently heard complaint in the Southern regions was that colonists were not given weapons with which to defend themselves.[40]

ZONE 2: THE ADRIATIC AND CENTRAL EUROPE

Whilst there was continuity between pre-war and postwar paramilitary violence in the 'Classical South', the dissolution of Austria-Hungary and the formation of Yugoslavia at the end of the war created a new zone of conflict in the region. Here, Italy, which had designs on Yugoslav territory in the Adriatic, supported, even created, transnational paramilitary networks which survived long after 1923. In addition to this, the newly-formed Yugoslavia partially comprised lands formerly belonging to Austria-Hungary but which, at the end of the war, became a violent Central European 'shatter zone'.

The most immediate and largest manifestations of violence connected to the disintegration of Austria-Hungary in the region were the armed gangs of peasants, the so-called 'Green Cadres', which roamed the countryside of Croatia and Slavonia during 1918. The Green Cadres were a composite and amorphous group whose aims and intentions were, for the most part, less ideologically charged than many other European paramilitary groups active during 1917–23. The Green Cadres comprised Habsburg military deserters, local peasants who had fled conscription,

---

[36] Correspondence of some of these societies can be found in AJ, fond 74 'Kraljevski dvor', fas. 219, 220, 221.

[37] According to a suggestion sent from the Ministry for Agrarian Reform in September 1919. See Borozan and Dimić, *Jugoslovenksa država i Albanci*, 323.

[38] AJ, fond 74 'Kraljevski dvor', fas. 50, jed. 69.

[39] Vladen Jovanović, 'Tokovi i ishod međuratne kolonizacije Makedonije, Kosova, i Metohije', *Tokovi istorije*, 3 (2006).

[40] Krstić, 60.

and 'returnees', former POWs back from revolutionary Russia. In the eyes of authorities they were evidence of the 'Bolshevik infection' spreading to the region. In fact, communist ideology amongst the Green Cadres was diffuse at best: the 'cadrists' wanted to escape from serving in the Habsburg army.[41] The Green Cadres really belonged to the waves of pacifist, anti-war revolutions that engulfed Central Europe in the last phases of the First World War.[42]

The Green Cadres formed the largest cohort of ex-Habsburg soldiers involved in paramilitary violence after 1918. Nevertheless, a smaller group of former Habsburg officers of Croat descent who had fought willingly on behalf of Austria-Hungary until its demise resisted the transition of the South Slav lands from Empire to (Yugoslav) nation-state. Instead, they formed transnational connections with, inter alia, ex-officers from Hungary and Austria who were committed to counter-revolution after 1918. Over the course of 1919–20, these officers in emigration formed a 'Croat Committee', a propaganda council dedicated to promoting the cause of Croatian independence from Yugoslavia, and the Croat Legion, a paramilitary group.[43] Yugoslav authorities knew about the formation of these groups and estimated that they comprised about 300 men: 250 officers and fifty 'higher officers'.[44] Through making links with Hungarian and Austrian paramilitary groups, the Croats hoped to compensate for the small size of their own paramilitary force. The 'central European Counter-revolution', as Robert Gerwarth has termed this paramilitary network,[45] was a more formidable force than a tiny group of Croat émigrés cut adrift by the collapse of Austria-Hungary. Furthermore, the ex-officers were united not only through wartime experiences in Habsburg uniform (which evidently left an important imprint on many members of the Central European counter-revolution), but also through a desire to revise the peace treaties and reverse the Allied victory.

The officers' most powerful sponsor in the region was Italy, Serbia's wartime ally, which had entered the war after being promised territory in Dalmatia by the Allies, only to be denied this territory at the peace conferences.[46] In response, Italian policy in the region pursued a double-move, on the one hand attempting to gain territorial concessions by reminding the Allies of promises made during the war, but on the other hand sponsoring and coordinating anti-Yugoslav groups throughout the region. It was this second component of Italian policy which linked the two zones of conflict in the region to each other and created transnational networks of paramilitary groups which would endure throughout the interwar period.

---

[41] The report of an official in Zemun, in July 1918, is representative. He spoke of an encounter with a 'returnee': a Habsburg soldier who had fought in Russia, witnessed the revolution, and now refused to fight for Austria-Hungary. The ex-soldier promised that 'of all those returning from Russian captivity, not a single [soldier] will fight on the front, whichever front that may be.' In Hrvatski Državni Arhiv (Croatian State Archives, hereafter HDA), fond 1363, 'Politička situacija', kut. 3.

[42] For analysis of this revolutionary zone, see Tibor Hajdu, 'Socialist Revolution in Central Europe 1917–1921', in: Roy Porter and Mikulas Teich (eds.) *Revolution in History* (Cambridge, 1986).

[43] See Vuk Vinaver, *Jugoslavija i Mađarska 1918–1933* (Belgrade, 1971), 120–4.

[44] Croatian State Archives (Hrvatski državni arhiv—HDA), fond 1363 'Politička situacija', box 5.

[45] Gerwarth, 'Central European Counter-revolution'.

[46] See Dragoljub Živojinović, *America, Italy, and the Birth of Yugoslavia 1917–1919* (Boulder, 1970).

In Vienna, the émigrés of the Croat Committee and Legion were introduced to the Italian ambassador to Austria by Hungarian legitimists/revisionists, and via him were supplied with weapons from Italy for their putative 'coup' against Yugoslavia.[47] Furthermore, the Legion's chief recruiter, Stjepan Duić, a former lieutenant-colonel in the Habsburg army, was allowed to tour Italian POW camps garnering support for the Croat cause amongst South Slavs.[48] Yugoslav authorities also saw, with justification, the hand of Italy in their Southern regions. In the weeks immediately after the war, the Serbian army in Kosovo complained that agitation and an Albanian uprising were being backed by Italy, their supposed ally.[49] The suspicions persisted. In summer 1919 a report to the Ministry of Interior complained that efforts to disarm the population were being undone by Italy, which was supplying anti-Serb elements with 'Austrian weapons'.[50] Then again at the beginning of February 1920, the Commander of the Third Army division in Skopje complained that Albanians were being recruited and trained by Italians for anti-Yugoslav activities.[51] The Italian 'double-move' was in full effect in the case of Montenegro, as Italian diplomacy supported the pro-independence forces of deposed King Nikola Petrović and pro-federalist 'Greens' in the armed conflict against unification forces inside Yugoslavia. The IMRO, too, were beneficiaries of Italian support against Yugoslavia during this period.[52]

In order to understand the nature of these paramilitary networks and the role they played in the Balkans during the interwar period, we can turn to Patricia Clavin's metaphor of transnationalism as a 'honeycomb', a structure which sustains and gives shapes to the identities of nation-states, institutions and particular social and geographic space.'[53] Although Italy's territorial interest in the Balkans was restricted to the Adriatic littoral, its support of various small anti-Yugoslav forces, Croatian, Macedonian, Albanian, created a paramilitary network shaped not by geography, but by revisionism. This was the structuring factor that linked the Southern zone of conflict to the Central European and Adriatic zone of conflict, and tied together paramilitary forces of greatly varied provenance (Habsburg officers, Montenegrin federalists, the IMRO). Whilst channels of support flowed outwards from Italy, these groups also cooperated amongst themselves against Serbia/Yugoslavia, for example, the joint Macedonian/Croatian plot to assassinate King Aleksandar of Yugoslavia at his wedding celebrations in 1922. The operation was apparently planned by the émigrés formerly of the Croat Legion, and involved a Macedonian gunman and erstwhile member of the IMRO.[54] This structure—Italian support for Balkan revisionists who in turn cooperated with one another—was sustained throughout the interwar period. Yugoslavs watched Italy's diplomatic

---

[47] Vinaver, 120.

[48] HDA, fond 1363 'Politička situacija', box 5.

[49] According to a report from the Yugoslav Division of the Serbian army in December 1918. See Borozan, Dimić, *Jugoslovenska država i Albanci*, 211.

[50] Ibid., 309.

[51] Ibid., 533.

[52] See Stefan Troebst, *Mussolini, Makedonien, und die Mächte 1922–1930* (Cologne, 1987).

[53] Patricia Clavin, 'Defining Transnationalism', *Contemporary European History*, 14/4, 438–9.

[54] See The National Archives (hereafter TNA), FO 371/7679–8097.

manoeuvres before, during, and after the Paris peace conferences, and the 'revisionist networks' in and around their country were hardly concealed by those involved.[55]

Italy's threatening posture towards Yugoslavia was partly responsible for the appearance of unitarist Yugoslav paramilitary groups along the Adriatic and on the Italo-Slovenian border. In these regions, many saw Italy's postwar territorial ambitions as a continuation of their wartime efforts to expand into the region. The result was a sort of 'hardline' of anti-Italian, pro-unitarist sentiment along the Adriatic which added yet another layer of differentiation within the region and yet another zone of violence.

This was reflected in large paramilitary organization was formed in Split in 1921: The Organization of Yugoslav Nationalists, or ORJUNA claimed, with some justification, a heritage that extended back to the revolutionary wing of the pre-war South Slav youth movement. And indeed, a number of their leaders, such as Ljubo Leontić and Niko Bartulović had been involved in the pre-war youth movement. ORJUNA glorified both the individual acts of terrorism committed by the pre-war revolutionary youth (especially Gavrilo Princip's assassination of Franz Ferdinand) and the violence of 1914–18, the latter since it had led to the creation of Yugoslavia. It was this glorification, coupled with the palpable threat of Italy in the region, which spurred ORJUNA on to committing its own acts of violence after 1918. ORJUNA attacked communists, supporters of the Croatian Peasant Party, and retired officers of the Habsburg army. Former Serbian *četnik* leaders Ilija Trifunović and Kosta Pećanac both served as commanders of ORJUNA's military 'Action Units' in the 1920s.[56] ORJUNA were eventually supplanted by yet another militia group, TIGR (after Trieste, Istria, Gorica, and Rijeka, territories claimed by both Italy and Yugoslavia) which continued anti-Italian resistance in the region.[57]

Considered together, these 'zones of violence' show the way in which the Balkans were connected to the larger pattern of paramilitary violence and upheaval in the wake of the First World War. In the 'classical south' the fighting between Serbian paramilitary *čete*, Albanian Kaçaks was part of a tradition that predated the war and was linked to the specific circumstances of anti-Ottoman national revolutions in the region. It outlasted the Ottoman expulsion from the region because

[55] The leading Serbian daily newspaper *Politika*, in October 1919, reported on the 'Dark Forces' that were surrounding Yugoslavia, making reference to the anti-Yugoslav Croat émigrés and the support they were receiving from Italy. See *Politika*, 3 October 1919.
[56] See the main ORJUNA organ, *Pobeda*, 17 May 1924. Exact numbers of ORJUNA membership are difficult to determine. At its first congress in 1923, ORJUNA claimed to have 100,000 members, although historian Branislav Gligorijević notes that this figure may have soon dropped to as low as 2,000. See Branislav Gligorijević, 'Organizacija jugoslovenskih nacionalista (ORJUNA)', *Zbornik Radova XX veka* (1963). Ivan Avakumović gives 40,000 as the high water mark of ORJUNA membership. See Ivan Avakumović 'Yugoslavia's Fascist Movements', in: Peter Sugar (ed.), *Native Fascism in the Successor States 1918–1945* (Santa Barbara, 1971).
[57] See Boris Mlakar, 'Radical Nationalism and Fascist Elements in Political Movements in Slovenia Between the Two World Wars', *Slovene Studies*, 31, 1 (2009).

paramilitary groups had been just as concerned with imposing their own pro-gramme of national integration in the region as they were with expelling the weak-ening Empire from the Balkans. The 'internationalization' of these paramilitary conflicts as a result of the First World War exacerbated violence. This was partly because, in the name of peace, Serbia's allies such as Great Britain and France allowed war to continue in the region. More importantly, however, it was because Italy's unfulfilled territorial claims on the Adriatic led it to inflame and provoke existing conflicts. Italian activity in the region, in turn, drew Slav populated areas of the Adriatic closer to the new state of Yugoslavia, seeing in it security from Ital-ian territorial ambitions. TIGR and ORJUNA were in part violent manifestations of this desire for security from Italy.

Finally, the breakdown of Austria-Hungary and the vacuum left by that state linked the region to the central European zone of conflict, a zone populated by post-Habsburg paramilitary groups such as the *Heimwehren*, Béla Kun's 'Lenin Boys', and Hungarian counter-revolutionaries. The Green Cadres, the Croat Legion, and the Croat Committee were part of this Central European conflict zone, but also had multiple connections with Balkan paramilitary groups such as the IMRO after 1918.

IDEOLOGIES, LEGACIES OF VIOLENCE

When presenting their cases to an international audience, most of the groups cited in this chapter couched their demands in Wilsonian terms. The IMRO appealed to the League of Nations over the right of Macedonian self-determination, for exam-ple, claims that were countered by Yugoslavia. So did pro-independence Mon-tenegrins and dissident Croat émigrés. In most cases, Wilsonian self-determination was a new skin for an old wine, rather than a novel and emancipatory ideology which mobilized paramilitary forces into conflict. It gave groups like the IMRO, and later revisionist organizations such as the Croatian Ustashe a moral, legal, and universalist framework onto which they could hang their particular demands.

The other messiah of oppressed peoples after 1918 was, of course, Lenin. We have seen that Leninist ideology and rhetoric ricocheted into South-Eastern Europe via returnees of the Habsburg army. For these men, Lenin's promise to end the war made a deep impression, and it was primarily their unwillingness to continue fighting that drew them to him. A far smaller number of returnees did remain more ideologically engaged with Marxism-Leninism and they formed the nucleus of the Communist Party of Yugoslavia after 1918.[58] Nevertheless, their failure to foment a socialist revolution in Yugoslavia (when their comrades in Hungary had been more successful) can be attributed in part to the unwillingness of most

---

[58] On this topic, see Ivo Banac, 'South Slav Prisoners of War in Revolutionary Russia', in: Peter Pastor and Samuel R. Williamson Rr (eds.), *War and Society in East Central Europe Vol. 5: Origins and Prisoners of War* (New York, 1983); Ivan Očak, *U borbi za ideje Oktobra: jugoslavenski povratnici iz sovjetske Rusije (1918–1921)* (Zagreb, 1976).

peasant-returnees in the former Habsburg South Slav lands to pursue radical social revolution once the war had ended. Non-compliance with the Habsburg war effort caused revolution in the countryside in Croatia during 1918, and once the war was over, the violence became more muted.

But communism did enjoy mass support in Macedonia and Montenegro, as shown in the party's impressive gains during the elections to the Yugoslav constituent assembly in November 1920.[59] It seems that in these regions, voters chose communism in protest against the new regime and its violent excesses in the region. The Comintern would come to value the revolutionary potential of the region, and adopted a resolution that called for Yugoslavia's dismemberment as a precursor for separate South Slav national revolutions, which were themselves precursors to socialist revolution. This stance made Leninism a more promising anti-Yugoslav/anti-Serb platform than Wilsonianism.

In the case of the IMRO, the communist siren call from the end of the war onwards exacerbated an already existing ideological split within the organization between the 'left' and the 'right' factions.[60] Todor Aleksandrov's reconciliatory move in April 1924 opted to place both factions under the communist wing. The strength of this alliance was potentially very great indeed. On the one hand, the IMRO would benefit from the backing of international communism and, more importantly, 'the all-round moral, material and political support of the USSR'.[61] On the other hand, the USSR would have a potent revolutionary ally in the region. Far more than just a pawn on the Balkan chessboard (which is how it came to be seen by Italy) the IMRO was the largest paramilitary force in the region, and if united internally and allied to the communists, it could seriously upset the postwar political map. However, Aleksandrov's *démarche* with Moscow deepened divisions within the movement, and internecine fighting after 1924 resulted in his assassination and that of his 'successor' Aleksandar Protogerov.

The IMRO's 'turn to the left' may have been devastating to the unity of the movement, but in terms of international politics and transnational allies it made perfect sense. Moscow was a far better suitor for the Macedonians than London or Paris, since France and Great Britain were in favour of constructing a stable postwar system based on the Allied victory. In the Balkans this meant a strong and viable South Slav state in which Yugoslav territorial and political demands were given precedence. In the period immediately after the war this desire to support Yugoslavia had a twofold effect. On the one hand, Serbian paramilitaries saw their work in the Southern regions as part of a larger transnational effort to consolidate the inter-Allied victory and the new order in Europe. On the other hand, Allies such as France and Great Britain gave tacit approval to this violence since it furthered their own strategic interests in the Balkans. The records of the British For-

[59] See Banac, *The National Question in Yugoslavia: Origins, History, Politics* (Ithaca, 1984), 331.

[60] See Rossos, 'Macedonianism and Macedonian Nationalism on the Left', 238–9.

[61] 'Declaration of the Central Committee of the IMRO on the Unification of the Macedonian Movement of Liberation' in *Macedonia: Documents and Materials* (Sofia, 1978), 756–8.

eign Office show that the British were aware of this violence, but that they accepted it as a necessary evil.[62]

This legitimacy based on the Allied victory and the interests of the part over the whole contributed to the failure of consensual politics in Yugoslavia. Since governments frequently lacked popular support throughout the country, they turned instead to paramilitary and militia groups to prop up their support.[63] Groups such as ORJUNA, the 'Serbian Nationalist Youth' (SRNAO), and the postwar *četnik* movement became involved in the politics of the country by siding with parties and using violence to intimidate or suppress opposition groups, especially in Bosnia, Macedonia, and Kosovo. In order to understand the path of Yugoslavia from faltering democracy to dictatorship it is also necessary to understand the role played by these groups in the state's formation and development during the 1920s.

Did the *četnici* of 1912–23 take part in the anti-Axis resistance of 1941–45? Nusret Šehić, the outstanding historian of the interwar *četnik* associations, has found that whilst some did, many did not. Much of the manpower of the various Chetnik units during 1941–45 came from Serbian officers and soldiers of the Yugoslav army who had not surrendered during the defeat of Yugoslavia by the Axis. There were some aging veterans of the anti-Ottoman *četnici*, Ilija Trifunović 'Birčanin', for example, who, despite his age and physical condition (he had lost an arm during the First World War) fought in the 'Dinara Division' of the Yugoslav Army in the Homeland (the Chetniks) until his death in 1943. On the other hand, there was Kosta Milovanović 'Pećanac', who fought only very briefly against Albanian guerrillas in the South of the country before putting himself and his handful of men at the disposal of the occupation regime in Serbia.[64]

The links between the communist Partisan guerrillas of the Second World War and the communist movement immediately after the First World War are more tenuous. Although the Partisan leader, Josip Broz 'Tito' had been a Habsburg soldier (although not involved in any of the 'green' violence in the region at the end of the First World War), Yugoslav communism had been through many vicissitudes in the interwar period. The interwar regime in Yugoslavia had been very efficient in suppressing the party's activities, and Yugoslav communists were heavily purged in Moscow during the 1930s (Tito was a notable survivor). Instead of using veterans of the First World War during 1941–45, military expertise of the movement came from the so-called 'Spaniards', veterans of the International Brigades who had fought in the Spanish

---

[62] In the annual report on the Kingdom of Serbs, Croats, and Slovenes in 1922 the British Foreign Office noting the possibility of an outside investigation into continued 'Bulgarian raids' into Yugoslav Macedonia, wrote that 'It is imagined that the Serbian Government [sic]...would scarcely welcome a European commission examining its defective administration in Macedonia'. See TNA, FO371 8910-10134, Serb-Croat-Slovene Kingdom Annual Report 1922.

[63] See Nusret Šehić, *Četništvo u Bosni i Hercegovini (1918–1941): politička uloga i oblici djelatnosti četničkih udruženja* (Sarajevo, 1971), 164–71; Nadežda Jovanović, *Politički sukobi u Jugoslaviji 1925–1928* (Belgrade, 1974), 47–54; Sabrina Ramet, *The Three Yugoslavias: State-Building and Legitimation 1918–2005* (Bloomington, 2006), 58–9.

[64] His forces constituted a force of between 3,000–6,000 men, over whom Pećanac retained control until he was killed in 1944.

Civil War.[65] In both the cases of the Partisans and the Chetniks, it needs to be remembered that an entire generation had passed between 1917–23 and the beginning of the Second World War in the region. Many activists from the earlier period were now 'retired', that is, too old to be effective soldiers as they had been during and immediately after the First World War. Many others had since died.

However, the transnational network of anti-Serb/Anti-Yugoslav forces that Italy cultivated at the end of the First World War remained largely intact throughout the interwar period. So the Ustashe, the Croatian paramilitary/terrorist organization founded after the promulgation of King Aleksandar's Dictatorship, was to a great extent rooted in the first wave of anti-Yugoslav emigration that took place after 1918. Like early anti-Yugoslav emigration, the Ustashe comprised former-Habsburg officers and Croats associated with Croatian Party of Right (*Hrvatska stranka prava*, or the 'Frankists'), and was committed to overthrowing Yugoslavia by instigating an uprising of Croats against the state, or through acts of violence. Both manifestations of this anti-Yugoslav revisionist movement were supported by Italy, who provided the Ustashe with weapons and allowed them to establish training camps on their soil, just as they had provided material support to the Croatian émigrés immediately after 1918. Revisionism, supported by Italy, proved the most solid and enduring transnational network in the Balkans during the interwar period, and it is amongst these groups that the legacy of paramilitary violence during 1917–23 is most visible.

CONCLUSIONS

To a certain extent, violent attempts to impose an integral national programme onto contested regions in the Balkans shared many of the traits of the violent nationalizing projects of post-1918 paramilitary groups in Austria, Hungary, Germany, Poland, and Ukraine. As Uğur Ümit Üngör shows in his contribution to this volume, violence committed by Balkan paramilitaries against Muslim civilians during and after the Balkan wars was part of an attempt to remake the ethnic and national composition of territories, and was repeated throughout Europe during 1917–23. If Balkan paramilitaries and Balkan armies were able to expel the Ottomans from the region with great efficiency during 1912–13, nationalization of these regions was far less successful in the long term.[66] Indeed, the same paramilitary traditions that helped to expel the Ottomans from the Balkans also proved detrimental to the establishment of viable and democratic nation-states after 1918, which, ironically, was exactly the goal for which these paramilitary groups had fought before 1914. Paramilitary groups that supported the post-war status quo and Yugoslavia were satisfied with the results of 1917–23. Their revisionist rivals were not, and although diminished and defeated by 1923, they lingered on throughout the interwar period. Their time would come again, eventually, during the Second World War.

---

[65] Koča Popović, e.g, who commanded the First Proletarian Brigade of the Partisan army. See also Vjeran Pavlaković, *Our Spaniards: Croatian Communists, Fascists, and the Spanish Civil War 1936–1939* (unpublished Ph.D. thesis, University of Washington, 2005).

[66] When the communists came to power in Yugoslavia after the Second World War, they opted to abandon the failed interwar policy of assimilation in Kosovo and Macedonia in favour of granting a level of political autonomy to the regions.

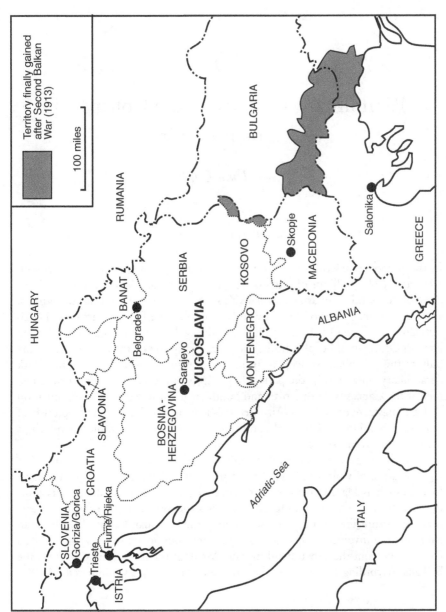

Map 3. The Balkans after the First World War.

Legend:

■ Territory finally gained after Second Balkan War (1913)

100 miles

10

Paramilitary Violence in the Collapsing Ottoman Empire

Uğur Ümit Üngör

INTRODUCTION

In the process of Habsburg, Ottoman, and Russian imperial collapse, between 1912 and 1923, millions of soldiers were killed in regular warfare war. But hundreds of thousands of unarmed civilians also died—victims of expulsions, pogroms, and other forms of persecution and mass violence. The Balkan wars of 1912–13 virtually erased the Ottoman Empire from the Balkans and marked a devastating blow to Ottoman political culture. The years 1915–16 saw the destruction of the bulk of the Anatolian Armenians, primarily (but not exclusively) by Young Turk paramilitary units. Lastly, the period 1917–23 is of great significance for the history of the Caucasus, both North and South, as it witnessed wars of annihilation and the massacre of civilians. All three episodes occurred amidst a deep crisis of inter-state relations and societal conditions, as well as inter-ethnic relationships between and within states.[1]

In all three episodes, paramilitary units played a decisive role in the initiation and execution of violence against both armed combatants and unarmed civilians. In areas such as Macedonia, the Pontos, and Nagorno-Karabakh these units committed acts of violence including large-scale destruction and arson of villages, beatings and torture, forced conversions, and indiscriminate mass killing. The Ottoman paramilitaries involved in this process were mostly but not exclusively unemployed young men from the urban demi-monde. Many of them were refugees from the Balkans. According to one researcher, at their peak the units numbered 30,000.[2]

---

[1] For four recent and different attempts to situate the violence of the period between 1870 and 1923 within a broader framework of modern mass violence as a result of disintegrating European continental Empires, see Benjamin Lieberman, *Terrible Fate: Ethnic Cleansing in the Making of Modern Europe* (Chicago, 2006); Donald Bloxham, *Genocide, the World Wars and the Unweaving of Europe* (Edgware, 2008); id., *The Final Solution: A Genocide* (Oxford, 2009); Cathie Carmichael, *Genocide Before the Holocaust* (New Haven, 2009). For a still useful overview, see Mark Levene, 'Creating a Modern "Zone of Genocide": The Impact of Nation- and State-Formation on Eastern Anatolia, 1878–1923', *Holocaust and Genocide Studies* 12 (1998), 393–433.

[2] Philip H. Stoddard, *The Ottoman Government and the Arabs, 1911–1918: A Preliminary Study of the Teşkilât-ı Mahsusa* (PhD dissertation, Princeton University, 1963).

Fig. 13. Armenian paramilitaries in the South Caucasus, 1919.

Their victims were Ottoman, Russian, and Persian Armenians and Syriacs, as well as Ottoman Greeks.

An ambitious undertaking would be to trace links between the above-mentioned episodes. Many studies of this kaleidoscope of violence have focused on their domestic dimensions. The Armenian genocide is often seen as a product of Turkish nationalist ideology or the machinations of the Young Turk party (the Committee of Union and Progress (CUP)). In a similar vein, the violence in the Caucasus has mostly been studied within the confines of Russian civil war history or Soviet studies. Without denying the importance of these frameworks, a transnational perspective might offer a new understanding of their genesis, scale and implications.

The subject of paramilitary violence offers a useful prism through which to attempt just this. I will argue that the collapse of state authority and functioning monopolies of violence in and after the First World War provided political elites and paramilitary warlords (a.k.a. *fedayis*) with a unique opportunity to establish or consolidate power in these post-imperial shatter zones. I shall focus on the roots and rationale of paramilitary violence rather than inter-state warfare of standing armies. How and why were paramilitary units established? What role did they play in the violence that engulfed these territories? What was the relationship between states and paramilitaries? I shall focus in particular on the relationship between victimization and revanchism. Research on other cases has suggested that traumatized and victimized people from one society who move to another can have a dual impact, destabilizing and radicalizing the domestic political

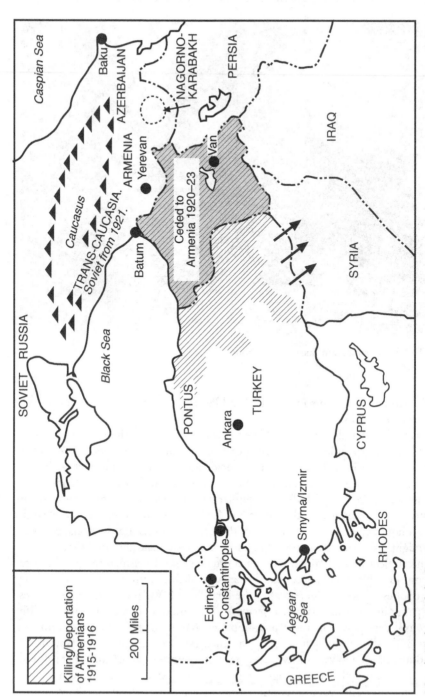

Map 4. Turkey and the Caucasus.

culture in the new society while providing paramilitary recruits for the its political elites.[3] Survivors of violence in one society can cross borders and become perpetrators of violence in another.

THE FIRST WORLD WAR AND THE ARMENIAN GENOCIDE

As explained by John Paul Newman in the previous chapter, paramilitarism in the Ottoman Empire had a long history. It became more and more prevalent in the Balkans in the late nineteenth century, as various groups fought each other in low-intensity civil wars.[4] Bulgarian, Macedonian, Serb, Greek, and Muslim bands engaged in skirmishes to protect their families and communities, advance ideological or religious beliefs or exact revenge for prior violence or perceived injustices. The Ottoman state grappled desperately with these conflicts and often resorted to paramilitarism and terror itself.[5] For example, whenever Muslim bands killed Bulgarians, they would leave a letter addressed to the local district governor that would read: 'This person has been killed in order to avenge the Muslim killed at such and such place.'[6] Internal correspondence of the CUP sheds light on how the Young Turks learned from the conduct of the bands. In an undated letter, Dr Mehmed Nâzım wrote to Dr Bahaeddin Shakir about a certain Hasan the Sailor:

> Hasan the Sailor's program is as follows: to slay ten Bulgarians for each murdered Muslim. He does not differentiate in order to fulfill his goal. No Bulgarian, man, woman, old or young, can escape alive from the axe of Hasan the Sailor until he reaches the number of ten. Hasan the Sailor has become the god of a few districts and Bulgarians tremble when they hear his name... The impact of these bands on the Bulgarians is greater than the impact of one hundred thousand troops dispatched by the administration.[7]

Spreading terror by killing civilians was thus seen as a legitimate method to secure submission of a potentially recalcitrant population.

A watershed in the nature of paramilitary violence in this period came with the Young Turk coup d'état of 23 January 1913. In the following months, the CUP, no longer wielding power from behind the scenes, would gradually impose a violent dictatorship upon the Empire. Enver reconquered Edirne, promoted himself to general, and became Minister of War. The new cabinet was led by Talaat, who went from party boss to Interior Minister. Political violence became commonplace. Assassinations were carried out by the paramilitary gangsters loyal to factions

---

[3] István I. Mócsy, *The Uprooted: Hungarian Refugees and their Impact on Hungary's Domestic Politics, 1918–1921* (New York, 1983).

[4] For a brief treatment see Giorgio V. Brandolini, *Low Intensity Conflicts* (Bergamo, 2002).

[5] Janet Klein, *Power in the Periphery: The Hamidiye Light Cavalry and the Struggle over Ottoman Kurdistan, 1890–1914* (PhD thesis, University of Princeton, 2002).

[6] Hanioğlu, *Preparation for a Revolution*, 223.

[7] Dr Mehmed Nâzım to Dr Bahaeddin Shakir, undated letter, quoted in ibid., 223.

around Talaat and especially Enver. Hüseyin Cahit (1875–1957), publisher of one of the most important newspapers of the period, witnessed one of these political murders as a hitman loyal to Enver Pasha shot a man in his presence for expressing criticism.[8] The Young Turks became the propelling force behind state terror. The *fedayi* paramilitaries who used to live as outlaws now rose to state power. They gained legitimacy and transposed the violence of their political culture to Anatolia. Their experience of paramilitary warfare in the Rumelian countryside was transplanted into the offices of the Ottoman government, which brutalized the state.

After January 1913, the doctors Mehmed Nâzım and Bahaeddin Shakir began merging the then relatively disunited and independent paramilitary forces into the 'Special Organization' (*Teşkilât-ı Mahsusa*). There were five groups of Ottoman paramilitary forces during the First World War. First, the rural gendarmerie (*jandarma*) functioned in both static units and mobile units. Trained to modern military standards and led by a professional officer corps, the gendarmerie was charged with keeping order in the countryside. Second was the tribal cavalry (*aşiret alayları*) that had grown out of the 29 Kurdish and Circassian cavalry regiments. These units were led by tribal chieftains and were responsible for various internal security duties. A third group were the 'volunteers' (*gönüllüler*), made up of Islamic ethnic groups from outside the Ottoman Empire. The majority of this group consisted of Turkish refugees from the Balkans, often vindictive and ready for battle. Fourth came the above mentioned 'Special Organization' (*Teşkilat-ı Mahsusa*), initially an intelligence service that sought to foment insurrection in enemy territory and conduct espionage, counterespionage, and counterinsurgency. The command structure of this organization would now absorb the other groups.[9]

Finally, a fifth group were simply called 'bands' (*çete*), a hodgepodge of non-military guerrilla groups not fully subject to centralized command and control but often acting as paramilitary wings of individual Young Turk leaders. Poor, unemployed young men, in Turkish named 'vagrants' (*serseri*) or 'roughnecks' (*kabadayı*), from the urban demimonde of louche coffee shops and criminal networks, were particularly receptive to recruitment into this group. Their contribution to regular warfare, counterinsurgency operations, and various 'dirty jobs' was deemed vital. Their rewards would consist of direct payments or carte blanche to pillage. As high-ranking Young Turk officials were implicated by association with their crimes, many of these ruffians enjoyed protection.[10] Apart from this bottom-up perspective, a top-down perspective on paramilitary units emerged: the CUP began drawing up paramilitary formations by releasing ordinary criminal convicts from prisons. Talaat and Enver oversaw the operation, administrated by Dr Bahaeddin Shakir and Dr Nâzım and organizationally supported by the party's large network in the provinces.

In August 1914, Talaat corresponded with the party secretary for Erzurum, Filibeli Ahmet Hilmi (1885–1926), himself a refugee from Plovdiv. Hilmi suggested

[8] Hüseyin Cahit Yalçın, *Siyasal Anılar* (Istanbul, 1976), 170.
[9] *Türk Silahlı Kuvvetleri Tarihi* (Ankara, 1971), vol. III, section 6, *1908–1920*, 129–240.
[10] Ryan Gingeras, *Sorrowful Shores: Violence, Ethnicity, and the End of the Ottoman Empire 1912–1923* (Oxford, 2009), 6, 51.

the release of convicts from the central prison of Trabzon and their enlistment into paramilitary units under the command of regular army officers. Particular preference would be given to prisoners 'who have a reputation for leading outlaw gangs'. Talaat's reply was affirmative: 'those people imprisoned who are needed for the irregular units will be released and a list will be prepared and sent'.[11] To facilitate the formation of these units, the Justice Ministry issued a special amnesty through a temporary law that became permanent in 1916.[12] As a result of these measures, thousands of criminals were released from Ottoman prisons and drafted into paramilitary units. The convicts, named 'savages and criminals' even by CUP officials,[13] were very often local outlaws and bandits who had committed crimes such as theft, racketeering, or manslaughter. According to one source, they were drilled in Istanbul for one week before being deployed in various regions: 'These gangs were composed of murderers and thieves who had been released from incarceration. They received a week of instruction in the courtyard of the War Ministry and were then sent to the Caucasus border through the agency of the Special Organization.'[14] Province by province, paramilitary units emerged as the clouds of war gathered over Anatolia.

From 11 November 1914 on, the Ottoman Empire was officially at war with Russia, France, and Britain. According to a recent study, the CUP entrance into the war was 'part of a strategy to achieve long-term security, economic development, and, eventually, national recovery'.[15] The CUP immediately began drawing up formations of irregular militia in order to invade Russia and Persia. These secret military units were integrated into the existing Special Organization. These new guerrilla bands was to be made up of convicts, Kurdish tribesmen and Muslim refugees, and would be led by the same cadres the CUP had used in the Balkan wars. On 18 November Talaat personally ordered the drawing up of lists of names of 'those convicts who were able to exert influence'.[16] The entire operation was led by Dr Bahaeddin Shakir and was kept out of the control of the Ottoman army as much as possible. Nevertheless, clashes of jurisdiction were inevitable and at times caused confusion and inefficiency during the war.[17]

In the early winter of 1914, the groups began penetrating into Russian and Persian territory to incite the Muslim populations to rise in rebellion and join the Ottoman forces.[18] Two operations were launched: into Persian Azerbaijan (North West Iran) and into the South Caucasus (current-day North East Turkey and

[11] A. Mil, 'Umumi Harpte Teşkilâtı Mahsusa', in: *Vakit*, 5 and 29 November 1933, republished as: Arif Cemil (Denker), *I. Dünya Savaşı'nda Teşkilât-ı Mahsusa* (Istanbul, 1997).

[12] Tarık Zafer Tunaya, *Türkiye'de Siyasal Partiler* (Istanbul, 1997), vol. 3, *İttihat ve Terakki*, 285–6.

[13] Denker, *Teşkilât-ı Mahsusa*, 196.

[14] Ahmet Refik, *Kafkas Yollarında: İki Komite, İki Kıtal* (Istanbul, 1998 [1919]), 157.

[15] Mustafa Aksakal, *The Ottoman Road to War in 1914: The Ottoman Empire and the First World War* (Cambridge, 2008), 191.

[16] *BOA*, DH.ŞFR 47/70, Talaat to provinces, 18 November 1914.

[17] Edward Erickson, 'Armenian Massacres: New Records Undercut Old Blame', *Middle East Quarterly* (Summer 2006), 67–75.

[18] For one of the first official Turkish histories of these campaigns, see Fevzi Çakmak, *Büyük Harpte Şark Cephesi Hareketleri: Şark Vilâyetlerimizde, Kafkasyada ve İranda* (Ankara, 1936).

Georgia). The former became a 'catastrophic success', the latter a monumental washout. The war on the Eastern Front gained momentum when Enver Pasha, driven by concerns of security and expansionism, attempted to attack the Russian army near Sarykamish on 29 December 1914 and suffered a decisive defeat, opening the way to Russian penetration into Ottoman territory.[19] After the battle, American diplomats stationed in Istanbul witnessed a sea change among the Young Turks they had frequent contact with.

The paramilitary units did not necessarily fight on the frontline itself. They penetrated through the lines and attempted to foment insurrection among Muslims in the Russian army's rear or wrought havoc in villages behind the front. Ottoman army officers serving on the Caucasian front provided detailed information about the paramilitaries' activities: 'The most distinguished officers and most courageous individuals in the units of the 9th Army Corps in Erzurum were given to the armed gangs formed by Bahaeddin Shakir. Later, I saw how these gangs did not go in ahead of us, but instead followed behind us and engaged in looting villages.'[20] Another Ottoman officer later reminisced:

> In the places they went, they... behaved cruelly and intimidated the local population. The gangs made sure that they were well taken care of. They did whatever they felt like... Enver Pasha trusted these groups of vagrants. He knew that they created mayhem and plundered villages. That he did not suppress these groups was his weakness. All who belonged to this Special Organization were bandits, shaikhs, dervishes, and deserters. We made great opposition to the formation of these organizations. But we could not stand up against Enver Pasha and the CUP's strong man Bahaeddin Shakir.[21]

In this guerrilla war, the paramilitaries attacked Armenian villages, plundering, raping, and killing with impunity. It was this behaviour that would strain the relations between the Special Organization and the army. Bahaeddin Şakir complained to Istanbul about the supposed low morale and unenthusiastic attitude of regular soldiers. Ottoman army officers in their turn were sceptical of the military efficacy of the paramilitaries. Enver Pasha often had to arbitrate the disputes between the two forces.[22]

The Ottoman Empire's allies, especially German military and consular personnel, were also distraught because of the violence. The German missionary activist Johannes Lepsius (1858–1926) secretly published a report that included the numbers of Armenians killed in the area: 1,276 in the districts of Ardanuç and Oltu, approximately 7,000 in the district of Artvin.[23] The German consul of Erzurum

---

[19] Edward J. Erickson, *Ordered to Die: A History of the Ottoman Army in the First World War* (Westport, CT, 2000), 51–74. For a detailed account of the Sarikamish disaster, see Alptekin Müderrisoğlu, *Sarıkamış Dramı* (Istanbul, 1997), 2 volumes.

[20] Quoted in Taner Akçam, *A Shameful Act: The Armenian Genocide and the Question of Turkish Responsibility* (New York, 2006), 138.

[21] Aziz Samih, 'Umumi Harpte Kafkas Cephesi Hatıraları', *Kurun*, 19 April 1935.

[22] Köprülü Şerif İlden, *Sarıkamış: Birinci Dünya Savaşı Başlangıcında Üçüncü Ordu: Kuşatma Manevrası ve Meydan Savaşı: Anı* (Istanbul, 1998), 158–60.

[23] Johannes Lepsius, *Der Todesgang des Armenischen Volkes: Bericht über das Schicksal des Armenischen Volkes in der Türkei während des Weltkrieges* (Potsdam, 1919), 78–9.

reported: 'Armenian population very concerned, fears massacres; in the village of Ösni near Erzurum Armenian priest was shot dead by Turkish *bashi-bozouks* [paramilitaries]. Excesses also reported from other villages.'[24] The complaints made it all the way up to Ambassador Hans von Wangenheim (1859–1915), who expressed his concern to Chancellor Theobald von Bethmann Hollweg (1856–1921) that the cross-border actions of the paramilitaries frequently escalated into 'abuses and excesses' (*Übergriffen und Ausschreitungen*) against Armenian villagers in that region.[25]

The Ottoman advance into and occupation of Persian territory spelled a similar fate for the local Armenians and Syriacs. Persia had been divided into a British and Russian zone of influence, with the north essentially occupied by Russian forces. As this was potentially a security threat to the Ottoman Empire, Enver Pasha gave the order to proceed towards the Caspian Sea and Iran became a battleground between Russia and Turkey.[26] Two armies thrust ahead: the First Expeditionary Force, commanded by Enver's uncle Halil Pasha (1882–1957), and the Fifth Expeditionary Force led by the Young Turk fanatic Tahir Cevdet Bey—governor of Van and Enver's brother-in-law. The paramilitary units, made up of gendarmerie, volunteers, and Kurdish tribesmen, devastated the area west of Lake Urmiye. Villages were razed to the ground, including schools, libraries, churches, shops, missions, houses, and governmental offices. Men were systematically murdered, women were raped and often killed. The unsuspecting victims were Armenian and Syriac citizens of Persia, a country that officially declared itself neutral in the Russian-Ottoman war.[27]

The Russian consul Pavel Vvedensky (1880–1938),[28] a graduate of the Russian Institute of Oriental Studies and fluent in Persian, was the first official to enter the area after the massacres on 10 March 1915. When Vvedensky entered a village near the town of Salmas he found a covered well full of decapitated corpses. The victims had apparently been hanged head down, had their heads chopped off, and were finally dropped into the well. Men had been made to face a wall in small batches in order to be executed one by one with pick-axes smashing the backs of their skulls. Vvedensky counted at least 15 wells and several barns filled with rotting corpses. In another place, he found prisoners who had been made to stick their heads through the rungs of a ladder, whereafter their heads were chopped off.[29] A Russian vice

[24] *PAAA*, Botschaft Konstantinopel 168, consul of Erzurum to embassy, 5 December 1914.

[25] *PAAA*, R14085, Wangenheim to Bethmann-Hollweg, 29 December 1914.

[26] Conventional accounts of the Ottoman Empire's two Eastern campaigns hold that it was an ideological attempt to open the way to Central Asia and establish a great Turkish Empire, named 'Turan'. Recent research has convincingly suggested that the Young Turks were driven mostly by security concerns. Michael A. Reynolds, 'Buffers, not Brethren: Young Turk Military Policy in the First World War and the Myth of Panturanism', *Past and Present*, 203 (2009), 137–79.

[27] For a detailed account of the violence against civilians in Persia see David Gaunt, *Massacres, Resistance, Protectors: Muslim-Christian Relations in Eastern Anatolia during World War I* (Piscataway, NJ, 2006), 81–120.

[28] During the Great Terror, Vvedensky was arrested on 10 April 1938 on charges of international espionage. On 15 September 1938 he was sentenced, shot, and buried at the infamous Kommunarka mass execution site in Moscow oblast.

[29] Vladimir Genis, *Vitse-Konsul Vvedenski. Sluzhba v Persii i Bukharskom Khanstve (1906–1920 gg.): Rossiiskaya Diplomatiya v Sud'bakh* (Moscow, 2003), 44ff.

commander who toured the area, reported: 'I saw with my own eyes hundreds of mangled corpses in pits, stinking from infection, lying in the open, I saw headless corpses, chopped off by axes, hands, legs, piles of heads, corpses crushed under rocks from fallen walls.'[30] The battle between the Russian and Ottoman armies, fought near Dilman, ended in a sound victory for the Russian Caucasus Army, aided by an Armenian volunteer battalion under the leadership of the famous commander Andranik Ozanian (1865–1927).

After returning from the Caucasian front, Enver wrote a letter to the Armenian patriarch of Konya, expressing his respect and admiration for the courage the Armenian soldiers had shown in the Sarykamish battle. He gave the example of a sergeant Ohannes who had received a medal for valour.[31] This may not have been how Enver really felt about the Ottoman Armenian participation in the war. In a personal discussion with publisher Hüseyin Cahit, he bitterly blamed the Armenians for the fiasco and proposed their deportation to somewhere they would not cause trouble.[32] Talaat too, accused the Armenians of having stabbed the army in the back.[33] The American diplomat Lewis Einstein (1877–1967) wrote in his diary that Talaat 'was different six years ago, when I used to see him daily... he had a seemingly engaging frankness, which contrasted favourably with the shiftiness of Hamidian officials.' But he noted how Talaat had changed after the Balkan wars: 'all his loyalty is to his organization, and his policy is ruthless Turkification... He declares openly that the persecution is revenge for the defeat at Sarykamish, the Turkish expulsion from Azerbaidjan, and the occupation of Van, all of which he lays at the Armenian door.'[34] The CUP leadership had reached a consensus that the disastrous defeats at Sarikamish and Dilman had been caused by 'Armenian treachery'. The Italian consul in Van reported that Halil Pasha's and Cevdet Bey's armies, forced back into Ottoman territory, took revenge on Ottoman Armenian villagers, indiscriminately massacring any and all they encountered, and pillaging their goods.[35] On the frontline in Bitlis, governor Mustafa Abdülhalik Renda summoned the Armenian civil inspector Mihran Boyajian and openly threatened him: 'Now it is time for revenge (Şimdi intikâm zamanıdır).'[36] According to American and German missionaries living in the area, the 50 Armenian villages in the area were raided, pillaged and destroyed by the regiments.[37]

[30] Letter dated 9 March 1915, in: Mkrtych G. Nersisian (ed.), Genotsid Armian v Osmanskoi Imperii: Sbornik Dokumentov i Materialov (Erevan, 1982), 276–7.

[31] Lepsius, Der Todesgang des Armenischen Volkes, 161–2.

[32] Hüseyin C. Yalçın, Siyasal Anılar (Istanbul, 1976), 233.

[33] Hülya Adak, 'Identifying the "Internal Tumors" of World War I: Talat Paşa'nın Hatıraları [Talat Paşa's Memoirs], or the Travels of a Unionist Apologia into "History"', in: Andreas Bähr et al. (eds.), Räume des Selbst: Selbstzeugnisforschung Transkulturell (Cologne, 2007), 151–72.

[34] Lewis Einstein, Inside Constantinople: A Diplomatist's Diary During the Dardanelles Expedition, April–September, 1915 (London, 1917), 175–6.

[35] Henry Barby, Au pays de l'épouvante (Paris, 1917), 230–40.

[36] Zaven Der Yeghiayan, My Patriarchal Memoirs (Barrington, RI, 2002), 273.

[37] Vahakn N. Dadrian, 'The Role of the Special Organization in the Armenian genocide during the First World War,' in: Panikos Panayi (ed.), Minorities in Wartime: National and Racial Groupings in Europe, North America and Australia during the World Wars (Oxford, 1993), 50–82, 63ff.

The twin military failures sparked a severe radicalization of anti-Armenian policy at the political centre, triggering persecution in the winter of 1914–15, including the dismissal of all Armenian civil servants from their positions.[38] This was followed by a second phase when a delusional fear of an organized Armenian insurrection reached boiling point as Allied forces landed at Gallipoli on 24 April 1915. In the same night, Talaat ordered the arrest of the Armenian elites of the entire Ottoman Empire. In Istanbul, 235 to 270 Armenian clergymen, physicians, editors, journalists, lawyers, teachers, politicians were rounded up and deported to the interior, where most were murdered.[39] Other provinces followed. This effectively decapitated a community of their political, intellectual, cultural, and religious leaders. A third phase followed when the regime ordered the general deportation of all Ottoman Armenians to the Syrian desert. Recent research has demonstrated how the deportations escalated into mass murder and cost the lives of about a million Armenians, amounting to genocide.[40]

The contribution of Young Turk paramilitary units to the genocide was particularly significant. Tens of thousands of Turks, Kurds, and Circassians had carried out the mass murder campaign. During the war they hardly denied or kept secret their involvement. One of the notorious paramilitaries was the Circassian killer Çerkez Ahmed, leader of one of the most ruthless death squads. During the war, a moderate Ottoman intellectual encountered him and asked him about his experiences:

> Çerkez Ahmed was an important source for the Armenian tragedy. I wanted to hear about the stages of this bloody event from its very perpetrator. I asked Çerkez Ahmed what he had been doing in the Eastern Provinces. He put his booted feet on top of each other, blew the smoke of his cigarette across: 'Dear brother', he said, 'This situation is affecting my honor. I served my country. Go and look, I turned Van and its vicinities into Kaaba land. Today you will not find a single Armenian there. I served the homeland this much, and then varmints like that Talaat can drink their ice-cold beers in Istanbul, and have me hauled in like this, no, this harms my dignity!' I wanted to get more information from Çerkez Ahmed: So what happened to Zohrab and them? 'Have not you heard? I whacked them all' (*hepsini geberttim*). He swung his cigarette smoke into the air, straightened his moustache with his left hand, and continued to talk: 'They had set out from Aleppo. We came across them on the road, I immediately surrounded their car. They realized they would be finished off. Vartkes said: "So, Mr. Ahmed, you are doing this to us, but what will you do to the Arabs? They are not content with you either." I said: "That's not up to you, you miscreant!" and I splattered his brain with a single Mauser bullet. Then I caught Zohrab. I took him under my feet. With a large rock I smashed and smashed and smashed his head until he croaked.'[41]

---

[38] Uğur Ümit Üngör, 'When Persecution Bleeds into Mass Murder: the Processive Nature of Genocide', in: *Genocide Studies and Prevention*, 1, (2006), 173–96.

[39] Mikayel Shamtanchian, *The Fatal Night: An Eyewitness Account of the Extermination of Armenian Intellectuals in 1915* (Studio City, CA, 2007).

[40] Raymond H. Kévorkian, *Le génocide des Arméniens* (Paris, 2006).

[41] Ahmet Refik, *Kafkas Yollarında*, 42.

Another member of the Special Organization justified the cut-throats' acts as follows:

> The committee is seen by some as plunder and robbery. On the contrary, I say that it
> is the epitome of patriotism. A committee member gives everything for the homeland,
> even his life. When the interests of the homeland and the people are at stake, the com-
> mittee member has no mercy. He destroys when he must destroy and burns when it's
> necessary, he breaks down and draws blood. Everything needs to be leveled, no head
> should remain standing on a body. We have been in such situations so often and have
> done what needed to be done. Now I look back, I think: 'Had we not been so radical,
> what would have happened to this country, under which feet would it be trampled, as
> whose slaves would we be doomed to live?'[42]

Whereas many paramilitaries escaped with considerable booty and full impunity,
some were deemed a liability to the Young Turk political elite. The memoirs of
Fourth Army Chief of Staff General Ali Fuat Erden (1883–1957) shed light on the
relationship between the paramilitaries and the state. Erden had found bloody gold
coins in the personal possessions of the militiamen. He mentions that on 28
September 1915, Cemal Pasha had received a short telegram from Talaat on Çerkez
Ahmed: 'Probably should be eliminated. Can be very harmful later.' Çerkez Ahmed
was arrested, court martialled, convicted and hanged, along with a consort in
Damascus on 30 September 1915. Erden added: 'The debt of gratitude to execu-
tioners and murderers is heavy. They desire to dominate those who express their
need of them and use them. Tools that are used for dirty jobs are needed in times
of exigencies; it is likewise necessary, however, not to glorify but to dispose of them
after using them, once they have done their job (like toilet paper).'[43]

Yet too often the paramilitary perpetrators of the genocide have been seen as
undifferentiated killers who acted for no other reason other than intrinsic (Turkish
or Islamic) cruelty and malignance. For many, however, prior victimization in the
Balkans may have served as a motive for collective vengeance against Ottoman
Christians. The roots of the Armenian Genocide can thus partly be traced to the loss
of power, territory, war, and 'honour' in the Balkans, with paramilitary violence
providing a linking vector. The affective context played a major role as the mobilization of rank-and-file killers depended on the manipulation of emotions of fear,
hatred, and resentment.[44] The genocide emerged as a child of the fatal combination
of existential fear and visceral hatred. It took shape on the distant Eastern Front as
a series of fiats issued after the invasion of Russia and Persia in December 1914.
Powerful cadres within the party, government, and army arrived at a genocidal consensus within the Empire during the months of heightened administrative network-
ing, strategic disputes, and factional infighting in the Empire's darkest hour.

The Ottoman Armenians were not the only victims of Young Turk violence. Greeks
living in the Aegean and Black Sea regions were subjected to an escalating campaign
of economic boycott, summary expulsions, and the killing of community leaders.

---

[42] Hikmet Çiçek, *Dr Bahattin Shakir: İttihat ve Terakki'den Teşkilatı Mahsusa'ya bir Türk Jakobeni*
(Istanbul, 2004), 110.
[43] Ali Fuat Erden, *Birinci Dünya Harbi'nde Suriye Hatıraları* (Istanbul, 2003), 267–9.
[44] For a study of this phenomenon, see Roger D. Petersen, *Understanding Ethnic Violence: Fear,
Hatred, and Resentment in Twentieth-Century Eastern Europe* (Cambridge, 2002), 17–84.

Already in the first half of 1914, over 100,000 Ottoman Greeks were expelled to Greece in an effort to render the littoral secure through ethnic homogenization.[45] During the war, Ottoman Greeks were terrorized, dispossessed, and deported, although this never escalated into outright genocide. One reason was that the Young Turk elite attempted to use the Greek minority as a bargaining chip in potential future negotiations. However, with the 15 May 1919 Greek occupation of Smyrna and ensuing mass violence against the Turkish civilian population, the Young Turks' anti-Greek policy radicalized considerably. They now realized that the presence of local Greek populations, whether a sizeable minority or majority, offered a real scenario in which the Greek government could occupy Ottoman territory. The Young Turk elite now turned its attention to two sensitive regions: the Eastern Black Sea region (Pontus) and Smyrna province. Both were inhabited by Greek communities that had been relatively spared during the war. That peace was ended when Special Organization units commanded by the notorious militia leader Topal Osman (1883–1923) razed the Greek villages of the Pontian coast in the summer of 1921, murdering and expelling its inhabitants.[46] Smyrna's end was near too. When Mustafa Kemal's triumphant army marched into Smyrna on 9 September 1922, the same paramilitaries that had destroyed the Armenians were now given carte blanche to purify the city of Ottoman Greeks. Young Turk death squads set fire to the Christian quarters and literally drove the Smyrna Greeks into the sea.[47] By the end of a decade of social catastrophe, the Ottoman Greek community was but a fragment of what it had been before the war. The survivors were dispossessed and exchanged for Muslims from Greece.

PARAMILITARY VIOLENCE IN THE CAUCASUS

A second episode of mass violence that occurred in the wider context of the Great War is the paramilitary activity in the South Caucasus after 1917. Conventional accounts of the violence in this period link it to deep-seated hatreds between Azeris and Armenians, the savagery of the Cossacks, or the breakdown of order as a result of Russian state collapse. But was there a transnational component springing from the Ottoman Empire? After all, many Armenian survivors had become refugees with vindictive attitudes not too dissimilar from those of the Balkan Turks. As Russian imperial rule collapsed with the revolution and the Ottoman Empire was defeated in the Great War a year later, the South Caucasus became a quintessential shatter zone where the authority of two dynastic Empires had collapsed and the nascent forces of nationalism strove to assert themselves against their rivals. The Armenian-Azerbaijani War was an important aspect of this process, with Armenian political parties siding with the Bolsheviks and the Azerbaijani parties opposing them as 'Whites'. The result was a series of mutual massacres between Armenians

---

[45] Yannis G. Mourelos, 'The 1914 Persecutions and the First Attempt at an Exchange of Minorities Between Greece and Turkey', *Balkan Studies*, 26 (1985), 388–413.

[46] Michael Llewellyn-Smith, *Ionian Vision: Greece in Asia Minor 1919–1922* (New York, 1973), 211.

[47] Hervé Georgelin, *La fin de Smyrne: Du cosmopolitisme aux nationalismes* (Paris, 2005), 201–26.

and Azeris. The most notorious examples were Black Sunday, the 31 March 1918 massacre of Azeris in Baku, and the massacre of Armenians in Nagorno-Karabagh's capital Shusha on 22–26 March 1920. Concretely, this period saw the breakdown of military discipline and the chain of command, the erosion of political consensus on the purpose of legitimate force and violence, and the collapse of the food supply. In these conditions, Armenian nationalist parties such as the Dashnaktsutiun also declared that they would take revenge for what became known amongst Armenians as the 'Great Crime' (*Medz Yeghern*)—that is the genocide of 1915–16.[48] Armenian acts of revenge occurred in three phases: in 1916–18 in occupied Ottoman territory, in 1917–22 in the South Caucasus, and internationally in the early 1920s against the former Young Turk leaders.

The first phase of Armenian revenge was executed under the Russian occupation of Eastern Anatolia. As they entered a foreign land, many Russian officers and commanders came to hold strong prejudices against the local Muslim population. Armenian units serving under Russian command presumably already held strong convictions about Turks and Kurds.[49] Armenian refugees' stories of mass murder had infected the Russian imagination with essentialist images of the Kurds' and Turks' supposed innate barbarism. The backlash against local Muslim civilians was ferocious. The Russian army launched 'punitive expeditions' (*karatel'naya ekspeditsiya*) against hostile elements in the occupied zone. Armenian paramilitary units and Cossack regiments were particularly receptive to the execution of these assignments. Although official Russian policy dictated containment of inter-ethnic tensions, some Russian officers only escalated them by launching a scorched-earth policy of Muslim settlements. General Liakhov, for instance, 'accused the Moslem natives of treachery, and sent his Cossacks from Batum with orders to kill every native at sight, and burn every village and every mosque. And very efficiently had they performed their task, for as we passed up the Chorokh valley to Artvin not a single habitable dwelling or a single living creature did we see.'[50] The Don-Cossack military officer Fedor Ivanovich Eliseev (1892–1987) wrote in his memoirs about their treatment of Ottoman Kurds:

> We occupied their land, razed their villages to the ground, took all their grain, slaughtered their sheep and cattle and paid next to nothing for them. The most junior [Cossack] officer felt he had the right to do whatever he wanted with a Kurd, including taking his last loaf of bread, kicking him out of his house and coming on to his wife and daughters... We only came to understand the psychological state of the Kurds when the Red Army and Soviet power descended from the north to our Cossack lands and treated us Cossacks just as we had treated the Kurds."[51]

These operations took the lives of approximately 45,000 civilians in the valley of the Chorukh river in the South-West Caucasus.[52]

---

[48] Michael P. Croissant, *The Armenia-Azerbaijan Conflict: Causes and Implications* (London, 1998), 14.

[49] For an overview of their military operations see Gabriel Korganoff, *La participation des Arméniens à la guerre mondiale sur le front du Caucase: 1914–1918* (Paris, 1927).

[50] Morgan Philips Price, *War and Revolution in Asiatic Russia* (London, 1918), 223f.

[51] Fedor I. Eliseev, *Kazaki na Kavkazskom fronte, 1914–1917: Zapiski polkovnika Kubanskogo kazach'ego voiska v trinadtsati broshiurakh-tetradiakh* (Moscow, 2001), 143–4.

[52] David M. Lang, *A Modern History of Soviet Georgia* (Westport, CT, 1962), 185.

The conduct of the Armenian paramilitary volunteer detachments was not much better. According to Eliseev, who served in the war with a Cossack regiment in the Caucasus, Turkish and Kurdish units would take no Armenian prisoners, and in retaliation the Armenian paramilitary units would not take Kurdish and Turkish prisoners. This was an ethnic war of annihilation.[53] The young writer Viktor Borisovich Shklovskii (1893–1984) wrote that Armenian units went into battle 'already hating the Kurds' and that this 'deprived the peaceful Kurds, and even their children, of the protection afforded by the laws of war'.[54] Turkish and Kurdish villages were pillaged, emptied, and burnt to the ground. Shklovskii added: '[During the war] I have seen Galicia, and I have seen Poland—but that was all paradise compared to Kurdistan.' He gave the example of a massacre in a Kurdish village, where Kurdish tribesmen had killed three soldiers who were foraging for booty. The punitive detachment that was dispatched retaliated mercilessly by slaughtering 200 Kurds, 'without regard to age or gender.'[55] The British war correspondent Morgan Philips Price (1885–1973) rode on horseback with the Russian army and Armenian volunteer units and wrote:

> One day I rode out from the camp and came across a little Kurdish village. The inhabitants had most of them fled with the Turks, but on riding down the street I came across the dead bodies of a Kurdish man and two women, with recent wounds in the head and body. Then two Armenians, volunteers from our camp, suddenly appeared carrying things out of a house. I stopped them and asked who these dead Kurds were. 'Oh', they said, 'we have just killed them.' 'Why?' I asked. A look of amazement came into their faces. 'Why ask such a question? Why, we kill Kurds at sight. They are our enemies, and we kill them, because if we leave them here they will do us harm.'[56]

In practice, the distinction between combatants and non-combatants had disappeared.

One of the Armenian paramilitary leaders was Murad Hakobian (1874–1918) from the central Ottoman province of Sivas. Murad had participated in demonstrations against the ill treatment of Armenians under the *ancien régime*, but as peaceful protests had proved futile, he formed his own bands and launched guerrilla activities. During the First World War he narrowly escaped death by a hair's breadth and made his escape with his *fedayeen* to Russian-held territory. He made it to Tblisi where he regrouped and joined the Russian army advance towards Erzincan and Sivas. Along the way his forces witnessed the destruction of Armenian villages, one after another, as they approached their home towns. By the time they reached Erzincan, they had lost their inhibitions against massacring civilians, and between December 1917 and March 1918, Murad's units vented their rage on the Turks and Kurds between Sivas and Erzurum.[57] There are few Armenian sources on these massacres. One of Murad's men, a young man who

[53] Eliseev, *Kazaki na Kavkazskom fronte, 1914–1917*, 85.
[54] Viktor Shklovskii, *Sentimental Journey: Memoirs, 1917–1922* (Ithaca, NY, 1970), 86–7, 99.
[55] Ibid., 100–1.
[56] Price, *War and Revolution in Asiatic Russia*, 140–1.
[57] Mikayel Varandian, *Murad of Sepastia* (Arlington, MA, 2006).

had been orphaned in the genocide and had survived and fled into the Russian-occupied zone, had joined Murad at the end of December 1917. In his memoirs, he admits to having killed many Turks to take his revenge.[58] Oksen Teghtsoonian, an Armenian refugee surviving in Yerevan during the Russian civil war, recalled:

> One day one of my co-workers declared that he was quitting his job to join the armed forces, any armed band, to go fight the Turks. He was a very likeable chap, about my age, but his burning hatred towards the Turks consumed his whole life. He had lost his parents and all his family during the escape from Van and had vowed vengeance. 'I must kill double the number of Turks against the dead members of my family,' he would say, 'Only then will I be satisfied and settle down to work.'[59]

The man then joined a paramilitary unit and was never heard of again.

The second phase of Armenian paramilitary violence followed the Treaty of Brest-Litovsk (3 March 1918). Talaat insisted that the provinces of Ardahan, Batum, and Kars be ceded to the Ottoman Empire, and these concessions were granted. At that point, the situation in Baku had been extremely volatile: tension between the Azeri-nationalist Musavat party and the Dashnaktsutiun had been rising, and Bolshevik forces in Baku were caught between a rock and a hard place. After the collapse of the Caucasian front, there was no army for the Baku Soviet to rely on. Head of the Baku commune, Stepan Shaumyan (1878–1918), desperately requested military reinforcements and humanitarian relief from Lenin, but his request was rejected.[60] Thus, the Baku Soviet saw no other choice than to resort to the Dashnaktsutiun to lend its assistance in the struggle against both the advancing Ottoman-Azeri army and the 'enemy within the gates': the Azeri nationalists in Baku. Obviously this alienated the Azeri community of Baku even more.[61] When the Bolsheviks provoked Azeris into firing at their soldiers, the Azeris responded, partly alarmed by the growing military strength of the Armenians. In the ensuing skirmishes, Armenian paramilitary forces were tacitly given impunity to subdue the 'insurrection'. This resulted in the massacre of up to 12,000 Azerbaijanis by Armenian paramilitary units in and around the city of Baku.[62]

Brest-Litovsk was followed by another victory for the Young Turks: Enver Pasha succeeded in bullying the Democratic Republic of Armenia into signing the Treaty of Batum (4 June 1918), which dictated very harsh territorial and infrastructural conditions for the Armenians. These two treaties brought profound changes in the power relations in the South Caucasus in the year 1918. The Young Turk regime saw the disintegration of Russian authority in the area as a power vacuum they could fill. The Treaty of Brest-Litovsk and the Bolsheviks' retreat from the 'imperialist war' was a blessing in this regard: now they could recover the Ottoman Eastern

---

[58] M. Esmerian, *Aksori ew baderazmi gragnerun mechen* (Boston, 1952).

[59] Oksen Teghtsoonian, *From Van to Toronto: A Life in Two Worlds* (New York, 2003), 92.

[60] Telegram from Stepan Shaumian to Vladimir Lenin, 27 August 1918, in: *Dokumenty vneshnei politiki SSSR* (Moscow, 1957), vol. 1, 411–12.

[61] Firuz Kazemzadeh, *The Struggle for Transcaucasia (1917–1921)* (New York, 1951), 75.

[62] Michael Smith, 'Anatomy of Rumor: Murder Scandal, the Musavat Party and Narrative of the Russian Revolution in Baku, 1917–1920', *Journal of Contemporary History*, 36 (2001), 211–40.

provinces and thrust into the South Caucasus.[63] Following Brest-Litovsk, a select group of Georgian, Azeri and Armenian political representatives proclaimed an independent Democratic Federative Republic of Transcaucasia.[64] Attracted by the oil fields of Azerbaijan and to a lesser extent by pan-Turkist ideology, the Young Turks invaded this fledgling state and marched on Baku. On 13 September 1918, the combined Ottoman-Azeri army of Nuri Pasha (1881–1949), brother of Enver Pasha, stood on the outskirts of Baku and was preparing to storm through its gates. Upon entering Baku, the paramilitary units hunted down Armenians and killed them indiscriminately in revenge for the 31 March massacre.[65]

By the summer of 1918, inter-ethnic warfare between Azeris and Armenians had enveloped several territorial pockets in the South Caucasus. On the Armenian side, the paramilitary violence in this period was committed by the volunteer units commanded by two noted commanders: Andranik Ozanian (1865–1927) and Drastamat Kanayan (1884–1956). Both were involved in battling the Ottoman army, defending Armenian interests, as well as committing violence against Turks, Kurds, and Azeris. Possibly the most important figure was Andranik, who was born in the Ottoman city of Shabin Karahisar. At an early age Andranik had joined the Armenian revolutionary movement, which pursued a policy of defensive and offensive political violence against Ottoman officials, Kurdish tribal chiefs, and Armenian opponents of their ideology. During the First World War, he organized and fought alongside volunteer units to combat the Ottoman army and thus made a contribution to the Russian war effort.[66] In 1918, Andranik rejected the Treaty of Batum as a Turkish dictate and moved to Zangezur with a paramilitary division estimated to have three to five thousand men, followed by many thousands of Ottoman Armenian refugees.[67] In the self-proclaimed 'Republic of Mountainous Armenia', comprising the multi-ethnic districts of Nakhichevan, Zangezur and Karabagh, Andranik's paramilitary units massacred and expelled the Azeri population. This was of course an embarassment to the Armenian government in Yerevan, who attempted in vain to reason with Andranik. Ultimately, Andranik was declared *persona non grata* and an order was issued for him to be disarmed if he ever entered the Republic.[68] On 23–26 March 1920, when an Armenian raid on Karabagh's capital Shusha failed, local Azeris took a 'pre-emptive revenge' in Shusha and murdered thousands of Armenians.[69]

[63] William E.D. Allen and Pavel P. Muratov, *Caucasian Battlefields: A History of the Wars on the Turco-Caucasian Border 1828–1921* (Cambridge, 1953), 421–9.

[64] For the declaration, see *Dokumenty i materialy po vneshnei politike Zakavkaz'ia i Gruzii* (Tblisi, 1919), 27–8.

[65] Michael Reynolds, 'The Ottoman-Russian Struggle for Eastern Anatolia and the Caucasus, 1908–1918: Identity, Ideology and the Geopolitics of World Order' (Ph.D. thesis, Princeton University, 2003), 436–513.

[66] Antranig Chalabian, *General Andranik and the Armenian Revolutionary Movement* (Southfield, MI, 1988).

[67] Richard G. Hovannisian, *The Republic of Armenia: The First Year, 1918–1919* (Berkeley, CA, 1971), 86–7.

[68] Richard G. Hovannisian, *Armenia on the Road to Independence* (Berkeley, CA, 1969), 194–5, 214.

[69] Richard G. Hovannisian, *The Republic of Armenia, vol. III: From London to Sèvres, February–August 1920* (Berkeley, CA, 1996), 152.

Andranik snubbed the Armenian government and travelled to the United States to plead with President Wilson for an Armenian homeland. But having arrived at the White House in November 1919, President Wilson's private secretary Joseph Patrick Tumulty (1879–1954) informed Andranik that the president's health did not permit him a personal conversation. Disappointed and frustrated, Andranik bitterly denounced Wilson and US policy on Armenia and went into exile in Fresno, California.[70] Other Armenian political leaders refused to accept what they perceived as a lack of justice for Armenians. The Dashnaktsutiun party decided at its 1919 congress to take justice in their own hands by organizing an assassination campaign against the Young Turk leaders, now in exile as the British and French victors occupied Istanbul. The undercover operation was called 'Operation Nemesis'. Talaat was murdered in Berlin on 15 March 1921 by Soghomon Tehlirian, who was acquitted in a German court by playing on the jury's sympathies for his family's murder. Bahaeddin Shakir and Cemal Azmi (governor of Trabzon) were shot dead in Berlin on 17 April 1922 by Aram Yerganian. Cemal Pasha was assassinated in Tbilisi on 21 July 1922 by Stepan Dzaghigian—the murder happened a block away from Lavrentii Beria's house, who witnessed the aftermath and according to some accounts was involved in the affair. On 5 December 1921 Said Halim Pasha, Grand Vizier from 1913–16 and unrelated to the genocide, was killed by Arshavir Shiragian. Dashnak agents also killed many Armenians whom they accused of collaborating with the Young Turks and denouncing other Armenians during the genocide.[71] Revenge had come full circle.

The Armenian militias of Dro Kanayan, Antranik Ozanian, and Murad Hakobia were not a part of any regular army or military bureaucracy but often held the monopoly of violence in certain areas. It is relevant to note that among the paramilitaries were many destitute refugees from the Ottoman Empire. Perhaps revenge was an important theme inspiring the acts of destroying villages and murdering civilians. It is also important to note that the Caucasian Azeris were in no way responsible for the Armenian genocide, just as the Ottoman Armenians were not responsible for the persecution and expulsion of Balkan Muslims in 1913.

PATTERNS OF PARAMILITARY VIOLENCE

In 1995, the Armenian Genocide specialist Vahakn Dadrian published his important book *The History of the Armenian Genocide*, a historical and legal treatment of the First World War destruction of Ottoman Armenians. The book's striking subtitle, *Ethnic Conflict from the Balkans to Anatolia into the Caucasus*, suggests both a continuity and a relationship between three large-scale processes of mass violence:

---

[70] Antranig Chalabian, *Dro (Drastamat Kanayan): Armenia's First Defense Minister of the Modern Era* (Los Angeles, CA, 2009), 152–6.

[71] Jacques Derogy, *Resistance and Revenge: the Armenian Assassination of the Turkish Leaders Responsible for the 1915 Massacres and Deportations* (New Brunswick, NJ, 1990); Edward Alexander, *A Crime of Vengeance: An Armenian Struggle for Justice* (New York, 1991); Rolf Hosfeld, *Operation Nemesis: Die Türkei, Deutschland und der Völkermord an den Armeniern* (Cologne, 2005).

the Balkan wars of 1912–13, the Armenian Genocide of 1915–16, and the ethnic civil war in the South Caucasus of 1917–22. Even though this is a promising and legitimate endeavour, Dadrian's explanations of the violence are not entirely satisfactory. He argues that the wars and conflicts in this period erupted due to a presumed primordial hatred between well-circumscribed ethnic groups that acted collectively with identical motives and affective dispositions, inherent convictions of superiority, and the vague concept of a 'culture of massacre'.[72] This concept is not developed further and is deployed in a rather static and essentialist way.

In this chapter I have attempted to re-problematize the subtitle of Dadrian's book and open it as a direction for research. The three conflicts are unmistakably related to one another. The nature of this relationship is one of direction and partly of causality. The violence of the paramilitary civil war of the Balkans and the 1912–13 Balkan wars was transposed to the Anatolian context in the First World War, which in its turn generated further violence in the Caucasus. Furthermore, political elites learned from each other. The success of Balkan nationalisms functioned as a model for Ottoman minorities, whose nationalist politicians concluded first that 'might is right' and that territory could be seized through violence as a fait accompli and, secondly, that European powers would not intervene if minorities were expelled or worse.[73] The chain reaction of this transnational process could be stopped neither by neighbouring powers nor by the Great Powers. The fact that Anatolian Armenians suffered a genocide under the watchful eye of German diplomatic and military personnel, or that Baku Azeris were massacred in the presence of the British army attests to the relative autonomy of political violence. Only further research would elucidate more precise linkages between the three episodes of mass violence.

The relevance of competing national claims and ethnic security dilemmas amidst a failed imperial system was unmistakable. The collapse of the state monopoly of force left in its wake a host of ethnic groups—Armenians, Kurds, Turks, Greeks, etc.—that were now bereft of the first amenity that states have historically supplied—security. Prevailing anarchy made security the first concern of the political elites of those groups. They had to determine whether neighbouring groups constituted a threat, hardly a difficult question to answer in the face of the past two wars. In particular a warped perception of the supposed group cohesion of the 'other' contributed to these fears of being dominated and destroyed. The elites believed in the effectiveness of offence versus defence in order to eliminate their own vulnerability and so launched pre-emptive wars such as the Young Turk reconquest of Eastern Anatolia and invasion of the Caucasus, or the Armenian move towards Zangezur and Nagorno Karabagh.

Paramilitarism was thus both an overlapping theme and a chain connecting these destructive episodes. Comparative research into the involvement of paramili-

---

[72] Vahakn N. Dadrian, *The History of the Armenian Genocide: Ethnic Conflict from the Balkans to Anatolia into the Caucasus* (Providence, RI, 1995), 121, 157. Elsewhere Dadrian uses the term 'subculture of primordial barbarism' and leaves it equally unqualified and undefined. Id., 'Children as Victims of Genocide: the Armenian Case', *Journal of Genocide Research* 5 (2003), 421–39.
[73] For a moralistic and modern Turkish-nationalist treatment of this process, see Salâhi R. Sonyel, *Minorities and the Destruction of the Ottoman Empire* (Ankara, 1993).

tary units in mass crimes such as genocide and ethnic cleansing demonstrates that governments benefit from relying on paramilitary groups as it provides them with plausible deniability for the violence the units commit against enemy populations. The regime can simply disavow any linkage with the paramilitary organizations by claiming they operated of their own volition.[74] Whereas this model certainly fits the Young Turk government of 1913–18, it is less applicable to the period 1919–23, when the Ottoman Empire was ruled by a dual government: the liberal Istanbul government attempted to undo the damage done by the CUP, but the Young Turks and their veteran paramilitaries retreated to Ankara, rejected the Treaty of Sèvres, and launched the 1919–22 'War of Independence' (the Turko-Greek war and Turko-Armenian war). In the case of the fledgling Armenian republic the dynamic is similar as we observe a split in the political landscape similar to broader contemporary European patterns. Whereas the state attempted to establish peace ('humiliating' or not) through treaties with its neighbours, independent paramilitary leaders continued the nationalist mission. These units committed grave crimes against humanity in their attempt to establish homogeneous territories, 'proto-nation states', by clearing as much territory of minority populations as possible. The massacres and expulsions of Azeris in the South Caucasus were part and parcel of this logic.

CONCLUSION

The Great War undoubtedly had an enormous impact on the Young Turks. It polarized Turkish society, leaving lasting scars and resentments, while foreign military successes created a permanent Young Turk fear of encirclement and vulnerability that contained elements of paranoia and xenophobia. Moreover, the war devastated the economy and, coupled with Young Turk persecution of Christians, industry and agriculture came to a standstill. This had economic but also social and political implications. It was in the context of world war that the Young Turks had their major experience of ruling a country. This shaped the party's subsequent development in several respects: it became a fighting brotherhood as war and politics became deeply entwined and military jargon percolated the language of government. Moreover, the war experience (para)-militarized the political culture of the Young Turk movement, and left a heritage that included a willingness to resort to violence, rule by decree, summary justice and centralized administration.

The war had also demonstrated the usefulness of keeping paramilitary groups 'on retainer' and deploying them during periods of crisis. The localized ethnic resistance against Young Turk rule by Armenians in Van (1915), Greeks in the Pontos (1920), Circassians and Albanians in the South Marmara (1920), Sunni Kurds in Diyarbekir (1925), and Shi'ite Kurds in Dersim (1937) was quelled by paramilitary violence. In the interwar period, Turkey's violent rejection of the Paris

---

[74] Alex Alvarez, 'Militias and Genocide', in: *War Crimes, Genocide, & Crimes against Humanity*, 2 (2006),1–33.

peace settlement also won it the respect and admiration of other losers in the post-war order such as Hungary and indeed Germany.[75]

In the longer term, paramilitarism became a time-tested tradition during crises in Turkey. The Kurdish-nationalist movement that was repressed from the 1920s on resurfaced in the 1950s and reached an important stage with the establishment of the Kurdistan Worker's Party (PKK). On 15 August 1984, the PKK declared war on the Turkish state as local skirmishes escalated into a full-scale guerrilla war, lasting 13 years and causing more than 40,000 casualties.[76] Deep-seated frustration about the war among the Turkish military elite led to the formation of extra-legal paramilitary units that conducted counter-insurgency operations and a scorched-earth campaign in 1994 and 1995. This state-sponsored terror left more than 3,000 villages devastated and millions of internally displaced people.[77] The similarities with the conflicts surrounding and including the First World War are remarkable and raise questions on the continuities of the political culture, as well as the geopolitical constellations resulting from the First World War. The main political challenges for the Turkish state continued to emerge from the Eastern borderlands where the two key ethnic groups excluded from the nation-state, Armenians and Kurds, persist in raising global awareness about their history. The legacy of the Young Turk era continues to bedevil the relations between these groups.

[75] Emre Sencer, 'Virtuous Praetorians: Military Culture and the Defense Press in Germany and Turkey, 1929–1939' (Ph.D. dissertation, Ohio State University, 2008).
[76] Ali Kemal Özcan, *Turkey's Kurds: a Theoretical Analysis of the PKK and Abdullah Öcalan* (London, 2006).
[77] Selahattin Çelik, *Verbrecher Staat: der 'Susurluk-Zwischenfall' und die Verflechtung von Staat, Unterwelt und Konterguerilla in der Türkei* (Frankfurt/M, 1998); id.., *Die Todesmaschinerie: türkische Konterguerilla* (Cologne, 1999).

11

Soldiers to Civilians, Civilians to Soldiers: Poland and Ireland after the First World War[1]

Julia Eichenberg

INTRODUCTION

Woodrow Wilson famously declared the end of the First World War to be the beginning of an era of national self-determination.[2] However, the political reality proved to be more complicated. Both Ireland and Poland became independent after the First World War. While the process of becoming independent was different, the trigger was the same: independence was made possible because the occupying Empires had been shattered (as in the case of the Habsburg or the Russian Empires) or badly affected (as in the case of Germany and the United Kingdom) in the course of the war. Wilson's promise, however, affected the two countries quite differently. A free Polish state had been one of Wilson's 14 points, making it a necessity in the postwar order. The Polish state gradually emerged behind the lines of the withdrawing powers Russia, Germany, and Austria-Hungary, but the consolidation of a central government and a state-controlled monopoly of the use of force took time. Ireland, on the other hand, had to learn that their hopes had been in vain: while national self-determination was welcomed if it concerned territories of the defeated Central Powers, a different measure was applied to areas and nationalities in the realms of one of the Allied Powers.

Ireland and Poland became two key sites of the 'war after the war'.[3] The armistice on 11 November did not end hostilities. Poland's independence in 1918 entailed further battle, defending—and expanding—the new Polish borders. In Ireland, the independence movement, betrayed by the Wilsonian promise and the Paris Peace Conference, increased the strength of the Irish Republican Army (IRA), challenged the British Crown Forces, started a war of independence and partly

[1] The author would like to thank Juliana Adelman, John Horne, Robert Gerwarth, and Joël Glasman for their comments on this chapter.
[2] Erez Manela, *The Wilsonian Moment: Self-Determination and the International Origins of Anticolonial Nationalism* (New York, 2007).
[3] Peter Gatrell, 'War after the War: Conflicts 1919–1923', in: John Horne (ed.), *A Companion to World War I* (Oxford, 2010), 558–75.

Fig. 14. Beat the Bolshevik! Polish Poster during the Russo-Polish War, 1920.

succeeded in ending British hegemony in Ireland, though fighting continued over the conditions of independence.[4]

In both countries, the conflict was dominated by irregular warfare. The genesis of paramilitary formations in Poland and Ireland shows a radicalization of independence movements, accelerated by the political disintegration of the former regimes. Distinctions between civilians and the military were eroded in the face of guerrilla warfare and ethnic, religious and ideologically motivated violence. The process occurred in the context of a bellicose transgression of boundaries and social mobilization in both countries following the World War.

SOLDIERS TO CIVILIANS, CIVILIANS TO SOLDIERS

The image of paramilitary combatants after the First World War has to a large extent been influenced by the stereotypical picture of the German *Freikorps*

---

[4] Michael Hopkinson, *The Irish War of Independence* (Dublin, 2004). Similarities between postwar events in Ireland and Poland after the Great War have recently been discussed in Tim Wilson, *Frontiers of Violence: Conflict and Identity in Ulster and Upper Silesia, 1918–1922* (Oxford, 2010).

Fig. 15. Polish Insurgents in Upper Silesia, 1920.

member: a young, physically fit man. Two threads of historiography have taken up this image and greatly influenced the interpretation of paramilitary movements of the period: first, the thesis that the war 'brutalized' postwar politics and, secondly, the idea of the ultra-masculinity of paramilitary violence.[5] Both debates have been applied to other theatres of postwar violence and have shaped the overall perception of paramilitaries. This chapter argues that both Ireland and Poland provide proof for, as well as evidence that challenges, this rule. Paramilitary violence in these two countries was not just induced by a brutalization resulting from the war experience. Nor was it only about male bonding and ultra-masculinity: combatants included younger boys and even women.

Violence after the end of the First World War marked a break in the relations between civil society and military formations, eroding the usual dichotomy between combatants and civilians. This chapter argues that combatants who perpetrated violence and civilians who were its victims became inextricably intertwined. Civilians could be injured or killed in the circle of violence owing to

---

[5] For the brutalization debate, see George Mosse, *Fallen Soldiers. Reshaping the Memory of the World Wars* (Oxford, New York, 1994) (note the French translation's title: *De la Grande Guerre au totalitarisme. La brutalisation des sociétés européennes*). On the perception of Mosse in historiography, see Pierre Purseigle, 'A Very French Debate: The 1914–1918 War Culture', *Journal of War and Culture Studies* 1 (2008), 9–14. For the debate on ultra-masculinity, see Robert Gerwarth, 'The Central European Counterrevolution: Paramilitary Violence in Germany, Austria and Hungary after the Great War', *Past and Present* 200 (2008), 223–57; Klaus Theweleit, *Male Fantasies*, 2 vols, (Minneapolis, 1985).

accident or to suspicion of being soldiers in disguise. Civilians, among them even women, boys, and old men, also became involved in combat formations. At the same time, combatants became vulnerable as civilians: they were attacked when off duty, or suffered threats and attacks on loved ones. In the process other social and cultural realities such as space and age were blurred, along with the distinctions between home front and battlefront, civilians and the military, masculinity and femininity.[6] The relations between civilian and military life in Ireland and Poland were re-negotiated after the First World War as new nation-states emerged amidst continuing military violence. Ending these conflicts and reuniting society required a degree of amnesia, or at least constructed silence, regarding 'uncommon' war experiences, especially those of women and children. The past had to be realigned with the present, but in the process much of the violence that had characterized the period faded from view.

WAR AND VETERANS

Combatants in both Ireland and Poland included a significant number of veterans of the First World War, underlining the 'aftershocks' of the global conflict.[7] Veterans were physically trained to fight, and psychologically used to doing so. Handling weaponry was nothing new to them, neither was the predominantly male companionship, the austerity of life in wartime, or experiencing and deploying violence.

However, because of the different histories of the two countries during the war of 1914–18, the number of veterans involved in Poland was much larger than in Ireland. Polish men—men living on the territory of the later Polish state—fought as conscripts and professional soldiers in the armies of the former empires Germany, Russia, and Austria-Hungary.[8] Far less had the opportunity to fight as volunteers in the Polish struggle for independence, within the ranks of the Polish Legions with the Central Powers, with Haller's Army (*Błękitna Armia*) in France, and the Polish Military Organization (*Polska Organizacja Wojskowa*, or POW). Haller's Army consisted of exiled or emigrant Polish volunteers (especially from the United States) and Polish prisoners of war from the German and Austrian armies, who fought alongside the Allies on the Western Front. As Poles were to be found on

[6] Louise Ryan, '"In the Line of Fire": Representations of Women and War (1919–1923) through the Writings of Republican Men', in: Louise Ryan and Margaret Ward (eds.), *Irish Women and Nationalism. Soldiers, New Women and Wicked Hags* (Dublin: Irish Academic Press, 2004), 45–61, 60.

[7] 'Aftershocks', special issue of *Contemporary European History* 19 (2010), guest-edited by Julia Eichenberg and John Paul Newman.

[8] No definite numbers exist for Polish soldiers fighting in 1914–18, but research suggests at least two million active combatants. Alexander Watson, 'Fighting for Another Fatherland: The Polish Minority in The German Army, 1914–1918' in: *English Historical Review* 126 (2011), 1137–1166; Piotr Wandycz, 'Se remobiliser pour renaître: Les voies polonaises de la sortie de guerre', in: Stéphane Audoin-Rouzeau and Christophe Prochasson (eds.), *Sortir de la grande guerre. Le monde et l'après-1918* (Paris, 2008), 307–28. Lesław Dudek, 'Polish Military Formations in World War I', in: Béla K. Király and Nándor F. Dreisziger (eds.), *East-Central European Society in World War I* (New York, 1985), 454–70, here 455. About half a million of these soldiers died, countless numbers were wounded. Rezmer, *Polacy w korpusie oficerskim*, 140.

either side at almost any front, battles—especially at the Eastern Front—sometimes turned out to be fratricidal.

Official restructuring of the Polish forces into the Polish army started even before the declaration of the Polish state (late October 1918) when all former Legionnaires and officers were called to Warsaw to be sworn into the Polish army.[9] However, it is difficult to speak of a national Polish army during the period in question and would be more accurate to describe the Polish formations as paramilitaries. During most of the period 1918–20, there was no functioning chain of command from Józef Piłsudski, as the new chief of state and official head of the Polish army, to the troops wandering the country.

Most formations returning from the fronts of the World War kept their former structure and command and only changed names. For example, the 3rd Podhale Rifle Regiment (Strzelców Podhalańskich, a mountain infantry unit) was set up in late October 1919 on the basis of the 2nd Training Regiment of Cavalry Grenadiers (Instrukcyjny Grenadierów Woltyżerów) of Haller's Army. The 4th Podhale Rifle Regiment was formed in May 1919 in France from the 19th Polish Rifle Regiment (Strzelców Polskich) of Haller's army. In June 1919 it was transported to Poland and re-organized in September according to new Polish standards as the 143rd Kresy Infantry Rifle Regiment (Piechoty Strzelców Kresowych). From October 1919 it was employed against the Ukrainians, then from March 1920 as 4th Podhale Rifle Regiment (Strzelców Podhalańskich) in the battle against the Soviets. Other formations gathered men formerly affiliated with the Polish paramilitary independence movement such as the Upper Silesian 11th Infantry Regiment, set up in November 1918 with one-time POW members, former Legionnaires, Polish soldiers from the former 13th Austrian Schützenbataillon, and volunteers. Furthermore, three months after the disarmament of the corps of General Dowbór-Muśnicki on 9 September, the 'Związek Wojskowych Polaków w Wilnie' (Alliance of Military Poles in Vilna) was set up, consisting of five battalions of artillery and a battalion of Uhlans, a formation of lance-carrying light cavalry.[10]

However, the perception that Polish combatants in this period were almost exclusively veterans of the First World War is not true. Formations filled their ranks with volunteers, often those who had been too young to serve during the war as well as demobilized soldiers. Individual soldiers or groups deserted from the former imperial armies to join the Polish formations. Only in March 1920 did the demobilization of the older soldiers and of the foreign Polish volunteers lead to a genuine reorganization of the Polish army. In the meantime, Polish formations fought what only at first sight looked like a traditional state war. Some engaged in excesses and banditry.[11] This participation in violence against civilians underlined their

[9] Ossolineum, 12925/III 1885–1939. Baczyński, 'Pamiętniki', 159 (17 October 1918).

[10] Biblioteka Narodowa (BN Rękopisy), Rps BN akc 10312, Andrzej Brochocki: Wspomnienia wojenne z 13-go pułku ułanów Wileńskich. Okres walk od Samoobrony Wileńskiej w 1918 r. do zawarcia rozejmu z Litwinami w 1920 roku, 4B. See also Wojciech B. Moś, *Wojsko Polskie i Organizacje paramilitarne* (Katowice, 1997), 20–6.

[11] 'Unit of men from Poznań (19 men) deserts from the German army to join [the Samoobrona]' Rps BN akc 10312; Andrzej Brochocki, 4B, 5. Moś, Wojsko Polskie i Organizacje paramilitarne,

nature as paramilitary rather than military formations since it displayed the lack of control of a central military command.[12]

After the end of the Great War, the IRA challenged the British Crown Forces, and started a war of independence that eventually ended British hegemony in the twenty-six Counties. The IRA was structured to become the core of a new army once an independent state was established, and much of it indeed supplied the Irish National Army, the Free State Forces of the new Free State from 1922. During the war of independence, the IRA fought as a pre-state army rather than as a paramilitary force, believing that they represented the new national army while another governmental power was (still) in place. While the Polish paramilitaries, without any control or central command, fought for their newly independent state, the Irish forces were fighting against the existing state. Initially, the IRA opposed what was understood as British colonization. After the conditional independence of the Irish Free State had been obtained, the anti-Treaty IRA fought the Free State Forces in the hope of gaining independence for the entire island of Ireland.

During the War of Independence, the IRA did not have the means to fight the British Forces openly, a situation that was repeated in the subsequent war against the Free State Army. In both instances, guerrilla warfare was adopted. The tactics of the War of Independence and the following Civil War eroded the traditional distinction between civilian and soldier, between military and civilian life. In clear distinction from what soldiers might have experienced during the First World War, there was no leave from guerrilla warfare. Likewise, the war was fought not only against the British administration, but also against many of those connected to it. Thus, while the First World War had not affected Irish territory (with the exception of the nationalist uprising in Dublin in April 1916), the War of Independence and Civil War introduced violence (including against civilians) to the Irish homeland.[13]

After their return, many Irish ex-servicemen of the British army joined or re-joined the Royal Irish Constabulary, but a significant number of them went on to join the IRA.[14] While Joost Augusteijn and Peter Hart have argued that the role of ex-servicemen in the IRA was influential, accurate numbers are still controversial.[15] The most prominent example is of course Tom Barry who, after

---

20–1, 24–5. For more detail on forms of violence employed against civilians, see Julia Eichenberg, 'The Dark Side of Independence. Religiously and ethnically motivated Violence in Poland and Ireland, 1918–1923', *JCEH*, 19 (2010), 231–48.

[12] 'Borderlands: Ethnicity, Identity, and Violence in the Shatter-Zone of Empires since 1848' (2003–2007) at the Watson Institute for International Studies at Brown University, coordinated by Omer Bartov; Donald Bloxham, *The Final Solution: A Genocide* (Oxford, 2009), 81ff.

[13] On the question of how far the experience of the First World War by British Soldiers affected their behaviour in Ireland, see Adrian Gregory, 'Peculiarities of the English? War, Violence and Politics 1900–1939', *Journal of Modern European History* 1 (2003), 44–59.

[14] A high number of ex-soldiers was among the IRA formations, and relied heavily on their experience in wartime and military tactics. Joost Augusteijn, *From Public Defiance to Guerrilla Warfare: The Experience of Ordinary Volunteers in the Irish War of Independence* (Dublin, 1996), 97.

[15] See the work on the social background of IRA combatants by Eve Morrison, 'Identity, Allegiance, War and Remembrance: The Bureau of Military History and the Irish Revolution, 1913–1923', Ph.D. dissertation, Trinity College Dublin (2011).

fighting in the Mesopotamian Campaign, eventually took over command of the Third West Cork Flying Column.[16] The most colourful example is perhaps Maurice Meade, who volunteered to join the British Army when he was still underage. Captured early in the war in France, he was transferred to a Prisoner of War camp where he was later recruited for the Irish Brigade, only to end up fighting for the German Army in the Middle East. Meade openly admitted that his own freedom was the one he was fighting for. Nonetheless, when he eventually returned to Ireland, he joined the IRA and was praised for his military experience and for being a good shot.[17] In general, ex-servicemen of the British Army were appreciated. In some regions, such as Derry, the local IRA and their officers consisted to a large extent of ex-servicemen. However, their military training and their contacts with the British army could also work against them, making them suspect of betrayal and turning them into targets of IRA attacks. Thus, with only a little exaggeration it might be said that British army ex-servicemen could either join the IRA or risk being attacked by it.[18]

VOLUNTEERING AND THE MYTH OF THE HEROIC MALE INDEPENDENCE FIGHTER

Beside these trained combatants, both countries had a large number of civilian volunteers. The conventional view sees volunteering in both conflicts as mainly the affair of the heroic young male, fighting for national independence. This image is conveyed not only in the autobiographies of the young men themselves but also in the memories of women who should have known better since they had also been involved themselves. As Louise Ward and Eve Morrison pointed out for the Irish case, female participation has been continuously underplayed to the point of almost being erased from the memory of the struggle for independence.[19] The same can be said for Poland, where many women were involved. The 'unlikely' combatants in the independence struggles also included boys and teenagers, the elderly, and even the physically disabled (war invalids). All these examples are more frequent in the Polish case, but can be found in Ireland too. Of course, this does not change the fact that paramilitary action was dominated by young men, but a more complete picture is required, and the obvious question is: when and why did 'the other' combatants disappear from it?

[16] See Tom Barry, *Guerrilla Days in Ireland* (Dublin, 1993) and Meda Ryan, *Tom Barry. IRA Freedom Fighter* (Cork, 2003).

[17] Bureau of Military History: Witness Statement 891: Maurice Meade: Private in the Casement Brigade, Germany; Section Commander, East Limerick Flying Column.

[18] Jane Leonard, 'Getting Them At Last: The IRA and Ex-servicemen', in: David Fitzpatrick (ed.), *Revolution? Ireland, 1917–1923* (Dublin, 1990); Augusteijn, *Public Defiance*, 242, 251, 316.

[19] Eve Morrison, 'The Bureau of Military History and Female Republican Activism 1913–1923,' in: Maryann Variulis (ed), *Gender and Power in Irish History* (Dublin, 2009), 59–83; Louise Ryan and Margaret Ward (eds.), *Irish Women and Nationalism. Soldiers, New Women and Wicked Hags* (Dublin, 2004).

Many paramilitaries, and especially those involved in violent excesses against civilians, were part of the 'war youth' generation. They were, in other words, too young to have fought in the 1914–18 war but old enough to have been fascinated by stories of heroism and keen to make their own impact on what were considered as 'wars of independence'.[20] Veterans did not have to be brutalized by the war to join the fighting and to commit violence. Some were looking for adventure or were simply unemployed.[21] As Joost Augusteijn points out, some might have joined paramilitary formations simply to impress women.[22] The war and the rising hopes of achieving national independence had also led to a decline of emigration from both countries.[23] Young men now stayed at home rather than leaving for abroad and became likely recruits for fighting units.

Polish commemoration of the war of independence cherished the myth that all of the Polish young male population rose up to fight.[24] However, the recruitment of volunteers was not as straightforward as the leaders might have wished. Even though official statements claimed a steady flow of volunteers, their own military leaders contradicted this assertion. Karol Baczyński, lieutenant of the Polish Legions fighting in Lwów complained: 'Announcement No. 6 tells of an incredible flow of volunteers. This is not the truth. In my unit I had to start putting together patrols to look for volunteers for the military among anybody between 20 and 40 years of age.' Even this enforced recruitment was not met with sympathy by all sides. 'We searched every single house [...in the whole quarter...] and handed those taken over to the medical commission. Despite any opposition (of which there was a lot) these men were put into uniforms and immediately informed where to fight.' Recruitment was easier in other parts of the country, not yet as strained by war. Some groups stressed their identity as a volunteer unit, but many were made up mainly of former soldiers who simply kept on fighting.[25] In the case of the Związek Wojskowych Polaków in Vilna, most men and most officers formerly belonged to the 1st Eastern Corps of General Dowbór-Muśnicki. Andrzej Brochocki, who was part of this group, praised them as being 'experienced in battle with the Bolsheviks', which made it certain that they 'knew their enemies'. At the same time, he argued that the Samoobrona, the dominant 'self-defence' units in the Vilna region, did not take a political side in the revolution but focused on Polish interests, 'grabbing all the arms and ammunition they could lay hands on'. The number of volunteers differed in the various regions, but all complained about

---

[20] A common phenomenon in paramilitary formations after the Great War. See Gerwarth, 'Counterrevolution,' 181.

[21] Ossolineum, Wrocław, 12926/II pol. 1939 Autograf, Odpis z pamiętnika ppłk. Karola Baczyńskiego '...z przeyżyć jego po...powierzeniu mu komendy punktu zornego rekrutów dla Legjonów Polskich w Jastkowie od dnia 5 sierpnia 1915 roku, 8' (15 August 1915).

[22] Augusteijn, *From Public Defiance to Guerrilla Warfare*, 144.

[23] Philip Orr, '200,000 volunteer soldiers', in: John Horne (ed.), *Our War. Ireland and the Great War* (Dublin, 2008), 63–94.

[24] Christoph Mick, ' "Wer verteidigte Lemberg?" Totengedenken, Kriegsdeutungen und nationale Identität in einer multiethnischen Stadt', in: Dietrich Beyrau (ed.), *Der Krieg in religiösen und nationalen Deutungen der Neuzeit* (Tübingen, 2001), 189–216.

[25] Ossolineum, 12925/III 1885–1939. Baczyński: 'Pamiętniki', Mikrofilm 2429, Zeszyt 5, 187 (7 November 1918); 192/193 (about 11 November 1918); BN Rękopisy; Rps BN akc 10312.

being insufficiently equipped with ammunition and weaponry.[26] The paramilitaries were also short of other essential equipment, such as winter clothes, shoes, boots, horses, and first aid materials. When the equipment finally slowly improved, Brochocki proudly noted that his unit assumed a 'more and more military look'.[27] Many bought guns from soldiers of the withdrawing armies—or simply disarmed them forcefully.[28]

This method of recruiting any available 'volunteer' for the national cause led to a decline in quality of the paramilitary units. The ex-servicemen who served in them frequently complained about the lack of discipline. Some units were formed by revolutionary soldiers who tried to be equipped by Bolshevik commissars. Other units, according to their critics, were little more than gangs of bandits, formed by 'local peasants, mostly veterans of the Russian Army who formerly fought with the communists [but who are] now just anti-communist and anti-Semitic gangs, never disdaining armed robbery.' Discipline was also tempered by the impact of alcohol and by war weariness.[29] These developments favoured violence against civilians in a transitional period and regions of low state control.

UNLIKELY COMBATANTS: BOYS AND WOMEN

Unlike regular military units, paramilitary formations in Ireland and Poland accepted unconventional combatants, thereby further dissolving the dichotomy of civilian and military. Even though fighting as a quasi-military force, the paramilitary formations in both countries displayed their ambiguous nature in their recruitment strategies. In this respect the definition of paramilitary included civilians acting as soldiers. Knowing their own tactics and recruitment included children, women and even invalids in the fighting, paramilitary combatants were more likely to expect the opponent to do the same, thus increasing suspicion and aggression towards civilians, and lowering the threshold of violence against them. The recruitment of younger men frequently included those too young for normal military service. In the Polish case, teenagers and boys were accepted. Karol Baczyński, one of the leading figures of the battle for Lwów, sent a letter to the commandant of the Polish Legion asking him to order the First Brigade to release his 12-year-old son Zdisław from military service, but in vain. His son was not the only child involved; the sight of children carrying weapons during the battle was common. Of the 6,022 defenders of Lwów, 1,421 were under 18. 1,027 of them were involved in active fighting while 394 acted as auxiliary units or nursed the wounded. The youngest fatality was the 12-year-old Jan Dufrat, while the youngest combatant

[26] BN Rękopisy; Rps BN akc 10312; Andrzej Brochocki: Wspomnienia, 4A; Ossolineum, 12925/III 1885–1939. Baczyński: 'Pamiętniki', Mikrofilm 2429, Zeszyt 5, 188, (8 November 1918).

[27] Rps BN akc 10312; Andrzej Brochocki, 6, 15.

[28] 'The alcohol record rests with the 4th Squadron, where the daily consumption is more than 1 Litre of spirits per day'. Rps BN akc 10312; Andrzej Brochocki, 82. Rps BN ack. 11400; Józef Fiedorowicz: Wspomnienia. (1980), 34. For Germans seizing weapons, see ibid., 72.

[29] Rps BN akc 10312; Andrzej Brochocki, 36–7.

was only nine years old. Forty-three children up to the age of 12 were involved.[30] Even men who had been wounded in the World War or considered unfit for service were not rejected as volunteers for the national cause, with several invalids included in the paramilitary forces.[31]

In Ireland, adolescents and teenagers participated in paramilitary activities, though to a lesser extent than in Poland. Joost Augusteijn identifies the proportion of teenage members of IRA units as nearly 20 per cent in 1921.[32] The tendency was helped by the importance of Gaelic sports clubs, family affiliations and local structures which, even if they did not engage in recruiting themselves, motivated and mobilized young men and boys for the cause.[33] However, while individual examples of very young boys (early teens) exist, most teenagers involved in the Irish struggles were more likely to be over 16. Some boys were actually turned down with regard to their age, when trying to volunteer—which sometimes did not prevent them from pretending they were members of the IRA anyway.[34] But even at the age of 16—or 18, for that matter—teenagers were likely to be overwhelmed by sudden immersion in fighting and violence—and had difficulties coping with their new role. Charles Dalton, only 17 when he participated in the killings on Bloody Sunday, was haunted by this experience.[35] Still, even though a significant number among their combatants would have been under age for a traditional state army, the paramilitary formations embraced these men as the young generation of a pre-state army, fighting for the national cause.

By contrast, the role of women was more controversial. Women also played a significant role in the independence struggles for both Ireland and Poland despite their subsequent marginalization in commemoration and historiography. Once the fighting ended, the former fighting women were reduced to passive figures such as mothers, sisters and nurses, or else portrayed as depraved 'wild women' and 'fighting whores'.[36] In fact, women were actively involved in the armed forces of the independence movements. Baczyński mentions in his diaries the daughter of one of his acquaintances, Zofia Kamińska, whom he helped to enlist, at her request, as a volunteer. She fought as an Uhlan, under a male *nom de guerre*, and was respected for her courage. Karol Baczyński, a lieutenant in the battle for Lwów and

---

[30] Ossolineum, 12926/II pol. 1939 Odpis z pamiętnika ppłk. Karola Baczyńskiego, 28 (1 October 1915), 32 (11 October 1915); 12925/III 1885–1939. Baczyński: 'Pamiętniki', Mikrofilm 2429, Zeszyt 5, 189–90, (9 November 1918); Obrona Lwowa. 1–22 listopada 1918. Vol. 3 'Organizacja Listopadowej Obrony Lwowa; Ewidencja Uczestników Walk; Lista Strat.' (Warsaw 1994), Appendix.

[31] The volunteers in the Silesian uprisings included a number of invalid veterans, e.g. Jan Ludyga-Laskowski, retired from front service in France after a serious injury, but became the Chief of GHQ in the insurrection.

[32] 19.7%, with a peak in Owenwee and Laffansbridge of 31%, Crossabeg being the only company without members of that age cohort. Augusteijn, *Public Defiance*, 355. While most members were 20 to 24, some companies' age range went from early teens (13 in Aughagower) up to the seventies (ibid., 354). Augusteijn argues this was a sign of better integration of the IRA into rural life. Ibid., 355.

[33] Peter Hart, *The IRA and its Enemies. Violence and Community in Cork 1916–1923*, 210ff.

[34] Hart, *The IRA and its Enemies*, 227.

[35] Anne Dolan, 'Killing and Bloody Sunday, November 1920,' *Historical Journal*, 49 (2006) 3, 789–801, here 798.

[36] Ryan, 'In the Line of Fire', 47.

in charge of the defence of one of the headquarters, was proud to be her mentor and praised her courage as greater than that of many men, including her own husband: 'I recall she is doing this out of good patriotism and because her husband did not volunteer to join the legions.'[37] Officially, Piłsudski had banned women from the Polish Legions. However, a number of women joined up under male pseudonyms, the best known among them being Wanda Gertz, who joined the Polish Legions in February 1916, using her cousin Kazimierz Żuchowicz's documents. From 1919 on she fought at the front in the Polish-Bolshevik War. Her POW commandant in Vilna, well aware of her being a woman, described her as 'a heroine, to whom most men should bow low', one of the 'heroic girls' who were 'marching to the front at a time when the boys were hiding.'[38]

Many more women fought for Poland over the following years. In the Battle of Lwów alone 427 women were involved, at least 17 of them fighting in the first line, the others serving in auxiliary units in charge of communications, provision of weapons and ammunition, providing first aid or acting as guards.[39] While Lwów might have been the most prominent case, other women paramilitary units were set up. There were female subdivisions of the Polish Military Organisation (POW) but the 'Ochotnicza Legia Kobiet' (OLK, Voluntary Legion of Women), formed in Lwów in 1918, soon established branches all over Poland during the following border wars. At its peak, the OLK counted about 2,500 official members.

Other women received less recognition for their work. In Ireland, they have been often dismissed as either barely involved, only in charge of despatches and nursing, or as political furies, harder and more bitter than the men.[40] But women were present as the public face of political activism, as republican men went into hiding or were arrested. Most influential and best known were the women of Cumann na mBan (The Women's League), founded in 1914. By 1921 it had established over 800 branches and had at its peak about 3,000 members. During the War of Independence, Cumann na mBan branches became affiliated to IRA units and acted as 'an army of women'.[41] They wore uniforms, engaged in military training, organized rallies and disrupted political meetings. Far from only being 'public representatives of the militant movement', they were also 'secret participants in military activities'.[42]

Several well-known female activists, such as Molly Childers, Mary MacSwiney and the Countess Markievicz, actively supported the IRA along with many less well-known women. Political activism in both countries led to the formation of what in many respects aspired to be a conventional army with a male-dominated hierarchy. However, male and female roles were called into question by the specific

---

[37] Ossolineum, 12926/II pol. 1939 Odpis z pamiętnika ppłk. Karola Baczyńskiego, 34 (22 October 1915). Ibid., 26 (28 September 1915).
[38] In a letter to the M.S. Wojsk to recommend her for the Virtuti Militari. Słownik Biograficzny Kobiet Odznaczonych orderem wojennym virtuti militari. (edited by Elżbieta Zawacka) (Toruń, 2004), Vol.I, 202–5. Other examples were Ludwika Daszkiewiczówna-Kepisz as Stanisław Kepisz; M. Wołoszynowska as Alfred Wołoszynowski and M. Błaszczykówna as Tadeusz Zaleski. Ibid., 128–31.
[39] Obrona Lwowa, vol. 3 'Ewidencja Uczestników Walk', Appendix.
[40] Ernie O'Malley, On Another Man's Wound, 290. Ward, Revolutionaries, 86.
[41] Ibid., 163.   [42] Ryan, 'In the Line of Fire', 46.

nature of conflicts that involved relying on civilian support. In the early months of the conflict, 'women did just about everything men did. Women fought, drilled, organized, canvassed, collected, and were willing to go to gaol for it.'[43] However, their active participation was regarded critically by many. When the *Cork Examiner* reported that 'young girls' had thrown bombs at a lorry of the national troops, this was officially denied by republican sources. Republican women were denounced as 'die-hards', as irrational and as 'hysterical "furies"', and they were accused of sexual 'impropriety'. Their impact on the independence struggle was denigrated and the masculine stereotypes of the struggle enforced. Because fighting women upset traditional social roles, official propaganda and the public focused on the more 'female qualities' and roles, such as first aid, and nursing, cooking, and providing shelter. [44] As the IRA became organized more professionally, women's part in the struggles changed and they were gradually relegated to supporting roles.[45]

From the early days of the Easter Rising there was no clear policy on women's participation in nationalist activities. The Irish Volunteers accepted Cumann na mBan as an auxiliary unit and the Irish Citizen Army proclaimed equality of sexes within its ranks, but a majority rejected the very idea of women fighting on the basis of traditional Catholic views on appropriate social behaviour for women. The Citizen Army Ambulance Corps was the only formation to give women revolvers for self-protection. About 90 women eventually took part in the Rising, 60 of them Cumann na mBan, the rest belonging to the Irish Citizen Army. Cumann na mBan were mainly restricted to 'female tasks' such as nursing, cooking, and dispatch carrying, but it should be noted that their tasks also included holding up vans and commandeering their contents (food).[46]

The guerrilla conflict during the War of Independence reorganized the internal structures of both the IRA and Cumann na mBan and linked them more closely. Each Cumann na mBan branch had to be set up in coordination with one IRA branch. Most of the women involved were in their early twenties. Cumann na mBan officers were trained in military camps, that taught them first aid and nursing skills, but also 'drill, signalling, map reading, care of arms'. Appreciation came only slowly with the Civil War, when the IRA had to rely on the women's support because their male members were imprisoned or in hiding.[47] Even though a lot of the tasks delegated to the Cumann na mBan branches were about communication and provision of goods, these were not always peaceful and 'ladylike'. Carrying dispatches often entailed cross-country cycling at night without lights, in danger of being captured or shot. 'Running errands' included not only shopping for food, but also providing petrol for arson attacks on military barracks, and sometimes even assembling the materials for tarring and feathering those who had fallen into

---

[43] Hart, *The IRA and its Enemies*, 236.

[44] *Cork Examiner*, 16 October 1922; Poblacht na hÉireann, 21 October 1922; William Cosgrave, *Irish Times* 1 January 1923, quoted in Ward, *Revolutionaries*, 86. Ryan, 'In the Line of Fire', 50, 60. Also see Sinead McCoole, *No Ordinary Women. Irish Female Activists in the Revolutionary Years 1900–1923* (Dublin, 2003); Ryan, 'In the Line of Fire', 50.

[45] Hart, *The IRA and its Enemies*, 257.

[46] Ward, *Unmanageable Revolutionaries*, 107, 110–11.   [47] Ibid., 157–5; 187–8.

disgrace. Sometimes, the female paramilitaries took individual action. Reacting to the murder of the McMahon family, the Cumann na mBan member Eithne Coyle decided to enforce the boycott of Northern Irish newspapers and goods. Helped by women comrades, she organized armed hold-ups of trains and carriages and burned their deliveries from the North.[48]

POLICE, MARTYRS AND FRANC-TIREURS

Civilians acting as soldiers were not the only ones to blur the traditional boundary between civilians and soldiers. There is also evidence of combatants deliberately using civilian disguise. This raised the danger of all civilians being treated like an enemy army. Those who were professionally trained soldiers repeatedly complained about outrages and the lack of military discipline in the paramilitary movement. Yet rumours of franc-tireurs frightened them into suspecting any civilian of being a potential combatant.

The term 'franc-tireur' originated in the Franco-Prussian War of 1870 and was used to describe irregular forces. Fear and 'autosuggestion' of combatants about civilians being franc-tireurs, about combatants dressing in civilian clothes and fighting a 'people's war', provided frequent justification for assaults against civilians. The franc-tireur myth represented the individual fear of death, especially from an unexpected quarter. In some cases the fear of franc-tireurs was even used by those in command in order to manipulate their troops. The reproach of faceless anonymity on the part of the enemy was central to all transgressions of restraint. In civil and guerrilla war, the enemy is regarded as treacherous and the civilian becomes a potential combatant in disguise, a supporter of the enemy, a traitor, or terrorist. Both in Poland and Ireland, each side in the conflict nurtured its own rumours and myths about franc-tireurs.[49]

The social prejudices against 'uncommon' combatants, especially women, were linked to the deep fear of franc-tireurs. The introduction of newly established formations added to the confusion. Repeatedly, Irish witness statements refer to crimes committed by agents, who 'did not appear to [be] a regular Soldier, nor...the customary Black and Tan'. The British equally perceived the IRA as faceless terrorists who could easily vanish among the supporting civilian population.[50] Describing an ambush in County Galway in November 1920, the Head Constable James Healey seems to have been even more upset that '50 young men had all vanished into peaceful workers over the countryside' than he was about the ambush itself.[51] This insecurity about who was civilian and who combatant continued into the Irish Civil War.

---

[48] UCD Archives, P61/4, Eithne Coyle Papers. Statement of Mrs Charlotte Dempsey (née Heney), 22–8.

[49] John Horne and Alan Kramer, *German Atrocities, 1914. A History of Denial* (New Haven, 2001), 149–50.

[50] The same was true for both sides, as Anne Dolan points out in her contribution to this volume.

[51] Imperial War Museum, London (IWM) 2949 Misc 175 (2658), Account of the life of Major General Sir H. H. Tudor KCB CMG (1871–1965), 29, 314.

The same 'facelessness' and blurring of distinctions between combatant and non-combatant were described in Poland, where volunteers often fought in civilian clothes.[52] The distinctions between regular army, paramilitaries, armed peasants or self-defence units on the one hand and armed gangs and bandits on the other hand were so blurred, that they could even overlap.[53] In Poland, the Battle of Lwów in an urban setting displayed aspects of both guerrilla and civil war and led to the suspicion of any inhabitant of the city. Since each side cherished the myth that 'everybody was fighting, regardless of age, gender, social background', anybody belonging to another community was suspected of doing the same.[54] The collective self-suggestion of being attacked illegally in a partisan war contributed to the escalation of violence.[55] Rumours of enemy outrages often provoked reprisals of the same kind, so that the accusation became self-fulfilling.[56]

In the Irish case the members of the IRA were usually still connected to their families and communities, even while in hiding or on the move. Also, many IRA men fought in their home county, thus being closely acquainted with both countryside and population. The Polish paramilitaries, on the other hand, were composed of a mix of local volunteers and a high number of mobile ex-veterans and adventurers. The dynamics of civil war and national uprising mixed with those of a war of conquest. Paramilitaries were often strangers to the regions and outsiders to their communities, among them the soldiers of the Haller's Army, who were highly active in the Eastern territories.[57] This, among other reasons, contributed to the difference in the scale of violence in the two countries.

Religion, too, shaped how participants in paramilitary violence understood their role.[58] A deep-seated belief in national martyrdom facilitated a rise of violence under the veil of a national struggle for independence. Polish and Irish Catholicism provided a symbolic language for presenting and justifying violence, most notably through the figure of the martyr. Of course, the paramilitaries were not all saints—far from it. While risking their lives for the national cause, most IRA volunteers would not stop living it, and some were even, as Augusteijn argues, 'diverted from their tasks by a strong interest in socializing'.[59] However,

---

[52] L'viv, DALO, f. 257, op. 1c, spr. 44, 5.

[53] As this note states, taken during the battle of Lwów: 'Two Jews killed by bandits, who at the same time were soldiers of the Polish army'. L'viv, DALO, f. 257, op. 1c, spr. 44, 5.

[54] Ossolineum 14059/II: Józef Wraubek, 'Moje wspomnienia'. Lata 1895–1945. Mikrofilm 3951, 139.

[55] Horne and Kramer, *Atrocities*, 124; John Horne and Alan Kramer, 'War between Soldiers and Enemy Civilians, 1914–1915', in: Roger Chickering and Stig Förster (eds.), *Great War, Total War. Combat and Mobilization on the Western Front, 1914–1918* (Cambridge, 2000), 153–68 (here 157).

[56] Stanley Tambiah, *Leveling Crowds: Ethnonationalist Conflicts and Collective Violence in South Asia* (London, 1996), 237.

[57] Kapiszewski, Andrzej, 'Controversial Reports on the Situation of Jews in Poland in the Aftermath of World War I', *Studia Judaica* 7 (2004), 257–304 (here 270, 276).

[58] Wilson discusses religion and its function as a major distinctive social boundary enabling crowd violence in Upper Silesia and Ulster: Wilson, *Frontiers of Violence*, 41–4.

[59] Which included meeting the opposite sex. Augusteijn, *Public Defiance*, 143. He also refers to 'some unconfirmed reports of illegitimate children' between male and female IRA members. Ibid., 144.

the (self-)representation of most male combatants clearly described them exclusively as chivalrous, well-disciplined and pious. In sharp distinction to accounts by the German *Freikorps*, their recollections emphasized brotherhood, camaraderie, and discipline instead of pleasure in killing, or sexual encounters with women. The image of the republican campaign was completely de-sexualized, representing the ideal of celibate devotion. Louise Ryan argues that this presentation can be read as a potential overlap between love of Ireland and devotion to Mary as the virgin mother of God.[60] The pious and chivalrous image was underlined by the later witness accounts provided by wives and relatives. By doing so, and by diminishing their own impact, these women contributed to the re-establishment of traditional dichotomies.[61] The idealization of the combatants placed them in the canon of Irish martyrdom, alongside figures such as Patrick Pearse, James Connolly and the other executed heroes of 1916, and also Terence MacSwiney in 1920.

The Polish martyrology of the defenders of Lwów also drew on the well-established commemoration of the 'national' uprisings in the nineteenth century, especially those of 1830 and 1863. However, in clear distinction to the Irish commemoration, the youngest participants were included in, or were sometimes even the centre of, this narrative of martyrdom. Schoolboys and young students were praised as 'the eaglets of Lwów'.[62] Some of the youngest fighters became national icons in the interwar period and the object of a number of poems and songs. The same was not true for the female participants. Their experiences had to be contained, as they did not suit the postwar restitution of a traditional gendered order. Wanda Gertz, though praised by her commanders for her courage, was denied the 'Virtuti Militari' medal, because she had been fighting with the Legions disguised as a man, ignoring the ban on women.[63]

In Ireland, the Catholic Church vehemently condemned women's participation in the conflict.[64] During the Civil War, it eventually excommunicated all Republicans who, 'in the absence of any legitimate authority to justify it [were carrying on] a system of murder'.[65] When women prisoners were called on to accept this before confession, Eithne Coyle provoked the priest by arguing that 'bishops were hardly right when they burnt Joan of Arc', thus claiming for the female contribution to the Irish struggle a martyrology similar to that of male combatants.

---

[60] Ryan, 'In the Line of Fire', 52–3. For Freikorps, see Theweleit, *Male Fantasies*, and Gerwarth, 'Counterrevolution.'

[61] Ward, *Unmanageable Revolutionaries*, 193.

[62] Stanisław Sławomir Nicieja, *Lwowskie Orlęta. Czyn i Legenda* (Warszawa, 2009).

[63] When she was eventually awarded the medal, it was only for her participation in the resistance movement during the Second World War: *Słownik Biograficzny Kobiet Odznaczonych orderem wojennym virtuti militari*, vol. I, 202–5.

[64] Ward, *Unmanageable Revolutionaries*, 86.

[65] Quoted in ibid., 192. This step of alienation from the Catholic Church might have removed their Catholic moral guidelines and thereby further encouraged the rise of radical violence (John Borgonovo, *Spies, Informers and the 'Anti-Sinn Féin Society.' The Intelligence War in Cork City, 1919–1921* (Dublin, 2007), 38–40).

CONCLUSIONS

After the end of the postwar independence conflicts, both Ireland and Poland experienced processes of consolidation and purges that reasserted the monopoly of force on the part of the new state. Paramilitary forces, which had helped gain independence, were now a potential threat to political stability, especially as they were not centrally controlled and were usually loyal first and foremost to their immediate leader. In the absence of functioning state authorities, or in opposition to authorities that were regarded as illegitimate, paramilitary formations in both countries defined themselves as legitimate forces. Believing in their responsibility to establish order and in their future designation as corps of the national armies, members of these irregular formations regarded themselves as pre-military rather than paramilitary forces. To them, this belief meant that their actions would be legitimized by their future function. While aiming to defeat their opponents, in their own understanding they were defending their country. During the years of the struggle, the fighting was considered as a national rising, a demonstration of the 'nation in arms', which united the national forces to achieve independence. Therefore, the range of combatants included women and children, and the organization of the national struggle relied on civilians for support and auxiliary service. In this respect the paramilitary formations in the two case studies had common features that distinguished them from the counter-revolutionary nature of paramilitary violence in some other countries.

Yet, their role in forming the nation also left an awkward, subversive legacy that hindered the acceptance of 'the unlikely' combatants and eventually rendered their integration into national commemorations difficult or even impossible. The participation of boys and students was retrospectively more acceptable than that of women, as the former would grow up and eventually become soldiers. This is at least true for Poland with a system of military conscription—the Irish seem to have experienced more taboos about the participation of minors. However, women's participation as combatants and the blurring of gender boundaries in irregular warfare presented a major challenge in both countries.[66] In the course of re-establishing 'normality' after the fighting was over, traditional dichotomies had to be reinstated. Minors and adults, men and women were restored to their 'proper place' in society. The male soldier in a 'pre-state' army, embodying both the national hero and the martyr for the national cause, contributed to the national pantheon, whereas subversive women did not. More generally, the paramilitary forces that fought for independence were now regarded as a potential threat to political stability, both because they embodied these transgressions of social roles and because (especially in the Irish case) they remained an alternative source of national myth and self-legitimization. As the national struggle was reconstructed in hindsight as a legitimate, conventional war, the figure of the irregular remained a troubling one. Commemorating the soldiers exclusively as able-bodied young men was part of a narrative that helped transform pre-state irregulars into the cadres of a national army and retrospectively consecrated the founding of the nation by war.

---

[66] Ryan, 'In the Line of Fire', 60–1.

12

The British Culture of Paramilitary Violence in the Irish War of Independence

Anne Dolan

FROM PARAMILITARIES TO PARAMILITARISM

On 28 February 1933 Major Henry Procter went to the House of Commons like any other day since he had become a member of parliament in 1931. It was an ordinary day by Parliament's standards but when late into the evening debate settled on the question of subsidies for housing, when Procter criticized the Labour Party and the trade unions for hindering the progress of building 'houses that are worth while for the working classes of this country', that long straightforward day took a slightly strange turn.[1] F.S. Cocks delivered Labour's retort: Procter had no authority to speak on the question of housing. It was nothing to do with his knowledge or expertise; Procter had, after all, just told the House that he was a qualified engineer. It seems Procter had no right to speak because of where he was and what he might have been eleven or twelve years before:

> I do not question the sincerity of the hon. and learned and gallant Member for Accrington [Procter], but I do question his authority to speak on this question of housing. I should have thought that after his wide experience with the Black and Tans in Ireland he was a greater authority on burning down houses than on constructing them.[2]

It was an irrelevant and utterly extraneous response. At best, it was parliamentary gamesmanship, at worst, a taunt, a jibe, and it was certainly understood by Procter as such. He was not going to stand for it: 'I was an officer in His Majesty's regular Army and not a Black and Tan'.[3] He understood how 'Black and Tan' had become shorthand for all that was unruly and undisciplined, all that was considered wanton and destructive about service in Ireland in 1920–21. His instinct was to protect his own record, to distinguish 'His Majesty's regular Army' from the taint of this implicitly irregular lot. He rose to the bait, made no attempt to point out the irrelevance of his Irish past to the issue at hand, and made no more contributions on the housing debate.

This exchange between Cocks and Procter is not very significant, and yet it manages to say quite a lot about Britain's paramilitary past, or at least something of its

---

[1] *Hansard* 5 (Commons), vol. 275, col. 269, 28 February 1933.
[2] Ibid., col. 2 73.   [3] Ibid.

Fig. 16. Group of three Black and Tans.

discomfort with it. Being called a 'Black and Tan' was an insult that needed no explanation; it tripped off the tongue with a readiness that suggested a sort of agreed cer-
tainty about what it had come to mean by 1933. It was something that any good
upstanding army man would not abide; it was demeaning, debasing, humiliating to
be counted among such men. It suggested that paramilitarism, this 'Black and Tan-
nery', was everything that 'regular' army life was not. For old army men like Procter
the distinction was obvious and easily drawn between military and paramilitary, but
after Ireland, the wider willingness to make this distinction seemed somewhat blunted,
much to this particular old soldier's distress. When he denied that he had been a Black
and Tan, Cocks just broadened the scope of his attack: 'Anyone who served in Ireland
during that terrible time must have a far better knowledge of burning down houses
than constructing them'.[4] 'Anyone'—no matter if regular soldier or Black and Tan—
they were all the same, all tainted by the worst associations that had come to define
the phrase 'Black and Tan' itself. There was no room for finer feelings about battalion
or platoon, military or paramilitary: all served Crown and state and all had come to be
associated in their service with the indiscipline and disorder, the reprisals and murders
that Ireland's war of independence had already come to signify. Britain's paramilitary
past in Ireland was one that bled into its military past. And this suggests a definition of
paramilitarism that strays far beyond those groups conventionally identified as paramilitaries there. It suggests paramilitarism as disruption, as defiance or disarray, as a state of
mind where the bounds of acceptable behaviour were aggressively crossed by army,

---

[4] *Hansard* 5 (Commons), vol. 275, col. 269, 28 February 1933.

paramilitaries and police, as something that served and was easily understood as an insult over a decade after the event. British paramilitarism was certainly shaped by the IRA's violence, by the nature of Ireland's guerrilla warfare, by the imagined dangers as much as the real threats. It was inspired and driven by the demands of metropolitan politics and by Ireland's place in its midst; it was an answer to a domestic problem before it became a colonial phenomenon. In part, it was a consequence of victory in 1918. Calls for men from Silesia to Constantinople and beyond, the pressure to demobilize beyond the already dramatic reduction of the forces by November 1920, together with the 'fear that the weary British soldier—conscript or volunteer—might not continue to serve unquestioningly now that the war was over' created the circumstances that made paramilitarism possible.[5] Paramilitarism was not the preserve of Europe's defeated powers like Germany and Austria or its dissatisfied victor, Italy. It was an unsettling part of Britain's postwar predicament and Procter's unease speaks eloquently of how this kind of paramilitarism was perceived. He understood all it meant to be called a 'Black and Tan'.

'Black and Tan'—the sobriquet that spoke of hastily assembled uniforms, part Royal Irish Constabulary (RIC) dark green, part army khaki—quickly became and remains a convenient, sometimes incorrect and quite charged shorthand for all the auxiliary forces sent to Ireland to supplement the RIC throughout 1920 and into 1921.[6] It was a common blurring of the nomenclature then as well as now. The Black and Tans were the ex-servicemen recruited as RIC constables throughout Britain in late 1919 and constituted a force of approximately 9,000 men before the war's end.[7] However, 'Black and Tans' also came to refer to the Temporary Cadets of the Auxiliary Division of the RIC, a force of some 2,200 ex-officers, formed in July 1920, and in practice virtually independent of military and police control.[8] Both forces were made up of veterans from all services. The Auxiliaries included members of the Burmese police, of Canadian regiments, even one from the Chinese Labour Corp. Both Auxiliaries and Black and Tans had Irish members. Samples of the Auxiliaries suggest that more than 80 per cent were Protestant, over 70 per cent unmarried. They came from a variety of backgrounds, including clerks, shop assistants, professionals, manual labourers, even actors and musicians and for equally varied reasons they found themselves at war in Ireland.[9]

---

[5] In November 1918 the Chief of the Imperial General Staff, Sir Henry Wilson, had over 3.5 million men. By November 1920 his forces had been reduced to 370,000 but still had to cope with vastly expanded military commitments. Keith Jeffery, *The British Army and the Crisis of Empire 1918–22* (Manchester, 1984), 13.

[6] See A.D. Harvey, 'Who Were the Auxiliaries?', *The Historical Journal*, 35 (1992), 665–9; David Leeson, 'The "Scum of London's Underworld"? British Recruits for the RIC, 1920–21', *Contemporary British History*, 17 (2003), 1–38; Richard Bennett, *The Black and Tans* (London, 1959).

[7] Charles Townshend, *The British Campaign in Ireland 1919–1921: the Development of Political and Military Policies* (Oxford, 1975), 40. Recruits were sought in the major cities in Britain and the first ex-service man recruited in this way was appointed on 2 January 1920.

[8] Ibid., 110–11.

[9] For a detailed analysis of the Auxiliaries see Leeson, 'The "Scum of London's Underworld"?' and Harvey, 'Who Were the Auxiliaries?'.

Ireland's war of independence began in January 1919. The country had been promised Home Rule before the outbreak of the Great War, but radicalized by that war, by the war's promises about the rights of small nations, radicalized by Britain's heavy-handed response to a rebellion in 1916, it emerged from the Great War with a changed political landscape. Whether Ireland's voters wanted a violent fight for independence when they returned a majority of Sinn Féin candidates in the general election of December 1918 remains a moot point, but it was clear that the 73 new members of parliament were not going to take their seats at Westminster, that they intended to form a parliament of their own in Dublin. On the first meeting of this new parliament, An Dáil, on the day that the Dáil declared Irish independence in Irish, English and French and vested its hopes for recognition in the conference at Versailles, the pattern of Ireland's war of independence was already set. Two policemen where shot dead by members of the Irish Volunteers in Co. Tipperary. No orders had been issued by Volunteer headquarters; the men wore no uniforms; they shot and killed and disappeared back into the everyday, starting a guerrilla war that crept towards an unmanageable intensity by the summer of 1920. Attacks on isolated policemen and police barracks left swathes of the country effectively unpoliced.[10]

The intimidation of police, of their families, the increased acceptance by enough of the people of the Dáil's alternative system of justice, from fear or conviction and from everything in between, meant that the country became increasingly ungovernable by traditional means.[11] An army stretched by new postings across the postwar world on top of its traditional drafts, an army stretched further by the imposition of martial law across a number of Irish counties in December 1920, caused and intensified the recruitment of Britain's paramilitaries for Ireland.[12] And of course the choice of paramilitary forces, of auxiliary forces to supplement the RIC, made sense in the context of the British government's official response. Britain was not officially at war. 'The Irish job', Lloyd George told his Cabinet, 'was a policeman's job'.[13] 'You do not declare war against rebels',[14] you do not admit the existence or legitimacy of anything more than murder and assassination, outrage and insurrection; nothing more than an outbreak of civil disobedience, to be treated as crime, as lawlessness, to be put down, with military and paramilitary aid to the civil powers. The lines were already blurred by Westminster. 'The RIC', Charles Townshend argues, 'had to become military in order to survive.'[15]

The British troops in Ireland were on a war footing for the purposes of discipline, crime and punishment; they were on peacetime pay, privileges, allowances

---

[10] For a full discussion of the war see David Fitzpatrick, *Politics and Irish Life: Provincial Experience of War and Revolution* (Dublin, 1977; new ed., Cork 1998); Peter Hart, *The IRA at War 1916–23* (Oxford, 2003); Michael Hopkinson, *The Irish War of Independence* (Dublin, 2002).

[11] William Joseph Lowe, 'The War Against the RIC', *Eire-Ireland*, 37 (2002), 79–117.

[12] See Leeson, 'The "Scum of London's Underworld"?' and Harvey, 'Who Were the Auxiliaries?'.

[13] Tom Jones, *Whitehall Diary Volume 3: Ireland 1918–25* (Oxford: Oxford University Press, 1971), 73.

[14] 'Note of conversation', 30 April 1920, TNA, CAB 23/21/23/20A.

[15] Townshend, *The British Campaign in Ireland*, 40.

and compensations.[16] They worked often in mixed patrols with the RIC, with the Black and Tans and the Auxiliaries. The Black and Tans wore a mixture of police and military uniforms; the Auxiliaries, the ex-officers recruited to supplement the RIC, wore military uniforms, and never tried or attempted or pretended to look like police. The paramilitaries were repeatedly portrayed and perceived as ex-servicemen, while the military repeatedly complained about playing at policemen, about not being allowed to respond as soldiers to the guerrilla war they found themselves in. Soldiers described Ireland as a curious mixture of war and peace, spoke of an army carrying out policing and later judicial duties, waiting, as one soldier put it, to be shot at before they were allowed to shoot back.[17] Many soldiers wrote of how humiliating they found their duties; that while some guard duties were more palatable than others, searching homes, stopping and searching men on the streets was undignified, even 'repugnant' for all concerned.[18] It was just not an army's work. There was too much blurring of the lines of service, too much under-mining of too many traditions, and it lent itself too easily to frustration, to the kind of behaviour that came to define 'Black and Tan'.

VIOLENCE AND PARAMILITARISM

Across forces, what initially seemed to define, and what was used to defend Brit-ain's paramilitarism in Ireland, was the nature of the violence encountered there. It was explicitly given as the cause of this paramilitary response. The Chief Secretary for Ireland, Sir Hamar Greenwood, frequently told Westminster that charges of reprisals and indiscipline against the troops and Black and Tans simply failed to take account of what he called the 'prime causes'.[19] Accounting for the burning of three villages in Clare by Crown forces, the nature of IRA violence was clearly blamed:

> I admitted the burning of these villages by forces of the Crown, but the House has forgotten the cause. One day six policemen were ambushed, murdered by explosive bullets, and their bodies disembowelled by those bullets. A short time afterwards some other forces of the Crown, coming along, saw this frightful mess of their comrades. I admitted in the House months ago, and I admit now, that they lost control of them-selves, and these villages were burned, people were turned out of their houses, and men were shot in the heat of a hot-blooded reprisal. I regret it beyond words...[but] let us have some tears for the 28 soldiers and policemen who have been brutally mur-dered...the responsibility for the commencement of this orgy of murder is not upon any Government on these Benches. It is not upon soldiers or police. It is upon these Sinn Féin conspirators...who have never ceased, and are not ceasing now, to murder.[20]

---

[16] E.M. Ransford, Imperial War Museum (IWM), 80/29/1.
[17] J.V. Faviell, IWM, 82/24/1.
[18] F.A.S. Clarke, LHC, 1/6 1968; Lt. Gen. Sir Hugh Jeudwine, IWM, 72/82/2.
[19] *Hansard* 5 (Commons), vol. 138, col. 630, 21 February 1921.
[20] Ibid., cols. 639–45. 28 refers to the number of murders in Co. Clare at that time.

The men Greenwood defended made these connections between cause and effect more explicitly still. In a variety of contemporary accounts, they measured the IRA's guerrilla war, against what they knew of war. Whether it was the Great War, or service in India or elsewhere, they defined their time in Ireland against these experiences. By the way it failed to measure up to the rules and conventions of modern warfare, by the manner in which it flouted and disregarded and broke those rules, these men seemed to be defining paramilitary violence in terms of what it was not. It was not about winning long-running battles, not about killing vast numbers in the field, it was not considered honourable, not regulated, not recognizable by a soldier's definition of war. It was defined by frustration and exasperation. As one man put it: 'Straightforward fighting is our job, but this sort of thing!...Why, fighting the IRA is fighting assassins. It's low, cowardly cunning they excel at. I tell you straight I'd sooner do another two-and-a half years in France than the same length of time here...Yes, it's a rum kind of war.'[21] And because they were fighting this 'rum kind of war' they had to change their own definition of war.

J.S. Wilkinson, who served with the Sherwood Foresters, wrote of Ireland: 'all in all I far preferred the War to civil duties in Ireland. In war one does know roughly where the enemy is, but in the conditions in Ireland in those times one never knew.'[22] This sense of never knowing bred a palpable paranoia. With the Camerons in Cork, Douglas Wimberley felt that 'all around us [were] those who were now our enemies, the Sinn Feinners, [sic] all wore plain clothes, had their arms hidden, and spoke good English. It was very difficult for some weeks to teach the Jocks that we were now in what was largely a hostile country, and that maybe 75 per cent of all the local inhabitants, both men and women, viewed us with enmity, active or passive...we had to learn our job the hard way.'[23] While Douglas Duff began his service as a Black and Tan unable to 'believe that the kindly, lovable Irish folk that I had known so well had become the dastardly murderers that they were represented to be', he left Ireland relieved 'to be returning from that hell-broth of murder and secret shootings on [his] own feet and not in [a] wooden case.'[24] Bernard Montgomery wrote from Cork in February 1921 that 'the war over here is the very devil; half the people are friendly and the other half bitter foes'.[25] Two years later he admitted that 'I think I regarded all civilians as "Shinners", and I never had any dealings with any of them.'[26]

From many of these men's perspectives there were plenty of reasons and rumours to fuel the anger and indiscipline of their own response. There were rumours that the IRA had the means and the will to spread typhus, that poisoned sweets and cigarettes were being dispensed, that nothing was to be trusted not even the most

[21] Wilfrid Ewart, *A Journey in Ireland 1921* (Dublin, 2008) (1st edn. 1922), 69–70.
[22] J.S. Wilkinson, IWM, 88/56/1.
[23] Douglas Wimberley, IWM, PP/MCR/182.
[24] Douglas V. Duff, *Sword For Hire* (London, 1934), 55, 91.
[25] Montgomery to A.H. Maude, 6 February 1921, IWM, Spec. Misc. G4.
[26] Montgomery to Percival, 14 October 1923, IWM, Percival Collection, P18 4/1.

innocent of apparent kindnesses.[27] More menacing than the rumours, there were
plenty of examples to make them more wary still. There were the RIC men shot
inside churches, the gunmen that faded in and out of crowds, the shots fired from
behind walls, the sudden ambushes, the mutilated bodies of 17 Auxiliary Cadets at
Kilmichael, the murdered, the assassinated, the bodies left labelled as spies. Douglas Wimberley was not alone in admitting that he slept with a loaded pistol under
his pillow. That he continued to do so for several months after he had left Ireland
is more revealing still.[28] 'It is worse than in the trenches', Lionel Curtis wrote.
'They are never free from the risk of bullet or bomb. There are no rest billets in
Ireland.'[29] Paramilitary violence was simply not knowing who to be afraid of, not
knowing who or at what point someone might come and shoot you dead. British
paramilitarism cannot be classified and calibrated without this sense of its opponents, without its measure of what was and was not war 'carried out in a sportsmanlike manner'.[30] Both auxiliaries and Black and Tans admitted their frustrations;
that they watched and participated and did things they were not proud of as a
result. And so much of this was explained or justified by the nature of the IRA:
'Our men don't know friends from enemies, there are no rules of warfare, consequently they take justice into their own hands'.[31]

Men spoke of the tension this bred in them, travelling in trains with a revolver
in each pocket, issuing orders that forbade civilians to walk in the streets with
their hands in their pockets, restricting leave, starting classes in guerrilla warfare,
insisting officers practice firing their revolvers; all precautions which in their own
ways heightened the fear further still.[32] Many of the men recorded that they had
no idea where they were even going, or what they were going there to do.[33] E.M.
Ransford, of the Suffolk Regiment, came to Ireland after Mesopotamia and India.
He complained that there was no 'frontier', that the possible dangers kept the
men confined to barracks, left them little or no opportunity for training or recre-
ation, that there were problems of indiscipline, poor health and even poorer
morale. He shot himself in the foot and narrowly escaped a court-martial because
he could prove that it was accident, but he noticed a lot of what he called 'self-
inflicted injuries', that the men seemed prepared to do anything to get home.[34]
Others noted that nothing in their training had prepared them for this kind of
war, for how to respond. There were complaints that they had only been trained
for trench warfare, that many were simply not fit for their new purpose at all. The
Deputy Adjutant-General wrote after one shooting incident: 'They all had the

---

[27] For a variety of rumours and reports see TNA, CO904/168, also in C.S. Foulkes papers, Liddell
Hart Centre, London (LHC).

[28] Douglas Wimberley, IWM, PP/MCR/182.

[29] Lionel Curtis, 'Ireland 1921', *A Belfast Magazine*, 20 (2002), 61. Curtis was advisor on Irish
affairs at the Colonial Office from 1921–24.

[30] 'To members of the IRA', TNA, CO904/168.

[31] Joice M. Nankiville and Sydney Loch, *Ireland in Travail* (London, 1922), 127.

[32] See, e.g, H.C.N. Trollope, IWM, PP/MCR/212; 'Guerrilla Warfare in Ireland', Lieut-Gen. A.E.
Percival, IWM, P18; 'History of the 5th Div. in Ireland', Lieut-Gen. Sir Hugh Jeudwine, IWM,
72/82/2.

[33] J.P. Swindlehurst, IWM, P538.   [34] E.M. Ransford, IWM, 80/29/1.

wind up, blood up, and did what they used to do in the trenches in France. In the circumstances you cannot hold them criminally responsible, but they are not fit to be policemen—but are any Auxiliaries?'[35]

They were disturbed and unsettled by the violence they encountered and it shaped their paramilitarism in Ireland more than some may have wished to concede. Craig-Brown of the Essex Regiment wrote home that 'there has been a very marked increase in the number of cases of drunkenness since we left Aldershot'.[36] Lionel Curtis conceded that 'under such conditions the bravest man is tempted to find relief for his nerves in drink.'[37] Many admitted their frustrations; that they watched and participated and did things they were not proud of as a result. 'The troops that wrecked Fermoy', Craig Brown wrote, 'put themselves on the level of the Bosches', but 'there is of course a limit to the pin pricks that troops will endure quietly'.[38] The provocation and the frustration were too much to take. Paramilitary violence had changed the nature of being a soldier, had damaged the discipline, morale, structure of the forces to such a point that H.C.N. Trollope of the Suffolk Regiment admitted that 'due to the Irish war the state of the Army was so low that it was not considered reasonable to do any training by battalions, barring one or two static battalion schemes.'[39] For some of these men the violence they encountered, or perhaps just the threat or rumour of it, had undermined the very essence of their army and service. F.A.S. Clarke of the Essex Regiment put it plainly: 'I did not like myself in Ireland. I don't think anybody else did either.'[40]

These testimonies suggest scope for a far wider definition of paramilitarism than one restricted to specific groups or organizations. And yet, the perception remains that Britain's only paramilitaries were the Auxiliaries and the Black and Tans. For most commentators these groups, particularly the Auxiliary officers and cadets, by their uniforms, by their appearance, are clearly set apart from the regular police, at the time, and in the sense of the conflict since. And they are distinguished by more than just their appearance and their pay, which in the £1 a day paid to the Auxiliaries, was quite distinctive in itself, making them the best paid force of their kind in the world at that time. But what sets them, their service, their violence, apart? What defines their particular paramilitarism, if paramilitarism is restricted to these forces?

Looking at the Irish sources it is clear. Dorothy Macardle, 'hagiographer royal to the [Irish] Republic',[41] subscribed in her own way to the brutalization thesis in the 1930s: she called them 'men of low mentality whose more primitive instincts had been aroused by the war and who were now difficult to control.'[42] Contemporary republican interpretations damned them as 'thief, drug addict, madman and murderer';[43]

[35] Quoted in Harvey, 'Who Were the Auxiliaries?', 667.
[36] E. Craig Brown, IWM, Con Shelf & 92/23/2.   [37] Curtis, 'Ireland 1921', 61.
[38] E. Craig Brown, IWM, Con Shelf & 92/23/2.
[39] H.C.N. Trollope, IWM, PP/MCR/212.   [40] F.A.S. Clarke, LHC, 1/6 1968.
[41] Joseph Lee, *Ireland 1912–1985: Politics and Society* (Cambridge, 1989), 270.
[42] Dorothy Macardle, *The Irish Republic* (London, 1937), 354.
[43] 'David Hogan' (Frank Gallagher), *The Four Glorious Years* (Dublin, 1953), 103.

they were the 'British Hun...let loose'.[44] But then what else were they likely to be in Irish nationalist eyes—often as caricatured there as the depictions by David Low in *The Star*, as the rabid dogs set loose by Lloyd George and now running amok beyond his control.[45] That the 'Black and Tans', in their broadest sense, drew upon them such ire, such enmity that they still occupy so much attention in what is still sometimes called the 'Tan War' despite their relatively small numbers—close to 9,000 Black and Tans and up to 2,200 Auxiliaries, together nothing close to the near 60,000 troops in Ireland—is itself indicative of how they very quickly came to represent a force apart. As one journalist remarked in 1922 'the Black and Tan business has sunk deep already into the national mind'.[46] While there may have been a degree of tarring all men with the same brush—'Every man serving the Government seems to be called a Black-and-Tan'[47]—even Irish propaganda and memoirs drew distinctions between the Black and Tans and the officers of the Auxiliary Division. Seen as swaggering with guns on their hips 'like miniature arsenals', talking as if 'this trouble was made specially to amuse them',[48] there seemed to be a quite common almost grudging respect for these ex-officers, which in itself became a kind of compliment for the IRA man who could match or murder him.[49] But this was an image which the Black and Tans and the Auxiliaries themselves seemed happy to encourage as rumours of their recklessness, their ferocity, preceded them and possibly made their opponents, made civilians, less likely to trouble them on their way. The Archbishop of Dublin was counselled to keep the nuns of his archdiocese confined to their convents with such desperate men about, to remember 'what our glorious Irish virgins suffered in the past...at the wicked hands of the Cromwellians', 'that the same fiendish cruelty is being enacted today by *British Barbarians*'; they were thought capable of nothing and everything and every dastardly deed in between.[50] They were said to be 'miserable creatures from the hell holes of London', and this reputation, the wider public belief in it, the act of encouraging and living up to it, seemed to become an almost fundamental part of their paramilitarism.[51] They were said to be 'dirty tools for a dirty job', and part of their nature seemed to be intent on becoming what so many people wanted to behold.[52]

There are many instances of outrage, indiscipline, of indiscriminate shooting, of strange and unusual techniques of interrogation, of torture and murder, there are plenty of accusations of even rape and rapine. And they come from a variety of sources: naturally from IRA publicity and propaganda, but more tellingly from British military and RIC reports, some even from the Black and Tans and Auxiliaries themselves.[53] Some came from the Auxiliaries' former chief, Brigadier General

---

[44] Archbishop Walsh Papers, Dublin Diocesan Archives (DDA), 29 November 1920, file 380/5 laity.

[45] e.g., *The Star*, 4 October 1921. [46] Ewart, *A Journey in Ireland*, 137.

[47] Nankiville and Loch, *Ireland in Travail*, 74. [48] J.P. Swindlehurst, IWM, P538.

[49] e.g., Charlie Somers Memoir, UCDA, P104/1395(22).

[50] Archbishop Walsh papers, DDA, 29 November 1920, File 380/5 Laity.

[51] Quoted in Leeson, 'The "Scum of London's Underworld"?', 19.

[52] Piaras Beaslaí, *Michael Collins and the Making of a New Ireland* vol. 2 (Dublin, 1926), 24.

[53] See, e.g., J.P. Swindlehurst, IWM, P538; William Maltby, IWM, Interview, 12258; Douglas Wimberley, IWM, PP/MCR/182.

Crozier, who resigned in February 1921 because of their behaviour, but also because it seemed like the British government had no will or inclination to curtail them.[54] Whether to excuse them, or to condemn them, the one element which seems to define these men across the sources is their lack of discipline and restraint, their capacity for reprisals, for burning and looting and seeking vengeance, with an acknowledgement or expectation that a blind eye was going to be turned to whatever they did. Again, this idea of 'dirty men for a dirty job', recruited and accepted as such with a nod and a wink from Lloyd George, reached down to the men themselves in Gormanstown training camp where it was said to be like 'the wild west' on pay night.[55] They went without proper rules, proper training, without a clear sense of function or purpose: 'no discipline, no esprit de corps, no cohesion, no training, no musketry, no mess, no NOTHING'.[56] They became associated with a certain type of activity—looting, burning, drunkenness—with certain events, most particularly the burning of Cork, the sack of Balbriggan—with certain murders—the death of Canon Magner in Dunmanway, the killing of a former soldier, Captain Nicholas Prendergast, in Fermoy. In effect they became very easy to blame for all that went wrong in Ireland in these years. Playing the scapegoat became part of their paramilitarism; and for the price of a £1 a day they took on the burden of more sins than their own.

Although many soldiers and policemen recorded their retrospective disgust at the actions of the Black and Tans and Auxiliaries, more perhaps recorded a certain envy of the means and methods they felt those auxiliary police forces were permitted to employ. While one army officer admitted that 'they were totally undisciplined by our regimental standards... they seemed to make a habit of breaking out of their barracks at night, illicitly, and killing men they thought were suspect rebels', he at least acknowledged that this 'habit spread surreptitiously even to a few army officers and men'.[57] Yet there is more than sufficient evidence to suggest that in certain quarters in the army, they were behaving in similar ways all by themselves. Evelyn Lindsay Young, an officer in Bandon, Co. Cork, confirms it. He seemed to revel in the details of how he tortured prisoners, claiming to show them corpses to try and frighten them to confess.[58] The men who burned Tuam in July 1920 were all old RIC. And while many in both the army and the police seemed to define the paramilitaries by their capacity to give 'as good as they got and often better', many within the army and the RIC were doing precisely the same.[59] When paramilitarism is being defined by indiscipline, by reprisals, by 'giving as good as you get', it is perhaps more accurate to refer to a state of paramilitarism rather than locating it exclusively within one or two groups of auxiliary police. They are being set apart superficially, perhaps, by pay and appearance, by reputation, by propaganda. But in effect, if their paramilitarism is defined by their actions, how different are those actions to the actions of any of the rest of the Crown forces in Ireland,

---

[54] See F.P. Crozier, *Ireland For Ever* (London, 1932; Bath, 1971).
[55] John D. Brewer, *The Royal Irish Constabulary: an Oral History* (Belfast, 1990), 85.
[56] Wilson Diary, 12 May 1920, IWM.
[57] Douglas Wimberley, IWM, PP/MCR/182.
[58] 'Under the Shadow of Darkness—Ireland', GB99 Lindsay-Young, LHC.
[59] H.C.N. Trollope, IWM, PP/MCR/212.

who came through their service there with the same mixture of obedience, indiscipline, shooting, murder, regrets, accusations and mistakes? The excuses made by Auxiliaries and Black and Tans for their reprisals were the same ones made by the soldiers. One Major, wearing a DSO ribbon, explained it to a journalist in 1921: 'How can you expect anything but reprisals when our pals and our men's pals are killed like this.'[60] All forces seemed prepared at some point to meet 'fire with fire', both shaped by fighting, what the army's director of Irish propaganda called, 'a secret society of assassins' rather than 'a disciplined regular army' at war.[61]

POLITICS OF PARAMILITARISM

While their paramilitarism was shaped by their sense of what they were fighting, it was also fuelled by the type of war they were not allowed to wage, and it was a frustration both soldiers and Black and Tans shared. The Black and Tan, Douglas V. Duff, wrote:

> [G]iven a free hand we could have restored order in Ireland in a month, even if it had been Peace of the Roman style, the kind that required the making of a desolation. But egged on to be brutal and tyrannizing one day, imprisoned and dismissed the service the next if we dared to speak roughly to our enemies, it is no wonder that the heart was taken out of the men and that most of us merely soldiered for our pay.[62]

There were constant pleas for martial law, for the government to call it war, to allow them to unleash the methods of war as they were known. Montgomery admitted 'that to win a war of that sort you must be ruthless; Oliver Cromwell, or the Germans, would have settled it in a very short time. Now-a-days public opinion precludes such methods'.[63] He conceded that 'squashing' rebellion, as he termed it, would probably only have been a temporary measure anyway, but there was no small amount of regret in what he wrote. Many blamed the government for pulling out of the fight when they felt that it was almost won. F.A.S. Clarke wrote of the shame of handing over a fort held for 350 years, that 'our politicians had given to them...a fort which they could never have captured' themselves.[64] G.W. Albin was just a little more forthright in his feelings than that: 'It was alright for the Government and the Intelligentsia, at home sitting on their fat arses; but it was the troops that were getting the shittie end of the stick'.[65]

Yet despite this despair of government, there are more frequent returns to what was and was not honourable in the IRA's war, and it is within this framework that these men continued to define themselves. In many respects it was this kind of idiom, the elevation of 'fair play', the notion that 'war between white men should be carried out in a sportsmanlike manner, and not like fights between savage tribes',

---

[60] Ewart, *A Journey in Ireland*, 70.
[61] C.S. Foulkes, 'Is the IRA a Murder Gang?', Foulkes papers, LHC, 7/43.
[62] Duff, *Sword for Hire*, 77.
[63] Montgomery to Percival, 14 October 1923, IWM, Percival Collection, P18 4/1.
[64] F.A.S. Clarke, LHC, 1/6 1968.   [65] G.W. Albin, IWM, PP/MCR/192.

that became the very thing that called into question the behaviour of the Crown forces in Ireland.[66] Their behaviour began to be measured against their own standards and it was found wanting in terms of the ideal of war. Reprisals and secret shootings were not the ways for His Majesty's forces to fight. The winners of the Great War, the defenders of plucky Belgium, could not be allowed and, certainly could not be seen, to offend in this way; it was an 'un-British' way to fight a war.[67] In the Commons, the Liberal Party's Lieutenant-Commander Kenworthy made a pointed comparison:

> In Germany the excesses in Belgium were excused in the Reichstag by stories of the Belgians firing from their houses on the brave German troops…The same defence is being made by the Government today for this system of burnings in Ireland. If we do not condemn it, we shall be as guilty as the German people, and worse. This House may not condemn it, but I hope the people outside will. If not, then Germany will have won the War. The Prussian spirit will have entered into us. The Prussian spirit at last will be triumphant, and the 800,000, the flower of our race, who lie buried in a score of battle-fronts will really have died in vain…and Germany has won and we have lost. That is the tragic, wicked part of it.[68]

Labour's Arthur Henderson questioned how the government could put itself in the position of being 'likened unto the policy of the Huns in the Belgian villages during the War'.[69] For Sir Henry Wilson, Chief of the Imperial General Staff, paramilitarism was not just 'a fatal policy and the negation of Government', but 'a most dangerous and indefensible proceeding'.[70] Wilson was not against violence in Ireland. He rarely referred to the IRA as anything other than murderers; he wanted full Martial Law; he wanted to calm the country by shooting by roster.[71] He wanted government to take responsibility, to govern as he felt and believed a British government should. 'To me all this is the bankruptcy of all Government and it must lead to chaos and anarchy'. The Black and Tans were nothing more than 'wild devils', that 'L.[loyd] G.[eorge] and Winston's ideas of sending over a gang of murderers to out-murder the murderers was, and is a scandalous thing'.[72] He noted in his diary that the King similarly disapproved: 'He wants to abolish all Black and Tans'.[73] They were not part of George V's ideal of a British war.

If paramilitarism offended against a wider ideal of war, it is even more difficult to discern the ideal or ideology many of the men in Ireland felt they were fighting for. While some, like Duff above, openly admitted to soldiering for nothing more than their pay, while many joined and rejoined because there was no other work, or no work to be got commensurate, as they felt, with their wartime rank, others did not seem to know where or why or who they were going to fight in Ireland. For one

---

[66] 'To Members of the IRA', TNA, CO904/168.

[67] Crozier, *Ireland For Ever*, 107.

[68] *Hansard* 5 (Commons), vol. 133, cols. 961–2, 20 October 1920. See John Horne and Alan Kramer, *German Atrocities 1914: a History of Denial* (New Haven, 2001).

[69] *Hansard* 5, ibid., col. 931.

[70] Wilson Diary, 27 September 1920, 6 September 1920, IWM; Keith Jeffery, *Field Marshal Sir Henry Wilson: a Political Soldier* (Oxford, 2006).

[71] Ibid., 23 September 1920.   [72] Ibid.   [73] Ibid., 28 March 1921.

Auxiliary, it was just 'something to do at last'.[74] While someone like Wilson was clear and committed and confirmed in his unionism, in his belief in Ireland as the test-case of the Empire, motivations were as mixed as the men themselves. For some it was a commitment to hatred, to enmity, to Empire, to the fight for the fight's own sake. Others believed in little more than getting by, in serving their time, in malingering or making the most of what was just another posting away from home. For some there was a kind of racism, as one Auxiliary said: 'The German is honourable. The Turk is honourable. The nigger is honourable. But not a Shinner. Stick up for any mongrel race you like, but not the Irish.'[75] But this lack of an obvious ideology is in direct contrast to many of Europe's paramilitaries. The 'Black and Tans' were not driven in the same way by ideology, by nationalism, by socialism, by a cause. If anything their paramilitarism was defined by the fact that they fought an enemy that had a much more coherent cause: 'most of us were more than a little sympathetic towards the poor devils that we hunted over the hills and bogs. They, at least, conceived themselves to be fighting for a just cause, whereas we knew that we were not, and that we were merely the catspaw of a political junta in London.'[76] While most did not go as far as Duff, who admitted that 'if I had known how, I should have served in the Irish Republican Army', there were enough cases of guns being passed out or sold from barracks, enough desertions and resignations in Ireland, to suggest that he was not an exceptional case.[77] 'We were definitely not patriots, anxious to die for our country'; and that perhaps set them apart from other paramilitary groups.[78] There was no loyalty to leader or policy; for many there was a drift to paramilitarism for want of any alternative coherent response. Politics, religion, ethnicity, even incoherence, there are shades and hints and varieties of all, but not enough to shape an ideology overall, to say that their paramilitarism in Ireland meant anything more than the sum of its parts.

If ideology cannot explain or categorize them then the traditional view of the 'Black and Tans' is that they 'were the brutal products of a demoralising war'.[79] Contemporary British propaganda in Ireland even played on their Great War past in the hope of frightening the IRA. 'They know what Danger is. They know what Fighting means. They have looked Death in the eyes before and did not flinch.'[80] But so too had many members of the IRA, and the brutalization thesis is as open to criticism in the case of the Black and Tans as it is in the context of any paramilitaries in postwar Europe. There is no way to gauge it beyond individual experience. There were those who explained their service in terms of the thrill of the fight, any fight, there were those who boasted, in one instance, of 37 kills.[81] But equally there

---

[74]   Ernest Lycette, IWM, 08/43/1.

[75]   Nankiville and Loch, *Ireland in Travail*, 132.

[76]   Duff, *Sword for Hire*, 77.

[77]   Douglas V. Duff, *On Swallowing the Anchor* (London, 1954), 106; Lieut-Gen. Sir Hugh Jeudwine, IWM, 72/82/2.

[78]   Douglas V. Duff, *May the Winds Blow* (London, 1948), 78.

[79]   Leeson, 'The "Scum of London's Underworld"?', 1.

[80]   *The Weekly Summary*, 27 August 1920, TNA, WO 35/205.

[81]   J.E.P. Brass, IWM, 76/116/1.

were decorated officers and men dismissed the service appalled by what they saw of Ireland's war.[82] While it would 'be a mistake', as Adrian Gregory argues, 'to conclude that there were no "violent" veterans in British life', it would be more appropriate in the Irish case to consider the reaction of many of these British veterans to the violence and conditions of their service in Ireland rather than to blame it simply on the Great War.[83] They were paramilitaries responding to a paramilitary situation, with all the confusion and potential for indiscipline that that involves. The Great War shaped this time in Ireland in the sense of how the war left so many unprepared for the kind of violence they found. In many respects the brutalization thesis is far too easy. The nature of their paramilitarism has to allow for more complexity than that.

There is also room for far more complexity in terms of defining Britain's paramilitarism as something detached and removed from Britain itself. Gregory argues that 'English self-congratulation over the lack of a post-war Freikorps mentality needs to be heavily qualified by the observation, "except in Ireland"', that this violence in Ireland even 'caused a fierce counter-reaction against political violence in Britain'.[84] This siphoning off of the problem to the 'other island' does not quite fit with the much more complex and intimate position Ireland occupied in too many minds at the time.[85] Sir Henry Wilson moved battalions from Ireland to Liverpool to London, always conscious that need in Ireland was always rivalling the urgency of labour unrest at home, that one force was aware and playing on the stresses imposed by the other on His Majesty's forces.

> The Irishmen who are clever enough are gradually looping into their toils Labour in England... in the very near future the Irish question will be so complicated with the Labour question in England that it will become insoluble, and this would mean the loss of Ireland to begin with; the loss of the Empire in the second place; and the loss of England itself to finish up with.[86]

In the fight for Ireland he believed he was 'fighting New York and Cairo and Calcutta and Moscow who are only using Ireland as a tool and lever against England'.[87] He was fighting anarchy and Bolshevism in Ireland just as he was fighting anarchy and Bolshevism on the Liverpool Docks and in the Lancashire mines, as sure as the *Union Civiques* were in France, as sure as the *Freikorps* or the White Army itself, even if, for Wilson and Britain, that threat was more perceived than real. Fight one, fight them all, and Ireland was as integral to his sense of Britain as Ulster, as England, as the King himself. Paradoxically, Oswald Mosley's opposition to paramilitarism was fundamental to his sense of what it meant to be British in 1920. He crossed the floor of the House in disgust at the government's continued use of the Black and Tans.[88]

[82] See Harvey, 'Who Were the Auxiliaries?', 665.
[83] Adrian Gregory, 'Peculiarities of the English? War, Violence and Politics: 1900–1939', *Journal of Modern European History*, 1 (2003), 53.
[84] Ibid., 53.
[85] Ibid., 54.
[86] Wilson to G.F. Milne, 2 June 1920, IWM, HHW 2/37/16.
[87] Wilson Diary, 11 May 1920, IWM.
[88] R.M. Douglas, 'The Swastika and the Shamrock: British Fascism and the Irish Question, 1918–1940', *Albion*, 29, 1 (1997), 71–2.

Ireland was not the same as any other part of the Empire. It was part of the Union of Great Britain and Ireland; there were Irish MPs in the Imperial Parliament itself. Yet regardless of the constitutional niceties or distinctions, the practicalities of the IRA's war meant that it was not so easy to disassociate or distance paramilitarism as Gregory suggests. The IRA had companies, battalions, in England, Scotland and Wales. The fires at Liverpool, the shootings, the planned assassinations of British ministers, the eventual murder of Sir Henry Wilson in June 1922, suggested that this was slightly more intimate than just some distant colonial war. The hoardings that were erected around Downing Street, the policemen who shadowed Lloyd George and his ministers well into 1922, suggested that this was a much closer fight.[89] Lieutenant-Commander Kenworthy also raised the thorny question of what was to become of Britain's paramilitaries when they came home:

> [I]f they are allowed to shoot men out of hand on suspicion of being Sinn Feiners or of being murderers what will they do in England tomorrow? ... if we think that we can stop at the other side of St George's Channel, we have an optimism which history does not warrant.[90]

Ireland and paramilitarism was not at such a convenient remove. Indeed, the thought of a defence force to cope with union unrest in Britain, was a direct consequence of the over-extension of forces in Ireland and beyond.[91] Indeed, plans to protect the capital during the Irish troubles were again put into use during the General Strike.[92] Britain was prepared, unlike the French, to give its paramilitaries at home, its Special Constabulary, its Civil Constabulary Reserve, police functions in 1926.[93] But even then the GOC London, Major General Lord Ruthven, detected the echo back to Ireland of 1920–21: these constabularies were 'undoubtedly looked upon as a species of strike breaker and "black and tan"'.[94]

LEGACIES

The legacy of Britain's paramilitarism in Ireland was a long one. The 'Black and Tans' slipped easily into a pantheon of perfidy along with Cromwell, the famine and rack rent. In 1972 the Minister of State for Northern Ireland, Lord Windlesham, asked for a report on the Black and Tans, questioning 'whether there are any lessons to keep in mind at the present time'. The report concluded that 'any body of men from Great Britain who should find themselves in the difficult position of

[89] See TNA, MEPO 38/125, 126, 127, 133, 157.
[90] *Hansard* 5 (Commons), vol. 133, col. 964, 20 October 1920. See also Jon Lawrence, 'Forging a Peaceable Kingdom: War, Violence and Fear of Brutalization in Post-First World War Britain', *The Journal of Modern History*, 75 (2003), 557–89.
[91] Jeffery, *The British Army and the Crisis of Empire*; Charles Townshend, *Britain's Civil Wars* (London, 1986).
[92] Keith Jeffery, 'The British Army and Internal Security 1919–1939', *The Historical Journal*, 24 (1981), 387.
[93] Ibid., 390–3.   [94] Quoted in ibid., 393.

having to interfere in Irish affairs, are all too likely to be accused of behaving like Black and Tans.'[95] The number of references and invocations of the term 'Black and Tans' in the Houses of Parliament alone since 1972, would suggest that that civil servant's predictions were unfortunately right. Their more immediate legacy was Palestine and service for many with the Gendarmerie. Some admitted that Ireland had changed them, that when it came to their time in Palestine they just 'turned a blind eye', shot first and did not care to ask questions later.[96] Douglas Duff's memoirs of Palestine are far more brutal than anything he experienced or expected in Ireland.[97] He was effectively dismissed from the force in 1931. But in many respects Palestine was a new problem, a far different and much more distant problem than Ireland. 'Black and Tan' remained a term of accusation or abuse long after Palestine. It was heard in parliamentary debates on Cyprus, Kenya, Malaya, in parts of the world where British policy and British action might be thought heavy-handed, ineffective, or somehow wrong. It remained a moniker for disorder and indiscipline, a state of mind, a state of paramilitarism, not tied necessarily to any particular kind of force.

The 'Black and Tans' in their broadest sense may not have been Britain's *Freikorps* although Harvey is prepared to suggest that they were made up of the same kind of men.[98] They were not driven by a coherent ideology, whether religion, ethnicity or race. They were only as extreme as those who saw 'Shinners' around every corner, only as indifferent as those who admitted to 'soldiering' for nothing more than their pay. They were born from the exigencies of an overstretched police and army, they were not an alliance of the driven and the disaffected that the state needed to marshal and control. Gregory's sense of a 'lack of a post-war Freikorps' past holds if the definitions are drawn too narrowly.[99] But if paramilitary gives way to paramilitarism, if it is allowed to mean more than particular groups of auxiliary troops or police, if it admits something more fluid, something closer to the state of mind of all the Crown forces in Ireland, whether army, RIC old and new, if it admits to something closer to disorder and indiscipline, and fighting with scant regard for regulations and rules and due process, then Britain's paramilitarism becomes a much more complicated, intrusive and unsettling prospect. Major Procter did not want to be called a Black and Tan for a reason. 'Black and Tan' was too reminiscent of the 'dirty tools' in Britain's Irish paramilitary war.

---

[95] TNA CJ4/152.   [96] J.V. Faviell, IWM, 82/24/1.   [97] Duff, *May the Winds Blow.*
[98] Harvey, 'Who Were the Auxiliaries?', 669.   [99] Gregory, 'Peculiarities of the English', 53.

13

Defending Victory
Paramilitary Politics in France, 1918–1926.
A Counter-example

John Horne

The stable democracies of Western Europe constitute a counter-example to the overall thesis of this volume by virtue of the near complete absence of paramilitary violence in domestic politics during the postwar period. Britain and France were 'victorious' in November 1918. Their political systems coped successfully with the strains of the war. Postwar social conflict, while serious, did not fundamentally challenge the established order. With the major exception of the War of Independence in Ireland, their geographical integrity was not called into question.

Yet the point of a counter-example is to provide a conceptual trigonometry for measuring the main phenomenon—in this case paramilitary violence in other parts of Europe. France is perhaps a better case than Britain since domestic paramilitary formations did emerge there and paramilitarism was advocated both in support of the parliamentary republic and as an alternative to it. Understanding why this was so, and what factors limited paramilitarism, may cast light on its far more extensive and violent manifestations elsewhere. However, for reasons that will become clear, explaining French paramilitarism requires a time-frame that goes beyond 1923.

MYTHS OF VICTORY AND REVOLUTION

'Cultures of defeat', which have only recently emerged as a subject of study, helped drive the emergence of paramilitary violence in the half dozen years after the Great War.[1] The attempt to stave off the worst consequences of military defeat in Germany and Austria-Hungary, and, on the part of nationalist circles in Italy, to reject a perceived diplomatic defeat, resulted in self-organized groups of returned officers and soldiers, and of young adventurers who had not participated in the war, acting as surrogates for the army. The

---

[1] Wolfgang Schivelbusch, *The Culture of Defeat. On National Trauma, Mourning and Recovery*, 2001; translation from German (London, 2003); see also John Horne, 'Defeat and Memory in Modern History', in: Jenny Macleod (ed.), *Defeat and Memory. Cultural Histories of Military Defeat in the Modern Era* (London, 2008), 11–29.

Fig. 17. A 'culture of victory' threatened with defeat. The voice of the war dead summons the living to defend victory: 'Let the living arise! Will you let it be said that we died for nothing.' Drawing by Maxime Real del Sarte, member of the extreme right Action Française, wounded near Verdun in January 1916, and a leading French artist and sculptor. Used on the front cover of the journal of The League for the Union Frenchmen Who Have Not Reneged on Victory, 9 March 1924, ahead of the elections won by the Cartel des Gauches.

regular military was seen as no longer able to defend the cause of the nation or the established order either at home in class warfare against the radical and revolutionary movements that erupted as the war ended (and which were reviled as Bolshevism) or on the contested ethnic frontiers of the new international order as this began to take shape during and after the Paris Peace Conference. From Finland and the Baltic states via Central Europe to North and Central Italy, legionaries, militias, *Freikorps* and other armed groups drew on the ideals and experience as well as the training and armaments of the Great War in order to resist what they saw as defeat, social or national, and to reverse it.[2] They defined their cause in ideological and ethnic terms but their impact came from the

[2] For the transnational dimension, see Robert Gerwarth, 'The Central European Counterrevolution: Paramilitary Violence in Germany, Austria and Hungary after the Great War,' *Past and Present*, 200, 2008, 175–209. For an excellent overview of the postwar conflicts (with bibliography), see Peter Gatrell, 'War after the War: Conflicts, 1919–23', in: John Horne (ed.), *A Companion to World War I* (Chichester, 2010), 558–75.

use of force in quasi-military formations as an antidote to perceived chaos. In Italy, with the emergent fascist movement, paramilitarism went on to provide the organizing principle for how an authoritarian state was imagined and implemented.[3]

France had the opposite experience, that of the elaboration of a 'culture of victory'—a theme that, as such, has not yet engaged the attention of historians. The French army's size and prestige were unrivalled since the Napoleonic wars. Not only had it 'liberated' Alsace-Lorraine, it also occupied the Rhineland (together with British and American forces) and remained there until 1930 to ensure the implementation of the peace treaty. It performed this role forcefully by occupying the Ruhr in 1923 in order to maintain repayment of reparations. French forces also advanced from Macedonia to the Danube and helped suppress the brief revolution of Bela Kun in Budapest in 1919. They intervened in the Russian Civil War (as did a French fleet in the Black Sea) and helped the Polish army to defeat the Bolsheviks in the Russo-Polish War of 1920. Some soldiers, anxious to go home, protested at the maintenance of over half the army under arms until the Treaty of Versailles had been signed on 28 June 1919.[4] But military demobilization proceeded apace in the second half of the year, and as the regiments that were not needed for foreign duties returned to their garrison towns, they were welcomed with civic ceremonies that underlined the scale of their victory and the debt the nation owed them.[5]

That debt was recognized by the invention of the national ritual that commemorated the war dead and the sacrifice of the ordinary soldier in the same period. From the victory parade of 14 July 1919, headed by a thousand handicapped veterans, to the inauguration of the tomb of the Unknown Soldier on 11 November 1920 under the Arc de Triomphe, the state recognized the victory and its price in a way that accommodated most of the political, confessional and cultural strands of the nation.[6] The proliferation of war memorials in the following half-decade installed the victory and the suffering it had entailed at the very heart of French civic and religious life.[7]

Yet the nature of the peace was anything but clear-cut. The ambiguities of the Armistice were translated into the anxieties of the peace conference as the French delegation sought to confirm diplomatically the victory they believed France had won on the battlefield. According to state surveillance reports on public opinion, the bulk of people 'wished for severe conditions that would make it impossible for the Germans to think about any new act of aggresssion.'[8] As is well known, Clemenceau was squeezed between the views of more militant nationalists (and Marshal Foch as supreme commander of the Allied armies), who wanted the Rhineland to be annexed permanently, and the desire of Woodrow Wilson and Lloyd George to avoid an 1871 in reverse by being more lenient towards Germany. For Lloyd George,

---

[3] Emilio Gentile, *The Origins of Fascist Ideology, 1918–1925*, 1996; translation from the Italian (New York, 2005).

[4] Bruno Cabanes, *La Victoire endeuillée. La sortie de guerre des soldats français (1918–1920)* (Paris, 2004), 314–33.

[5] Cabanes, *Victoire endeuillée*, 425–94.

[6] Avner Ben-Amos, *Funerals, Politics, and Memory in Modern France 1789–1996* (Oxford, 2000), 215–24.

[7] Annette Becker, *Les Monuments aux morts. Mémoire de la Grande Guerre* (Paris, 1998); Daniel Sherman, *The Construction of Memory in Interwar France* (Chicago, 1999).

[8] Service Historique de la Défense (SHD), 6N 147, Bulletin confidential résumant la situation morale à l'Intérieur, 15 April 1919; Pierre Miquel, *La Paix de Versailles et l'opinion publique française* (Paris, 1972), 236–7.

the threat of Bolshevism throughout Europe and especially in Germany required a more moderate settlement.[9] In the end, all but the Socialists (who declared: 'This peace is not our peace!') ratified the Treaty of Versailles in the Chamber of Deputies.[10] But the fear that what had been won at such cost in the war might be lost with the peace continued to gnaw at French political consciousness.

Domestic politics were also troubled in 1919–20 even if they were not subject to the violent social conflicts and revolutionary episodes that occurred in other countries. Strikes reached an all-time high in 1919–20 and would only disappear with the slump of 1920–21 as the economy moved back to peacetime production and sought to absorb demobilized labour.[11] The strikes were often linked to the implementation of wage increases that had been granted by mechanisms set up during the war on a tri-partite basis between the state, business and labour. But they also expressed more sweeping demands for reform that were driven by the belief of the main trade union confederation, the Confédération Générale du Travail (CGT), that labour's support for the war effort should be rewarded by some form of economic democracy. Under the threat of strikes in late April 1919 and in the teeth of opposition from employers, who believed that France could not afford the measure, Clemenceau granted a key labour demand, the eight-hour working day.[12]

A more militant current of trade unionism inspired by pre-war revolutionary syndicalism aspired to a more radical, even revolutionary confrontation with the state. This became apparent with an intense engineering strike in Paris in June 1919 and a short-lived railway strike in February 1920, before culminating in a general strike on 1 May 1920. While the minority militants saw this as a revolutionary assault on the existing order, the CGT fronted the strike as a demand for the nationalization of the railways (which the state had temporarily taken over during the war) and for widespread reforms. It marked the high-water mark of postwar labour militancy.

The social unrest was not confined to industrial workers. White collar workers began to unionize and agitate in response to the erosion of their living standards by inflation, while state employees, who under the French trade union law of 1884 were prohibited from unionizing, now demanded the right to do so. As elsewhere the domestic tensions of 1919–20 were closely connected to the sacrifices of wartime and to the 'moral economy' (to borrow E. P. Thompson's term) that had emerged in response to these.[13] While workers and white collar employees contin-

[9] Jere Clemens King, *Foch versus Clemenceau: France and German Dismemberment, 1918–1919* (Cambridge, MA, 1960); Margaret Macmillan, *Peacemakers: Six Months that Changed the World* (London, 2001), 205–14.

[10] Edouard Bonnefous, *Histoire politique de la Troisième République*, vol. 3, *L'Après-guerre (1919–1924)* (Paris, 1968), 57. *L'Humanité*, 9–12 May 1919, for the Socialist position.

[11] Leopold Haimson and Giulio Sapelli (eds.), *Strikes, Social Conflict and the First World War* (Milan, 1992).

[12] John Horne, 'The State and the Challenge of Labour in France, 1917–20', in: Chris Wrigley (ed.), *Challenges of Labour. Central and Western Europe, 1917–1920* (London and New York, 1993), 239–61 (here 250–1).

[13] E. P. Thompson, 'The Moral Economy of the English Crowd in the Eighteenth Century', *Past and Present*, 50, 1971, 76–136; John Horne, 'Social Identity in War: France, 1914–1918', in: Tom Frazer and Keith Jeffery (eds.), *Men, Women and War. Studies in War, Politics and Society* (Dublin, 1993), 119–35.

ued to blame inflation on 'speculators' and 'hoarders', hard pressed middle and lower middle class families were only too ready to believe that war workers (including women *munitionnettes*) had benefited from soaring wages and military separation allowances, thus inverting the pre-war hierarchy of income and social status. While the family farm had benefited from buoyant demand, a measure of prosperity was bought at the cost of unrelenting labour by women, children and the elderly. It was accompanied by the resentful belief that war workers, and even the urban working class in general, had been 'shirkers' *(embusqués)* whose privileged employment status removed them from suffering and death at the front. And while the benefits of the war economy had been spread widely owing to small-scale contracts, the war 'profiteer' was an even more reviled figure than the *embusqué*.[14]

Residual anxieties over the peace settlement, fear of social disorder and a wartime social morality of which the soldiers' sacrifice was the supreme measure, all helped shape French politics in 1919–23. In particular, they determined the outcome of the general election for the Chamber of Deputies in November 1919 when the centre-right triumphed and ex-servicemen predominated in parliament. The 'culture of victory' ensured a continuity between the new majority and the values that were held to have presided over national success in the wartime ordeal. The last 18 months of the war had witnessed the 'remobilization' of French opinion by a host of propaganda organizations operating under the Union des Grandes Associations contre la Propagande Ennemie.[15] This effort vilified the Germans and condemned the treason of those urging a negotiated peace. If anything the campaign intensified after the Armistice, as anxieties switched to the peacemaking. But onto the figure of the *Boche* was now grafted that of the *Bolchévique*, the class enemy who had formerly served German interests by his 'pacifism' and his demand for a negotiated peace, and who now became the collaborator of a Moscow-backed revolution. The same imaginary structure applied to both myths, *Boche* and *Bolchévique*. Each took the form of an external conspiracy replete with agents, spies and Moscow (or German) 'gold' that sought to manipulate an 'internal enemy' ready to betray the *patrie*. As one right-wing fly sheet put it in December 1918: 'He who is a Bolshevik today was a German-lover yesterday and will still be one tomorrow.'[16]

The propaganda of the Union des Grandes Associations addressed both themes, *Boche* and *Bolchévique*. The election campaign of the centre-right in 1919 turned not only on the victory over Germany but also on the threat of Bolshevism, producing the notorious poster showing a Bolshevik with a 'knife between his teeth'.[17] It was at this moment that the Bolsheviks announced their refusal to honour the

---

[14] Jean-Louis Robert, 'The Image of the Profiteer' in Jean-Louis Robert and Jay Winter (eds.), *Capital Cities at War. London, Paris, Berlin 1914–1919* (Cambridge, 1997), 104–32; Charles Ridel, *Les Embusqués* (Paris, 2007) and François Bouloc, *Les Profiteurs de guerre, 1914–1918* (Brussels, 2008).

[15] John Horne, 'Remobilizing for "total" war: France and Britain, 1917–18', in: J. Horne (ed.), *State, Society and Mobilization in Europe during the First World War* (Cambridge, 1997), 195–211.

[16] Archives Nationales (AN) F7 13090, Anon., *Les Influences allemandes et bolchévistes dans la presse et le role de l'Europe Nouvelle* (10 December 1918). *L'Europe nouvelle* was a radical new review accused of pacifist and pro-German tendencies.

[17] Bonnefous, *L'Après-guerre*, 66–7.

bonds raised by the tsarist government on the Paris bourse, which so many small French investors had bought. In one of his last speeches as premier, Clemenceau, borrowing a metaphor from trench warfare, declared that: 'So long as Russia remains in the state of anarchy that we see at the moment, there can be no peace in Europe. We have agreed [with Britain] that [...] we wish to place a network of barbed wire around Bolshevism in order to prevent it from breaking out across civilized Europe.'[18]

In short, though built on French military pre-eminence, the culture of victory was tempered by the compromises of coalition diplomacy and preoccupied by the possibility of a resurgent Germany, especially once the USA had failed to ratify the Treaty of Versailles and the British had declined to offer the French a permanent military alliance. It was also haunted by the spectre of revolution, seemingly backed from abroad by Bolshevism and promoted from within by the agents of class warfare. It was hard in these circumstances to be sure that victory was really secure.

NATIONAL MOBILIZATION AGAINST BOLSHEVISM: THE CIVIC UNIONS OF 1920

The most likely trigger for paramilitary formations in the immediate postwar period was the railway strike of February 1920 and the general strike of the following May. The railways were an obvious battleground since the conservative government of Alexandre Millerand, supported by the new centre-right majority in the Chamber, intended to return them to their private owners. Both the reformist majority and the militant minority of the labour movement were determined to resist this. Hope of revolution also waxed strong in syndicalist and socialist circles in the spring of 1920 with a reciprocal fear of revolution among the middle classes and in much of the countryside. As the government broke the accord which had ended the February strike (guaranteeing the strikers immunity from sanctions) in order to challenge and destroy the revolutionary minority of the CGT, feelings on both sides reached their apex. This resulted in the formation of Unions Civiques, or Civic Unions, whose goal was to rally behind the state and keep the railways and other services running.[19]

We are fortunate in knowing a good deal about the mood in both camps and in the population more generally as the Civic Unions were founded. The prefects (who were the principal agent of the government in each of the 89 *départements*) routinely informed the government on the state of public opinion. But in March 1920 the Ministry of the Interior asked the prefects to report on the nature of strikes locally, the outlook of the working class and other social classes, and the likelihood of an attempted revolution. Responses survive for 77 *départements* (87

---

[18] Ibid., 83.

[19] On the 1920 strikes see Adrian Jones, 'The French Railway Strikes of January–May 1920: New Syndicalist Ideas and Emergent Communism', *French Historical Studies*, 12/4, 1982, 508–40; Annie Kriegel, *La Grève des cheminots 1920* (Paris, 1988).

per cent of the total).[20] The prefects confirmed that the railway workers had taken over from the engineering workers as the principal source of union militancy. They indicated that local trade unionism in 32 per cent of the *départements* either belonged to the revolutionary minority of the CGT or was impregnated with revolutionary language. In only ten *départements* (13 per cent) did they anticipate an independent revolutionary initiative, but these included major urban centres such as Lyons (Rhône), Grenoble (Isère) and Marseilles (Bouches-du-Rhône). Paris (Seine) is one of the *départements* for which there is no reply but it certainly fell into this latter category.[21] More significantly, however, the prefects considered that in 28 *départements* (36 per cent) the local unions would obey a general strike order from the CGT.

The state knew in advance that the real danger was less revolution than the use the CGT might make of the solidarity built up over the previous three years to oppose the government's determination to dismantle wartime controls and pursue economic recovery by favouring market forces and private enterprise. An attempt by the syndicalist minority to use that solidarity for revolutionary ends posed a particular threat, but the government's formal case in taking on the CGT was the right to work and the illegality of paralysing public services. However, the prefects' reports also show that whatever the reality, minority syndicalist and socialist militants believed fervently in the imminence of revolution while the reciprocal fear of revolution was even more widespread, often masking a reluctance to contemplate any change in class relations. According to the Police Commissioner of Marseilles:

> The truth is that for some time now the 'future Revolution' is the object of every conversation. In cafés, in bourgeois clubs [*cercles*], in salons, everywhere, people talk of revolution as of something that is almost inevitable. In workers' circles and among advanced socialists the question of the Revolution is no longer just the favourite theme of violent and extremist speakers, it has become the subject of everyone's conversation. In these milieux it is now talked about as something that will occur inevitably and very soon. In the groups that organize propaganda, the forthcoming seizure of public powers by the Proletariat, or rather by the CGT and the United Socialist Party, is no longer in any doubt; it is just a matter of the date and means. In the countryside, the fear of social upheaval is as strong as in the towns; but there, the great majority is hostile to all revolutionary movements...[22]

Reports for 54 *départements* (61 per cent of the total) gave information on the attitudes of the 'bourgeoisie' and lower middle classes. In 45 of these (or 83 per cent), the bourgeois were seen as committed to the social order and in 21 (39 per cent) they expressed anxiety (*inquiétude*) about the social situation. In six *départe-*

---

[20] AN F7 12970–13023 (and F7 13963 for Marseilles). The percentages calculated refer to this base.

[21] Roger Magraw, 'Paris 1917–20: Labour Protest and Popular Politics', in: Wrigley (ed.), *Challenges of Labour*, 125–48; Jean-Louis Robert, *Les Ouvriers, la patrie et la révolution. Paris 1914–1919* (Besançon: Annales Littéraires de l'Université de Besançon, no. 592, 1995), esp. 357–76 ('Une grève révolutionnaire?') on the metalworkers' strike of June 1919.

[22] AN F7 13963, reply of the Marseilles Police Commissioner, 6 April 1920.

ments the bourgeois and lower middle classes were seen as dependent on the state for the maintenance of order, but in 12 *départements* (22 per cent) they were felt to have shown a 'volunteer' spirit. With a few exceptions, the peasantry was seen as no less hostile to the idea of revolution, according to the returns for 55 of the 66 *départements* for which the prefect reported on the countryside. In over a quarter of cases peasants resented workers in general or striking railwaymen in particular. One commune in the Bouches-du-Rhône protested against railway workers who were 'so well housed and paid and who were exempt during the war from the suffering that we peasants endured in the trenches, let alone the cruel anxieties of our families.'[23] But the peasants were also too remote from the sites of conflict to intervene. The Civic Unions arose from the activism identified by the prefects in the urban middle and lower middle classes, which feared revolution and opposed even a moderate-led railway strike as a threat to the social order and national recovery.

The first French Civic Union was set up in January 1920 by Pierre Millevoye, a Lyons lawyer, though there was a precedent in Geneva. As a member of the Union des Grandes Associations contre la Propagande Ennemie and also president of the Union des Pères et Mères dont les fils sont morts pour la Patrie (Union of Fathers and Mothers whose Sons died for the Fatherland), Millevoye stood firmly within the 'culture of victory'.[24] It was no accident that Lyons should have been the cradle of the movement since the city was embroiled in industrial disputes with some 40,000 workers on strike by early March.[25] It was also a nerve centre of the major rail network linking Paris to the Mediterranean. Millevoye insisted that his Union, which recruited among engineers, technicians and students, had no desire to intervene in legitimate labour disputes but intended to help the authorities in defeating what he considered to be politically inspired attacks on public order, if not attempted revolution. Volunteers kept electricity and public transport operating during the February strike.

In fact, the state had become worried the previous autumn that demobilization was depleting the military forces on which it could rely to combat major domestic disturbances and had already contemplated mobilizing civilian auxiliaries. Millerand took up the idea and the Ministry of the Interior appealed for voluntary help during the February railway strike. But the Lyons experiment gained national attention and the government sought to extend it to the whole country before the general strike in May.[26] In Paris, an elderly general acknowledged the Lyons precedent in setting up the capital's Civic Union, arguing that only the comradeship between classes in the trenches made such an experiment possible ('these bourgeois have learned to get their hands dirty, to trade blows and to crawl in the mud.

[23] AN F7 12975, address by the 'peasants' of Mouries to Milhaud, the local mayor and representative on the conseil general of the *département* (n.d.).

[24] AN F7 14608, Unions Civiques, initial circular of the Lyons Civic Union, dated January 1920, with an accompanying note by the Prefect, dated 17 January, containing details on Millevoye.

[25] Report of Prefect of the Rhône to Minister of the Interior, 5 March 1920, Archives Départementales (AD) Rhône, 10 MP C66 (Grèves, 1920).

[26] AN F7 14608, Direction de la Sûreté Générale, 'Note pour M. le Ministre de l'Intérieur... [on] Grèves de services publics; personnel de remplacement' (February 1921). The Minster of the Interior sent the prefects circulars addressing the issue of Civic Unions on 8 March and 14 April 1920.

It doesn't take any more than that to fight against the revolutionaries').[27] In Saint-Etienne, a major industrial conurbation in the eastern Massif Central and the second most important centre of arms production (after Paris) during the war, whose labour movement had a militantly revolutionary leadership, the Civic Union was formed in view of the 'gravity' of the Bolshevik peril.[28] Over 500 people turned up to its inaugural meeting and it recruited from the liberal professions, industry and commerce (whether owners, employees or workers), 'all of them, with one or two exceptions, [being] former mobilized soldiers who had valiantly done their duty at the front, and none of them being actively involved in political battles.'[29]

Forty Civic Unions existed by the time the general strike was launched by the CGT on the first of May and at least 65 by the time it ended.[30] In Paris and Lyons they kept public transport running and ensured the maintenance of gas, water and electricity. They also helped distribute essential supplies of food and fuel to shops and depots.[31] The railway companies recruited specialists and over 9,000 technical students to keep trains running throughout the strike.[32] Four hundred students at the leading business school in Paris, the Ecole des Hautes Etudes Commerciales, 'at least half of them former mobilized soldiers, most of them officers, all decorated with the Croix de guerre and some with the Légion d'honneur', supplied drivers, firemen, telephonists and signalmen.[33] Women participated too. The three national Red Cross organizations (all run by women) offered their services officially to Millerand in the event of a general strike. But they also allowed their members to join Civic Unions provided that they did not wear Red Cross uniforms or badges.[34] Inevitably there were violent clashes as strikers accused the volunteers of being blacklegs, but the latter avoided a policing role. They saw their function in replacing an illegal withdrawal of labour as essentially 'civic'.

Were the Civic Unions paramilitary? The emphasis on civic action suggests the deliberate refusal of military organization, let alone a recourse to arms. The issue surfaced when Steeg, the Minster of the Interior, proposed that Civic Unions should take on a police function by guarding the railways and telegraph lines. A decree on the eve of the general strike allowed for the creation of volunteer police detachments, but the result was an 'almost total failure' because veterans who were prepared to defend the national interest felt 'repugnance' at the idea of becoming police. In the wake of the May strike, 'civic guards' were discreetly established under the orders of the prefects. But when this became known, the Civic Unions were condemned by the left as 'White Guards'. According to a report by the

---

[27] General Bailloud, 'L'Union Civique Parisienne', *L'Echo de Paris*, 28 April 1920.

[28] AD Loire, M Sup. 504, policy statement of the Civic Union. For the syndicalist movement in the Loire, see AN F7 12995, police and prefect's reports.

[29] AD Loire, M Sup. 504, report by the prefect in response to the circular from the Ministry of the Interior of 14 April seeking information on the state of Civic Unions.

[30] 'L'Union civique', *Le Temps*, 6 May 1920 and 'Les Volontaires', *Le Temps*, 14 May 1920.

[31] SHD 6N 152, Auber report, 7–16.

[32] Kriegel, *Grève des cheminots*, 116–20.

[33] 'Les Volontaires', *Le Temps*, 14 May 1920.

[34] AN F7 14608, President of the Croix Rouge to Millerand, 21 April 1920.

national police service, great care was taken subsequently to ensure that they were seen 'not as organizations of attack but of simple social defence'.[35]

The experience of war and a veteran identity were important factors. The culture of victory clearly played a major role in motivating the volunteers. Moreover, the Civic Unions were the hub of a larger mobilization, which included not only the Red Cross societies but also some veterans' organizations, notably the Ligue des Chefs de Section (former non-commissioned officers) and many members and local groups of the Union Nationale des Combattants (UNC), the more conservative of the two major associations of *anciens combattants*.[36] The war experience became the touchstone for a view of the national cause in terms of the renewed defence of the victory of 1918. From this perspective, 'Bolshevism' and the revolutionary minority of the CGT were a new incarnation of the wartime enemy. Equally unacceptable was the use of a political strike by the CGT majority to force through a major reform, nationalization of the railways, especially in view of the urgent reconstruction the devastated North-East. The executive of the Paris Civic Union publicized these arguments at the end of the May strike. It did not deny the need for reform in recognition of the moral economy bequeathed by the war, calling in particular for tax changes to deal with the 'war profiteers'. But it defended its own action in breaking the strike as the preservation of freedom in a democratic Republic against all forms of dictatorship, precisely the freedom that had been defended in the war.

> France is not Russia. She has taken a century and a half to win one after another all the freedoms that are the condition of social and political progress: freedom of assembly, freedom of the press...Against the forces that seek the violent overthrow [of the regime] and against retrograde reactionaries, France will maintain the sacred gains of our glorious revolutions.[37]

In effect, the Millerand government avoided recourse to paramilitary violence as it mounted its campaign to break the CGT (which it pursued for breach of the 1884 trade union law, which forbade political strikes) and to crush the syndicalist minority, 18,000 of whose activists were sacked by the railway companies following the May strike. Confident that it had sufficient police and military strength to deal with breaches of the peace, it used a model of national mobilization inspired by the (mythic) memory of 1914—what Millerand called a 'civic battle of the Marne'— along with the very real memories of service and comradeship at the front. This allowed it to isolate the strikers almost like a wartime enemy that was unworthy of public support. As Steeg told parliament:

> Inspired by ideas from the Orient which have found a few conscious agents among us and a far greater number of blind instruments, a struggle has been fomented against the economic vitality of the fatherland.[38]

---

[35] AN F7 14608, Direction de la Sûreté Générale, 'Note pour M. le Ministre de l'Intérieur...[on] Grèves de services publics: personnel de remplacement' (February 1921).
[36] Antoine Prost, *Les Anciens Combattants et la société française 1914–1939* (Paris, 1977), 3 vols., vol. 1, *Histoire*, 72–4.
[37] *Le Temps*, 22 May 1920.
[38] *Journal Officiel, Chambre des Députés, Débats*, 20 May 1920, 1579.

In the face of such a menace, the Civic Unions were presented as a renewal of the *Union sacrée* and an impartial expression of the real nation. They established a federation in November 1920, and maintained a presence for the remainder of the decade, but the decline in industrial unrest meant that they were never mobilized in the same way again.[39] They illustrate the lack of space in France, even during the most tense social confrontation of the postwar period, for paramilitary violence. The solid parliamentary majority of a conservative government, underpinned by the culture of victory, allowed the spectre of revolution and the challenge of organized labour to be defeated by voluntary mobilization, especially of the urban middle classes, in support of the Republic and the existing social order. The journal of the new Federation of Civic Unions pointed out a couple of years later that Italian fascism shared the ideals of social peace and strong government with the Civic Unions but that its methods were entirely unnecessary in Republican France.[40]

DEFENDING VICTORY: PARAMILITARISM AND THE 'CARTEL DES GAUCHES', 1924–1926

By 1924, the paramilitary violence that had been provoked by defeat, revolution, counter-revolution and ethnic strife over the composition of new nations was ebbing away in much of Europe or had been converted into domestic politics. In Germany after the occupation of the Ruhr in 1923, stability was restored to both parliamentary government and the economy, paving the way for the 'prosperity' of the mid to late 1920s. The Bolsheviks became less of an international threat as they embarked on a halting normalization of diplomatic relations with other states.

The French, too, entered a period of détente with the former enemy as the passions of wartime waned. While the occupation of the Ruhr had renewed the flow of reparations, the cost in terms of polarizing German politics encouraged the French to take a more conciliatory approach to their former enemy. By 1926 this had produced the era of Locarno diplomacy, German entry into the League of Nations, and the partnership of Aristide Briand and Gustav Stresemann (the French and German Foreign Ministers), who were both determined that neither country should relive the catastrophe of the Great War.[41] The change was both signalled and reinforced by the legislative elections in May 1924, which returned a centre-left majority to parliament and allowed the Radical Party to preside over governments with the support of the Socialists in the so-called 'Cartel des Gauches'.[42] Political leaders who had been prosecuted during the war for pacifist tendencies (Caillaux, Malvy) resumed their ministerial careers. Some of the social

---

[39] *Union Civique. Bulletins de liaison*, 1921–1933, for the post-1920 history of the Civic Unions.

[40] *Bulletins de liaison de l'Union Civique*, 1922.

[41] See Zara Steiner, *The Lights that Failed. European International History, 1919–1933* (Oxford, 2005) and Jonathan Wright, *Gustav Stresemann. Weimar Germany's Greatest Statesman* (Oxford, 2002).

[42] Jean-Noël Jeanneney, *Leçons d'histoire pour une gauche au pouvoir: la faillite du cartel, 1924–1926* (Paris, 1977).

reforms favoured by moderate syndicalists and Socialists during the war returned to the political agenda. Above all, by a process of 'cultural demobilization', hatred of the wartime enemy abated. The soldiers' sacrifice was invested in strong anti-war sentiment and thus in a new internationalism designed to reduce national enmity.[43]

All of this eroded the culture of victory and made its major supporters on the nationalist right extremely anxious.[44] While others might believe that the new Germany was different from the Empire that had provoked the war, the right was convinced that beneath a democratic façade, the threat remained unchanged. The very fact that diplomatic relations had been established by Soviet Russia with France as with other European powers was a variation on the revolutionary conspiracy, and the emergence of a small but highly provocative French Communist Party (PCF) formalized the ideological confrontation between democracy, communism and authoritarianism in domestic politics.[45] *Boches* and *Bolchévique* thus remained the enemy but to the list was now added the Cartel des Gauches itself, which was accused of undermining both the victory of 1918 and the veterans who had achieved it. The language of diplomatic détente and a cultural demobilization that portrayed war itself as the supreme evil seemed tantamount to betrayal. Developments that weakened paramilitarism elsewhere thus had the opposite effect in France, where paramilitarism emerged as a serious idea and a perceptible current in politics. The nature and limits of this paramilitarism can be assessed by briefly considering the most prominent groups that espoused it

Pierre Taittinger, founder of the Jeunesses patriotes (JP), was a modest clerk in the Paris department store, Printemps, who married into a banking family and went on to become a successful businessman and founder of the Champagne firm of the same name. Through his wife's family, he developed a lifelong commitment to the Bonapartist strand of French politics, entering the Ligue des Patriotes (founded in response to the defeat of 1871) before the war. He was elected a deputy for Paris in the 1919 election. All of this placed him in the well-established tradition of the authoritarian right. However, Taittinger returned from the First World War, during which he had been cited for bravery on four occasions, with 'a pronounced taste for military things'.[46] In 1920 he considered even the reformist CGT leadership to be revolutionary; he condemned the strikers for trying to 'sabotage victory' and called for the 'tricolor railwaymen' who had kept working to be rewarded. But he was content to support the Millerand government.[47] In 1924, by contrast, the victory of the Cartel des Gauches seemed to endanger the state itself,

---

[43] John Horne, 'Locarno et la politique de la démobilisation culturelle, 1925–30', *14–18 Aujourd'hui-Heute-Today* (Paris), 5, 2002, pp. 73–87, and id., 'Demobilizing the Mind: France and the Legacy of the Great War, 1919–1939', *French History and Civilization*, 2, 2009, 101–19 (also at <http://www.h-france.net>).

[44] For disillusionment since 1918, see Benjamin Martin, *France and the Après-Guerre, 1918–1924: Illusions and Disillusionment* (Baton Rouge, 2002).

[45] Ronald Tiersky, *French Communism, 1920–1972* (New York and London, 1974).

[46] Robert Soucy, *French Fascism: The First Wave, 1924–1933* (New Haven and London, 1986), 41.

[47] *Journal Officiel, Chambre des Députés, Débats*, 18–21 May 1920, 1533.

prompting Taittinger to found a new political organization, the JP, on paramilitary lines.

The trigger was provided by the events of 23 November 1924 when, in a state ceremony, the remains of Jean Jaurès, the socialist leader and peace advocate assassinated in 1914 on the eve of the war, were transferred to the Panthéon. For the right, the occasion symbolized all that was wrong with the Cartel. Not only did it mark the official approval of Jaurès' anti-war stance, and thus repudiate the sacrifices of the Great War, it placed organized labour at the heart of the proceedings, as the coffin was accompanied by miners from Jaurès' own constituency dressed in full mining gear and black hats. Far more troubling was the appearance of communists in the cortège bearing red flags, singing the *Internationale* and shouting 'Down with war!'. They were joined by workers, many of them immigrants, of whom there were significant numbers in postwar France drawn by the reconstruction of the North-East.[48] For Taittinger, it was a call to action; the sight of communist flags and the foreign workers suggested that 'in a few more days, the streets might be prey to the Revolution.'[49]

Taittinger set up the JP the following month as a youth group within the Ligue des Patriotes and with the full approval of the leadership of that organization, which had itself been renewed to meet the threat of the Cartel des Gauches. Initially, the organizational model was similar to that of the 'national' mobilization of 1920, with local 'action groups' open to all Frenchmen, whatever their political affiliation. Nonetheless, the goal of contesting the street power of the communists, who were supposed to be armed and drilling in quasi-military fashion, suggested that violence was envisaged. An early set of statutes defined the goal of the JP as 'the coordination of the all the living forces of France in defence of the social order and national prosperity, using homeopathic means against communism, revolutionary socialism and the destructive forces of freemasonry.'[50]

In the course of 1925–26, following the absorption of two other right-wing groups, the Jeunesses Patriotes assumed full independence and reorganized on an explicitly paramilitary basis. The basic unit now become the 'century' composed of a hundred men from a given locality and distinguished between 'shock centuries' who were always ready for combat and would lead JP marches if fighting broke out, 'active centuries' who could be called on at short notice, and 'reserve centuries' who would be available in the event of a full-scale mobilization.[51] Consciously or not, the structure paralleled that of the national army (with the 'active' army composed of current conscripts, the reserve of the active army, and the territorials). The JP wore uniform (a blue coat and beret) and carried a walking cane. There was also an elite corps, the 'Brigade de Feu' or 'Battle Brigade', which constituted Taittinger's

[48] 'Les Cendres de Jaurès au Panthéon', *Le Matin*, 24 November 1924.

[49] Jean-Charles Kieffer, *De Clemenceau à Lyautey. Les Origines, les buts, l'action des Jeunesses Patriotes de France de 1924 à 1934* (Nantes, 1934), 10.

[50] AN F7 13232, note of May 1925 on the Jeunesses Patriotes. For the Jeunesses Patriotes more generally, see Soucy, *French Fascism: The First Wave*, 39–86, and Philippe Machefer, *Ligues et fascismes en France, 1919–1939* (Paris, 1974), 10–12.

[51] AN F7 13232, 'Au sujet des Jeunesses Patriotes', September 1926.

personal bodyguard. The police estimated that by 1926 the JP had some 50,000 members, with 48 'centuries' in Paris and a presence in the major provincial cities.[52]

The JP engaged in street fights with the PCF, who had organized their own revolutionary guards. Yet this amounted to serious rioting rather than armed combat, although four members were killed in 1925 in a particularly fierce encounter in the rue Damrémont, in Paris. During the municipal elections of that year, a JP march-past deliberately taunted communists who had themselves been looking for an opportunity to confront the nationalists. In the ensuing fracas, four members of the JP were shot and killed, thus providing the movement with the martyrs that were essential to a paramilitary cult.[53] As to the purpose of violence, the JP remained ambivalent. The goal of contesting the revolutionary threat of French and international communism was clear. Sometimes the JP saw themselves as auxiliaries of the state in this regard—precisely what the Civic Unions had refused to become in 1920. Taittinger enjoyed the support of some 70 parliamentary deputies and maintained his connections with the Ligue des Patriotes, even after formal separation. Yet in his own manifesto issued in 1926 when the Cartel was still in office, Taittinger also targeted the government.

> We have had enough of anarchy in this country. We are resolved to fight against this anarchy in all its forms: bloody and active anarchism, that is, communism; latent and passive anarchy, that is to say the regime that we have to put up with at the moment.[54]

The proposed alternative was a 'regime of order' based on authority, class collaboration and social reform, and the means of achieving it were to be peaceful if possible, but violent if not. The ultimate goal was to restore the victory of 1918:

> At the end of the war, there was a unanimous hope in the country that a new France could be created from the victory [which the Cartel had turned into defeat]. This was also the desire of all those who had lost their lives on the field of battle.[55]

Invoking the martyrs of the rue Damrémont, Taittinger called on the country to realize that goal. Yet two years later, when the Cartel des Gauches had fallen and centre-right governments held sway, a model speech circulated among members insisted that: 'The JP are not fascists... There are other ways of emerging from the current difficulties than by overthrowing our institutions, which are capable of producing strong and energetic governments.'[56]

The Faisceau founded by Georges Valois apparently removed the ambiguity by taking its name and at least its superficial inspiration from Italian fascism. The starting-point was the same as that of the JP. But Valois' background as a self-made intellectual of humble origins, who before the war had sought to link the monarchist Action Française with revolutionary syndicalism in order to attack the parliamentary republic, made him intellectually more inventive and politically more radical

---

[52] AN F7 13232, Jeunesses Patriotes, 'Activité de ce groupement de mars 1925 à janvier 1926'.
[53] Kieffer, *Jeunesses Patriotes*; AN F7 13236, Jeunesses Patriotes. Affaire rue Damrémont.
[54] AN F7 13232, programme of the JP in 1926, printed version signed by Taittinger.
[55] Ibid.　　[56] AN F7 13232, note of 24 February 1928 with three model JP speeches.

than Taittinger.[57] Like the latter, however, wartime combat had given him a vision of both community and hierarchy, and above all, authority. His experience of General de Castelnau's leadership at Verdun in 1916 had a durable effect, not least because de Castelnau played a role on the political right in the 1920s. On 11 November 1924, Valois called a meeting of veterans in Paris to protest against the outcome of the election in May. In April 1925, this became the Légions pour la Politique de la Victoire (the Legions for the Politics of the [1918] Victory), in which Valois joined with two other right-wing intellectuals, Philippe Barrès and Jacques Arthuys, to summon the 'artisans of the victory' to reject both communism and the new spirit of reconciliation with Germany (*Boches* and *Bolchéviques* once again).[58] The intention was to impose 'the politics of victory' by extra-parliamentary means, resulting in a dictatorship.'[59] On 11 November 1925, this organization mutated into the Faisceau des Combattants et des Producteurs.

Valois' programme turned on restoring victory by appealing to the Great War veterans as the legitimizing authority for a corporatist state and a dictatorship that would overthrow both the Cartel and the Republic. 'Victory, our victory, has been broken by the politicians and the *embusqués*,' declared an early Faisceau tract. With fascist-inspired theatricality, Valois summoned the veterans in 1926 first to Verdun and then to Rheims, the sacred sites of the Western Front, in order to realize the living body of the new politics that would result in the 'dictatorship of the combattant'. With a term that would resonate for 20 years, he called for a 'National Revolution'.[60] Unlike Taittinger, Valois decried the 'counter-revolution' of the November 1919 elections because it had imprisoned the right in an electoral straightjacket from which the Faisceau were to liberate it. Violence and paramilitary organization were thus intrinsic to the Faisceau, which had no pretentions to act as an auxiliary to the state in fighting communism and maintaining public order. Its local 'legions' wore a blue-shirt uniform closely modelled on that of Italian fascists, and like the JP they engaged in street fighting—as happened when the local left resisted the Faisceau's national crusade to Rheims on 27 June 1926.[61] The Faisceau was smaller than the JP, with some 40,000 members at its peak in 1926.[62] Once the Cartel des Gauches had fallen, it also declined before breaking up in 1928.

Paramilitarism emerged as a theme in right-wing politics in 1924–26 in response both to the disintegration of a culture of victory (already beset by doubts and anxieties) and to a shift in the electoral balance of power to the left, which threatened the ability of the state to defend a conservative political and social agenda. While the international context played a role (the fear of détente with Germany and Russia,

---

[57] Paul Mazgaj, *The Action Française and Revolutionary Syndicalism* (Chapel Hill, 1979).

[58] AN F7 13208, police note 'Les Légions', Paris, 19 November 1925, detailing the history since the founding of the Légions in April.

[59] AN F7 13211, André d'Humières, 'Le Faisceau. Ses origines. Son développement. Son esprit,' *Le Nouveau siècle*, 3 January 1926. For the Faisceau see also Soucy, *French Fascism. The First Wave*, 87–125, and Machefer, *Ligues et fascismes*, 12–13.

[60] AN F7 13211, Faisceau tract no. 5, 'La Politique de la victoire'.

[61] *Le Matin*, 28 June 1926, and police report, 'L' "Assemblée Nationale" du Faisceau à Reims le 27 juin 1926' in AN F7 13211.

[62] Soucy, *French Fascism. The First Wave*, 112.

the consolidation of the fascist government in Italy), domestic reasons predominated. The moral and political capital of the veterans provided Valois with an alternative source of authority with which to attack the 'cartellist' Republic. The forms and experience of military organization were especially important for Taittinger as he sought to forge an instrument that could contest the control of the streets with communism in order to defend the social order, though not necessarily the Cartel government.

These militant right-wing groups were not the only ones to protest. Some veterans' organizations, including the UNC, also mobilized against the communists and criticized rapprochement with Germany. General de Castelnau presided over a Fédération Nationale Catholique (FNC), which sought to defend the spirit of the Union sacrée and to resist the anticlericalism of the Cartel government, which reverted to a pre-war anti-Catholic sectarianism. Yet although individuals straddled both conservative and far right organizations, the UNC and the FNC, each of them a large movement, were careful to avoid any semblance of illegality, let alone street violence.[63] General de Castelnau, for example, remained in close touch with the ecclesiastical hierarchy and used the diocesan structure as the local basis for the FNC, which was presided over by a broad spectrum of Catholic notables.[64]

The years 1924–26 saw the invention of a right-wing politics of street demonstrations that was turned against the government by people whose social roles and background usually led them to shun such activities. Between December 1924 and July 1926 there were 185 such manifestations.[65] The same impulse took root in a number of organizations that proclaimed their belief in some form of paramilitarism. What is less clear is how prone they were to actual, as opposed to symbolic, violence. Nor does there seem to be evidence of other kinds of paramilitary violence such as the arson, assaults and intimidation routinely conducted by Italian fascists from March 1919 on. Moreover, the groups that espoused violence at least in principle were vastly outnumbered by organizations that were also committed to defending the 'victory' of 1918 but which were unwilling to place themselves even potentially on the side of disorder. By 1927–28, the Cartel des Gauches had gone. But many of the themes of cultural demobilization had been absorbed by the new governments of the centre-right. Briand retained the Foreign Ministry until his death in 1932 and the policy of détente with Germany reached its peak after the end of the Cartel. Temporarily at least, paramilitarism was over.

CONCLUSIONS

The French counter-example underscores some of the factors that fuelled paramilitary movements and violence elsewhere. First, the absence of actual, as

[63] Prost, *Les Anciens Combattants*, vol. 1, 99, for the cautious respect paid by the UNC to the Cartel as the legal government.
[64] AN F713219, Fédération Nationale Catholique, esp. *Bulletin Officiel de la Fédération Nationale Catholique*, no. 1, February 1925, which reported that the federation had branches in 82 dioceses.
[65] Daniel Tartakowsky, *Les Manifestations de rue en France 1918–1968* (Paris, 1997), 129.

opposed to imagined, revolution at the height of the postwar social tensions in 1920 meant that the mobilization of middle class solidarity behind the 'national' cause remained essentially economic and civic, rather than assuming a violent, paramilitary form. This is the opposite of what happened at the same moment in Italy, as the *biennio rosso* peaked with the factory occupations in autumn 1920 and in Germany where *Freikorps* units bloodily repressed the last 'red' militias in the Ruhr.

Second, it was next to impossible for paramilitary organizations to undermine or challenge the monopoly of force of a victorious state possessing immense military and police strength. In 1920 the Civic Unions were at most a useful supplement, and saw themselves as nothing else. The demonstrations of 1924–26 never jeopardized public order, and both the JP and the Faisceau remained relatively small. Despite the appeal of both to the veterans of the Great War, the latter were far too numerous to be reduced to a political cause—some three million of them belonging to various associations. Again, this was in marked contrast to cases where the state had lost much of its authority and where defeat, or its refusal, placed political authority in contention, to be seized by the best armed groups which often appealed to at least one version of veteran identity.

Third, because of the solidity of the political culture of the parliamentary Republic, the three-way ideological conflict between fascism, communism and democracy was confined to the margins of French politics, and often seemed tinged with foreign exoticism (as when the JP disclaimed any similarity with Italian fascism). This in turn limited the political space in which either extreme could mobilize paramilitary support against the other or against the parliamentary regime. True, the pretensions of the centre-right to a monopoly of 'victory' and the 'national' interest opened the way to some pressure against a left wing government in the streets, as well as in parliament and the press. But the ambivalence of the JP over just this issue (by contrast with the much more clear-cut attitude of the Faisceau) showed that even here the margin for paramilitary organization against the state, as opposed to communism and the threat of 'Revolution', was slim.

Fourth, the almost complete absence of ethnic and frontier tensions reduced the purchase of paramilitary politics on national life yet further. True, the supposed failure of the Cartel to satisfy the susceptibilities of opinion in Alsace-Lorraine, which reinforced the movement for Alsatian autonomy, was another example for the JP and the FNC of the Cartel's failure to defend the victory of 1918. But it was a minor theme compared to the effects of frontier turmoil elsewhere.

Finally, the limits to French paramilitarism, and the extent to which it remained a matter of rhetoric and organization rather than violent practice, should make us wary of the claim that the experience of the Great War necessarily 'brutalized' postwar societies. This argument has been deployed well beyond its original application by George Mosse, which was to German *political* life after the war.[66] French

---

[66] George Mosse, *Fallen Soldiers. Reshaping the Memory of the World Wars* (New York, 1990), 159–81.

politics had been subject to domestic violence before the war—perhaps owing to the precocious nature of democratic politics in France from 1870. Yet violence remained restricted in the postwar period, at least compared to much of Central, Southern and Eastern Europe. Paramilitary violence is precisely one of the symptoms that can help us establish where the brutalization of postwar politics really took place, and why.

Index

Printed in the USA/Agawam, MA
December 19, 2014

602657.022